# ENGLISH AND FRENCH NEUTRALITY

AND

## THE ANGLO-FRENCH ALLIANCE,

IN THEIR RELATIONS TO THE

# UNITED STATES & RUSSIA,

INCLUDING

AN ACCOUNT OF THE LEADING POLICY OF FRANCE AND OF ENGLAND FOR THE LAST TWO HUNDRED YEARS—THE ORIGIN AND AIMS OF THE ALLIANCE—THE MEANING OF THE CRIMEAN WAR—AND THE REASON OF THE HOSTILE ATTITUDE OF THESE TWO POWERS TOWARDS THE UNITED STATES,

AND OF THE MOVEMENT ON MEXICO,

WITH A STATEMENT OF THE

GENERAL RESOURCES—THE ARMY AND NAVY OF ENGLAND AND FRANCE—RUSSIA AND AMERICA—SHOWING THE PRESENT STRENGTH AND PROBABLE FUTURE OF THESE FOUR POWERS.

---

BY REV. C. B. BOYNTON, D. D.

---

CINCINNATI:
C. F. VENT & CO., 38 WEST FOURTH STREET.
CHICAGO: 112 DEARBORN STREET.
1864.

# PREFACE.

"You have not come to the bottom of the conduct of "Great Britain, until you have touched that delicate and "real foundation cause, we are too large and strong a "nation.

"This is in my judgment the right of the whole matter. "A distinguished clergymen of London, personally kind, "and friendly to me, said to me in these very words, 'Mr. "Beecher, you may just as well have it said to you, you "have been growing so strong that we had got to take you "down, and we were very glad when the job was taken out "of our hands by your own people.' When Mr. Roebuck "declared the same fact in Parliament, it was cheered "immensely."—*Mr. Beecher's Speech in Brooklyn.*

In the same speech, Mr. Beecher analyses English society, and states what he believes to be the spirit of the different classes in regard to this country. His conclusions, in substance, are as follows:

"The great commercial class is against us. The influen- "tial clergymen and laymen of both the Established Church "and the Dissenters are, as a body, against us. The nobility, "as a class, are against us.

"Parliament, in sympathy and wishes, is five to one "against us.

"The conservative intelligence of Great Britain is "against us, and all there is on the surface of society repre-

"senting its dignities, its power, its intelligence, is anti-"American."

The force of these statements, as fully sustaining the tone and purpose of this book, will be felt, when we consider that they are made by one, who, more than any other of our public men, seems anxious to place England in the most favorable light before his countrymen, and would lead us to expect, that in the future, Great Britain may become our friend.

He relies, as others do, upon the assumed fact, that the nonvoting, and in a sense, uninfluential laboring classes are in favor of the North. That a majority of them are thus friendly may be admitted, but few probably are ready to believe, that in spite of all the great forces arrayed against us, these nonvoting laborers of England have power to shape her policy.

There is no such enthusiastic love of America or Americans even among the people of England, as would lead them to band themselves together as our champions, against the Government and the Church, the army and navy, the nobility, the literary power, and the commercial interests of the kingdom.

The people have, it is hoped, exerted some influence in the change which has been lately wrought in British policy, but the main causes are to be sought in the sudden exhibition which we have made of military power, in the strength of our army, the formidable character of our navy, the superiority of our new cannon, and the waning of the power of the rebellion.

The central purpose in the American policy of France is declared by the Emperor himself to be, to restore the ascendancy of the Latin race in the New World, and this necessarily involves the supremacy of the Papal power, and the repressing, if possible, the growth of free Protestant institutions. This, with its consequences, is the settled design of France.

The purpose of Napoleon in proposing a Congress of nations is not yet fully revealed, but nothing is hazarded in believing that his intention is to make France more completely than ever the mistress of Europe, to strengthen himself by new alliances with the Latin Powers, so as to compel England to follow his lead, or expose herself to a formidable attack—in short, to render France so powerful that she can dictate terms and policy to England, Russia, and America. That these are the intentions of the French Emperor, no one who has studied his past course, will be likely to doubt, and for these new European combinations, it would be well to prepare in season.

It is then evident, that the Great Rebellion will introduce a new era, not only for our own country, but for Europe and the world.

It will change the political relations of European States to each other, and to us, and will improve the condition and prospects of the *people* in all lands.

The late movements here and in Russia, by which the proper rights of millions of laboring men have been acknowledged and secured, form a new starting point in human history.

Under the pressure of this war "The United States" have become an American Nation, and this new-born nation has been brought, by a combined home and foreign conspiracy, within the circle of European relations, has been compelled to take its place a Power among the Powers, and henceforth its policy and its ability to attack or defend, will form an important element in the councils of the nations.

A new-born Russia has also presented itself to the world.

The old military despotism is gone, and in its stead there comes a Constitutional Monarchy, proposing to use its vast powers only for the protection and elevation of humanity.

Hand in hand, Russia and America are crossing the threshold of the new era, the Great Powers of the future, while Western Europe is plotting against both, and threatens and fears them. This book has been written, in the hope that it may help to explain the policy of France and England, and what we have to hope or fear from them, to set forth the resources and mission of that great nation, which alone has remained our friend, and to show the probable future of this New, Free, Christian American Nation.

# AUTHORITIES CONSULTED IN PREPARING THE WORK.

BARON HAXTHAUSEN'S NOTES ON RUSSIA.
EHRMAN'S TRAVELS IN RUSSIA.
OLIPHANT'S SHORES OF THE BLACK SEA.
ALLISON'S HISTORY OF EUROPE.
RUSSEL'S MODERN EUROPE.
BANCROFT'S HISTORY OF THE UNITED STATES.
PRESCOTT'S PHILIP II.
KINGLAKE'S INVASION OF THE CRIMEA.
STANLEY'S GREEK CHURCH.
KAY'S SOCIAL CONDITION OF ENGLAND.
HUNT'S MERCHANT'S MAGAZINE.
LONDON QUARTERLY.
FOREIGN QUARTERLY.
EDINBURGH REVIEW.
NORTH BRITISH REVIEW.
SCIENTIFIC AMERICAN.
NATIONAL ALMANAC, 1863 AND 1864.
UNITED STATES SERVICE MAGAZINE.
REPORTS OF THE NAVY DEPARTMENT.
REPORTS OF THE ORDINANCE BUREAU.
OFFICIAL DOCUMENTS OF THE AMERICAN AND ENGLISH GOVERNMENTS
HON. CHARLES SUMNER'S SPEECH ON OUR FOREIGN RELATIONS.

# TABLE OF CONTENTS.

# CHAPTER I.

## FREE INSTITUTIONS PLACED ON TRIAL BEFORE THE WORLD.

The results already attained in the progress of our war, and the sure promise of the future, justify us in believing, that one purpose of God in permitting this rebellion, was to draw the attention of the nations to the free institutions of the North, and then, by putting them to the severest possible proof, show their excellence unto the people of every land, and thus advance the general cause of human freedom.

It has been proved that a popular Government is not necessarily a weak one, and that a free, unwarlike people, unused to the restraints of thorough organization and discipline, can yet assume almost at once the highest forms of national life, can reshape, without confusion, their whole industrial energy to meet the demands of sudden war, can bring forth and organize, and hold in hand all their resources, and with all the skill and science of the age, can wield a thoroughly compacted national strength, greater in proportion to population than has been exhibited by any other power of earth.

The *people* of the whole civilized world are studying with intense interest the events which are passing here, and the prominent friends of freedom in Europe declare that we are fighting here the great battle of universal humanity.

Doubtless our complete success in overthrowing slavery here, the emancipation of all our laborers, will give a new impulse to popular liberty all over the world, and therefore, as it would seem, God has made the nations spectators of this desperate fight.

This American war closes a political era for Christendom. New powers are being prepared as rulers in the coming age, and the race will feel the power of a higher life.

But in order to show fully the quality and the power of the life of the free North, it was necessary not only to unveil the weakness, the cruelty, the loathsome corruption, the ignorance, and barbarism of slavery, but to give to the slave-power great advantages in the contest, and cause the free States to be taken by surprise, and compel them to begin a great war under all possible disadvantage, not only without arms, and without friends, but with thousands of foes within giving aid and comfort to the enemy without.

If a Government of the people could pass such a peril safely, and win at length a triumph, if it could come forth from the trial not only a mighty compacted nation, but with all its proper liberties secure, it would be a lesson to which kings and people must alike give heed. The North at first had nothing to oppose to this great conspiracy, all armed and equipped, but its own free, irrepressible life. And this was well; for thus only could the might of freedom be known.

Never were a people more completely surprised, and even bewildered, than those of the free States were for a time. when the conspirators showed that they had fully resolved to destroy the Government, and were ready to begin a war. The preparations of treason went forward on all sides, and men refused to believe that the traitors were in earnest. They would not credit the evidences of their own senses. They could not be persuaded *then*, that Americans could be guilty of such a shocking crime.

The incredible nature of the meditated villiany, secured it it for a season, and gave time to perfect its plans, and when at length the war was actually begun, the North found itself not only unarmed but disarmed. Small arms and cannon, forts, navy yards, arsenals, the Southern coast and cities, the Gulf, the Mississippi from the Ocean to the mouth of the Ohio, all these, with few exceptions, were in the hands of the traitors; the small "regular army" was surrendered on the frontier, the little "navy" was in distant waters, a single sloop-of-war only on all the Atlantic coast. In addition to all this, the Potomac was blockaded by batteries, a hostile army was within two days march of Washington, and the Capital was cut off from communication with the North. Naturally, in this hour of extreme peril, the people of the North and their Government, turned to the European States, expecting, that at the very least, they would sympathize with a regularly established Government, in its effort to suppress an uncalled-for rebellion. They thought that those who had ever dealt so sternly with treason at home, would be found on the side of the regular authorities here.

They expected that France, who had generously aided us to establish here a Republic, would manifest her former friendship in this our new danger, and they thought that England, who had done and sacrificed so much in the cause of human freedom, would come promptly to our aid with living sympathies, when the object of the conspirators was declared to be, to build a slave empire on the ruins of a free Republic.

If the free States were amazed at the conspiracy itself, they were confounded at the treatment they received from the two great allied powers of Western Europe. They placed themselves at once virtually on the side of the rebels. They declared that the "Great Republican Bubble" had burst. They gave the traitors officially, and at once, the position and privileges of proper belligerents, they took from them the odium, and so far as they could, the guilt of rebellion, and relieved their corsair cruisers from the name and fate of pirates. We were informed that not one dollar of money should be loaned us wherewith to carry on our war, and we met both at London and Paris only coldness and repression, while the rebels were cheered and encouraged by every act short of recognition, alliance, and war against the North. Helpless almost, as the free States were, in the first days of this conflict, nearly overwhelmed at the first onset by the vast weight of such a conspiracy, not only fully organized, but well armed with its stolen weapons, and backed by the sympathies of nearly all Europe, Russia only excepted, they showed little less than a miraculous energy by the manner in which they first stood firm, and then rallied their strength, and increased their resources and power, until the conspiracy was put under their feet, and they stood forth a new-born military nation, the equal of the foremost.

We have now reached a point in our national progress, where it is needful to study with jealous care the nature of our relations with Western Europe.

The swift waning of the power of the rebellion will probably free us from all fear of intervention, or even recognition, and England shows at present a more kindly spirit which may possibly ripen into friendship, bnt France, her ally, and with whom she declares herself in perfect accord in regard to American affairs, France has planted an army just over our border, and proposes to erect a throne there also, and to exercise an important influence over American affairs, and to dictate, if she can, a policy for our continent.

It becomes us, therefore, quickly to inquire what these things mean. We should know why England and France are so ready and cordial with their sympathy for the rebels, as if by previous agreement, and why we were met with coldness and ill-concealed hostility from the beginning, as if in accordance with a policy which France and England had in concert adopted beforehand.

We cannot safely trust to uncertainties hereafter. We must not again delude ourselves with false hopes. If hostility to the American Nation is one feature of the Anglo-French Alliance, if their scheme of policy include the crippling of America as well as Russia, it is high time that this were fully understood by both nations, that in the future we may be prepared in season. Russia and America may, perhaps, consider it prudent hereafter not to permit each other to be separately attacked by the Allied Powers of Western Europe.

It becomes all Americans then, to study now afresh the origin and aims of the Anglo-French Alliance, as shown by their own declarations and corresponding acts, to understand the policy and resources, the military and naval strength of these two Powers, and in connection with these, to become familiar with the real character, power and policy of Russia, and to measure at the same time our own national strength and capabilities, and to comprehend our national mission.

# CHAPTER II.

## ENGLISH AND FRENCH NEUTRALITY.

Our war with the rebellion is evidently near its close. The conspirators have exhausted their means of resistance, and submission or destruction is now their only choice. When the end of this conflict is reached, may we then safely disband our armies, and lay up in harbors our dismantled war ships, and securely give ourselves as heretofore, exclusively to the pursuits of peace? Shall we continue, as before, isolated from the affairs of Europe, and shall we be permitted to pursue in quiet our own home policy, an independent American career?

Or has this war been brought upon us merely to prepare us for conflicts to come, which will test still more severely our courage, skill and power? Has the God of nations appointed us to a great mission in behalf of the rights of man, which we could not execute until we were delivered from that sin and curse which paralyzed our energies, prevented us from becoming a national power, corrupted our morals, and stripped us of our manhood? Was this political and social upheaval ordered for us as a preparatory discipline, and through this baptism of blood and tears has our God consecrated us unto a nobler work?

Did God take note of the secret plottings of Western Europe, and foreseeing that they would attack us whenever an occasion could be found; has He brought upon us the stern necessity of casting from us the weakness of slavery, adding thereby half a million of fighting men to our available strength; has He compelled us to consolidate our national power; has He shown us our resources and capabilities; has He made us familiar with our strength, and forced us to become a great military nation, in order to prevent the meditated blow from Europe, or enable us to meet it without disaster?

If these questions can be answered, it will be by first observing the conduct of France and England as neutral powers, and then we may find the meaning of this, in the nature and purposes of their alliance, and in the necessities of their settled national policy.

In judging the past acts of nations, even of such as call themselves Christian, or if we would know what we may expect in the future, we must remember that the abstract right, the principles of the Gospel, have very little direct influence upon national policy. We have not yet arrived at that state of perfection, where righteousness and faithfulness are the girdle of the loins of rulers. Kings, Presidents, Cabinets, are not expected to do anything contrary to apparent interests, merely because it is right, or to refrain from any act, merely because it is wrong.

Each great power of Europe has a national policy of its own, which it will carry out so far as it has the power, with very little regard for the rights or welfare of others, while under that artificial system devised to maintain what they call the "balance of power," any one is liable to be attacked, merely because it is more prosperous than its neighbors.

Nor must Americans overlook the all-important fact, that the Allied Powers of Western Europe do seriously propose to apply the European political system to the affairs of this Continent. Steam navigation has virtually condensed the population of the world; the spaces between nations are scarcely one-fourth of what they once were; the ocean which divides us from Europe is now only a strait; and placed as we are, almost side by side with France and England, they see and fear the advancing shadow of our greatness, and they seek earnestly the means of hindering our progress and crippling our power. If other means fail, if we should come forth from this rebellion with our national unity unbroken, and our strength unimpaired, they will combine, and attempt by State craft, or by force if they dare, to preserve here the "balance of power," which simply means to prevent us by all and any means, from becoming an American Nation, great enough to be independent of them.

Whoever expects less of hostility, or more of friendship than this from any power of Western Europe, will surely be deceived.

It is perhaps barely possible that England may yet seek an alliance with America to save herself from France, but that is among the secrets of the future.

Nor must we forget, when we attempt to forecast the future, that the great forces which move the nations of Christendom are religious ones. By this is meant, not that national counsels are controlled by Christian principles, but that the alliances and antagonisms of nations are largely shaped by the influence of the ties of race, and the religious faith and traditions of the people. It is quite certain now, that the civilized world is fast arraying itself under three great political divisions, which correspond to the three great religious organizations. Russia heads and wields the Eastern Church. France is already the actual leader of the Latin race, and the Papal Church, while the Protestant power is not as yet so thoroughly organized and united. It has not as yet selected its head and champion. Where shall we find the great Protestant national leader of the future? Will it be Germany or England? Not unless great changes are speedily wrought. Will it be America? Perhaps so, if she is found worthy.

The political tendencies of the three great religious divisions of Christendom are perfectly apparent. Protestantism embodies itself naturally in free institutions. It seeks everywhere, and at all times, to elevate the people, it desires to enfranchise universal humanity. Russia and the Greek

Church are moving in the same direction, and give noble promise for the future.

The Papal Church is, as ever, the friend of political and ecclesiastical despotism, the bitter enemy of popular rights and free institutions; and France, in striving to become the Imperial Head of the Latin race and Church, is the Leader of a new conspiracy against the peace of nations and the liberties of man.

These facts must all be considered in any attempt to form an opinion of the future of Europe and America. They show us the true reasons for the course which France and England have pursued since the beginning of the rebellion, they show why these Powers united for an attack on Russia, and that the same motives have shaped their policy towards both Russia and America; and in the light of these facts, we may turn to the misnamed neutrality of these Governments and read aright its meaning.

# CHAPTER III.

## THE NEUTRALITY ILLUSTRATED BY ACTS.

In referring to the conduct of France and England, no friend of his country or of his race, would dwell upon their unfriendly acts for the purpose of creating bitterness of feeling, or merely to keep alive the memories of wrong.

America desires only peace. She asks of Europe that she should be left in quietness to work out her own national destiny, and to manage her own affairs, as seems best to her, without interference from any. But the spirit which has been manifested by France and England, the evident and earnest desire that the Republic should be destroyed, the prompt and cheerful giving of sympathy and aid to our rebel enemies, these things should surely warn us to watch with jealous care their every movement, to study carefully the principles and objects of their policy, that they may have no chance hereafter to take us unawares.

While we rejoice at, and frankly and kindly accept for what it is worth, every friendly or forbearing act, which seems to indicate some change of temper or intention, we are bound by every consideration of prudence and national safety, to judge of the present by the past, and to expect that these nations hereafter will be guided as they have been thus far, not by any friendly feelings towards this Western Power, but by those very principles of policy which have controlled them since the beginning of our war.

Their plans are settled and far-reaching ones. They are not to be suddenly or lightly abandoned. The national necessities of France and England, as their leaders view them, and the policy which they have jointly adopted for the control of Christendom, do not permit them to look quietly on while Russia and America are making such rapid progress.

Their alliance was framed in view of a real antagonism between their interests, and those of Russia and America; they have made the antagonism an actual one by a war with Russia, and their treatment of us; and this should be borne steadily in mind if we would understand the past, or be prepared for the future. The future will be peace, if we are strong enough to compel a peace, not otherwise.

It is important for Americans to remember that the course pursued by France and England was the result of previous consultation, and positive agreement between them. At the outset, they informed our Government that the two Powers would be perfectly united in their policy, whatever it might be, and in declaring this policy by acts, England took the lead.

Her first open and decided step then, was taken in accordance with the plan which the French and English rulers had decided upon beforehand, and with definite purposes in view. The very manner and time chosen, must have been fixed by a previous decision.

By formal Proclamation of the Queen, the Confederate rebels, in the very first hours of their insurrection, were declared to be rightful *ocean* belligerents before they had a single ship afloat, and when, even if they had ships, there was not a port on earth where they could send a prize for trial.

This Proclamation was issued when the British rulers knew that Mr. Adams, our newly appointed Minister, was at Liverpool, prepared to represent the cause of our Government, but with a haste which revealed clearly the hostile intent, the design to prejudge and settle the whole matter against us, before we could be heard, and to grant the rebels privileges and a national standing, which no effort of ours could recall.

They had resolved, after consulting with France, to commit the English and French nation to a policy from which they could not retreat. It was essentially an unfriendly act. It was known to be so, it was intended to give aid and comfort to the traitors, to relieve them from the name and crime of treason and piracy, and to win for the rebellion the respect and sympathy of the world. In moral guilt, as a heartless, selfish violation of national friendship, this act was equal to an alliance with the rebels, and a declaration of war against the American Government, and every subsequent event has shown that it was designed to be war in disguise, war without risk to the two Allied Powers, but which brought destruction to our commerce, and ministered the strength of an alliance to our enemies.

No change in conduct, nor even friendship shown hereafter, can alter the character of this first unfriendly act. It is the one life fountain from which the rebellion has received vitality and power. France and England, with perfectly agreeing hostility, have employed the Confederates to use against us their powder, rifles, cannon, blockade runners, and war ships, and these have been employed to advance their designs against this Republic as really as if they had been covered by the French or English flags, and a majority of Englishmen and Frenchmen have rejoiced over every Rebel success as if it were a victory of their own, and so it really was. It is mockery of the most bitter kind, to remind us, as Englishmen have so often done, that they have furnished us also with munitions of war, and that as neutrals they sell alike to each belligerent. The wrong, flagrant and designed, lies in the previous act by which, for purposes of their own, and to our deep injury, they proclaimed our enemies to be lawful belligerents.

They found a company of rebels engaged in an insurrection against a lawful Government, in a treasonable conspiracy, and because they desired the overthrow of this Republic, and they saw the traitors could be used for this foul purpose, and because they were determined to give all possible aid to these rebel enemies, and could not assist them *as traitors and rebels*, without disgrace, the French and English political magicians touched these rebels with the wand of royal proclamation, and lo! the conspirators were transformed into lawful and highly respectable belligerents, on equal footing with the lawful Government, and France and England were, of course, neutral powers, and with rights derived solely from their own proclamation, they proceeded to strengthen the rebels with all manner of moral and material support, because they had changed them from traitors to belligerents for this very purpose.

The two Powers are mentioned together as concerned in the Proclamation, because from the first they declared that they were perfectly united in their American policy.

Every subsequent act of these two Powers seems to have been conceived in the spirit of the Queen's Proclamation; there has not been a single instance, down to the seizing of the Rebel Rams, in which the English or French Government deigned to assume even the appearance of friendship. A cold, harsh, unfriendly temper, a spirit that sought occasion against us, watching for a cause of quarrel, was evident in all their intercourse. They did not attempt to conceal that they sympathized with the rebels, that they desired their success, and the overthrow of the Republic; they assumed constantly that the Union was destroyed already, and would never be restored, and their every act was intended, it would seem, to prove the assertion true.

And unless it was a part of the original plan to interfere by force, when the occasion should come, and crush us in our hour of peril and weakness, there seems no way to explain the conduct of England in the affair of the Trent. Unless British statesmen had then determined upon war, as a certain means of securing the independence of the South, and the destruction of our Government, what meaning can we attach to their acts? They knew perfectly well that the seizure of the Trent was not intended by our Government; they knew that not only did our officer act without orders, but that his act was repudiated by our authorities; they had official knowledge of all this, and yet they purposely withheld all this from the knowledge of the English people, while all means were being earnestly used to inflame the popular mind to a degree that would render a war inevitable. If the English Government did not then intend war, why did it withhold the information which it had of our peaceful disposition, and of our willingness to make honorable amends for the seeming wrong.

It seems impossible to resist the conclusion, that England then thought that with a single blow she could establish the South and free herself forever from the fear and the rivalry of a great American Nation. She knew perfectly that America desired nothing more than peace and friendship with France and England, and unless she intended to force us into a war that would be fatal to our nation, why did she suppress the truth, why did she suffer the English people to be imposed upon, and goaded into fury by falsehood, and appeals to national jealousy and pride?

These things are referred to, not to stimulate ill-feeling or a desire for revenge, but because we should be admonished by the past what to expect in the future. These acts were the result of settled policy on the part of France and England both, as will be seen before the subject is dismissed, and that policy will not be abandoned, until great changes are wrought in the political relations of Europe. These Allied Powers may be actively hostile, or ostensibly friendly toward us, as circumstances may demand, but their national policy, in regard to both America and Russia, will remain unchanged until revolution sweeps over Europe.

The objects aimed at by the Proclamation are set in the clearest light by what has since occurred. It opened at once for England a great market for all kinds of munitions of war, and every other species of goods which, by swift steamers, and from her adjacent ports, could be run through the lines of our blockade. These goods would greatly increase the courage and power of our enemy, and enable the conspirators, in all probability, to compel a separation of our territory, and this would render impossible a great American Nation.

It enabled England to build a navy for the Rebels, arm and man their ships in her own ports, as she did the Alabama and others, and these could cripple our commerce in two ways, by the destruction of our ships at sea, and by rendering them everywhere insecure, so as to transfer even our own trade to the British flag.

These two things have come to pass with immense injury to us, they are results easily foreseen, were inevitable even, and we have a right, therefore, to believe that this was aimed at in the Proclamation. Nor can Americans safely forget one important part of the sad evidence of the hostility of England in particular, that nearly the whole literary power of the Kingdom was employed, as if in concert, to injure the cause of the American Government in the eyes of the world.

The most popular letter-writer of England was sent to this country with the scarcely veiled intention of presenting the North and its cause, in the worst possible light to the world, and of painting the conspirators as making a heroic effort for independence.

Not alone the TIMES, which in spite of all denial, reflects in the main more faithfully than any other paper the prevailing temper of England, but the graver Quarterlies, which had hitherto shown some candor in regard to our country, joined in the general outcry, and lent their powerful aid in misleading and inflaming the public mind, and exciting against us and our cause the prejudices of Continental Europe.

These things were not accidental. They were evidently parts of a general plan, all bearing upon one purpose, the success of the Rebel cause, the destruction of our National Union. The statements and arguments of the British Press were contrary to all the main facts in the case, and we cannot think that educated Englishmen were utterly ignorant of our condition and our purposes. We cannot but believe in the clear light of all the facts, that the intention was to make a case that should justify the hostile attitude which they had assumed.

No one will believe that it was any surprise, or thoughtless haste, or sudden irritation, that could induce cool, experienced British statesmen to ignore both the principles and practice of their Government in regard to conspiracy and rebellion, to forget that their island has been crimsoned with blood shed to maintain the authority of the regular Government, to cast behind them all the testimony and all the acts of England against human slavery, and place themselves, and the nation which they represented, by the side of conspirators, who were not only banded together to overthrow a regular Government, but to establish a slaveholding despotism.

It is evident, that motives of no ordinary power must have swayed the British Government in adopting such a course, and equally strong must have been the influence which swept France away from all her precedents, and severed the friendly relations which had been the growth of more than half a century.

The motives of both nations must be sought in the nature and purposes of their alliance, which will be more fully explained hereafter. In carrying out the policy agreed upon by the allies, a separate part was assigned to France, in the execution of which, England cordially sustained her, as she herself declared, for she was careful to assure the world, that she approved the movement of France upon Mexico, and she supported her words by the presence and co-operation of her fleet. Nor does the withdrawal of her ships, after the landing was effected, prove by any means that the ultimate aims of France were either unknown or not approved. Far otherwise. Great Britain has uttered no note of remonstrance; but, on the contrary, France is commended for daring to defy us on the subject of the Monroe Doctrine, and is given to understand that England will be pleased to see what is called a stable Government in Mexico, and this is a full endorsement of a most iniquitous scheme of invasion and conquest, the most wicked and causeless attack of the strong on the weak, which modern times have seen.

The work of France then, was not one of personal ambition only, it was a part also of the general scheme of both nations to humble and cripple the Great Republic, to check the growth of a naval, commercial, and manufacturing nation, England the while indifferent to the fact, that the success of the plan would overthrow free institutions and the Protestant faith on all this Western Continent.

Spain and England politely escorted the French fleet and army to Mexico, and then left France to plant her army on shore, to begin a causeless war, and capture the Mexican cities, to proclaim a Government in opposition to the wishes of the people; to establish, indeed, a vast French camp on the flank of the Republic, with wishful eyes turned on California, Texas, and the mouth of the Mississippi, declaring her purpose to be, to check the progress of the Protestant Republic, and reassert on this Continent the supremacy of the Latin race and Roman Church. Such are some of the acts of these miscalled neutral powers, and prudence demands that we should study carefully their meaning. What are the national necessities of these two Governments, out of which this policy has sprung? This question requires an answer.

## CHAPTER IV.

### THE REMOTER CAUSES WHICH HAVE SHAPED THE NATIONAL POLICY OF FRANCE AND ENGLAND.

In studying the course of these Allied Powers toward America, it is not necessary to assume that it has been dictated by any special hatred of the American people, that all the old friendship of France has been suddenly turned to gall and bitterness, or that England is watching to repay the ancient grudge caused by the separation of our colonies.

There is no such animosity between these nations and our own as demands a war. Left to their own impulses, the people of these countries would not only live in peace, but would gladly cultivate friendly relations. But whoever builds a hope of continued peace, merely upon the absence of hostile feeling, or upon such popular friendship as may exist, will surely be deluded. France and England will be governed only by considerations of national policy. Back of all friendly feelings, whatever they may be, back of all influences of the ties of race, language and religion, which might otherwise move England, are the stern necessities of her British policy, by which she will be inevitably controlled.

England's commercial and manufacturing interests, England's power and supremacy among nations, these will be first considered; all else will be coldly thrust aside. The English people may be suddenly kindled into a perfect blaze of wrath, as in the case of the Trent, but the moment it was seen that British policy did not then demand a war, the angry fires burned harmlessly out.

On the other hand, it is by no means safe to suppose that, because Mr. Beecher's efforts were applauded by so many thousands, that therefore all apprehensions may be laid aside, and our safe course now is to caress the British Lion into quietness and friendship. It would be a short-sighted and dangerous policy to place any reliance upon such manifestations as these.

The necessities of England's position will override all this. If the Anglo-French Alliance continues, and these powers pursue the policy with which it was formed, they will remain in real antagonism to Russia and America, and the struggle for the mastery will surely come. Let us do our part in the preserving of peace; yet by all means, prepare for the future.

In studying the policy of the Great Powers of Christendom, we must remember, that the greatness and power of a nation in this age, depend upon the extent of its commerce and manufactures.

War itself has become as much a question of capital and machinery, as the working of a cotton mill. But the capital made for a great and long war can only be created through manufactures and commerce, and therefore, a nation must be commercially great in order to become a first-rate military power—and to great wealth must be added skill, in the production and use of machinery.

Battles by land and sea are fought more and more each year by machinery. These remarks apply with peculiar force to France and England. Their future supremacy depends upon their commerce and manufactures, and armies and navies are needed by them mainly to extend and secure these great interests, which are the sources of their wealth and power. Bonaparte found that, although he could overrun Europe by mere military power and skill, that he could lay no permanent foundation of a great Empire, except upon a manufacturing and commercial basis, such as England had created; and from that time France has been endeavoring to obtain for herself extensive colonies, and to create both a great navy and a commercial marine.

If we add to these interests, the influence of the great religious organizations of Europe, we shall have the key to the whole policy of England and the great powers of the Continent.

European wars just now are not waged for an idea, notwithstanding what France has said. England will make war, if necessary, to protect the sources of her wealth, and to crush a commercial rival; France may do the same to add to her colonies or increase her territory, that her commerce and manufactures may grow, and she may use the *idea* of restoring the prestige of the Latin race as best suited to her purpose; but she will prepare no armies or navies merely to propagate or defend a principle.

In order to understand the commercial necessities of the Great Powers of Modern Europe, it is necessary to trace from afar the movements of the commerce of the world.

From the earliest ages, to which history reaches even with an uncertain light, it is found that wealth, civilization, and power are connected with the commerce of eastern Asia, India, China, and the East Indian Archipelago. Wherever a depot could be formed for the reception of the precious merchandise of the "far East," there was a magnificent center of dominion. From this source Egypt derived much, or most of her enormous wealth. Her upper and lower Capitals were each connected with the Red Sea and so with India, one by the celebrated ship canal, portions of whose bed still are visible, and the other by a graded road from Karnac to Kosseir, and their wonderful ruins sufficiently attest how Egypt fattened both upon the military and commercial spoils of India and the eastern Islands. Solomon with his Indian seaport at Ezion Geber on the Elanitic Gulf, directed a portion of that commerce by sea toward Jerusalem, while Palmyra, that beautiful miracle of the desert, was created by the trade of the caravans, and the enriching effects upon Judea are graphically described in the Scriptures, where it is said, that iron became as stones, and silver as iron, and gold as silver in the streets of Jerusalem.

Again, when this trade was centered upon the eastern

shore of the Mediterranean, it produced Tyre, that ocean queen, and Sidon, scarcely inferior. It was a vast commercial idea, and not simply a mad thirst for useless conquest that originated the eastern expedition of Alexander. It was one of the most remarkable conceptions of any man in any age, considering the birth, education and position of the young Macedonian, dying as he did almost in youth, in his thirty-third year. It was the establishment of a mighty empire, with an Eastern capital as its center, to be enriched by the control of the commerce of India. For this purpose he founded Alexandria, and attempted to control all the East.

A French writer bears the following testimony to the sagacity of Alexander: "Alexander opened to Europe the commerce of the Indian seas, and of Eastern Africa, by a road, which if it was at the present day free and perfected as it ought to be, would cause the way by the Cape of Good Hope to be entirely abandoned." At the same time, Alexander and his successors did not overlook that more northern route upon which Russia has her eye now fixed, by the Caspian and Black Seas, and whose advantages were so long enjoyed.

Alexander built cities on the south and east of the Caspian, while one of his immediate successors attempted to unite the Black Sea and the Caspian by means of a canal connecting the River Kouban, which empties into the Euxine, with the Kouma which flows into the Caspian, thus stretching a line of navigation eastward toward India.

The idea of Alexander was long and fondly dwelt upon by Napoleon, and gave rise to his expedition into Egypt. He saw that if the East Indian commerce could be diverted from its route by the "stormy Cape," and brought once more along its ancient channels, through the Red Sea to Egypt, that it would change the seat of the world's wealth and dominion, and restore to their former importance the eastern shores of the Mediterranean. England has undertaken to monopolize this trade, by conquering and holding the very countries where it originates, and while she makes

Europe echo with her bitter condemnation of the aggressions of Russia, she seems to forget that the annals of earth do not present a record of a more grasping, selfish, and cruel policy than that which has marked her course in India. There is no act of ambition or fraud, selfishness or oppression, which Great Britain has ever charged upon Russia in her acquisitions in Europe and Asia, for the purpose of opening a highway to China and northern India, for which impartial history will not find at least a parallel in the manner in which England has sought occasions of quarrel and interference in India, and trampled down the weak and wrested their possessions away, for the purpose of controlling this very commerce of which Russia once enjoyed a part, and which she is now seeking to share with the rest of Europe.

The importance of that portion of this trade which once poured into Europe by the Black Sea, must not be forgotten in an estimate of the present course and aims of Russia. An active commerce between India and the West was carried on along this route, in the remotest antiquity to which the light of history has reached. The Phœnicians who are said to have possessed a powerful navy two thousand years before the Christian era, established colonies and built cities both on the Dardanelles and the shores of the Black Sea, which flourished upon the trade of the remote East. The description of the traffic of Tyre, in the twenty-seventh chapter of Ezekiel, shows that horses, mules, slaves, and other articles were brought from the Black Sea and the Caspian, while from thence also, she hired the soldiers by which her walls were defended. The route traversed by those merchants who brought her the silks and spices of China and India is not mentioned, but we should infer from other facts, that the course of a part of this trade was by the Sea of Aral, the Caspian and the Euxine.

Troy, at or near the entrance of the Dardanelles, was also an opulent emporium of eastern commerce, whose power is attested by the ten years siege. This city seems to have been attacked because, as Constantinople now does, it commanded the gates of the Black Sea, whose commerce was coveted by the rising and aspiring Greeks; and thus, many centuries before the coming of Christ, the theater of the Crimean war was the scene of bloody conflicts, whose objects were similar to those which have stirred up the strife of modern times—the command of the Euxine and the adjacent waters, with the traffic of the East.

The Colchians, at the foot of the Caucasus, having sprung, as is supposed, from an Egyptian colony became greatly enriched by this commerce with China, India and the intermediate regions, and their wealth and luxury having attracted the cupidity of the piratical Greeks, gave rise, probably, to the famous Argonautic expedition, in which some of the towns of the Colchians on the Black Sea were pillaged. This lucrative commerce was soon after monopolized by the rising power and maritime superiority of the Greeks, who not only controlled the trade which flowed into the Euxine by its numerous rivers, but extended a line of towns and citadels, or fortified halting places for the caravans far eastward toward India. For centuries, the highway from Greece to India lay along the Black Sea, the Caspian, and the Sea of Aral, the precise route which Russia is intent upon re-establishing now.

About one hundred and fifty years before Christ, the countries on the eastern shores of the Mediterranean contended with Rome for the riches of the Black Sea commerce. In this contest Rome was victorious, and the Euxine became a closed sea, a Roman lake, and under Pompey the country was explored toward India for the purpose of extending the commerce by which Asia Minor had been enriched. The civil wars which followed, occupied soon after the whole attention of Rome, and when Egypt fell into her hands the old highway to India by the Red Sea was occupied again, and immense Roman fleets, in the time of Augustus, passed by the ship canal from the Nile to the Red Sea, on their eastern voyages. But this commerce was burthened by the emperors with excessive duties, and this tended to force it gradually back upon the northern routes toward the Black

Sea once more. Even at this remote period the iron and furs of Siberia were among the articles of Roman traffic, the mountains of the Ural then yielding their precious deposits.

The importance of the commerce on this northern route to India at this time, may be understood from a single fact. A short time before the Christian era, Phasiona, on the river Phasis, was the great mart of eastern trade, and such was its extent that there were one hundred and fifty bridges across the stream to accommodate the business carried on upon its shores. For some time previous to the Christian era, and for several centuries subsequent, the direct trade between China and the West, centering upon the Caspian and Euxine, was exceedingly active and important, and few probably are aware of the extent of the Chinese overland trade which Russia at the present time enjoys, and which she is steadily and rapidly increasing. It is a struggle, as is perceived, between the ancient highways of traffic, and the modern new routes from India, which directing the wealth of the Indies upon Western Europe have built up London and Paris, as the eastern marts were reared of old around the Mediterranean and Black Sea, and upon the banks of the Nile.

The removal, by Constantine, of the capital of Rome from the Tiber to the Hellespont, formed a new and most advantageous center for commercial interchange between the East and the West, and Constantinople soon rose to be the foremost city of the world. To her markets crowded the merchants from China, India, Arabia, Persia and Europe, and her magnificence in consequence was without a rival. The advantages of her admirable position between Europe and Asia, and between the Mediterranean and the Black Sea, were understood and wisely used. She was, in all senses, the mistress of the East and West, with the single exception of the spiritual power of Rome. Thus for some centuries she flourished, and then the Arabian power was interposed between her and China and India, and Bagdad and other lesser Arab cities rose on the fruits of this intercepted commerce, and dazzled for a time all the East with their splendor.

Constantinople suffered in consequence, but was still, in the twelfth century, the most splendid city of the world. Bagdad alone was worthy to be in any degree compared with the Queen of the Hellespont.

But the hatred of the Roman Church and the ambition of Venice and Genoa to possess themselves of an eastern commerce, directed an army of the crusaders against Constantinople which they besieged and plundered, glutting at once religious hatred and commercial ambition, and Venice obtained the control of the Mediterranean and the Black Sea together. She excluded as far as possible Genoa from any participation in her advantages, and monopolized and fattened upon the business of Constantinople.

For the possession of this commerce long war was waged between Venice and Genoa, but in the fifteenth century the conquest of Constantinople by the Turks, and the discovery by the Portuguese of the new route to India, seaward, by the Cape of Good Hope, changed the whole face of Europe. Commerce deserted its ancient seats on and around the Mediterranean, and planted the centers of future dominion in western Europe, whose cities soon became the depots for the eastern trade.

But previous to this, as has been already stated, one great commercial and manufacturing city, with half a million of inhabitants, had been built up in central Russia where the merchandise of India and China was brought to be distributed through Europe, and thus centuries before England had any importance, as a manufacturing or maritime nation, Russia received by the way of the Black Sea, an enriching portion of the traffic of India and China.

But in the meantime, Russia was desolated by a Tartar conquest and then by civil strife, ending in a stern, unyielding despotism, that for a time not only crippled her energies but threw her back toward barbarism, and during this period the Portuguese, the Spaniards, the Dutch and English, by their maritime enterprise and skill, had turned into their newly-opened ocean route, the trade of India.

When once more Russia emerged from obscurity, in the time of Peter the Great, the world's great centers of power were altogether changed. Desolation and silence reigned in the once busy marts of the East, the old highways of commerce were all deserted, the Mediterranean fleets and cities had moldered together; in all the East the Turk ruled only to oppress, and exhaust, and ruin, and ocean fleets were conveying the riches of China, India, and the Eastern Archipelago, to the rapidly advancing cities of southern and western Europe.

At this point begins the modern struggle for the commerce of the East, which also involves the control of the wealth of Western Europe. On this question of the trade of Asia, in connection with the antagonisms of religions and races, the whole policy of Western Europe hinges, and especially has it shaped each movement of France and England in regard to Russia and America.

A brief review of these efforts to secure the trade of India and the East, is necessary to explain the meaning of the Anglo-French Alliance, the attack upon Russia in the Crimean war, the invasion of Mexico, and the hostility which France and England have manifested to our own Republic.

The policy and efforts of Russia should be first considered, because it will reveal the true reason why she was attacked by the Western Powers.

At the time when Russia was beginning to recover from the effect of her Tartar invasion, and the subsequent civil wars, the Dutch, the French and the English, were all seeking to establish themselves in India, and to obtain control of its commerce, and hold it for their own exclusive benefit. In this condition of things—the most important and enriching trade of all the world in the hands of the western Powers, which commerce would soon make them the center of power and civilization, as it had already done for all who had previously enjoyed its advantages—Russia perceived clearly that her only hope of becoming a great nation lay in her recovering for herself a portion of the Eastern commerce, and that her only route to India and China was the ancient one—by the Black Sea, the Caspian, and the Ural. She saw the necessity of producing those commodities which she might exchange for the precious stuffs of the East, and therefore created a manufacturing system of her own, for the double purpose of stimulating her own industry, opening up her own resources, and to obtain within herself an independent supply of manufactured goods, suitable for the Eastern markets.

Russia, like England, desired to share in the trade of northern India and China. For her no path was open across the waves, but the old highways leading from the Euxine eastward, though mostly deserted, might, perhaps, be opened and occupied again. But between her and her goal lay the Tartar and the Turk. The question at once arises, was it more criminal, more heartless and despotic for Russia to remove these from her path, than for England to sweep away the natives of Hindostan. Great Britain was marching northward, conquering and absorbing India as she went; Russia was marching south-eastward, conquering, but also incorporating what she subdued, and making it an integral part of her empire. She has been displacing and incorporating Turkey, while England has been swallowing India, and both for the same purpose, viz: the securing that world-enriching commerce of the East.

Russia has thus advanced to the Crimea, southward to the Danube, northward round the Black Sea, and eastward still to the Caspian, embracing that also in her acquisitions, and now, and thus, she has enclosed Constantinople in a semi-circular line of her possessions, from the mouth of the Danube, northward and eastward, round to near the neighborhood of Ezeroum and Trebizond. In addition to this, such is her influence with the court of Persia, that her route lies open eastward. In all this, Russia has invaded no right of England, has touched neither her territory nor her property. She has been endeavoring to open for herself a land route eastward, while England held the sea and was conquering and overrunning India for her own exclusive advantage.

Tried by the rules of Christian morality, the course of Russia can not be defended; but on the other hand, when compared with the policy of any one of the great nations of Europe, she will scarcely suffer in the comparison. She stands before the world as one among those powers, swayed by the same ambition, and using against others the same means and the same arts which were directed against herself, and which every strong one was using like herself for the subjugation of the weak. Not to defend or justify the acts of the Russian court, have these remarks been made, but to expose the hypocrisy of those who, deeply stained as Russia with the sin of ambition, and selfish and wanton aggression, wiped their mouths with an affectation of innocency, and cried out against the Czar as if he were the only disturber of the repose of Europe—and where this was done merely as a cover for their own ultimate designs. Let England compare her own march from the trading-post of Clive, northward over the subjugated provinces of India, with that of Russia from Moscow to the Caspian, and she will find little cause for self-congratulation. She has established a rule there over one hundred and fifty millions of a downtrodden people, the rule of strong and exacting masters over comparatively weak and defenseless races, that will be crushed out and displaced, not elevated to the position of free and civilized communities, who will neither share the glory nor the prosperity of the nation by which they have been subdued. India is a vast plantation owned by England, and worked exclusively for the benefit of the dominant race.

But to return to a consideration of the commerce of the East. Russia aims at the trade of the East Indian Archipelago, China, Northern India, Persia, and the countries around the Hellespont, the Euxine and the Caspian. To place herself in communication with the wealth of the East Indian Islands she has stretched her dominions to the Pacific, and along its shore, till she now embraces the mouth and the valley of the Amoor, including a large and fertile province obtained from China. This river opens up a commercial highway, as has been stated, far westward through northern China into Siberia, toward the Ural, whence a railway is practicable into Europe, toward Moscow and Odessa. Rivers and canals already connect all parts of the Empire with the Euxine and the Caspian, and then a great northern route stretches out before her, by the way of the Sea of Aral, toward Herat and Northern India. Already this trade has been nourished into great importance. This will appear by the following statement copied from MERCHANTS' MAGAZINE, in an article whose authority can scarcely be questioned:

"The Russian caravans carry the furs of foxes, beavers, castors, of Kamkschatka and of America, coral, clocks, linens, woolen cloths, wool, leather, looking-glasses, glass, etc., and give them to the Chinese in exchange for silk, precious stones, tea, cotton, rice, porcelain, rhubarb, gauze-crape, mourning-crape, musk, anniseed, silks with threads of gold, velvets, tobacco, sugar candy, preserved ginger, pipes, combs, dolls made of silk and of porcelain.

"In the time of Catherine, this business was valued at 20,000,000 of francs, equally divided between the Russians and Chinese. The business has constantly progressed ever since, and in 1850 the Russians exported to China 28,000,000 francs worth of merchandise. The caravans of Kiatka have not alone the privilege of the commerce between China and Russia; the independent Tartars carry to Oremberg and Troizkai the provisions which they purchase in India and China. A part of this merchandise, and of that brought by other caravans from Thibet, from India, from Khiva, from Bokhara, from all central Asia, from Persia, from Georgia from Armenia, arrive at the great fair at Nijnei-Novgorod, at the confluence of the Volga and the Olka, where, it is said, 600,000 merchants assemble. To give an idea of the importance of the commerce of Russia with the different countries of Asia, it is sufficient to say that she imports by the Caspian 8,000,000 francs' worth of merchandise, to which must be added about 10,000,000, to represent the productions which she receives by land from the Turkish and Persian provinces. She buys 116,000,000 francs' worth of Chinese productions, and brings from Bokhara and Tartary 76,000,000. Her exports by land to Asia amount to 170,000,000 of francs.

"It would be easy for Russia to bring all this commerce to the Black Sea, without doing any prejudice to her provinces in the north of Europe. She is doing everything for the accomplishment of this result, and nature has traced the route by which this immense commerce would easily flow into the Euxine. The most considerable rivers in Russia—the Dnieper, the Dniester, and the Don—empty into this sea; and with them, all the agricultural and manufacturing riches of Russia would descend into the Euxine, attracted there by the merchant vessels of the maritime nations of southern Europe, of western Asia, and of the north of Africa. In order to prevent any obstacle to this powerful current of commerce, which would bring to the south the productions of the north-east of Europe, the rivers just mentioned were connected with the Baltic and the White Sea by means of a vast system of canalization, conceived and commenced by the genius of Peter the Great.

"The Danube alone could bring into the Russian ports of the Black Sea the commerce of a large part of western Europe; for the Danube, united to the Rhine by the canal Louis, which puts it in direct communication with France, Belgium, and Holland, offers to commerce the most direct line of communication between Europe and Asia. The Caspian is connected with the Northern Sea by means of an immensely important canal, which joins the Volga to the Meta, a tributary of the Volchov, which falls into the Lake of Ladoga. This lake communicates with the Baltic (Gulf of Finland); the Volga itself is connected with the Lake of Ladoga by the canal of Tchkvin; and the canals of Koubensk, and of the north, unite the Caspian with the White Sea.

"However great the importance of this net-work of

canals in Russia in Europe, still they do not suffice to carry out but a part of the commercial projects of Peter the Great. It was still necessary to bring eastern Asia and the Black Sea into communication with the Caspian Sea. Peter, as we have already seen, had traced on a map the plan of a canal between these two seas; this was no more than the renewal of the project of Seleucus, of which we have spoken in its place. At a later period he decided to join these seas by means of a canal between the Clavlia, a tributary of the Don, and the Kamychenka, a tributary of the Volga—an enterprise which had been attempted by the Venitians and the Tartars of the Crimea.

"There were great difficulties to overcome before completing this canal, for the Don is higher than the Volga. But Peter undertook to overcome them, and employed an English engineer named Perry, who, after three years labor, was obliged to abandon it to complete fortifications of immediate necessity. Catherine II. caused the enterprise to be carried on for two years; but the ravine of Peter the Great, as it is called, is still unfinished.

"Now, it is probable a railroad will take the place of a canal. The Black Sea has already become almost a Russian lake. The Caspian belongs to the Czar, for Persia has lost the right to keep an armed force there, and her communication with the Black Sea becomes at once of the greatest importance to Russia. Besides, the Caspian receives the Volga, that immense stream which traverses all southern and eastern Russia, which, by the aid of the Kama—one of its tributaries—is connected with the Ural Mountains, so rich in mines of gold, platina, iron and copper; also the rich productions of all eastern and central Asia, of Persia, of Armenia, and the neighboring countries, flow into the Caspian by different routes. Now, to carry out the commercial views of Russia, it remains to put the Caspian in direct communication with all central Asia, as far as India and China. Nature had primitively established this immense line of communication, by making but one great internal sea of the Aral and Caspian. Ever since the epoch of the separation of these two seas by the vast steppes of Manquischlaks, a communication still existed, if it is true that as late as the tenth or eleventh century of our era the ancient Oxus (Amou Daria) emptied into the Caspian, placing her in a direct communication with the south-west frontiers of China and the north of India; but in the present day this river empties into the Aral, but still could, by its numerous tributaries and by caravans, easily bring the productions of Chinese Tartary, of Thibet, of Cashmere, and of India, by Khiva, to the Aral, which receives the Scria Daria (Jaxade), which is the route of an active commerce, and the best communication with the table-lands of China, Turkistan, southern Russia, and the Black Sea.

"From the preceding, it is easy to understand the efforts made by Russia to get possession of Khiva, which is at the head of the Amou Scria (Oxus). Once mistress of this place, Bokhara would soon see her at her gates, and Khokanee, which is near, would become her prey. Then she would at pleasure direct the caravans of China, of Thibet, and of India. After that, it would be easy to create a communication between the Caspian and the Aral, and the Black Sea would be connected with the extreme East. Independently of the facilities of communication by water, just mentioned, a prodigious quantity of merchandise would come by caravans from the East to the Black Sea.

"In two hundred days, the caravans can make the journey from Chin-Si, on the western frontiers of China, to the eastern shores of the Caspian. From there the numerous steamers can easily transport the merchandise to Astrakan. A large part of the commerce of western Persia, of Armenia, of Mesopotamia, and other countries bordering on the Tigris and the Euphrates, on the north-east of Asia Minor, goes to the Black Sea, and Trebizond is its principal depot. Now, Trebizond is within a few leagues of the Muscovite frontiers. Russia is preparing to extend herself on the South. She already covets Kurdistan and Armenia, and would like the possession of the Tigris and the Euphrates, so important to her commercial interests; and in 1829, during the war against the Turks, General Paskiewitch, who was at Ezeroum, had the intention for a moment of taking possession of Bagdad, rendered an important city by its commerce with Egypt, Arabia, India, Turkistan, and Persia, and depot of the merchandise from the East which is directed to Syria, Asia Minor, Trebizond, and Constantinople.

"Russia, in order to firmly establish her commercial power, tries, like an immense polypus, to stretch her thousand arms over the Eastern world. At the same time, she attempts to naturalize in her provinces all the industrial arts of the West, and has made a real progress, which is easy to be proved, and of which Europe makes too little account. The Czars, in their haughty pride, do not wish to be obliged to have to ask anything from the rest of the world, and profiting by the different climates united in their vast empire, endeavor to cultivate the productions of every clime. They have no colonies for the production of sugar; but the provinces of Oral and of Sacalof are covered with immense plantations of beets, from which sugar is manufactured. Their southern provinces furnish wheat for part of the west; in 1850 the exportation was enormous. The northern provinces produce prodigious quantities of flax and of hemp. Cotton is cultivated in Georgia, and the country taken from Persia; since 1845 indigo has been introduced into the Caucasian provinces; merino sheep, by hundreds of thousands, are all around Moscow, towards the Baltic, and on the shores of the Black Sea—they prosper every where, and produce abundantly. Silk is produced in the southern provinces, and in 1833 the Emperer Nicholas caused 4,000,000 of shoots of the mulberry tree to be planted. The gold mines of Asiatic Russia are very productive, and furnish annually 100,000,000 of francs to the treasury. Finally, the Czars wished to have their wine independently of France, and the Crimea is covered with vineyards."

From what has now been presented, the grand commercial idea of Russia will clearly appear. It is certainly second to no conception of modern times, and it ill becomes other nations to accuse her of ignorance and barbarism, when she is working out before the world so vast a problem as the restoration of the commerce of the East, in part at least, to its old highways, that commerce which filled once all the space between the Mediterranean and the Indies with populous cities, and whose ebbing tide left these seats of old dominion to waste and desolation.

There is one feature of the operations of Russia which seems to indicate a design to render her commercial scheme independent of the possession of Constantinople. While the Allies were arrested at Sebastopol, she was exceedingly active in Asia, in the neighborhood of Trebizond and the south-eastern extremity of the Black Sea. She evidently intends to possess herself of permanent stations there. With a seaport at that point, and communication with the Euphrates and the Persian Gulf, she would possess a commercial line to India and the East, which would be entirely independent of Constantinople and the Mediterranean.

These statements present a view of the policy and commercial views of Russia up to the time of the Crimean war. As will be more fully explained hereafter, she was endeavoring, in a perfectly legitimate manner, to develop her own great resources by cherishing her manufactures, and to secure for herself an independent channel for her trade with India. If now we turn to the policy and acts of France and England, we shall understand why Russia was attacked, and why America is menaced.

Russia was attacked because France and England feared her growing power, and for no other reason whatever. They feared that she would soon become a great commercial power by the overthrow of Turkey, and a manufacturing nation by the development of her immense resources, and therefore they wanted to cripple or destroy her—and the very same reasons have caused their hostility to us.

Let not Americans forget that these reasons remain in full force, whatever the present aspect of these powers may be.

# CHAPTER V.

## ENGLAND'S DOMESTIC AND FOREIGN POLICY.

"I would not suffer even a nail for a horse-shoe to be manufactured in America."—(Declaration of the elder Pitt).

"Nicholson, the royal governor of Virginia, calmly advised that parliament should forbid the Virginians to make their own clothing." Spotswood repeats the complaint: "The people, more of necessity than inclination, attempt to clothe themselves with their own manufactures; adding, it is certainly necessary to divert their application to some commodity less prejudical to the trade of Great Britain.—(Bancroft, vol. iii., 107).

In the same connection, Bancroft also cites the following act of Parliament: "After the first day of December, 1699, "no wool or manufacture made, or mixed with wool, being "the produce or manufacture of any of the English planta- "tions in America, shall be loaden in any ship or vessel, "upon any pretense whatsoever—nor loaden upon any "horse, cart, or other carriage, to be carried out of the "English plantations to any other of the said plantations, "*or to any other* place whatsoever." Thus, says Bancroft, the fabrics of Connecticut might not seek a market in Massachusetts, or be carried to Albany to traffic with the Indians. An English mariner might not purchase in Boston woolens of a greater value than fifty shillings, lest a larger amount should injure the manufactures of England at home.

Another Colonial measure is thus stated by Bancroft, vol. iii., 103–4: "To make most of the money centre of England, "the Lords of trade proposed a regulation of the colonial "currency, by reducing all the coin of America to one "standard. The Proclamation of Queen Anne was not "designed to preserve among the colonies the English basis; "on the contrary, it confirmed to all the colonies a depre- "ciated currency, but to make the depreciation uniform and "safe against change; and England therefore," he says, "monopolized all the gold and silver."

To these statements may be added what the English historian Russel (vol. ii., 181,) says in regard to the character and design of the "famous navigation act, which prohibited "foreign ships, unless under some particular exceptions, "from entering the harbors of the English (American) colo- "nies, and obliged their principal produce to be exported "directly to countries under the dominion of England.

"Before this regulation, which was with difficulty sub- "mitted to by some of the colonies, and *always evaded by "the fanatical and factious inhabitants of New England*, the "colonists used to send their produce whithersoever they "thought it would be disposed of to most advantage, and "indiscriminately admitted into their harbors ships of all "nations. * * * The navigation act remedied this evil; "and the English parliament, though aware of the incon- "venience of such a regulation to the colonies, were not "alarmed at the probable results."

To all these settlements, England thenceforth exported without a rival her various manufactures.

These quotations set forth with perfect accuracy the spirit and policy which have governed England for more than two hundred years. Her scheme is very simple in its elements, and its main points are perfectly obvious. They are first to manufacture, as far as possible, for the rest of the world; second, to confine the commerce of the world, as much as in her lies, to her own ships; and third, as the consequence of these, to draw to herself the gold and silver of the nations, and make herself the Banker and Capitalist for all nations.

To accomplish these ends, Great Britain has steadily

employed all her sagacity and all her power, and in the pursuit of her purpose, she has been just as selfish and unscrupulous in all her course as she was in her treatment of her American colonies.

Were she able to prevent it, she, in the spirit of Pitt, would not permit any nation of earth to manufacture a horse-shoe nail for themselves, or own a single ship.

She has hesitated at nothing that promised her success. If, in order to increase her manufactures, her commerce, and her wealth, it was necessary to oppress her colonies, and cripple their industry, it was done. If she needed a country like India, she seized it, annihilated its domestic manufactures, and reduced its millions to mere serfs, laboring for her mills, and to employ her ships. If China would not buy her opium, she battered down her towns, and slaughtered her inhabitants, and then forced China to pay the expenses of the robbery.

When Russia is making such rapid advances in manufactures and commerce, as to threaten her with rivalry, she smothers the enmity of centuries, and unites with France to attack and cripple her, and then on the first opportunity, joins with France and the Rebels in an attempt to destroy this manufacturing and commercial Republic, and she has done this in the same spirit and with the same end in view, as when she crushed, so far as she could, the manufactures and the commerce of the infant colonies. The spirit that protested against the Virginians manufacturing their own clothes, is the same which now cries out against a tariff which cherishes our home industry, and declares the Morrill tariff a proper cause of war, and the policy which forbade the colonists to ship on any but English bottoms, is the same that now furnishes privateers to the Rebels, which by rendering our commerce unsafe, transfers to British ships our own proper carrying trade.

England desires to see the nation divided, both in order that a rival may be crushed, and because she hopes that thus the South would be virtually an agricultural colony, to supply her looms with material, and furnish a market for

4

her fabrics, while France covets Mexico, Texas, and California, for similar reasons, but at the same time religious ambition is largely shaping her policy. We may judge whether they will be moved from these purposes by pleasant words.

Having thus given the key-note to the policy, both of England and France, it is necessary to look at their course somewhat in detail, in order to understand fully their present attitude and aims.

# CHAPTER VI.

## ENGLAND AND THE EASTERN QUESTION.

The present state of Europe, with its alliances and antagonisms, the union of France and England, and their hostility to Russia and America, is the result of commercial causes which have been in operation for at least two hundred years, while the religious influences that are shaping the present and the future, reach much farther into the past.

And even should France and England separate, the combinations of the future will be governed by the same general causes which have produced the present, unless one of those great revolutions should occur, which close up eras in the world's history, and form a new starting point for the nations.

In the sixteenth century, for the first time, the commercial interest in European politics became prominent. In the language of Bancroft, "it formed alliances, regulated "wars, dictated treaties, and established barriers against "conquests. Now, for the first time, great maritime powers "struggled for dominion on the high seas. The world "entered on a new epoch."

When the discovery of the ocean route to India by the "stormy Cape" had turned the Eastern trade away from its ancient marts in western Asia, and even from the Italian cities, and was directing it upon western Europe, Portugal, first of all, by the daring, enterprise, and skill of her mariners, became the center of this enriching traffic; and Lisbon for a time was the great commercial mart of Europe. She was soon, however, compelled to share this commerce with the Dutch, who wrested from her an important portion of her East Indian possessions. They rapidly amassed immense wealth by this enriching trade, and Amsterdam and Antwerp became the "great heart of commercial circulation."

The commercial prosperity of the Dutch, however, received a severe check by that navigation act by which England compelled her colonies to buy from, and sell to, her alone, an act by which she not only injured her Dutch rival, but hoped to prevent the rise of any commercial or manufacturing power in America. The power of Great Britain increased exactly in proportion as she extended her commerce and manufactures, compelling her colonies, and all else whom she could control, to sell to her their raw material, to be transported in her ships, manufactured in her mills, and then resold it to those by whom it was produced, and who were forbidden to make from it even their own clothing.

The decline first of the commerce of Portugal, and then of the maritime power of the Dutch, and at length the fall of the Spanish Monarchy, left England with only one formidable rival. France alone had power to confront and threaten her, and thenceforth for about a hundred years, these two great powers were contending directly for the control of the commerce and manufactures, and consequently for the wealth and the power of the world. It will be interesting for Americans to study the reasons which suddenly ended their conflict, and united them, first against Russia, and now against America.

About the middle of the seventeenth century, we find Great Britain actively engaged in carrying out her colonial and commercial policy, alike in the East and the West. From her American possessions, both insular and continental, she had excluded the rest of the world, and with little regard for the rights or interests of the colonists, subjected them all to a commercial system, which repressed their industry, and drained them of their wealth, in order that her own merchants and manufacturers might be enriched, and that England might be made the money centre of the world. Had she proposed to accomplish this by a fair development of her own resources, there would have been no cause for complaint. Had she become more wealthy and more powerful than others by her superior skill, energy or industry, she would have been worthy only of admiration and praise. But when she said to the millions of her colonial subjects, you shall make no use of the resources of your country, except such as our home interests demand; you shall manufacture nothing, but buy all from the English mills and shops; and you shall build you no ships, but your trade shall all be in our hands at home; she was simply a selfish oppressor, enslaving to the extent of her power, the industry of the world.

The colonial system of England, like that of all Western Europe at the time, was only an application on a large scale of the principles of monarchical and aristocratic governments, to such communities abroad as she could control. As the noble and wealthy landholders considered it quite right to use the laborers merely to increase their own wealth and luxuries, so each home government, esteeming itself to be the lord proprietor of all colonial territory, scrupled not to use the land, its resources, and its inhabitants, in any manner by which it might be most speedily enriched.

It was the serf or slaveholding principle applied to nations so far as was possible, and England grew haughty with the increase of her power, nursed her ambition and her pride until she thought to become the great slaveholder of the nations; she aimed to hold in subjection the territory, the resources, the labor of the world.

When her colonists were spirited and intelligent, like those of America, she hedged them round, and fettered them with oppressive enactments; and where they were weak and ignorant, she reduced them, as in India, very nearly to the condition of serfs upon the soil, laboring to supply cargoes for her ships, and material for her mills.

So far as lay in her power, she made of the earth one vast plantation, owned in England, and worked for the benefit of British capital. It is not surprising that, with such a spirit and aims, the English aristocracy should sympathize with our slaveholding rebels.

The present position and policy of France and England, and the motives in which their alliance originated, will be better understood, if we consider the nature of the conflict which these two powers waged with each other for a hundred years previous to their new-born friendship.

It was a contest for the dominion of the world, and as commerce, and particularly the trade of the East, was the chief source of wealth and power, it was a struggle for commercial supremacy, both in India and America. It will appear that the war which France and England carried on with each other from about the middle of the eighteenth century to the fall of the first Napoleon, sprung from the same general cause that originated the alliance itself. Many other causes, doubtless, contributed to produce the European wars of the last hundred years—still the great question which convulsed Europe was, whether England or France should be the great naval and commercial power of the world—and when they found that the power of both might be endangered by the rapid progress of Russia and the United States, they united in the unexpected alliance, in order to cripple these two rivals, declaring from the first, that this alliance reached in design beyond the settlement of the Eastern Question, that it had also a reference to the affairs of the West.

"France and England united, will be strong enough to control the world," this was the central idea of the alliance. They fought each other in order that the victor might govern the nations—and when it was found that neither could do this separately, they agreed to attempt it together. During the conflict, and in the alliance, however, their motives have not in all respects been the same. While England has been controlled mainly by commercial considerations, by the wish to be the money centre of the world, France has aimed not only at this, but she has been swayed also by a religious idea, and by the affinities of the Latin race.

She has sought to strengthen or establish the Papacy wherever her power could reach. To govern Europe as the head of the Latin races and the Papal Church, is an idea never lost sight of by the French Priesthood or the French Rulers, and to secure this ecclesiastical and political power, she, like England, has striven for a hundred years to control the commerce both of the East and the West.

Because of these different motives, which have guided the course of these two powers, it will be necessary to observe them separately, although they were engaged in the same field, and in conflict with each other.

As the great colonial enterprise of England has been the seizure and occupation of India, and because her deep interest in the Eastern Question had no reference to the welfare of Turkey, but sprung from her anxiety for her Eastern possessions, we may look to her operations on that vast field for an illustration of that spirit which so eagerly desires the destruction of this Republic, in order that America may be reduced again to colonial weakness and dependence, and which is quite willing that France should imitate in Mexico her own East Indian example.

In no other quarter of the globe has Great Britain had an opportunity of exhibiting her real character on a large scale as she has done in India. In dealing with her American colonies, she was restrained by intelligence and power, on the part of those whom she attempted to tread down; but the feeble Hindoo could offer no effectual resistance, and on that vast field where there was no let nor hindrance, we have a right to infer that the real national spirit of England was revealed.

There, she had none to judge and none to restrain; she was not forced to any act which her judgment or her heart rejected, and she was not compelled to refrain from anything which she desired to do, and if any one asks what is the real temper and conduct of England in dealing with others, it is a perfectly legitimate answer to point him to her course in India, from the landing of Clive in 1751, down to the close of the Sepoy mutiny. Since that event, external influences, the opinion of the world, and the fear of another and successful revolt, are modifying her spirit and her course.

The rise and rapid growth of Great Britain's East Indian Empire, is one of the marvels of modern times, and Americans will better understand the nature of the nation that has sought to destroy us through this rebellion, if they will study the manner in which she has obtained and governed her Indian possessions.

In 1750 England possessed a few trading factories, or ports, on the coast of Malabar and Coromandel, with the same right, and no more, of enlarging her territory by conquest, that Louis Napoleon would have of conquering the United States, if we should grant the French permission to have cotton trading ports opposite Matamoras—or to state the case more accurately, if he should make a bargain with some local authorities there for land, and then declare war if the United States should object to his occupation of our territory. The rapidity with which the Indian Empire grew from this small beginning, is thus stated by the Edinburgh Review, for January, 1863: "In 1757 England had obtained not quite 5,000 square miles. In 1793 she had enlarged her dominion to 200,000 squares miles, with a population of 40,000,000. The former had grown when the charter was renewed in 1813, to 320,000 square miles, and the latter to 60,000,000, which again were increased in 1833, to 462,000 square miles, peopled by at least 100,000,000 of natives. At this day," adds the Review, "the surface extent of land actually contributing to the Indian treasury falls little short of 600,000 square miles, with a population of 120,000,000."

The manner in which this vast territory has been acquired, this great population trodden down, is very forcibly presented in the Westminster Review, for January, 1863, from which the following extracts are taken:

"To us annexation is only a long word. By the natives of India it is felt to be an awful reality. As Mr. Ludlow well says, we should view the annexation 'not as swathed mummies in a Parliamentary Paper, but as bleeding corpses before the eyes of the multitude, with many a dark-skinned Mark Antony to put tongues in every wound.' The only way in which to bring the consequences of annexation home to us is to put such a case as the following. Let us suppose, that France is the dominant Power in Europe; that neither England nor any other country is a match for her; that she does not wish to commence hostilities against any of them, but offers to be peaceful on condition that her claims to supreme power are recognized. Let it also be supposed that a treaty is concluded, by which, on the Queen of England surrendering one-half of her territories, the remaining half is guaranteed to her and her successors for ever. Suppose further, that suddenly and without cause, France decrees the annexation of England, occupies London with troops, dethrones the Queen, dismisses her Ministers, deprives every one connected with the Court and Government of their places, salaries, and pensions, shuts every public employment against Englishmen, except perhaps the honorable posts of letter-carriers, policemen and scavengers. How should we feel under these circumstances? Should we content ourselves with a little extra grumbling, and then adapt ourselves to our altered stations? Or, if we felt sure that grumbling and resistance would not better our condition, should we not cherish bitter animosity against those who had treated us so badly, and should we not expect impartial onlookers to pity our fallen fortunes? It is to such straits as these that we have reduced the upper and middle classes of every principality which has been annexed. All have been put on an equal footing; left without hope of change and deprived of gratifying a natural ambition to distinguish themselves in the world. Under native rulers, natives are advanced to places of honor and emolument; under English rule, natives of every class are contemned and degraded. When governed by natives, most principalities yield surplus revenues; of this Sattara was a striking example. Lord Dalhousie coveted the large sum which was thus produced; he annexed that State, and the result has been an annual deficit. If independent States are well governed, they teach us a lesson; if badly governed, their inhabitants can draw a comparison in our favor. Should independent princes acquire wealth, they either expend it among their people, or else invest it in Indian securities; in either case India is a gainer. When Englishmen acquire wealth they remit it to Europe, and thereby help to impoverish India.

"To the policy of annexation let there be an end. Let us begin to conciliate those who have good cause to detest us, and consider it a nobler thing to govern humanely and well, than to acquire fresh territory at the expense of our honor, and by disregarding every rule of law and every human right. By acting thus we shall be the gainers in the long run. In 1800 the Duke of Wellington declared, what is even truer now than when he made the declaration, that the extension of our territory and influence had exceeded our means. 'Wherever we spread ourselves we increase this evil. We throw out of employment and means of subsistence all who have hitherto managed the revenue, commanded, or served in the armies, and have plundered the country. These people become additional enemies, at the same time that, by the extension of our territory, our means of supporting our Government and of defending ourselves are proportionately decreased.'

"To his policy of annexation we owe it that much of what Captain Bruce told Robert Southey more than twenty years ago is true to the letter still: 'If our empire in that country were overthrown, the only monuments which would remain of us would be broken bottles and corks. Along the whole coast our Government is popular, because the people share in the advantages of a flourishing trade. But in the interior we are hated. There is a grinding system of exaction; we take nine-tenths; and the natives feel the privation of honors and places of authority more than the weight of imposts. One of them compared our system to a screw, slow in its motion, never violent or sudden, but always screwing them down to the very earth.' It is improbable that we shall ever cease to tax, but we can easily cease to torment the natives. Although we may never gain their love, yet we need not continue to merit their unmitigated hate. We may and we ought to refrain from reducing every class and degree among them to the same level of abject dependence on our bounty and subjection to our decrees, thereby wilfully shocking their prejudices and cruelly exciting their fears, causing the man of rank to live in continual dread for the suppression of his title, the landholder for the confiscation of his property."

It is fortunate for an American who would describe the nature and results of British rule in India, that all the facts are furnished by English witnesses, and that England has drawn her own portrait as a ruler of colonies. Evidence of the same character, coming from any other source, would certainly be discredited.

One fact is quite sufficient to show the main cause of the wretchedness of the great mass of the people of India, and reveals very clearly the pressure not of a Government, but of an oppression. The Government holds all the lands of the country as the supreme Landlord, and the laborers are tenants at will, or hold only by leases at stipulated rates—the rent required leaving for the cultivator nothing but the most scanty food, and clothing, and shelter, so that the laborer can obtain no interest in the soil, has no motive for improvement, and has no hope for himself or his children beyond his mud hut and his handful of rice. Some beneficial alterations are being made in this respect; the leases are being given for longer periods than they once were, but still there is no approach to that system which is the strength and glory of America, the absolute ownership of the land by those who till it.

Americans at least understand that it is absolutely essential to the elevation of the laboring classes, that they should be the owners of the soil. Wherever this is not the case, they are speedily reduced to the rudest hut, and the coarsest and scantiest food and clothing, as the sole reward of their labor.

It is perhaps quite natural, that Great Britain, whose lands at home are nearly all in the hands of the aristocracy, and whose peasantry are but a single step above the condition of serfs, should deem it quite proper that the East Indian Government should own all the lands of India, which they could seize, and allow the native cultivators to retain only the slave's portion of their earnings; and it is not strange that this same aristocracy is in active and earnest sympathy with the slave lords of the South, in their attempt to destroy the free labor institutions of the North.

Every oppressor is by instinct in league with all other oppressors, in every attempt to reduce the laborer to the condition of the slave.

The actual condition of India, under British rule, and the spirit of the English Government, is well exhibited in the following extracts from the EDINBURGH REVIEW, for January, 1853:

"Still the utmost that can be predicated even of the Ryots, considered as subjects of the English Crown, is that they seldom, if ever, trouble themselves with discussing the merits of the system under which they live; being content to do as their fathers did before them, and satisfied so long as life and property are safe. But it is not so with any of the classes above the mere cultivators: quite otherwise. They see in the English Government a power which, however evenly it may profess to hold the scales between man and man, entertains no sympathy for them or for the traditions of their ancestry. They may acquire fortunes by trade; they may build ships and obtain the honor of knighthood; and whatever they earn by honest industry they feel that they will be permitted to keep: but all beyond this is a blank; and they are fully alive to its dreariness. There are no such avenues to advancement opened to them as stirred the ambition and stimulated the exertions of their forefathers. They cannot attain in the civil service of the State to a station more elevated than that of an ill-paid rural magistrate, or a clerk in one of the public offices. Even the status of a practising attorney in the Courts of Law seems to be denied to them, though the decision of the judge who settled the question was manifestly delivered under a painful sense of its iniquity. And as to the army, we shall have occasion presently to explain, that it offers no prizes for which it would be worth while for a native gentleman to strive. Now people so circumstanced cannot be loyal in any sense of the term. They may submit to their fate with more or less of resignation; either because they see no chance of escape from it, or through the influence of that fatalism which enters largely into the faith of all the religionists of the East. But it is impossible that they can nourish the slightest feeling of love for the government which thus grinds them down, far less be prepared to make sacrifices of any kind in defence of it. Nor do they. By the native gentry of India,—and it is a great mistake to suppose that India has not its gentry of ancient lineage and proud reminiscences,—the rule of the English is regarded not only without favor, but with settled detestation. There is not one among them all but would rejoice to see it overthrown to-morrow.

"In a word, it is idle to talk of the contentment of the *people* of British India with the particular form of government which we have established among them. They submit to it, because they cannot help themselves,—the masses with the same degree of apathy which caused their co-religionists to submit to the government of the Ameers in Scinde, and to that of the Sikh Sirdars in the Punjab. But no living soul entertains the slightest predilection for us or for our government, while all who may be crossed by it in their schemes of personal or family ambition execrate, while they endure, what they feel to be the wrong.

"That we are taking no prejudiced view of this important matter, nor broaching opinions that lack authority on which to rest, a very little research on the part of our readers will enable them to ascertain. The statements adduced here have been held and promulgated by almost every man of note who has made India and its institutions the subject of his inquiries. Open Mountstuart's Elphinstone's able History, and you will find the same tone pervading every page. He speaks of the people whom we thus slight and keep down as having attained to a high degree of civilization and prosperity before the march of Alexander across the Oxus. He describes them as retaining these advantages in the midst of endless wars, revolutions, and schemes. And he attributes the circumstance to their admirable municipal institutions, which survived every change of dynasty except the last. 'Dynasty upon dynasty,' he says, quoting from Sir Charles Metcalf, 'tumbles down; revolution succeeds revolution,—Hindoo, Pagan, Moghul, Mahratta, Sikh, English, are all masters in turn; but the village community remain the same. This union of the village communities, each one forming a separate little state in itself, has contributed more than any other cause to the preservation of the people of India through all the changes and revolutions they have suffered; and is in a high degree conducive to their happiness and to their enjoyment of a great portion of freedom and independence.' Again: 'The main evil of our system is, the degraded state in which we hold the natives. We suppose them to be superstitious, ignorant, prone to falsehood, and corrupt. In our well-meaning zeal for their welfare, we shudder at the idea of committing to men so depraved any share in the administration of their own country. We exclude them from every situation of trust and emolument; we confine them to the lowest offices, with scarcely a bare subsistence; and even these are left in their hands from necessity, because Europeans are utterly incapable of filling them. We treat them as an inferior race of beings. Men, who under a native government might have held the first dignities of the State, who, but for us, might have been governors of provinces, are regarded as little better than menial servants, are often no better paid, and scarcely permitted to sit in our presence. We reduce them to this abject state, and then look upon them with disdain as men unworthy of high station. Under most of the Mahomedan princes of India, the Hindoos were eligible to all the civil offices of Government, and they frequently possessed a more important share in them than their conquerors.'

"They are more secure from the calamities both of foreign war and internal commotions; their persons and property are more secure from violence; they cannot be wantonly punished, or their property seized, by persons in power; and their taxation is, on the whole, lighter. But, on the other hand, they have no share in making laws for themselves, little in administering them, except in very subordinate offices; they can rise to no high station, civil or military; they are everywhere regarded as an inferior race, and often rather as vassals or servants than as the ancient owners and masters of the country. It is not enough that we confer upon the natives the benefits of just laws and moderate taxation, unless we endeavor to raise their character; but, under a foreign government, there are so many causes which tend to depress it, that it is not easy to prevent it from sinking. It is an old observation, that he who loses his liberty, loses half his virtue. This is true of nations as well as of individuals. To have no property scarcely degrades more in one case, than in the other to have property at the disposal of a foreign government in which we have no share. The enslaved nation loses the privileges of a nation, as the slave does that of a free man. It loses the privilege of taxing itself, of making its own laws, of having any share in their administration, or in the general government of the country. British India has none of these privileges; it has not that of being ruled by a despot of its own; for, to a nation which has lost its liberty, it is still a privilege to have its countrymen, and not foreigners, as its rulers. Nations always take a part with their government, whether free or despotic, against foreigners. Against an invasion of foreigners, the national character is always engaged, and in such a cause the people often contend as strenuously in the defence of a despotic as of a free government. It is not the arbitrary power of a national sovereign, but the subjugation to a foreign one, that destroys national character, and extinguishes national spirit. When a people cease to have a national character to maintain, they lose the mainspring of whatever is laudable, both in public and in private life, and the private sinks with the public character. This is true of every nation, as well as of India. It is true of our own. Let Britain be subjugated by a foreign power to-morrow; let the people be excluded from all share in the government, from public honors, from every office of high trust and emolument; let them, in every situation, be considered as unworthy of trust, and all their knowledge, and all their literature, sacred and profane, will not save them from becoming, in another century or two, a low-minded, deceitful, and dishonest race.'

"These are words of wisdom, put upon record by one who better, perhaps, than any servant of the Company, understood the subject which he was discussing. Nor was he, while thus reasoning, blind to the well-nigh universal degradation of the people whose cause he pleaded. No one knew better than he that the inhabitants of the Company's dominions are the most abject race in India; no one was more keenly and bitterly aware of the causes which had produced such a result. For even the wretched satisfaction of seeing the strangers who seek their shores for the purpose of growing rich at the public expense, settle down, and become, by degrees, one of themselves, is denied them. Other conquerors had overrun their territories before, assumed supreme power, and dispensed patronage; but they did so upon the spot, and excluded no man, of whatever race descended, from a share in it. We send out our youth by shoals from England to amass wealth and exercise power for a season; each batch returning to England, when it has satisfied its own wishes, only that it may be succeeded by another. What bond of good feeling can exist between the hundred and twenty millions whom we thus govern and the few thousands of white-faced men whom we appoint to plunder while they profess to govern and protect them."

Such is the British dominion in India, extending at this

time over 150,000,000 of people; such, according to her own witnesses, is the manner in which it has been acquired, and these in general are the results of her government for the millions she has thus subdued.

A reference to these facts was necessary, in order to show clearly the nature of her policy, and the unscrupulous selfishness with which she has carried it out, when she was dealing with those weaker than herself. It was important to know that in all her course in India, no moral or religious consideration was permitted to interfere with any plan for extending her power or increasing her revenues, that neither the rights or welfare of others were allowed to have the slightest influence in deciding a question of conquest or annexation, and that the only inquiry was, will this increase the British power, and add to the wealth of Englishmen? It was necessary to know this, in order to prepare us for her subsequent attack upon Russia, and her recent joy at the prospect of our destruction, the desire to attack us in our weakness, so strong, that we barely escaped a war, and for the malicious blow struck upon our commerce through the Confederate privateers. This East Indian history will also enable us to judge exactly how much we can depend upon pleasant words or argument, or appeals made to conscience, or honor, or justice, when dealing with England, unless back of all these, are the ships and the cannon which excite her fears.

This glance at the doings and policy of Great Britain in India, will enable us to estimate aright her motives in the Crimean war, and to judge whether we have any reason to expect her friendship in the future. Her policy in India is the same that guides her in her dealings with every other nation. She carries it out on all sides so far as she has the power, and she crushes, if she can, whatever opposes.

The one central idea of this policy is, to make Great Britain the manufacturing, the commercial, the money centre of the world. For this purpose she has seized upon every available spot of earth and made it tributary to herself, taking the Lion's share of all that could be produced, stripping her American colonies by oppressive enactments, and leaving the people of India just enough to enable them to continue their toil for her.

As shown in quotations previously made, she struggled hard to render manufactures, commerce, and a navy, impossible in America, for the same reasons that she would gladly destroy them now; and she ruined the domestic manufactures of India, in order to compel the Hindoos to raise the raw material for her own mills, and then to purchase from her the manufactured articles, the Indian consumer paying thus not only the profit of manufacture to England, but the freight to her ships for carrying it twice across the ocean.

The position of England at the time just preceding the Alliance with France, and the Crimean war, her necessities, dangers, hopes and fears, were the natural result of the policy which she had been pursuing for more than a hundred years, to compel the nations to be tributary to her capital, skill, machinery, and ships, to make them virtually mere colonial appendages of her own central power.

Her aim was, to control, and bring to her own mills, as far as possible, the raw material of the world, and having manufactured it, resell it in all markets, levying upon the people the tribute of her profits, and the freight of her ships. To the full extent of her ability she prevented every other nation from manufacturing for itself, or building up a commerce or a navy of its own. While her own manufactures were in their infancy, she excluded every rival from the markets that she could control, as she did from the American colonies; but so soon as her accumulated capital, her skill and experience, and her perfected machinery, gave her the necessary superiority, then she proclaimed the doctrine of free trade to all the nations, knowing well that if she could thus gain access to the markets of the world, her capital and skill would thus enable her to crush the growth of manufactures elsewhere. Particularly did she desire a perfectly untrammelled trade with Russia and America, because exactly in proportion as she could introduce her own goods, would she prevent the erection of mills, and the growtn of a commerce and a navy.

In this policy the South has continually sympathized most earnestly with England, because she feared as much as Great Britain the rapid growth of the Free States, and the Southern leaders have persistently opposed any substantial protection to Northern manufactures, because of the wealth, the commerce, and the navy, which they would create.

If the North could only be restricted to the raising of grain, wool, stock, etc., the supremacy of the Slave States would be permanent and complete.

At the time of the formation of the French Alliance, the power of England was based, not upon her military strength, nor upon the extent of her territory, nor upon the number of her people, but upon her capital, her mills, and her navy, and these again depended upon her power to control the lands producing her raw material, and the markets for the sale of her goods. At this time France was becoming a formidable naval power, and England feared that she would attempt to avenge the disgrace of Waterloo; Russia was cherishing her manufacturus, opening up on all sides her resources, increasing her navy, and *growing* on towards India. In the West, the United States were meeting her already in the world's markets with the produce of their own looms, while their commercial marine was equal to her own. Such was the condition of England just previous to the alliance.

# CHAPTER VII.

## REMOTER CAUSES OF THE PRESENT POLICY OF FRANCE.

In addition to the motives which have governed England in her struggle to compel all nations to become tributary to her, there are others of almost equal power that are peculiar to France, and which must be studied, in order to understand her attack upon Russia, her present attitude towards the United States, and her movement upon Mexico.

First—France has never forgotten that she was once the Imperial Head of the nations of Europe; in fact, the political and religious Dictator of the world. The Empire of Charlemagne is regarded as presenting France in her rightful position, as Ruler of the Latin nations, and these, it is believed, ought to be supreme in Europe. The Kingdom of Charlemagne is looked upon as the luminous point, the triumphant era in the history of France, and the idea of re-establishing her lost supremacy, of making her throne once more the Imperial center of the world, has influenced the policy of her ablest statesmen, and her most ambitious kings. It is well known that this thought was a leading one in the mind of the first Napoleon, and he indicated this most clearly by causing himself to be crowned with the iron crown of Charlemagne, as a sign of what he intended to be, and to do.

His expedition into Egypt was connected with this idea of making France the central power of Europe. He hoped to wrest from England the control of the Eastern trade, by holding Egypt, and other Eastern shores of the Mediterranean, and by bringing the wealth of the Indies to the French cities, through the old canal of the Pharoahs. He thought in this manner to possess himself of Constantinople, to revive the Eastern Empire, and so render impossible the further progress of Russia towards the East.

The declarations and the acts of Louis Napoleon have given explicit notice to the world, that he has fully adopted the main ideas of his uncle, and that he intends to carry them out. His alliance with England, for the double purpose of ridding himself of a powerful adversary while he perfected his plans, and of using her for his own purposes; his attack on Russia, his movement upon Italy, and the occupation of Rome, his position in Syria, the finishing of the ship canal across the Isthmus of Suez, in which he is now engaged, the plans which years ago he made of a ship canal across the American Isthmus at Panama, the explorations which he has made of the mineral wealth of our Pacific coast, and now his occupation of Mexico—all are parts of one gigantic scheme, to make France once more the recognized head of the Latin races in all parts of the world, and give to her more than the power and splendor of the Empire of Charlemagne. Whoever attempts to study the career of Louis Napoleon without understanding this scheme, will have no key to his policy. Viewed in connection with this, every movement is plain.

But the religious sentiment has also exerted an important influence upon the policy of France. In the time of Charlemagne, she was the one Empire which, with the one Church, ruled all the Western world. The Roman Church and the Roman Empire, with the French king at its head, they were jointly supreme. The Empire was the earthly ally and supporter of the Church, and the Church gave to the Empire the full authority of what was deemed by all a Divine sanction. Charlemagne was crowned as Emperor of the Romans, and the Roman Church, and Roman Empire, with France as its head, were expected to go down into the future together.

The Imperial crown then passed from France into the

possession of Germany; but France has not forgotten that she was once the political head and recognized defender of the Latin Church, and from the time of Charlemagne to the present, the French clergy have mourned over their lost glory, and have hoped that in some manner it might be regained. For the double purpose of restoring the Roman Empire, with France at its head, and he the Emperor of France, and of bringing to his support the power of the church, Napoleon caused himself to be crowned by the Pope with the crown of Charlemagne, reviving in the French clergy the hope of the restoration of their former power. For precisely similar reasons, Louis Napoleon has connected his movements with the old ambitions of the French clergy, and of the Catholic Church as a whole, espousing the cause of the Roman Church at Jerusalem and Constantinople, and taking on that occasion the part of champion of the Western Church, and then pushing Austria aside in Italy, and lifting France to the foremost position among the Latin races; and, finally, invading Mexico, and threatening the United States, with the solemnly avowed intention of restoring in America the prestige of the Latin race, and of course, the power of the Roman Church.

These two ideas, the restoration of the Empire, and the supremacy of the Roman Catholic Church, must not be lost sight of by any one who wishes to understand the policy of France, and they should be very carefully considered by Americans, because thus only can we know the power of the motives by which the French Emperor is governed, both in his attack upon Mexico, and in his hostility to the Republic.

Thus only can we judge whether it is probable that he will abandon for slight reasons what he has undertaken on this continent, or whether it will be necessary for us to decide by arms the question of imposing a French Monarchy by force upon a people inhabiting our border, with the avowed intention of using the territory, the resources, and the proximity of position, as a standing menace to this Republic, and to our Protestant Faith.

We shall find that our danger from this quarter is greater than from England, for while Great Britain declares that she does not contend for an idea, the French movement has in it the dangerous element of religious enthusiasm. True, it is almost dormant as yet, or living only in the bosom of the clergy; but the history of the church shows how easily a movement for the universal restoration of Romanism might rouse whole nations for a crusade, for what the people would deem a truly holy war.

We shall find, that with the exception of a short period in her history, wherever France has carried her arms, she has borne with her a zeal for the Papal church.

These facts, in the past history of France, have for us a very grave significance, when they are coupled with the exact words of the Emperor himself, explaining his intentions in the movement upon Mexico: "We propose," he says, "to restore to the Latin race, on the other side of the "Atlantic, all its strength and prestige. We have an inter-"est, indeed, in the Republic of the United States being "powerful and prosperous; but not that she should take "possession of the whole Gulf of Mexico, thence to com-"mand the Antilles, as well as South America, and to be "the only dispenser of the products of the New World."

Whoever will weigh these words in connection with the history of the Latin race, and Latin church, with the schemes of Napoleon, and the course of the present Emperor, will be convinced that the almost immediate future will present to us, and to Europe, the most solemn questions of modern times. It seems almost certain, that our contest with the slave power, fierce and bloody as it is, will be but the opening act in a war drama, and that gigantic, though it be, it may prove the most insignificant of the series.

The words of Louis Napoleon appear like the throwing down the gage of battle to all Protestant nations, to all free institutions; nay, more, to every people outside of the Papal church,—and the most alarming feature of the declaration is, that this is precisely its meaning. Such a threat in regard to the Western Continent presupposes the intention to restore the lost prestige and strength of the Latin race and Papal church in Europe also, and the reality of this intention is clearly set forth in every step which the French Emperor has taken, from the Crimean war to the present time, including that proposal for a European Congress, which means simply an attempt to chrystallize the Latin powers around France as the Imperial centre,—and to make the Emperor not only independent of England, but, as he hopes, to give him the power to crush her if he pleases.

We know too well what is implied in the proposition to restore the strength and prestige of the Latin race and Papal church, both here and in Europe.

It means the destruction of civil and religious liberty, the suppression of free speech and free thought, the elevation of nobles and priests, the ignorance, the poverty, the degradation of the people. We know that this cannot be accomplished without such a conflict as the world never saw; and yet every sign of the times compels us to the conclusion, that such a stupendous conspiracy against the liberties of humanity is being matured, and that the Latin race and the Papal church will make the attempt under the lead of France, and that we must take the Emperor at his word, when he sets forth the invasion of Mexico as a part of the plan. The scheme is so bold, and so vast, that it seems more like a Satanic inspiration than a mere conception of an ambitious man.

The following extracts from a very able article on the Monroe Doctrine, in THE NEW ENGLANDER, for Oct., 1863, exhibit the subject in a very clear and forcible manner:

"The other dangerous element in the case before us is the growing arrogance and strength of the Papal Power in connection with all the progressive developments of French ambition and conquest. It is curious to see how everything that France does or gains or aims at becomes subservient to the Papal Power, and turns to the disadvantage of religious liberty and of enlightened civilization. Beginning with the overthrow of the Roman Republic, and the still continued armed occupancy of Rome by a French army, as the only means of upholding the Pope in his throne as a temporal prince, we see in Cochin China, in Madagascar, in Turkey, in Spanish America, in Poland, and everywhere, that it is the support and favor of the Pope which constitutes Louis Napoleon's reliance in the last resort; and it is the extension and consolidation of the Papal Power which gives unity to all his aims, and the strength of a common interest to all his schemes. It is now clearly understood that the outbreak in Poland was but a plan for establishing in the centre of Europe a Franco-Romish interest that should serve as a point of defense and aggression against Russia and the Greek Church. It is Popery, struggling against the advance of freedom and civilization, that has for forty years kept the Spanish American states in turmoil, and kept them from consolidating their governments or improving their conditions. In Venezuela, in Colombia, in Ecuador, everywhere, it is the Priests' Party against the body of the people; the people striving to recover the right of governing for themselves, and the Priests, aided by a few bigots, a few rich men, a few European Know-nothings, and a good many reckless and marauding brigands, trying to keep the power of the government in the hands of a class, and subject the many to the control of a few. This power has at length been happily put down, at least for the present, by the gallant and patriotic President Mosquera in Colombia. It has succumbed, at least temporarily, to a compromise in Venezuela; while, in the adjoining republic of Ecuador, it has apparently achieved an absolute triumph, in the treaty which was concluded in April last, by President Morena with Cardinal Antonelli in the name of the Pope.* And

* This treaty, which has been published in *El Nacional*, the official journal of Ecuador, contains the following articles, which serve to illustrate the Pope's idea of religious liberty, where he has things in his own way:

"1. The Roman Catholic and Apostolic religion is the religion of the Republic of Ecuador. Consequently, the exercise of any other worship, or the existence of any society condemned by the Church, will not be permitted by the Republic.

"2. The education of the young in all public and private schools shall be entirely conformed to the doctrines of the [Roman] Catholic Religion. The one of the chief ends of the conquest of Mexico by France, is announced to be the ascendency of the Latin race, and the restoration of the Church of Rome to its ancient honor and power in the country. The confiscation already begun of the estates of all Mexicans guilty of the crime of supporting their own constitutional government, will prepare the way for the restoration of the estates of the Church, valued at a hundred millions of dollars, heretofore sequestered for the uses of the state.

"In former days, the civilized world has been accustomed to rely for protection against any unwarrantable aggressions of Rome, upon the vigilance and strength of the two great Protestant Powers, Prussia and England. And it is a most unfortunate coincidence, that just at this time, when the Papal Power is so rapidly consolidating itself, Prussia is well nigh powerless for any good purpose, by the insensate relapse of the present monarch into the wildest madness of absolutism; while the government of England is under the administration of a chief who seems to have become practically, but a mere satrap of Louis Napoleon. Mr. Kinglake, in his remarkable volume on the Crimean War, before

teachers, the books, the instructions imparted, &c., &c., [the provisions are given in a very condensed form], shall be submitted to the decision of the bishops.

"3. Government will give its powerful patronage and support to the bishops in their resistance to the evil designs of wicked persons, &c.

"4. All matrimonial causes, and all those which concern the faith, the sacraments, the public morals, &c., are placed under the sole jurisdiction of the ecclesiastical tribunals, and the civil magistrates shall be charged to carry them into execution. The priests shall confine themselves to consulting the lay judges, if they think proper to do so.

"6. The privileges of churches [the ancient right of asylum is consecrated buildings] shall be fully respected."

The Philadelphia *Catholic Herald and Visitor*, August 5th, exults:

"*A most satisfactory Concordat* has been concluded between the Holy See and the Republic of Ecuador, in South America. In that exclusively Catholic country, *the public exercise of no other worship than the Catholic is to be allowed. The bishops are to have the control of the education of youth,* and to propose three candidates for the vacant episcopal sees to the selection of the President and of the Pope. No *Exequatur,* no Piedmontism, no Gallicanism, no shortcomings. The Hispano-American population, in the State of Ecuador, mean to *be truly and generously Catholic!*"

referred to, has described the process by which Great Britain was drawn, wholly beyond her intentions and against her interests, into that most bootless conflict. And there is no reason to expect that the same fallacious *entente cordiale* will not be made available to draw her onward, *nolens volens*, into whatever ulterior national embroilments the conquest of Mexico may lead to, in the interest of Popery and Absolutism.

"But the Monroe Doctrine is not dead. It will not die, for truth never dies, and the Monroe Doctrine is an axiomatic truth in political science. It is as true now as it was when Washington issued his Farewell Address, that 'Europe has a set of primary interests, which to us have none or a very remote relation. Hence she must be engaged in frequent controversies, the causes of which are essentially foreign to our concerns.' It is as true now as it was when Mr. Monroe issued his Declaration, that 'any attempt on the part of European powers to extend their system to any portion of this hemisphere,' IS 'dangerous to our peace and safety.' And we of this day have been brought at length by the cogent force of events, to see as clearly as that golden administration saw, that 'any interposition' with any of the American nations, 'by any European power,' for the purpose of 'controlling their destiny,' IS 'the manifestation of an unfriendly disposition towards the United States.' Those who have doubted, now see it plainly. The efforts for forty years, of selfish partisans, of timid statesmen, of political sciolists, of venal scribblers, or of covert reactionaries, to make it out that the Monroe Doctrine was a *brutum fulmen*, which struck no blow and made no mark, and then vanished into thin air, are all blown to the winds. The clouds which temporarily shrouded it from general view, have been rolled away by the winds from the South-west, and the Doctrine shines forth as the political cynosure by which we are to steer our national course through this sea of difficulties, until the Imperial Republic shall resume her place among the nations, as a light to oppressed millions, and the political regenerator of the world."

"What is next to be done, is not for us to prescribe. By what steps or through what struggles on our part the Monroe Doctrine is to be restored to its ancient respect in the counsels of European dynasties, will depend more upon the wishes of those Powers than on our own. The United States long ago reached that condition of conscious strength anticipated by Washington, when under any European intrusion 'we may choose peace or war, as our interest, guided by our justice, shall counsel.' Should the European Powers receive the lessons of our recent successes, and speedily withdraw their criminal aggressions on a neighboring republic, thus paying their old homage to the Monroe Doctrine, that is well. Should they make open war upon us, we shall meet them as best we may, notwithstanding our embarrassments with the rebellion. Such a country as this, inhabited by such a people, and blessed with such institutions and such a history, is worth a struggle of a hundred years against the world in arms, before we allow the Political System of Europe to be extended over us by all the military force that can be brought against us. Should they merely continue their intrusions and impertinencies, we can afford to consult our own convenience, and choose our own time for appealing to the last resort of injured nations for redress of the wrong.

"And if the European Powers should see fit to press the matter to its ultimate issue, we shall not shrink from our proper responsibility, as a free people and the friends of free institutions. And the Powers may be sure that we shall not stand wholly on the defensive. We will say no word and do no act implying an admission that the Political System of America is less honorable than that of Europe, or less true, or less beneficent, or less worthy of heroic sacrifices in its cause, or less deserving of universal adoption. The question will then lie between the European System for America, and the American System for Europe. If, by their machinations or aggressions, we are once involved in their conflicts against our will, there will be no more peace for us or for them, until the American ideas of national independence and responsibility have been spread over the countries of the Old World, and the doctrines of national interference and the Balance of Power have been cast among the rubbish with the systems of absolutism and popular ignorance which they were devised to support. And let God give the victory to the right!"

With the statement of these general views we shall be better prepared to follow France intelligently in her direct struggle with England for colonial and commercial supremacy. Near the close of the seventeenth century, when the power of Louis XIV. was at its heighth, France had nearly reached the position which she held under Charlemagne. The French Monarch assumed the attitude of Judge and Dictator of Europe. The French navy was then the most formidable in the world, numbering no less than one hundred ships of the line, in addition to the usual proportion of smaller vessels.

From this point the power of France again declined, and at the close of the long exhaustive war, which ended with the peace of Aix La Chapelle, she had no longer the power to carry on a great conflict, and her once formidable navy had been completely ruined. She was anxious for peace, in order that she might renew her strength for another effort to control the world. At the very time when she was negotiating the peace of Aix La Chapelle, she was already forming her plans for future aggressions. The commercial idea, as Bancroft has stated, had become about that time the leading one in European policy; and it was clearly seen that whatever nation should control the trade of the East, in connection with extensive colonies, would become the centre of power for Europe. Acting upon this idea, France formed the design of obtaining for herself vast colonial possessions, both in the East and West, and as a necessary part of the plan, began at once with great vigor, and on a large scale, the reconstruction of her navy.

M. Dupleix was at this time Governor of Pondicherry, a trading post which the French then held in India, and he urged upon France to possess herself of the whole of Hindostan, and then make that a base of operations for the subjugation of all Eastern Asia, and make it a colonial empire subject to the French crown.

The magnificence of this conception is well attested by the manner in which the dazzling project has been executed by Great Britain—and it shows, also, the largeness of the ambition of which the French mind is capable.

Galissioniere, who was then Governor of Canada, proposed to his Government a scheme of conquest in America of equal grandeur. This was no less a project than to draw a military cordon around the English colonies, from the St. Lawrence to the mouth of the Mississippi, and thus confine at the outset these colonies to a narrow strip on the Atlantic, then gradually expel them from the continent, and place America permanently in the hands of the Latin race and Papal church, France holding the North, and Spain the South of the Western world.

Almost immediately after the peace of Aix La Chapelle, in 1748, France engaged in the most active measures for carrying out these great designs by which she hoped to cripple the power of England, and make herself mistress of Europe and the world. In both hemispheres she began aggressive movements that were intended to lead to war.

In India M. Dupleix began that system which England has so successfully practiced since, of intriguing among the native princes, espousing the quarrel of one party for the purpose of weakening and plundering both. He conceived the ideà of controlling India by procuring for France the appointment of princes for the provinces, and was himself appointed Nabob of the Carnatic, a valuable province in the Eastern part of Hindostan.

By various arts, and acts of violence, the French possessions in India were rapidly extended, until they held the Eastern or Coromandel coast for six hundred miles. At this point, the progress of the French in India was arrested by the English through the genius of Captain, afterwards Lord Clive, who first established the British Empire in the

East on a firm foundation—and opened one of the darkest chapters in all human history, if England's own witnesses are worthy of belief.

The attempt of Dupleix was only the carrying out of an idea which long before occupied the French mind, and the leaders of the Papal church. He whom history has named the great Colbert, the leading statesman of the early part of the reign of Louis XIV., had established an East Indian Company at Pondicherry in 1664, nearly an hundred years before Dupleix's time. At the same time he created a navy, which made France for the time the first maritime power of the world. His intentions were exactly the same with those of Dupleix and the French statesmen of his time; the same with those of Napoleon, when he made such gigantic efforts to crush the naval power of England, and by the possession of Egypt and Syria to control for himself the commerce of the East, the same which governs the whole policy of Louis Napoleon now.

Leading ideas control the movements of nations for centuries, and the battle of the ages is continually renewed. France, age after age, struggles to realize the French idea of the political and ecclesiastical supremacy of Europe and the world. The political and the religious have not always been obviously united, and France has even for a time been guided by the irreligious, the infidel sentiment. Still the Papacy, with a brief exception, has been ever a power in the State; and now Louis Napoleon bases his grand movement upon the affinities and prejudices of race, and upon the revived ambition and superstitions of the Latin Church. It has, therefore, become the widest and most dangerous movement of modern times.

The enterprize, the zeal, the activity of the Papal church, and its power, is well illustrated by its movements in the East. A hundred years before France had made any important settlements in India, the missionaries of the Latin church were traversing India and China with a heroic daring and endurance of hardship, unmatched since the days of Paul, they spread every where in the East such knowledge of

Christ as they had themselves, their zeal for God apparently bounded by the one idea of extending the dominions of the Pope, and salvation being in their view secured by baptism into the communion of the Papal church.

But whatever their motives, their enterprise and their enthusiasm were both boundless. Nothing seemed too great to attempt, or too difficult to perform. Such missionaries as Zavier defied all dangers, whether from heat, or deserts, or pestilence, or wild beasts, or hostile men. These operations show us the prodigious power of religious enthusiasm, and history informs us how well the Romish church understands its nature and its use. It is this power to which the leaders of the Papacy, in union with the statesmen and Emperor of France, intend to appeal in their present designs. The ancient supremacy of the Romish church, the former prestige and strength of the Latin race, the glory of France, these form the spell words with which Louis Napoleon's Jesuits hope to rouse the Catholic nations of Europe, and unite them under France as Imperial Head. Thus are the schemes of to-day connected with those of the past.

For more than half a century, from the landing of Clive in India till the fall of Bonaparte, the contest was carried on for the possession of the East, but France was unsuccessful, and forced back at all points, and the final result left her with only an inconsiderable territory around Pondicherry, while England rules over one hundred and fifty millions of East Indian subjects.

France, however, as we shall see, has not abandoned the idea of dominion in the East. Her plan for possessing herself of North America, and for securing all America for the Latin race, and Papal church, was as vast as the one she formed for India. In the exploration of the Western Continent, the missionary operations of the church had preceded the march of armies, and the progress of commerce—as they had also done in India. With the leaders of the Papacy, territory is sought only to extend the dominion of the Pope and the church, and with the newly awakening zeal of

Romanism as a stimulant, it is easy to foresee what would follow the establishment of French supremacy on this Western Continent.

At least a hundred years before the American Revolution, the Jesuit Missionaries were busy around the Lakes and in the Valley of the Mississippi. They had followed the great lakes to Superior, they had gone on southward to the Mississippi, and their stations were planted on the banks of the Ohio. From Quebec to New Orleans, the whole West has been one great Missionary field for the Church of Rome nearly two hundred years ago, and it is not strange perhaps, that the Catholic Powers should often consider whether it is possible for them to recover again this lost dominion of the West.

The French plan for the military occupation of North America embraced a series of fortified posts, extending from Louisburg on the Atlantic coast westward, to Quebec and Montreal, and along the great lakes, and then southward to New Orleans. Besides this general line, there were some strong positions on Lake Champlain, and in the upper portion of the Valley of the Mohawk, and on the upper waters of the Ohio.

The immediate effect of this chain of forts was to confine the English to the Atlantic coast, rendering the expansion of the colonies westward impossible; the ultimate result of the scheme, had it proved successful, would have been, to expel from America the English, and the Protestant Church together.

In the progress of the war which followed these encroachments of France, she was driven from all these positions in rapid succession, till on the plains of Abraham, Montcalm, in dying, yielded virtually to Great Britain all that France possessed in America, with the exception of New Orleans. This at length was ceded by Napoleon to the United States, and thus the colonial empire of France, both in India and America, vanished, leaving only a little patch of territory in India, and some insignificant islands in the West Indian group.

At the close of the war which ended with the fall of Bonaparte, France found herself stripped of her vast colonial possessions, which were all in the hands of the Power she hated, and feared more than all others—and by that same ancient enemy her navy had been utterly ruined. France was a mortified, defeated, and weakened Power, but she was not utterly discouraged. She accepted such a peace as was granted, and with bitter memories and meditated revenge, she silently bided her time. She had played a stupendous and bloody game for the control of the commerce and manufactures of the world, and with her the Romish church had attempted to extend the Papacy in all lands, and both had utterly failed.

Protestant England was the dominant power in all the earth, her navy had complete command of all seas, her commerce was the commerce of the world, and London was the great money centre of Christendom.

But mighty nations do not abandon a traditional policy, a national idea, because of severe defeat. They simply pause to recruit their strength—and such a people as the French, fertile in resource, energetic, and proud, recover very rapidly even from extreme disaster. In less than a century after the surrender of her North American possessions, forty-five years after the battle of Trafalgar, in which her navy was annihilated, and thirty-five years after Waterloo, where her military power was broken, France was prepared to renew the contest for the control of Europe and the world.

The French, through the period of their humiliation, could scarcely name Waterloo, or think of St. Helena, without an execration for England, and breathing a desire for vengeance. Actively and steadily she gathered her resources, improved her army, and enlarged her navy, and England soon began to be uneasy at the rapid progress of her formidable neighbor. France at this time had been placed permanently under the control of Louis Napoleon. The designs of the new Emperor none then could penetrate, but it was quite evident from his military and naval preparations, that he intended that France should play no inferior part among the nations of Europe. This brings us to consider the position of the great powers of the world just previous to the Anglo-French Alliance; and it is hoped that this rapid review of French policy for a hundred years, will enable us to understand the nature and objects of this unexpected compact.

# CHAPTER VIII.

## CONDITION OF ENGLAND, FRANCE, RUSSIA AND AMERICA, WHEN THE ANGLO-FRENCH ALLIANCE WAS FORMED.

Mr. Kinglake, in "The Invasion of the Crimea," comments with great severity upon the Alliance with France, as the one step which rendered inevitable a war with Russia, which might otherwise have been avoided. He says that the French Emperor subordinated all other considerations to the plan of forming with England a combination against Russia. In studying the policy of France it is very important to remember this fact. France originated the war against Russia, and it began in a quarrel between the Latin and Greek Churches about the holy places at Jerusalem, which was carefully nursed by France into a cause of war, as will hereafter be made to appear, while England with alacrity accepted the proposal of France to attack Russia. But England had motives of her own.

Mr. Kinglake seems to think that the prominent motive of Louis Napoleon in seeking the Alliance was to gain support and recognition for that throne which he had so lately set up with perfidy and in the blood of his countrymen, and he presents no very satisfactory reasons for the course of England.

Events have shown already, and will yet more clearly reveal the real intentions of these two powers in forming that strange agreement, in which, without sufficient ostensible reasons, they suddenly abandoned the policy which for centuries they had pursued towards each other, and all the humiliations and resentments of France were apparently forgot.

At this point Mr. Kinglake makes a statement in regard to the temper of his countrymen, which it would be wise for those Americans to consider, who think that the good feeling, the kindly sympathies of England, may be relied upon hereafter, if only soothing, friendly words are used by us, or who hope that such men as Mr. Cobden and Mr. Bright can stay the tide of British violence and passion when once the cry is war. After showing that the war was brought on by France, and that England was easily induced to join her, he says:

"Welcome or unwelcome, the truth must be told. A "large obstacle to the maintenance of peace in Europe was "the temper of the English people. In public, men still "used forms of expression implying that they would be "content for England to lead a quiet life among the nations, "and they still classed expectations of peace among their "hopes, and declared in joyous tones that the prospects of "war were glaring and painful; but these phrases were the "time-honored canticles of a doctrine already discarded. "The English people desired war; and perhaps it ought to "be acknowledged that there were many to whom war, for "the sake of war, was no longer a hateful thought." Again he says: "All whose volitions were governed by the ima-"gined freeing of Poland, or destroying Cronstadt and "lording it with our flag in the Baltic; or taking command "of the Euxine, and sinking the Russian fleet under the "guns of Sebastopol; all who meant to raise Circassia, and "cut off the Muscovite from the glowing South, by holding "the Dariel Pass, and those also who dwelt in fancy upon "the deeds to be done on the shores of the Caspian; all "these and many more saw plainly enough that separation "from the German Powers, and alliance with the new "Bonaparte, was the only road to adventure." The English people were eager for war, for the sake of war, for the sake of adventure—eager to strike down a power that had helped to save her from Napoleon, a power that had not harmed her, and that meditated no attack.

Connect this statement with the late picture of that same English people furious with passion over the affair of the Trent, shouting with joy over the flames of our vessels fired by pirates fitted out in their own harbors, and it may easily be seen what safety there is in depending upon the kind feeling of England—even of the English people. In dealing with England, our iron clads and Parrott rifles, and fifteen-inch guns, will be found more convincing arguments than the most good natured and eloquent words.

But the French Emperor and English statesmen were not moved by passion in forming the Alliance, or in the Crimean war. What then were the true reasons by which the two nations were governed? To answer this question, it is necessary to study the condition of France, England, Russia and America, at the time when the Alliance was formed, and the attack on Russia was made.

At the close of the war in 1815, when the Allied armies entering Paris, England occupied the proudest position in Europe. Both in India and America she had stripped France of vast colonial possessions; in fact, to quote the words of Alison, "During the course of this long struggle, "the colonies of all the European States successively fell "into the hands of England."

She had utterly destroyed the French maritime power, and with it her commerce, and Wellington at Waterloo crushed the military idol of France and with him her army. The navy of England was supreme every where, and with her immense colonial territories, her navy, and her moral power, she was well prepared to rule for a time the world. She saw very clearly the necessities of her position. She understood both her strength and her weakness. She knew that she could not remain permanently the chief military power of Europe, and that she must rule the nations, if at all, through her capital, her machinery, and her ships. If she could draw from all countries the raw material for her work-shops and her looms, and sell in all markets her manufactured fabrics, securing for herself the profits of her labor, her capital and machinery, and the carrying trade to her ships, then indeed all nations would become tributary to her. She pressed this scheme of aggrandizement in all lands to the full extent of her power, and far and near, her policy was crowned with a success that was equal to her ambition.

Her policy was to repress and destroy all commerce and manufactures except her own, and she found the South ready to aid her in any free trade scheme which would prevent the growth of manufactures or commerce in the free States, while many of the smaller States of Europe were merely factors of the merchants and mill owners of England, so that the wealth of the world flowed towards that small island as the rivers to the ocean.

In the meantime, as has been stated, France was recovering from defeat and exhaustion, and when Louis Napoleon seized the throne, grave apprehensions began to fill the English mind—nor was this anxiety without sufficient cause.

No sooner did the new monarch feel himself secure, than it was apparent that the one purpose which guided all his movements was to make France, in the shortest possible time, the leading military and naval power of Europe. The attention which was given to the enlargement, organization and discipline of the army, the artillery studies of the Emperor—and above all, the gigantic scale of his naval preparations, showed very clearly the intentions of the new ruler of France. Europe at first looked on puzzled and amazed. That France should become powerful, a European leader under such a man as Louis Napoleon, was deemed an impossible thing.

But as proofs of consummate ability in the guidance of French affairs began to multiply, and her military and naval power assumed grander proportions, as immense navy yards and fortifications began to menace the coast of Britain, English statesmen, in view of the past, had good reason for anxiety, if not for alarm.

It certainly was quite possible that France was preparing

to avenge herself for the humiliations of centuries. It was certain that a Bonaparte was on her throne, an ardent admirer of that uncle who had made the conquest or humbling of England one of the chief purposes of his life, and that uncle had not only been defeated by England, but she had mercilessly chained him to a rock, and shutting out all succor, left him there to die.

France had not forgotten, much less had the nephew forgotten or forgiven. Now that nephew wielded the power of France, his army was superior to any thing which England could command, and her navy was only the second in the world. Well might Englishmen inquire, how will this power be used? What purpose has this new Bonaparte in these vast preparations? What can he intend, unless to carry out the policy of his uncle in the invasion of England, and to revenge France and his family for national defeat, and especially for St. Helena and Waterloo. Those who remember the tone of the English Press at this period, know well how deeply the English nation was moved, even alarmed at the menacing attitude of France, from whom came no threatening word, but whose sphynx-like mystery was a source of terror, while especially at her great naval stations opposite England, the hum of preparation continually sounded.

What could this warlike activity mean, unless a sudden attack upon England was meditated? Between France and all other powers there seemed no cause for war. But the preparations and growing power of France were not the only causes which created uneasiness in England. Her supremacy had become a commercial rather than a military one, notwithstanding the immense strength of her navy, and it was necessary for her if she would rule the world, to retain her markets, to prevent, if possible, the growth of commercial rivals, and to secure the colonial possessions which she had wrested from others. As she surveyed the world, an eastern and a western vision troubled her. Hitherto Russia had been regarded as a mere military, barbarian Colossus, whose joints were not well compacted, composed of heterogeneous materials, that could not be united in one true, organic, political structure, with a common life, which would insure a regular and healthy growth.

But Russia, under Nicholas, began to give signs that she was more than a mere barbarian camp, more than a nation of serfs and wandering Tartars. She gave evidence of a true national life, of enlargement, which was growth from a national life centre. Under many disadvantages the Russian Emperor was striving to give his country the means of independent self-development, and was laboring to establish manufactures and internal commerce, and to make profitable use of the great resources of his empire. He was establishing schools for his people, literary, and agricultural, as well as military, opening roads, projecting railways and canals, and putting steamboats upon his numerous rivers.

He was improving his navy and his mercantile marine, and in all his operations he seemed to prefer American mechanics, and American machinery, a fact which, of course, did not escape the watchful eye of England.

He had constructed a large fleet upon the Black Sea, and its fortified rendezvous, Sebastopol, was only a few hours sail from Constantinople; Turkey, unless defended by other powers, was apparently within reach of the Czar, and once in possession of Constantinople, Russia would have the means not only of becoming a great military power, but she would certainly be a first class manufacturing and commercial nation.

Russia, moreover, had already extended the outposts of dominion far on eastward, from the Black Sea along the Caucasus, and the northern frontier of Persia, and England saw, that if Turkey were overgrown, even the peaceful march of Russia eastward, would bring her at no distant date to the borders of her Indian possessions. The English Press at this time was complaining, as if it were ill-treatment of Great Britain and Europe, that Russia was planting vineyards in the Crimea with the intention of making her own wine, and that she was multiplying her flocks of sheep for the purpose of manufacturing her own woolens, and that in general, she was disposed to cherish and protect her own workmen, and develop her own resources, instead of following those free-trade doctrines, which England was then proclaiming to the world.

It was apparent that by this course, Russia in time would not only manufacture to supply the wants of her own people, and to this extent curtail the foreign markets for English goods, but with her boundless mineral wealth, her great facilities for internal trade by her navigable rivers, with the control of the Black Sea, with Constantinople, and access to the Mediterranean, she might become in all respects a very formidable rival of both England and France.

Russia proposed to sweep from her path that usurping infidel power which had crushed her mother church, conquered her holy City Constantinople, and held in bondage eleven millions of Christians of her own communion; but she meditated no attack upon any European Power, she relied for progress upon the normal development of her own national life. Her crime was, in the opinion of France and England, that she was growing too fast. As Englishmen have lately expressed themselves in regard to our own nation, Russia was growing so strong that measures had to be taken to cripple her, "to take her down." She had done no wrong at that time to provoke or justify an attack, but she was too prosperous to suit the interest of England, and hence the Alliance and the Crimean war.

At the same time, England saw in the West a rising Empire, whose marvellous growth gave her more anxiety than even the progress of Russia.

The population of the United States was almost equal to her own. The Americans had just obtained California and the Pacific coast, Texas had been annexed, Mexico seemed ready to fall into their hands, and their commercial marine was even then second to none in the world.

In spite of inadequate protection, and the combined influence of the slave States and England, American manufactures were making rapid progress in many departments, American mechanics were already ahead of the world—and in all the markets of the United States, British fabrics were being rapidly displaced by the products of American skill. English statesmen knew well, that a people that could create for themselves an unmatched fleet for commercial purposes, that had covered their rivers and lakes with swift steamboats, could also produce a navy with equal ease whenever it should be needed, and with resources of all kinds to which man could assign no limit, fronting on two great oceans, what could prevent the United States from overshadowing even England with her greatness, unless indeed, as was said to Mr. Beecher, she could "be taken down."

The colonies of England on the North were too weak to resist their powerful neighbors, and her West Indian islands were in dangerous proximity to those harbors whence American fleets might issue, and the restless filibustering of the slave-holders coveting new lands, was an indication of what might be done if expeditions should be fitted out with the sanction, and supported by the power of the Government. England saw and dreaded the threatening preparations of France; Russia was swiftly rising in the East, and America was overshadowing the West.

It is easy to see, therefore, that Great Britain had been urged by what appeared very pressing reasons, to accept an Alliance which promised relief from a triple danger, an attack from France, and the too great prosperity of Russia and America.

The motives by which the French Emperor was induced to seek the Alliance with England were of a more complex character. France feared no attack from England, and the commercial idea swayed her because commercial greatness had become the foundation of political power, but French policy was also influenced by other reasons of nearly equal weight. Louis Napoleon and his associates, "the Brethren of the Elysee," as Mr. Kinglake calls them, had with the aid of the army seized upon France, and with the slaughter of innocent thousands in the streets of Paris, the banishment of other thousands that they might die in Cayenne, and the imprisonment of multitudes beside, had crushed out of her the power of resistance, and held her helpless in their bloody grasp. They styled themselves a government, the French Government, and Louis Napoleon declared himself an Emperor, the Emperor of France. He desired as a first necessity, recognition of his claims, and respect for the Empire thus created, as it was, in one day of slaughter.

If he could succeed in obtaining this recognition from England, it would have a double value, because she was not only the foremost State of Europe, but she was the ancient enemy of France. This was his first object, and this was easily gained, or if not easily, it certainly was quickly done.

But this, however important, was only one step towards an ultimate end. If what has been previously stated in regard to the traditional policy of France is received as correct, if one remembers that the leading purpose of the first Napoleon was the establishment of a European Latin Empire, with France at the head of the Empire and the Papal church, and that Louis Napoleon has devoted himself to the carrying out of the unfinished schemes of his uncle, then a clear light will be shed on the Alliance, the Crimean war, his hostility to the United States, and his invasion of Mexico.

If it is conceded that his design was to make France supreme in Europe, and to unite under her the Latin race, and restore over the world the lost "strength and prestige" of the Papal church, then it was necessary to accomplish these designs,—to crush England or make her his ally and tool, for a time, and then when strong enough, compel her to serve him, or risk destruction, to arrest the progress of the Greek church and Russia in the East, and to prevent the further growth of the United States, which was supplanting the political power of the Latin and the Catholic church in the West.

If such a supposition seems to invest Louis Napoleon with a greatness to which he has no proper claims, let it be remembered, that if he is not equal to the forming of such a vast design, that he has advisers within the Papal church, whose sagacity and ambition are quite sufficient to originate such a scheme, and that it lies, moreover, along the familiar line of thought of every able Jesuit in Europe or America.

In attempting to carry out so vast a plan, it was, of course, necessary, first of all, to make some safe disposition of England. Two methods were open to the choice of the Emperor. He might attack her with a superior army, and with a navy nearly equal in efficiency, but, to say the least, this would be a hazardous attempt, and Louis Napoleon might well hesitate at what his uncle had shrunk from when at the height of his power. Or he might propose to her an alliance, under cover of which, and even by the assistance of England, France might increase her strength, and perhaps assume the position of leader.

He chose this latter course, as not only safer, but as offering the fairest prospect of ultimate success. But how could he approach England with such a proposition? How detach her from her ancient friendships and link her to the fortunes of her most bitter foe? The bait was cunningly contrived—England, for reasons already stated, feared the growing power of Russia. It was her traditional policy to hinder her growth, and counteract the plots of the Czar that looked towards Constantinople and the East. She watched with jealous care each movement of Russia which appeared to threaten Turkey or the Mediterranean. France, on the contrary, had adopted no such steadfast and clearly defined policy in regard to "The Eastern Question." Her position at this time is thus stated by Mr. Kinglake:

"Among the very foremost of the Great Powers of Europe was France; and she was well entitled, if her rulers should so think fit, to use her strength against any potentate threatening to alter the great territorial arrangements of Europe; and especially it was her right to withstand any changes which she might regard as menacing to her power in the Mediterranean. But French statesmen have generally thought that, as the Mediterranean after all is only a part of the ocean, a new maritime power in the Levant might be rather a convenient ally against England, than a dangerous rival to France; and, upon the whole, it was difficult to make out, either from the nature of things or from the general course of her policy, that France had any deep interest in the integrity of the Sultan's dominions. At all events, her interest was not of so cogent a sort as to oblige her to stand more forward than any of the other great Powers, or to bear in any greater proportion than they might do, the charge of keeping the Ottoman Empire untouched. Indeed, it was hard at that time to infer from the past acts of France that she had any settled policy upon the Eastern Question. She had clung with some steadiness to the idea of establishing French influence in Syria; and from time to time during the last half century she had been inclined to entangle herself in Egypt; but upon the question whether the elements constituting the Ottoman Empire should be kept together, she had generally seemed to be undecided; for, although she took part in the conservative arrangements of 1841, her conduct in the previous year, and at several other times of crisis, had disclosed no great reluctance on her part to see the empire dismembered. Upon the supposition, however, that she intended to pursue the policy which she afterward avowed, and to concur in the endeavor to maintain the Sultan's dominions, her duty toward herself and to Europe required that she should herself refrain from disturbing the quiet of the East; and that in the event of any wrongful aggression by Russia upon the dominions of the Sultan, she should loyally range herself with such of the four great Powers as might be willing to check the encroachment by their authority, or, in last resort, by force of arms; but it was not at all incumbent upon France to place herself in the van; and it was not consistent with the welfare of her people that she should take upon herself a share of the European burden disproportionate to her interest in the state of Eastern Europe. Nor was there at this time any reason to imagine that the country could be brought into strife, or engaged in warlike enterprises without sufficient cause; for the institutions of France had not then shriveled up into a system which subordinated the vast interests of the State to the mere safety and welfare of its ruler. The legislative power and the control of the supplies were in the hands of an Assembly freely elected; and both in the Chamber and in print, men enjoyed the right of free speech. Also the executive power rested lawfully in the hands of ministers responsible to Parliament; and therefore, although the President, as will be seen, could do acts leading to mischief and danger, he could not bring France to a rupture with a foreign State unless war were really demanded by the interests or by the honor, or at least by the passions of the country. And, the people being peacefully inclined, and the interests and the honor of the country being carefully respected by all foreign States, France was not at that time a source of disturbance to Europe."

But for the purpose of winning England, and binding her to the fortunes of his throne by solemn contract, the Emperor adopted suddenly an Eastern policy suited to the English market. He first of all placed himself in an attitude of incipient hostility towards Russia, and when the wiles of his Jesuits had provoked the Russian Emperor, and induced him to threaten Turkey, he at once turned to England as an ardent convert to her Eastern policy, and offered to unite with her in checking the ambition of Russia. Mr. Kinglake has set forth this diplomatic manœuvre in the following passage:

"At length, nay so early as the 28th of January, 1853, the French Emperor perceived that his measures had effectually aroused the Czar's hostility to the Sultan, and he instantly proposed to England that the two Powers should act together in extinguishing the flames which he himself had just kindled, and should endeavor to come to a joint understanding, with a view to resist the ambition of Russia. Knowing beforehand what the policy of England was, he all at once adopted it, and proposed it to our

Government in the very terms always used by English statesmen. He took, as it were, an 'old copy' of the first English speech from the throne which came to his hand, and following its words, declared that the first object should be to 'preserve the integrity of the Ottoman Empire.'* From that moment until the summer of 1855, and perhaps even down to a still later period, he did not once swerve from the great scheme of forming and maintaining an offensive alliance with England against the Czar, and to that object he subordinated all other considerations. He had at that time the rare gift of being able to keep himself alive to the proportionate value of political objects. He knew how to give up the less for the sake of attaining and keeping the greater. Governed by this principle, he gradually began to draw closer and closer toward England; and when the angry Czar imagined that he was advancing in the cause of his Church against a resolute champion of the Latins, his wily adversary was smiling perhaps with Lord Cowley about the 'key' and the 'cupola,' and preparing to form an alliance on strictly temporal grounds.

"It would have been well for Europe if the exigencies of the persons then wielding the destinies of France would have permitted the State to rest content with that honest share of duty which fell to the lot of each of the four Powers when the intended occupation of the Principalities was announced. Neither the interest nor the honor of France required that in the Eastern question she should stand more forward than any other of the remonstrant States; but the personal interest of the new Emperor and his December friends did not at all coincide with the interest of France; for what he and his associates wanted, and what in truth they really needed, was to thrust France into a conflict, which might be either diplomatic or warlike, but which was at all events to be of a conspicuous sort, tending to ward off the peril of home politics, and give to the fabric of the 2nd of December something like station

* 'Eastern Papers,' part i., page 68.

and celebrity in Europe. In order to achieve this, it clearly would not suffice for France to be merely one of a conference of four great Powers quietly and temperately engaged in repressing the encroachments of the Czar. Her part in such a business could not possibly be so prominent, nor so animating as to draw away the attention of the French from the persons who had got into their palaces and their offices of State. On the other hand, a close, separate, and significant alliance with England, and with England alone, to the exclusion of the rest of the four Powers, would not only bring about the conflict which was needed for the safety and comfort of the Tuileries, but would seem in the eyes of the mistaken world to give the sanction of the Queen's pure name to the acts of the December night and the Thursday the day of blood. The unspeakable value of this moral shelter to persons in the condition of the new French Monarch, and St. Arnaud, Morny, and Maupas, can never be understood except by those who look back and remember how exalted the moral station of England was in the period which elapsed between the 10th of April, 1848, and the time when she suffered herself to become entangled in engagements with the French Emperor.

"It would have been right enough that France and England, as the two great maritime Powers, should have come to an understanding with each other in regard to the disposition of their fleets; but, even if they had been concerting for only that limited purpose, it would have been right that the general tenor and object of their naval arrangements should have received the antecedent approval of the two other Powers with whom they were in cordial agreement. The English Government, however, not only consented to engage in naval movements which affected—nay, actually governed—the question of peace or war, but fell into the error of concerting these movements with France alone, and doing this—not because of any difference which had arisen between the four Powers, but—simply because France and England were provided with ships; so that in truth the Western Powers, merely because they were possessed of the implement which enabled them to put a pressure upon the Czar, resolved to act as though they were the only judges of the question whether the pressure should be applied or not; and this at a time when, as Lord Clarendon declared in Parliament, the four Powers were 'all acting cordially together.' Of course, this wanton segregation tended to supersede or dissolve the concord which bound the four Powers, and, as a sure consequence, to endanger yet more than ever the cause of peace. Some strange blindness prevented Lord Aberdeen from seeing the path he trod, or rather prevented him from seeing with a clearness conducive to action. But what the French Emperor wanted was even more than this, and what he wanted was done. It is true that neither admiration nor moral disapproval of the conduct of princes ought to have any exceeding sway over our relations with foreign States, and if we had had the misfortune to find that the Emperor of the French was the only potentate in Europe whose policy was in accord with our own, it might have been right that closer relations of alliance with France (however humiliating they might seem in the eyes of the moralist) should have followed our separation from the other States of Europe. But no such separation had occurred. What the French Emperor ventured to attempt, and what he actually succeeded in achieving, was to draw England into a distinct and separate alliance with himself—not at a time when she was isolated, but—at a moment when she was in close accord with the rest of the four Powers."

England was thus gained for France. It was the most momentous step in her history since the Reformation, and the full results cannot be foreseen as yet. For reasons which, as Mr. Kinglake says, have never yet been satisfactorily explained, she separated herself secretly from Austria and Prussia, and, with no necessity laid upon her by the state of the negotiations with Russia and Turkey, joined France in a crusade against Russia.

The reasons, says her historian, have not been revealed.

Recent events in connection with our own country are now throwing back a clear light upon the reasons for the Anglo French Alliance, which at the time were only hinted at in sentences falling from English statesmen, and which appeared like enigmas when uttered—such as "the Alliance has reference to Western as well as Eastern affairs." We know too well now the meaning of those declarations.

England had been placed in safe position. France might now push her military preparation to any extent, and England could not complain. She could increase her navy till it should be a match for that of Britain, and it would merely be to prepare to execute her part of the contract. She could pursue her schemes for supremacy in any direction, and depend upon the powerful aid of England. England having been thus secured, the next step in the grand conspiracy against the nations would naturally be to use the power of Great Britain in an attempt to cripple the military strength of Russia, and check the progress of the Greek Church, and restore in the East the lost prestige and power of the Papal Church, precisely as France now proposes to do in Mexico and throughout this Western Continent. It need not be supposed that Louis Napoleon, or his political associates, have any special regard for any church or any religion, but it is through the church alone that the reheading of the Latin nations under one imperial crown can be effected. Their history, their former glory, their religious sentiments, hopes and fears, their traditions and superstitions, are all bound up with the Papal Church.

There can be no restoration of empire for them, without restoring at the same time the supremacy of the Roman Catholic Church. Without the church, the ambitious scheme of the two Napoleons could never be successful, and therefore it is that in every movement of France, the church and the empire are inseparably connected. While, therefore, the Emperor presented to England such political and commercial considerations as he thought would move her, it was at the same time carefully arranged that the opening contest with Russia should have a religious character—

should be, in fact, a renewal of the struggle of ages between the Eastern and Western churches, the Latin and the Greek; a conflict which had so often shaken all Christendom, and crimsoned the East and the West with blood.

So it was understood by the Czar and the Russian people, and so, also, it was understood by the present leaders of the Papal Church. Mr. Kinglake has this remark: "When "the angry Czar imagined that he was advancing in the "cause of his Church against a resolute champion of the "Latins, his wily adversary was smiling perhaps with Lord "Cowley about the 'key,' and the 'cupola,' and proposing "to form an alliance on strictly temporal grounds." Events have shown that Mr. Kinglake was mistaken; or, if he is right in his conjecture, then neither Lord Derby nor Louis Napoleon understood the full meaning of their own acts. There were deeper grounds of quarrel than any mere temporal interest. Beneath all else, was the undying, unresting ambition of the Papal Church and its Jesuit leaders.

Other considerations doubtless influenced Louis Napoleon. He knew that in the expedition which he was projecting in the Crimea, there would be no great opportunity for the English navy to win renown, and he rightly believed that the French army was superior to that of Britain. If, therefore, the joint effort should prove successful against Russia, the French Emperor might hope that France would win the principal glory, and be recognized once more as the great military power of Europe. All now know that this was the actual result. England came out of the contest with her glory dimmed, her influence diminished, her military weakness unveiled, and France was in the ascendant. Such was the general condition of the four great powers particularly affected by the Anglo French Alliance, at the time when it was formed, and it seems not very difficult to understand the motives in which it originated, or the purposes of the contracting parties. England was glad to exchange the old French enemy that she dreaded into a new French friend, and then, as the TIMES declared, the two Powers being strong enough to control the world,

England could use this allied strength, first, to humble and cripple Russia, and then give such attention to the rising empire of the West as should prevent us also from growing too strong.

Intimations of this kind fell from English statesmen, and the TIMES' oracle and the Quarterlies echoed their sentiments. The following are examples:

"The Alliance with France does not regard the East exclusively, but has reference to affairs in both hemispheres."*

"Our transatlantic cousins will become a trifle less insolent and overbearing, when they find that the fleet which 'summers' in the Baltic can, without cost or effort, 'winter' in the Gulf of Mexico, and our statesmen will not again need to speak with 'bated breath' in the cause of humanity and justice, from a dread lest the spirit of the country will not, or the energies of the country can not, bear them out in assuming a loftier tone."†

"When Russia is settled, France may safely abate her army, and England her navy, but neither must disarm. If they do, not only will other Powers cease to respect them, but they will cease to respect each other. *We must still be able to say 'No' to our lively young brother across the Atlantic, if he wants Cuba without paying for it, or takes any other little vagary into his head.*"‡

"England and France together are strong enough to bind nearly all the world over to keep the peace."||

There seemed to be a general English wish, that when

* Sentiment expressed by Lord Clarendon, and indorsed in France.

† *North British Review*, November 1854, written when England thought Sebastopol had already fallen, or might be regarded as captured.

‡ *Blackwood*, November, 1854.

|| *Blackwood*, November, 1854.

"Russia was settled" attention should be given to the United States, and a general expectation that it would be done—that, in some form, France and England would interpose and humble the pride of the Great Republic. On the part of England the Alliance was formed, first, to secure herself, at least for a time, against France, then, if possible, to crush or hinder her two rising commercial and manufacturing rivals, Russia and the United States; and when the secret notes and conversations of the time shall come to light it will be revealed that, in its original conception, this contract was an Alliance both against Russia and America, with the intention as definite and real, of attacking in some form the United States, as was the plan of war against Russia.

The occasion of our rebellion was eagerly seized as the fit instrument for our destruction, and every step of England and France has been taken to carry out the spirit and intention of the original Alliance. France, as has been stated, was operating upon a wider plan, and with a deeper purpose. Her scheme was one of universal empire, with the prestige of the Latin race and church restored both east and west. This was in sympathy with English policy, so far as it went, but sne had also a grander ambition of her own.

When France attacked Russia, it was not simply one State against another, it was the Western Latin Church striking once more for the supremacy of the world. When, subsequently, Louis Napoleon attacked Austria, it was not to free Italy, as Italy since has learned, but to place France instead of Austria at the head of Catholic Europe.

The French Emperor, with his troops guarding the Pope at Rome, is again the "eldest son of the Church." On this eldest son the Papal power now rests its hope, and the movement upon Mexico is simply another step in the scheme of recovering the lost power of the Latin race under the lead of France, and to restore on this continent the supremacy of the Papal Church by crippling a free Protestant Republic.

# CHAPTER IX.

THE CRIMEAN WAR.—IT WAS BEGUN BY FRANCE.—IT WAS IN ITS ORIGIN A RELIGIOUS WAR, AN ATTEMPT OF THE PAPACY TO REGAIN ITS ASCENDANCY IN THE EAST OVER THE GREEK CHURCH.

Americans cannot fully understand the motives which have governed England and France since the outbreak of the rebellion without studying the nature and purposes of the war against Russia in the Crimea. That war was the first part of a plan, of which the other was to cripple the United States either by State craft or by arms, whenever the opportunity should come after Russia was "settled."

The general principles and purposes which originated the war against Russia were the same which have guided these allied Powers in their hostility to the American Republic. The United States in the West occupied the same position as Russia in the East, and Mexico is the western Turkey to be sustained or occupied against our growing power. England looked at it then as now, from the commercial stand-point, fearing a rival in the West as in the East, while the object of the Papal leaders who urged France into hostilities, was to restore in the East the strength and prestige of the Roman Church, as they now propose to do the same thing in the West by a French occupation of Mexico, and as much more of the American continent as circumstances may allow.

For the same reason that the Allies interfered to prevent Russia from opening an eastern route to India by way of the Black Sea, the Caspian and the Aral, do they now propose to block up our American western road to Asia; and the same policy which causes the reopening of the ship canal across the Isthmus of Suez has also planned the French ship canal across our American Isthmus, and made surveys and maps, not only of Central America and Mexico, but of our whole Pacific coast. The plan of the Allies in the East was the exact counterpart of their plot against the United States, a plot which the rebellion has only in part revealed.

The Crimean war, then, should be carefully studied by Americans, in order to understand the real motives by which France and England are governed.

During the progress of the siege of Sebastopol, the author of this work wrote as follows in reference to the attack upon Russia, and the quotation is made for the purpose of showing how events have justified the warning, and to convince Americans that the views then set forth were correct, and that the dangers pointed out were real.

"The interest of the United States in this struggle is second only to that of Russia, and to a great degree is evidently identical with hers. 'When Russia is settled,' what remains but to settle the United States also, inasmuch, as the *North British* suggests, the Allied fleets can spend their summers in the Baltic and their winters with us. Let those whose sympathies have flowed so freely for the Allies consider the tremendous stake which our country has in this contest. It is quite natural, and entirely right, that American Christians should cultivate the most friendly feeling with our fellow Christians in England, and that we should be grateful for the kindness with which her public servants have regarded our missionary efforts in Turkey, and that we should feel a deep interest in her as our mother country and as a Protestant nation, and it would be an act not only of folly but of wickedness to excite against her a causeless hostility.

"But it would manifest still greater infatuation if we should suffer these things to mislead us in regard to the actual character of this war, or close our eyes to the manifest designs of the Allies, or fail to perceive the selfish, arrogant spirit that rules their policy. Let Americans be careful, lest by a misplaced sympathy they not only sustain a wrong, but endanger their own country.

"It was natural that Americans, in the beginning of this conflict, should cheer on France and England with their sympathies and their prayers, for then it appeared to be what they so loudly declared it was, a war of freedom against despotism, of civilization against barbarism; and it was expected that the yoke of enslaved nations would be broken. But can it be expected that Americans should still feel deeply interested in their success when it is so clearly shown by testimony and by actions, that this assault upon Russia has been prompted by no generous motive whatever, by no hatred of despotism, no desire for the deliverance of the oppressed, no kind regard even for tottering Turkey—but simply with the unrighteous design of checking the growth and hindering the prosperity of a neighboring nation, which might dispute with them their commercial supremacy, mingled, on the part of France, with the personal ambition and personal pique of her sovereign, and the intention of restoring supremacy to the Catholic Church; and when, moreover, it is virtually declared that so soon as Russia is 'settled,' the affairs of the western hemisphere will receive attention.

"The fact will not much longer be concealed from the world, that the true question involved in this war is whether France and England shall be the joint dictators of the world, domineering over all oceans with their navies, and prescribing limits to the growth of nations; whether they shall be permitted to say to Russia, 'You shall advance no further eastward,' or to the United States, 'You shall neither have the Sandwich Islands, nor Cuba, nor Mexico, and you, and all other Powers, shall dwell within the limits which we think proper to allow.' This is the real significance of the Eastern war, to which the United States will do well to give heed in time.

"It becomes us to consider in due season whether we are prepared to submit to such dictation, or whether we shall claim and exercise, at all hazards, the right of unrestricted development. The batteries of Cronstadt and Sebastopol are ranged in front of American as well as Russian rights, and the interest of the United States in the preservation of the Russian navy is second only to that of Russia herself. The last war for American independence is yet to come, if Russia can be humbled.

The United States and Russia sustain almost precisely the same *general* relations to France and England, and to the main objects of their Alliance. Both are animated by a vigorous life, seeking on all sides room for its expansion. Both are already formidable, and promise an overshadowing greatness in the future. Both are seeking commercial and manufacturing importance, and threaten to rival older States. Each is advancing at a rate unknown to other nations.

"Both are regarded with intense hostility by the Papal Church, and her priests and Jesuits are equally laboring for the overthrow of each. Both are seeking to secure for themselves a share of the commerce of the East, and meet alike the opposition of France and England. Both are seeking for themselves a theater of national life outside of the sphere of Western Europe, and Western Europe interferes with both. Both claim the right of making an experiment for themselves in a civilization of their own, and have been met, each in its turn, not only with sneers, but hostility; and both stand confronted by the Anglo-French Alliance—the one in the Baltic and at Sebastopol, the other in the Gulf of Mexico, in the Sandwich Islands, and in Central America, ready to say 'No' to our progress when 'Russia is settled.'"

These were not vain words, as subsequent events have shown, and the author, with the consent of the publishers, has made free use of such other portions of the work from which this was taken as seem suited to his present purpose;

and it is but justice to himself to state that the main thoughts setting forth the origin and purpose of the Crimean war were first written out and published some ten years ago, and while the war was in actual progress. Were it not for this statement, it might appear that they had merely been borrowed from later writers, especially from Mr. Kinglake, whose recent statement of the origin of the Crimean War is here presented as a complete justification of what the author of this book wrote and published nearly ten years ago. No other apology is needed for quoting nearly the entire chapter from Mr Kinglake than this. He wrote with every possible advantage for knowing the truth; his is the very latest work upon the subject, and its authority is not to be successfully disputed upon these points, and he sustains in full, the general view taken in this book of the origin of the war.

# CHAPTER X.

## HOLY SHRINES.

"The mystery of holy shrines lies deep in human nature. For, however the more spiritual minds may be able to rise and soar, the common man during his mortal career is tethered to the globe that is his appointed dwelling-place; and the more his affections are pure and holy, the more they seem to blend with the outward and visible world. Poets bringing the gifts of mind to bear upon human feelings have surrounded the image of love with myriads of their dazzling fancies, but it has been said that in every country, when a peasant speaks of his deep love, he always says the same thing. He always utters the dear name, and then only says that he 'worships the ground she treads.' It seems that where she who holds the spell of his life once touched the earth—where the hills and wooded glen and the pebbly banks of the stream have in them the enchanting quality that they were seen by him and by her when they were together—there always his memory will cling; and it is in vain that space intervenes, for imagination transcendent and strong of flight can waft him from lands far away until he lights upon the very path by the river's bank which was blessed by her gracious step. Nay, distance will inflame his fancy; for if he be cut off from the sacred ground by the breadth of the ocean, or by vast endless desolate tracts, he comes to know that deep in his bosom there lies a secret desire to journey and journey far, that he may touch with fond lips some mere ledge of rock where once he saw her foot resting. It seems that the impulse does not spring from any designed culture of sentiment, but from an honest earthly passion vouchsafed to the unlettered and the simple-hearted, and giving them strength to pass the mystic border which lies between love and worship. For men strongly moved by the Christian faith it was natural to yearn after the scenes of the Gospel narrative. In old times this feeling had strength to impel the chivalry of Europe to undertake the conquest of a barren and distant land; and, although in later days the aggregate faith of the nations grew chill, and Christendom no longer claimed with the sword, still there were always many who were willing to brave toil and danger for the sake of attaining to the actual and visible Sion. These venturesome men came to be called Pelerins or Pilgrims. At first, as it would seem, they were impelled by deep feeling acting upon bold and resolute natures. Holding close to the faith that the Son of God, being also in mystic sense the great God himself, had for our sakes and for our salvation become a babe, growing up to be an anxious and suffering man, and submitting to be cruelly tortured and killed by the hands of his own creatures, they longed to touch and to kiss the spots which were believed to be the silent witnesses of his life upon earth, and of his cross and passion. And, since also these men were of the Churches which sanctioned the adoration of the Virgin, they were taught alike, by their conception of duty and by nature's low whispering voice, to touch and kiss the holy ground where Mary, pure and young, was ordained to become the link between God and the race of fallen man. And, because the rocky land abounded in recesses and caves yielding shelter against sun and rain, it was possible for the Churches to declare, and very easy for trustful men to believe, that a hollow in a rock at Bethlehem was the manger which held the infant Redeemer, and that a grotto at Nazareth was the very home of the blessed Virgin.

"Priests fastened upon this sentiment, and although in

its beginning their design was not sordid, they found themselves driven by the course of events to convert the alluring mystery of the Holy Places into a source of revenue. The Mahometan invaders had become by conquest the lords of the ground; but, since their own creed laid great stress upon the virtue of pilgrimage to holy shrines, they willingly entered into the feelings of the Christians who came to kneel in Palestine. Moreover, they respected the self-denial of monks, and it was found that even in turbulent times a convent in Palestine surrounded by a good wall, and headed by a clever Superior, could generally hold its own. It was to establishments of this kind that the pilgrim looked for aid and hospitality, and in order to keep them up the priests imagined the plan of causing the votary to pay according to his means at every shrine which he embraced. Upon the understanding that he fulfilled that condition he was led to believe that he won unspeakable privileges in the world to come, and thenceforth a pilgrimage to the holy shrines ceased to be an expression of enthusiastic sentiment, and became a common act of devotion.

"But, since it happened that, because of the manner in which the toll was levied, every one of the holy places was a distinct source of revenue, the prerogative of the Turks as owners of the ground was necessarily brought into play, and it rested with them to determine which of the rival Churches should have the control and usufruct of every holy shrine. Here, then, was a subject of lasting strife. So long as the Ottoman Empire was in its full strength, the authorities at Constantinople were governed in their decisions by the common appliances of intrigue, and most chiefly, no doubt, by gold; but when the power of the Sultans so waned as to make it needful for them to contract engagements with Christian sovereigns, the monks of one or other of the Churches found means to get their suit upheld by foreign intervention. In 1740 France obtained from the Sultan a grant which had the force of a treaty, and its articles or 'Capitulations,' as they were sometimes called, purported to confirm and enlarge all the then existing privileges of the Latin Church in Palestine. But this success was not closely pursued, for in the course of the succeeding hundred years, the Greeks, keenly supported by Russia, obtained from the Turkish Government several firmans which granted them advantages in derogation of the treaty with France; and until the middle of this century France acquiesced.

"In the contest now about to be raised between France and Russia, it would be wrong to suppose that, so far as concerned strength of motive and sincerity of purpose, there was any approach to an equality between the contending Governments. In the Greek Church the right of pilgrimage is held to be of such deep import that if a family can command the means of journeying to Palestine even from the far distant provinces of Russia, they can scarcely retain the sensation of being truly devout without undertaking the holy enterprise; and to this end the fruits of parsimony and labor enduring through all the best years of manhood are joyfully devoted. The compassing of vast distances with the narrow means at the command of a peasant is not achieved without suffering so great as to destroy many lives. This danger does not deter the brave, pious people of the North. As the reward of their sacrifices, their priests, speaking boldly in the name of Heaven, promise them ineffable blessings. The advantages held out are not understood to be dependent upon the volition and motive of the pilgrim, for they hold good, as baptism does, for children of tender years. Of course, every man who thus came from afar to the Church of the Holy Sepulchre was the representative of many more who would do the like if they could. When the Emperor of Russia sought to gain or to keep for his Church the holy shrines of Palestine, he spoke on behalf of fifty millions of brave, pious, devoted subjects, of whom thousands for the sake of the cause would joyfully risk their lives. From the serf in his hut even up to the great Czar himself, the faith professed was the faith really glowing in the heart, and violently swaying the will. It was the part of wise statesmen to treat with much deference an honest and pious desire which was rooted thus deep in the bosom of the Russian people.

"On the other hand, the Latin Church seems not to have inculcated pilgrimage so earestly as its Eastern rival; and if it did, it obtained but slight compliance with its precept; for while the Greek pilgrim ships poured out upon the landing-place of Jaffa the multitudes of those who had survived the misery and the trials of the journey, the closest likeness of a pilgrim which the Latin Church could supply was often a mere French tourist, with a journey and a theory, and a plan of writing a book. It was true that the French Foreign Office had from time to time followed up those claims to protect the Latin Church in the East which had arisen in the times when the mistresses of the Most Christian kings were pious; but it was understood that by the course of her studies in the eighteenth century France had obtained a tight control over her religious feelings. Whenever she put forward a claim in her character as 'the eldest daughter of the Church,' men treated her demand as political, and dealt with it accordingly; but as to the religious pretension on which it was based, Europe always met that with a smile, yet it will presently be seen that a claim which tried the gravity of diplomatists might be used as a puissant engine of mischief.

"There was repose in the empire of the Sultan, and even the rival Churches of Jerusalem were suffering each other to rest, when the French President, in cold blood, and under no new motive for action, took up the forgotten cause of the Latin Church of Jerusalem, and began to apply it as a wedge for sundering the peace of the world.

"The French Ambassador at Constantinople was instructed to demand that the grants to the Latin Church which were contained in the treaty of 1740 should be strictly executed, and, since the firmans granted during the last century to the Greek Church were inconsistent with the capitulations of 1740, and had long been in actual operation, the effect of this demand on the part of the French President was to force the Sultan to disturb the existing state of repose, to annul the privileges which (with the acquiescence of France) the Greek Church had long been enjoying, to drive into frenzy the priesthood of the Greek Church, and to rouse to indignation the Sovereign of the great military empire of the North, with all those millions of pious and devoted men who so far as regarded this question were heart and soul with their Czar. 'The Ambas-'sador of France,' said our Foreign Secretary, 'was the 'first to disturb the status quo in which the matter rested. 'Not that the disputes of the Latin and the Greek Churches 'were not very active, but that without some political ac-'tion on the part of France, those quarrels would never 'have troubled the relations of friendly Powers. If report 'is to be believed, the French Ambassador was the first to 'speak of having recourse to force, and to threaten the in-'tervention of a French fleet to enforce the demands of his 'country. We should deeply regret any dispute that might 'lead to conflict between two of the great Powers of Europe; 'but when we reflect that the quarrel is for exclusive privi-'leges in a spot near which the heavenly host proclaimed 'peace on earth and good-will towards men—when we see 'rival Churches contending for mastery in the very place 'where Christ died for mankind—the thought of such a 'spectacle is melancholy indeed. . . . . Both parties ought 'to refrain from putting armies and fleets in motion for 'the purpose of making the tomb of Christ a cause of 'quarrel among Christians.'*

"Still, in a narrow and technical point of view, the claim of France might be upheld, because it was based upon a treaty between France and the Porte which could not be legally abrogated without the consent of the French Government; and the concessions to the Greek Church, though obtained at the instance of Russia, had not been put into the form of treaty engagements, and could always be revoked at the pleasure of the Sultan. Accordingly, M. de Lavalette continued to press for the strict fulfillment of

*'Eastern Papers,' part i., page 67.

the treaty, and being guided, as it would seem, by violent instructions, and being also zealous and unskilled, he soon carried his urgency to the extremity of using offensive threats, and began to speak of what should be done by the French fleet. The Russian Envoy, better versed in affairs, used wiser but hardly less cogent words, requiring that the firmans should remain in force; and, since no ingenuity could reconcile the engagements of the treaty with the grants contained in the firmans, the Porte, though having no interest of its own in the question, was tortured and alarmed by the contending negotiators. It seemed almost impossible to satisfy France without affronting the Emperor Nicholas.

"The French, however, did not persist in claiming up to the very letter of the treaty of 1740, and, on the other hand, there were some of the powers of exclusion granted by the firmans which the Greeks could be persuaded to forego; and thus the subject remaining in dispute was narrowed down until it seemed almost too slender for the apprehension of laymen.

"Stated in bare terms, the question was whether, for the purpose of passing through the building into their Grotto, the Latin monks should have the key of the chief door of the Church of Bethlehem, and also one of the keys of each of the two doors of the sacred manger,* and whether they should be at liberty to place in the sanctuary of the Nativity a silver star adorned with the arms of France. The Latins also claimed a privilege of worshiping once a year at the shrine of the Blessed Mary in the Church of Gethsemane; and they went on to assert their right to have 'a cupboard and a lamp in the tomb of the Virgin,' but in this last pretension they were not well supported by France,† and virtually, it was their claim to have a key of the great door of the Church of Bethlehem instead of being put off with a key of the lesser door, which long remained

* 'Eastern Papers,' part i., p. 84. † Ibid., p. 48.

insoluble, and had to be decided by the advance of armies,* and the threatening movement of fleets.

"Diplomacy, somewhat startled at the nature of the question committed to its charge, but repressing the coarse emotion of surprise, 'ventured,' as it is said, 'to inquire 'whether in this case a key meant an instrument for open-'ing a door, only not to be employed in closing that door 'against Christians of other sects, or whether it was simply a key —an emblem;'† but diplomacy answered, that the key was really a key—a key for opening a door, and its evil quality was—not that it kept the Greeks out, but that it let the Latins come in.

"After the change which was wrought in the institutions of France in the night between the 1st and the 2nd of December, 1851, increased violence seems to have been imparted to the instructions under which M. de Lavalette was acting, and his demand was so urgently pressed that the Porte at length gave way, and acknowledged the validity of the Latin claims in a formal Note;‡ but the paper had not been signed more than a few days, when the Russian Minister, making hot remonstrance, caused the Porte to issue a firman,|| ratifying all the existing privileges of the Greeks, and virtually revoking the acknowledgment just given to the Latins. Thereupon, as was natural, the French Government became indignant, and to escape its anger the Porte promised to evade the public reading of the firman at Jerusalem;§ but the Russian Minister, not relaxing his zeal, the Turkish Government secretly promised him that the Pasha of Jerusalem should be instructed to try to avoid giving up the keys to the Latin monks.

Then again, under further pressure by France, the Porte engaged to evade this last evasion, and at length the duty of affecting to carry out the conflicting engagements thus made by the Porte was entrusted to Afif Bey. This calm

* See Count Nesselrode's Dispatches, ibid., p. 61. † Ibid., p. 79.

‡ Note of the 19th February, 1852.

|| The firman of the mi-fevrier, 1852.

§ Col. Rose to Lord Malmesbury. 'Eastern Papers,' part i., p. 46.

Mahometan went to Jerusalem, and strove to temporize as well as he could betwixt the angry Churches. His great difficulty was to avert the rage which the Greeks would be likely to feel when they came to know that the firman was not to be read; and the nature of his little stratagem showed that, although he was a benighted Moslem, he had some insight into the great ruling principle of ecclesiastical questions. His plan was to inflict a bitter disappointment upon the Latins in the presence of the Greek priesthood, for he imagined that in their delight at witnessing the mortification of their rivals, the Greeks might be made to overlook the great question of the public reading of the firman. So, as soon as the ceremonial visits had been exchanged, Afif Bey, with a suite of the local Effendis, met the three Patriarchs, Greek, Latin, and Arminian, in the Church of the Resurrection just in front of the Holy Sepulchre itself, and under the great dome, and there he 'made an oration 'upon the desire of his Majesty the Sultan to gratify all 'classes of his subjects,' and when M. Basily and the Greek Patriarch, and the Russian Archimandrite were becoming impatient for the public reading of the firman which was to give to their Church the whole of the Christian sanctuaries of Jerusalem, the Bey invited all the disputants to meet him in the Church of the Virgin near Gethsemane. There he read an order of the Sultan for permitting the Latins to celebrate a mass once a year, but then, to the great joy of the Greeks, and to the horror of their rivals, he went on to read words commanding that the altar and its ornaments should remain undisturbed. 'No sooner,' says the official account, 'were these words uttered, than 'the Latin, who had come to receive their triumph over the 'Orientals, broke out into loud exclamations of the impos'sibility of celebrating mass upon a schismatic slab of 'marble, with a covering of silk and gold instead of plain 'linen, among schismatic vases, and before a crucifix which 'has the feet separated instead of one nailed over the 'other.' Under cover of the storm thus raised, Afif Bey perhaps thought for a moment that he had secured his escape, and for awhile he seems to have actually disentangled himself from the Churches, and to have succeeded in gaining his quarters.

"But when the delight of witnessing the discomfiture of the Latins had in some degree subsided, the Greeks perceived that, after all the main promise had been evaded. The firman had not been read. M. Basily, the Russian Consul-General, called on Afif Bey, and required that the reading of the firman should take place. At first the Bey affected not to know what firman was meant, but afterward he said he had no copy of it; and at length, being then at the end of his strategems, he acknowledged that he had no instructions to read it. Thereupon M. Basily sent off Prince Garan to Jaffa to convey these tidings to Constantinople in any Arab vessel that could be found, and then hurrying to the Pasha of Jerusalem, he demanded to have a special council assembled, with himself and the Greek Patriarch in attendance, in order that Russia and the Orthodox Church might know once for all whether the firman had been sent or not; but when the meeting was gathered, Hafiz Pasha only 'made a smooth speech on the 'well known benevolence of his Majesty toward all classes 'of his subjects, and that was all that could be said.'* So the Greeks, though they had been soothed for a moment by the discomfiture of their Latin adversaries in the Church of the Virgin, could not any longer fail to see that their rivals were in the ascendent, and it soon turned out that the promise to evade the delivery of the keys was not to be faithfully kept.

"The pressure of France was applied with increasing force, and it produced its effect. In the month of December, 1852, the silver star was brought with much pomp from the coast. Some of the Moslem Effendis went down to Jaffa to escort it, and others rode out a good way on the road that they might bring it into Jerusalem with triumph; and on Wednesday, the 22nd of the same month, the Latin

* Consul Finn to Earl of Malmesbury, October 27, 1852. 'Correspondence,' part i., p. 44.

Patriarch, with joy and a great ceremony, replaced the glittering star in the sanctuary of Bethlehem, and at the same time the key of the great door of the church, together with the keys of the sacred manger, was handed over to the Latins."*

The Russian Government was right therefore in viewing this conflict as a religious one, and declared truthfully that it took up arms in defense of the national religion. The Russians evidently believed this to be true, and the Russian soldiers were fired with religious enthusiasm in addition to their love of country.

These are dangerous elements to cope with, especially when an army thus excited is scientifically directed, and supplied with every weapon of destruction known to modern war. This was sufficiently shown by the wonderful defense of Sebastopol. But it was declared that the Russian Government imposed upon the people, and without cause maddened them with a fanaticism whose only purpose was to stimulate them for the conflict.

* Consul Finn to Earl of Malmesbury, Dec. 28, 1852; but see Mr. Pisani's note, p. 106.

# CHAPTER X.

## THE RELIGIOUS ASPECT OF THE EASTERN WAR.

The idea was contemptuously scouted that the struggle was in any sense to be regarded as a religious war. But notwithstanding these confident assertions, the facts in the case, as they will appear to any candid observer who will view the present in the light thrown over it from the past, will disclose a religious aspect to this contest as clearly marked as its commercial phase, and even more important. Russia is guilty of no falsehood when she asserts that the war was directed against her national faith. Such were not the motives of England; as stated in a preceding chapter, she was swayed by commercial considerations almost exclusively, holding herself indifferent alike to the Greek Church, Romanism, or Mohammedanism; or rather choosing, as she has deliberately avowed, that the power of the Papacy should be revived in Europe under France, than that Russia should not be humbled.

The real character of the war can not be fully understood without a careful study of its religious bearings, and of the present religious aspect of Europe, and this investigation should include at least the outline of the history of the Greek and Latin Churches. Whoever undertakes to explain "the Eastern Question" without giving a prominent position to the relations of these churches to each other, will only deceive himself and others. It belongs in part to the quarrel of the Ages between the East and the West.

The history and character of the Greek Church are comparatively little known to the mass of the American people. Far removed from the theater of its life, we have had little occasion to study its nature or its movements.

With Protestantism and Romanism only before our eyes, it has scarcely occurred to us that there is still another branch of the original Church which has not only been an important actor in the history of the past, but occupies a prominent place in the present, and must from its numbers and power influence largely the future. We have, and with good reason, been chiefly interested in the movements of the Roman Catholic Church, whose emissaries swarm around us, intent here as elsewhere, upon schemes for the overthrow of all power which stands opposed to Rome. We have been fully employed in defending our institutions, our liberties and the faith of our fathers, from the Jesuits and priests that fill our land with their intrigues, and little thought has been bestowed upon the Greek Church, and little has been known of it aside from the facts communicated by our missionaries, who have come in contact with it at Constantinople and at Athens.

These, however, are but fragments, and deeply corrupted ones, of the ancient body, while it is the Russian Church, fifty millions strong, which has taken its place among the great religious Powers of earth, and which is now in reality the Greek Church. Its character must be studied not at Constantinople, nor at Athens, but at home; for the policy of the Russian Church will in the end give direction and character to all. Because there has been persecution at Constantinople and Athens, it is ungenerous and deceptive to assume that the Russian Church is actuated by a similar spirit, and so endeavor to arouse against her the hatred of the world. Let the Church of Russia be judged by its acts.

A majority of readers will probably be better prepared to understand this portion of our subject, if their attention is first directed to some prominent facts in the history of the Greek and Latin Churches, and the Eastern and Western empires. Through these the origin and true character of the war, and the actual position of Russia will appear. Although the scholar will find here only the most familiar facts, yet it is believed that those who have little leisure for the investigation of such subjects, will derive some benefit from this brief epitome of a portion of history.

The Church of Christ was for some centuries a united body. From the regions beyond the Euphrates, westward to its utmost limits, in what is now western Europe, it was one undivided whole, its thousands of local churches belonging to one communion. Then, also, one civil power ruled over all the theater of the old civilization, and its *one* capital city was Rome. As was perfectly natural, the Bishops of the principal cities in the Roman Empire felt an importance proportioned to the positions which they occupied, and the prelates of Jerusalem, Antioch, Alexandria, Rome, and Constantinople, were jealous of each other's power, and struggled for the supremacy. The Bishop of Rome, located at the Capital of the Empire, possessed great advantages over his competitors, and soon secured for himself a proud pre-eminence, though not an undisputed one, among his jealous rivals.

He early asserted for himself the Primacy in the Church, and claimed the distinction of Universal Bishop. The prelates of Rome neglected no acts by which the power of the other Metropolitans of the Empire could be diminished and their own increased. They claimed nothing less than the supreme dominion of the world, and each year brought them nearer to the accomplishment of their purpose. At last the contest was narrowed down to the Bishops of Rome and Constantinople, which latter city having been made the Capital of the Roman Empire, by Constantine, soon rivaled and even eclipsed both the splendor and power of Rome. The Roman Pontiff found himself confronted in the East by a most formidable rival, wielding all those advantages which belong to the metropolis of a great empire, and which Rome had hitherto exclusively enjoyed.

The Bishop of Constantinople now naturally hoped to

hold himself the position of Universal Pontiff, and boldly asserted his claim to exclusive dominion over the Church. The proud prelate at Rome, however, was by no means inclined to abate one tittle of his loftiest pretentions. A bitter quarrel between the two ensued, which was handed down to their successors—a contest between the East and the West, between the Latins and the Greek race. The Prelates denounced, and even excommunicated each other, and bitter hatred sprung up and was cherished by the contending parties. Disputes of various kinds continually widened the breach.

The genius of Hildebrand conceived for the Roman Catholic Church that stupendous scheme of universal dominion, both over the Church and over the governments of the world, which from his time has shaped the unvarying policy of the Papacy, which distinguishes its vast ambition both from the Greek Church and every other body bearing the Christian name, and which directs her every effort, whether in her hour of weakness or of strength, to the subjugation of the world. As a consequence of her settled policy, the Roman Catholic Pontiff never ceased to claim authority over the Bishop of Constantinople, nor abandoned the design of finally subduing his power.

It is probably sufficient for the present purpose to state results, without dwelling upon the progress of events. An entire separation was finally produced between the East and the West—between the Greeks and Latins, or Roman Catholics. Constantinople remained the actual capital of the Roman Empire, and head of the Eastern or Greek Church, while the Pope at Rome was head of the Latin Church, the Church of the West. The western, or Latin, portion of the Roman Empire was overrun by the Northern Barbarians, and when out of its ruins several small kingdoms sprung up in western Europe, Charlemagne united them all in one empire, of which France was the head.

There was then a Greek Empire and a Greek Church, whose chief city was Constantinople, and a western Latin Empire under the crown of France, and a western Latin

Church, whose head was the Pope at Rome. The world was divided between the contending interests of the Greeks and Latins. When the countries which now form portions of the Russian Empire were converted to Christianity, they united themselves mainly with the Greek Church, and so from the earliest times Russia has been allied by religious sympathies with the East, and as such has been opposed and hated by the Latin Powers and Papal Church.

The constant effort of the Pope has been to bring the East into subjection to the power of Rome, and force and fraud have been alike freely employed to extend over Constantinople the influence of the Papacy. This hatred of the Greek Church and Empire was carried to such a height, that in the time of the Crusades, the Latin or Roman Catholic Crusaders turned away from their attempts to recover Jerusalem from the Turks, and besieged, captured and *pillaged* Constantinople, with the double purpose of centering its Eastern commerce upon the Roman Catholic cities of the western Mediterranean, and of subjecting the Greek Church to the power of the Pope.

From this severe blow Constantinople did not recover. The Eastern Empire had been previously partly spoiled of its provinces—first by the Arabs, and then by the Seljukian Turks; it grew weaker and weaker, and with the capture of Constantinople by the Ottomans, in 1453, the Greek Empire and Greek Church fell and disappeared together. The fragments of the Greek Church proper now found within the limits of the Turkish Empire are the descendants of the remnant which escaped the ferocity of the Mussulman conquerors.

For four hundred years, the fiercest foe that Christianity ever encountered has been encamped in Europe on the ruins of the Empire and the Church, which he trampled scornfully out in tears and blood, filling with cruelty and oppression, and withering up the beauty and fertility of some of the loveliest portions of the earth; and now, with the shocking barbarities of a thousand years from the time of the rise of Mohammedanism ringing in the ears of all

Christendom—with the blood and tears of millions of murdered Christians, victims of Turkish lust and fury, crying unto God from that fair but desolated land—American Christians are called upon to pray for the preservation of Turkey, to pray that the devastating deluge of Mohammedanism might not ebb away from the plains of Europe.

But while Constantinople was trodden under foot by the Turks, and the Eastern Empire spoiled, and while the western world was prostrate at the Papal throne, God was nursing a new power in the regions of the unknown North, which was to bring once more the Greek Church, in a most imposing form, upon the world's theater, and open before it another career of greatness. Russia adopted, from the first, the Greek faith and worship, and of course inherited the Eastern quarrel with the Romish Church, and was cordially hated in return by the Catholic Powers of the West, especially by the Pope.

She looked to Constantinople, as the Catholics regarded Rome. There was Russia's mother Church, and there was her holy city. From the time of the conquest of Constantinople by the Turks, Russia meditated their expulsion from Europe, and the regaining of her Holy City, which, like "Holy Moscow," at home, stirred the religious sympathies of her people.

This fact is thus stated in *Blackwood's Magazine*, for July, 1855:

"The close of the reign of Vassili III. was marked by the taking of Constantinople by the Turks. This event made a great sensation in Russia. 'Greece,' says Karamsin, 'was a second mother country to us; the Russians always recollected with gratitude that they owed her Christianity, the rudiments of the arts, and many amenities of social life. In the town of Moscow, people spoke of Constantinople as in modern Europe they spoke of Paris under Louis XIV.' It is among the annalists of that epoch that a remarkable prophecy was found, on the strength of which modern aggression on Turkey appears justifiable both to the church and state of Russia. The annalist, after mourning over the misfortunes of Constantinople, adds: 'There remains now no orthodox empire but that of the 'Russians; we see how the predictions of St Methodius 'and St. Leon the Sage are accomplished, who long ago 'announced that the sons of Ishmael should conquer By-'zantium. Perhaps we are destined also to see the accom-'plishment of that prophecy which promises the Russians 'that they shall triumph over the children of Ishmael, and 'reign over the seven hills of Constantinople.' It is worth while for us to consider, now that this prophecy, since the taking of Byzantium by the Turks, has become a fixed and ruling idea with the Russian people, quite as much as that of restoration to Judea is to the Jews. The priests and popes have taken good care to keep it up for their own purposes, as well as those of their masters, the Czars; and when we take the superstition of this people into consideration, it is easily seen what a powerful lever the real or feigned existence of such a prophecy must put into the hands of those whose object it is to move the Muscovite race."

This feeling has strengthened with the increasing power of Russia, and it evinces no unusual degree of national ambition or vanity that now, with fifty millions of Greek Christians within her own dominions, and twelve millions more in Turkey affiliated to her by a kindred worship, and with a million of soldiers at her disposal, she should regard herself as the proper head of the Greek Church, the defender of its faith, the representative of the Eastern Empire, and as commissioned to recover and to hold Constantinople. These facts, though they justify no wrong which Russia may have committed, yet serve to explain her policy, and to show why it is that she seems determined to construct for herself, even over prostrate nations, a highway to Constantinople and the East.

The following statement is also quoted from *Blackwood:*

"Ivan IV. was crowned by the Metropolitan, and saluted by the Byzantine title of Autocrat. Thus it seems that he wished to be recognized as the heir of the defunct Greek sovereignty, and the master *de jure*, if not *de facto*, of Byzantium. These are important facts, because they show that the idea of the acquisition of Turkey does not merely date from the time of Peter, but has been a fixed principle of action with Russian sovereigns ever since the fall of the Lower Empire. We can not help considering the other encroachments of Russia on the map of Europe as in a measure incidental, brought about often by an unforeseen concurrence of circumstances, at the same time eagerly caught at by the nation as a means to this one great end, the possession of Constantinople, and the centralization of all the Russias and their dependencies in the great capital on the Bosphorus. This has been and is the one definite and distinct object of the ambition of the Czars, the avarice of the courtiers, and the fanaticism of the people. That Russia or her sovereigns ever had any distinct design of conquering and absorbing the west of Europe we can hardly believe, although such would doubtless be to her a consummation devoutly to be wished. For instance, Germany was divided, bribed, and overawed, not with a view to immediate conquest, but with a view to silencing her protest against Russian aggression; and here Russia has fully gained her point. Only one thing was wanted—the revival of the old antagonism between England and France, a thing which seemed the easiest of all, but turned out, contrary to all expectation, the most difficult—that Constantinople should be once again the capital of the Eastern world."

It is only necessary to bear in mind the character of this ancient quarrel between the East and the West, between the Papacy determined to subjugate the Greek Church, and that Greek Church equally resolved upon self-defense and independence, to comprehend why Russia would guard with most jealous watchfulness against any interference of the Roman Catholic Powers with Turkey, and especially when coming from France, which is now the most powerful, as well as the most earnest defender of the Papacy in Europe; France, which to gratify the Pope trampled out the Italian Republic, and now with a Jesuit as chief adviser of the

Emperor, makes war on Russia in the name of civilization and liberty. The "Eastern question," then resolves itself mainly into the old contest between races and churches, between the East and the West, between Russia as representing the Eastern Empire and Greek Church, and the Latin Powers of western Europe, represented in France, to whom, for commercial purposes, England has for the time allied herself. The immediate struggle previous to the war, was between France and Russia, on the field of diplomacy at the court of the Sultan: France, by the aid of the Jesuits, was endeavoring to extend the Papal influence over Turkey, and through a Protectorate over one million of Roman Catholics in the Ottoman Empire, to obtain a pretext for interfering with its concerns at some convenient opportunity.

It was the old design, never abandoned at Rome, of adding ultimately Constantinople to its dominions. To carry out this design France originated the strife concerning the Holy Places at Jerusalem, and undertook to repair for Roman Catholic use a church which had hitherto been claimed by the Greek Church. To effect these purposes some musty claims, which had been sleeping a hundred years, were hunted up and revived—by Louis Napoleon—and in these questions, started by France for such purposes, the *immediate* causes of the war may be found.

By the custom of several generations, the occupation of the Christian churches and other "Holy Places" at Jerusalem had been divided between the Greek and Latin Churches, but Louis Napoleon, by the aid of Catholic priests and Jesuits, hunted up some old and neglected treaty stipulations which the Ottoman Government had once made in favor of the Roman Catholic Church, and then formally demanded that the "Holy Places" should be controlled strictly according to the letter of the old treaty, which had been dragged for the purpose out of its tomb.

To this Russia objected, and as Protector of the Greek Church demanded that the existing state of things, so long settled by custom, should still continue. Here was the originating point of the difficulty, the Papal Church searching out forgotten records in order to revive its old quarrel with the Greek Church, and manufacture an occasion for interference with the concerns of Turkey. Russia only asked that the course of several generations should still be pursued without disturbance. This very important point in the history of that war and the Eastern question, should not be forgotten. France, and not Russia, was the aggressor, and it began as a religious quarrel, precisely as Russia has declared.

It was a collision between the eastern and western churches produced by a demand of France, the very nature of which shows every feature of Jesuit intrigue, and that it was designed as an entering wedge of difficulty. Let it be remembered, too, that France had succeeded in obtaining a protectorate over one million of Roman Catholic subjects of the Porte, the intention of which was of course well understood by Russia. Austria also, another Roman Catholic Power, had obtained from the Turkish Government stipulations in favor of Catholic subjects, while the rights of Russia, in regard to twelve millions of Greek Christians, rested on verbal promises and customs, instead of treaty stipulations, excepting, perhaps, the treaty of Kainardji, the meaning of which was in dispute, the validity of which, as interpreted by Russia, had been acknowledged by an English minister, as previously stated.

With these evidences of a settled design on the part of the Catholic Powers, and especially France, to secure exclusive advantages for themselves, and with the manifest willingness on the part of the Porte to yield to their demands, what was the course of Russia? No opprobious epithet has been spared in denouncing her conduct at this point, and French and English talent has been lavishly employed to exhibit her as worthy only of the scorn and hatred of the world. What then are the facts? In regard to the the Holy Places, Russia simply demanded that no alteration should be made in the existing state of things, which had been peaceably acquiesced in for "several generations," according to English authorities. This was so eminently reasonable, that France did not choose to risk her reputation by refusing, and the question of the Holy Places was thus settled by the abandonment of the claims of the Papacy.

But France and Austria had obtained by treaty stipulation the right to a protectorate over the one million of Catholics in the Turkish dominions, while the right of Russia in her protection of *twelve millions* of Greek Christians rested, with the exception of the disputed treaty, on a *traditional* privilege, custom, and the verbal promise of the Porte, *not upon express treaty*, as did those of France. With this Russia had been satisfied until the designs of the Papal Powers had been disclosed in the matter of the Holy Places, and until it was evident that the Roman Catholic influence was likely to become the ruling one with the Sultan.

Russia then asked that the privileges which she had enjoyed, and which rested on custom, and promises, excepting only the disputed treaty of Kainardji, should now be secured by formal contract, as those of France had already been, thus placing her rights on the same footing with the other Powers. She asked for herself no peculiar or exclusive advantages; she demanded simply that the Greek Christians should be placed on the same condition as other Christian Powers, and that verbal promises and custom should be ratified by assuming the form of a treaty. It has nowhere been shown that Russia demanded any new privileges, anything not previously enjoyed, but she only desired that existing rights should have the solemn sanction of a treaty.

This point can not be too strongly insisted upon, because the charge was continually made against Russia, that after the settlement of the question of the Holy Places, she advanced entirely new pretentions, alike incompatible with the honor of the Porte and the safety of Europe. This has been brought forward on all occasions, to show that Russia was pre-determined upon a rupture with Turkey, or upon forcing her to accept such terms as would prove her ruin. Let it therefore be remembered that the *new demand* of Russia was *simply to be secured by treaty in the rights which she then possessed.*

She asked nothing which had not been previously granted and secured so far as customary use and verbal promise could avail, but fearing that Jesuit artifice and influence might induce the Ottoman Government to change its mind, Nicholas chose to ask the security of a written document, such as the other Powers had already obtained. This request, which history must yet pronounce a most reasonable one, Turkey, advised by France and England, refused.

France, England, Turkey, all were willing, perfectly so, to *re-affirm existing treaties as Turkey construed them.* But all parties were aware that *existing treaties* while they *secured the rights desired by Roman Catholics, did not in like manner provide for those of the Greek Church.* You have our word for it, was the reply of Turkey, and with that you should be satisfied. We agree to place the Greek Christians on the same footing with others. Let us have this in due form of treaty, was the answer of Russia, and we are satisfied. But Turkey refused.

We have the authority of the best English writers for stating that the promises given to Russia and the rights she enjoyed, did not differ from those of other Powers. "*That engagement with Russia did not differ in principle* "*from any similar promise given to any other Power.*" Such is the language of the *Edinburgh Review*, in speaking of the engagements entered into between the Porte and the European Powers, including Russia, concerning the Christians in Turkey. Russia then had claimed nothing unusual, nothing which other Powers did not possess, and nothing which had not been *verbally*, and as she claimed, by treaty also, conceded to her already, and sanctioned by long use. What then was the point of difficulty so grave, so incapable of removal, as to produce this terrible war? Once more let it be repeated.

Turkey, by the advice of the Allies, refused to give Russia

any formal written legal security for her acknowledged rights, when this had already been done in regard to other Powers. She was willing to be bound by formal treaty in regard to the one million of Roman Catholics, when demanded by France and Austria, but she insisted that her unsupported word was enough for Russia, and the twelve millions of Greek Christians, and in this position she was supported by England and France. They insisted that Russia should not have a *legal* and *formal* right to privileges which all parties acknowledged; and, of course, whenever France could persuade or overawe the Turkish Government, they could be denied altogether.

It was precisely the case of a man refusing to give any written obligation for a debt which he acknowledges to be just, leaving himself the privilege of repudiating it at his pleasure. No one could blame a creditor, under such circumstances, for endeavoring to secure himself; and history will justify Russia, first, in believing that Turkey did not intend to fulfill engagements to which she refused to bind herself in due form, and second, for attempting to secure her acknowledged rights—and more especially when every movement showed that France was seeking to make it the occasion either of quarrel or of reviving her supremacy in the councils of Turkey.

"If," says the *Edinburgh Review*, "the new demands of "Russia were of a nature to confer upon her in a *definite* "*and legal form*, rights of protectorate over the Christian "subjects of the Porte, they were demands which called "for the resistance of Europe." The world will be inclined to ask *why*? Precisely such rights of protectorate had already been granted to France in "*definite and legal form*;" why then should they be refused to Russia, particularly when for a long time she had enjoyed them without dispute, and "they did not differ in principle" from what had been formally secured to others?

If Russia would be content with a mere "*re-affirmation of existing treaties*," France and England would agree to such a note; but all well knew that this settled nothing, because the very sense insisted upon by Russia in the treaty of Kainardji was disputed by France, and finally by England also, when it suited her convenience, after her marriage with France. Russia asked only a stipulation confirming her construction of this treaty, but France and England refused to admit this construction, and consequently this proposal to re-affirm existing treaties was a mere specious device. The clause in the treaty of Kainardji is in these words: "The Sublime Porte promises constantly to protect the Christian religion and its churches."

This certainly in itself is sufficiently indefinite. But when Turkey, under this general rule, enters into certain specific relations with France and Austria, she fixes thereby her interpretation of the clause, or of her general obligations to Christian Powers, and Russia, beyond all dispute, has a right to insist upon a similar interpretation of the rule in her own case. This was her only demand, and this Turkey and the Allies refused.

When the blinding vail which diplomatic art has thrown over this transaction has been removed by time, the world will perceive that Russia was wronged by Turkey and the Allies, and that her only course was to submit to manifest encroachment, or prepare herself for resistance. But it may be asked, what motive could have influenced France and England to persevere, at the hazard of war, in resisting a just demand of Russia. The explanation is easy, and is given in few words by the *Edinburgh Review:* "That engagement with Russia did not differ in principle from any similar promise given to any other power. *Greater danger attached to it in her case,* from the alliance between the forms of Christianity in Russia and in Turkey."

This furnishes the key to the whole. Because there were in the Providence of God twelve millions of Greek Christians in Turkey, who could be influenced by Russia, and only one million of Roman Catholics that could be used by France, therefore if Russia should possess equal rights with other Christian Powers, she would have an advantage over them all; and *therefore,* while Roman Catholic interests must be secured by solemn treaty, Russia must rely upon the unsupported word of the Porte, a promise which could be repudiated at pleasure.

Such, when stripped of all the wrappage of diplomatic mystification, appears to be the real state of the "Eastern Question," in which the war originated, a war for which the world will yet hold France and England justly responsible. Russia saw that she was trifled with, and with reason felt that she was insulted, and she decided upon her course accordingly. In the whole history of earth, it will be difficult to discover an example where the real merits of a case have been more studiously concealed, and western Europe. and perhaps most in America, have been led to believe that France and England were forced, much against their will, to enter into this war with Russia. In one sense this is true.

They were forced into a war because Nicholas would not consent, after the intrigue of France in regard to the Holy Places, to suffer his acknowledged rights to rest any longer upon the mere word of the Porte, or upon the language of a disputed treaty, where the *similar rights* of other Powers were guaranteed in due legal form. They were forced into a war, rather than permit an act of simple and manifest justice toward Russia. From their own testimony this verdict will assuredly be rendered by history in due time.

# CHAPTER XI.

## THE PAPACY IN ITS CONNECTION WITH THE EASTERN QUESTION.

"War is going to break out between philosophy and faith, between politics and religion, between Protestantism and Catholicism; and the banner raised by France in this gigantic struggle will decide the fate of the world, of the Church, and, above all, of France herself."*

This feature of the religious aspect of the Eastern question is one which demands from us, as Americans, our most serious regard. The activity and zeal of the French Government in its efforts to obtain a controlling influence at Constantinople for the Roman Catholic Church, is only a part of a vast design which Rome has conceived for regaining her lost ascendancy over the world. She is making one last but mighty effort to place herself at the head of universal dominion.

She believes herself able even yet to carry out the design of Hildebrand and the Innocents, and subject all nations to her power once more. Americans should not forget that this claim to rule the world in the name of God, and as his only and proper representative on earth, has never for one moment been abandoned by the Papal Hierarchy, nor has their been an hour in her history, since the days of Gregory the Great, when she has not both designed and hoped to

* De Custine's Russia.

make it good. On this point no American should either remain indifferent, or suffer himself to be deceived.

The one essential and unvarying claim of the Roman Catholic Church is, that she is of right and by the appointment of God himself, not only the one true Church of the earth, but the supreme power of the world; that, as the vicegerent of Jesus Christ on earth she is, in the person of the Pope, the rightful sovereign of all other sovereigns, king of kings, and lord of lords; that all out of her pale are heathen or heretics; that all dissenting governments ought, as heretical Powers, to be subdued or exterminated; that it is her duty to do this whenever and wherever she obtains the power; that for this end, all means whatever are justifiable in the sight of God, and her stedfast intention is to overthrow every government of earth, whether monarchial or republican, that refuses to submit to her power.

The Roman Catholic Church has never abated one iota of this demand in its widest extent, and she never will. She can not surrender the very loftiest of the pretensions without abandoning all. They constitute her life. Without these demands, she would become simply one among religious denominations, or a local, national church, like that of England or Russia, instead of what she now claims to be—the one only church of God, and, as such, the sovereign of the nations.

Nor is it wise to dismiss with an idle sneer either the pretensions or the power of the Roman Catholic Church, nor blindly rely upon the boasted intelligence of the nineteenth century, nor trust implicitly in the present forms and spirit of Protestant Christianity, as affording a sufficient safeguard against the designs of the Papacy, without watchful and earnest effort. Few are now ignorant of the remarkable change which a few years have wrought in the attitude and spirit of the Romish Church. But a short time has passed since the Pope fled, a fugitive, from his capital, and the hopes of the friends of freedom and of Protestantism were raised to the highest pitch.

It was thought that the Papal power was broken forever, and the day of the world's deliverance had come. Yet in how brief a period was despotism more firmly established in Europe than before, and the very power that claimed to be the foremost apostle of liberty, crushed out republicanism in Italy, and reinstated the Pope upon his throne.

Nor has any thinking man failed to observe how, from that hour, the boldest, the most impious pretensions ever made by the Catholic Church have been revived, and doctrines which even the Middle Ages could scarcely bear are openly proclaimed and earnestly defended in republican America. A more vigorous life, a more hopeful and aggressive spirit,.is everywhere manifested by the Papal Power, and the persecuting hierarchy of the dark ages has suddenly re-appeared upon the scene, throwing once more over the nations its haughty shadow, breathing defiance and commanding submission.

Her priests and Jesuits are abroad in every land, a mighty band animated by one spirit, and fired with one common hope of victory, and revenge for the long dishonor of their Church; unscrupulous in the use of means, versed in every wile of diplomacy, and in every art by which the sources of public or private influence are reached, citizens nowhere, with no home or country, and bound by no feeling of allegiance, except to the Pope and their Church alone, they are making an earnest, world-wide effort for the complete subjugation of the nations. The attempt which for years has been made at Jerusalem and Constantinople, is but a part, yet a very important one in the general design.

The revival of the old quarrel with the Eastern Church, is one step only in a premeditated series of aggressions in the East for the purpose of humbling and crippling Russia, the representative of the Greek Church and empire, and, as such, hated and feared. Not from idle curiosity, but from settled design originating with his Jesuit advisers, did Louis Napoleon search through the forgotten records of two hundred years to find an occasion against the Greek Church, and the means of expelling it from its possessions in Jerusalem, and at the same time of striking a blow at Russia.

It must be understood that national pride, ambition, and commercial interests had also a powerful influence in this movement, but behind all these, and using these as the instruments of their working, were the leaders of the Romish Church, stirring up national pride and ambition, in order through them to advance the interests of the Papacy. A papal influence procured from the Porte concessions in favor of Catholics, which at the same time it was induced to refuse to Russia and twelve millions of Greek Christians, leaving them to the *bare word* of the Turkish Government, while Roman Catholic rights were solemnly secured by treaty. A Papal influence has secured an alliance between France and England for the crushing of Russia, the only formidable foe of the Papacy in Europe, and England has been led so to seek the gratification of her ambition, and to take such measures to secure her commercial supremacy, as will if possible check and limit the power of Russia, the defender of a rival Church, and thus the whole power of Protestant England has been made available to re-establish the supremacy of the Papacy in Europe.

Disguise all this as we will, these are the facts, and to these conclusions the world ere long must come: but, possibly too late to avert a long train of calamities which now are threatening Europe, if not Protestantism, throughout the world. Every interest of Protestant Christianity, and every interest of America, whether commercial or religious, would have been advanced by the defeat of the Allies, and the breaking up of the Anglo-French Alliance.

Their success tended to the triumph of the Papacy in Europe, and in all the East. In England the newly awakened vigor of Rome has been manifested in equally earnest efforts to win back even this Protestant Power to her embrace and control. These attempts and the powerful influence which they have produced upon the English nation are too well known to be dwelt upon here. Whatever may be said of the soundness of the heart of the English nation, all of which it is hoped will prove true, the astounding fact is before the world, that England has deliberately chosen a Papal alliance in a war whose origin was a religious one—that in a struggle between the Greek and Latin Churches, she espoused the cause of Rome, and coolly avowed that the war, if successful, would strengthen the Papal power in Europe, and that she preferred this to the progress of Russia. She is therefore the ally of the Latin Catholic nations against the Eastern Church and Empire. American Protestants may well inquire with some anxiety, what will become of English Protestantism?

In our own country, this new struggle for Papal supremacy is no less earnest than at Constantinople. Armies of foreign priests and Jesuits are not permitted to roam at will in Russia, fomenting strife and intriguing against the government, and therefore fleets and armies, shot and shell, are employed to cripple her; while our theory of liberty has been that Americans have not even the right to protect themselves or their institutions, lest it should abridge the liberties of those who are endeavoring to subvert them, and therefore the emissaries of a foreign despotism, and millions of emigrants wherewith they could work, have been directed to our shores—and to them our subjugation has been for the present entrusted. A concerted attack, as carefully planned and as determined as that upon Russia, has been made upon the very life of American institutions.

The very basis of American Protestant Republicanism, our schools and our Bible—these have been assailed by the combined talent of the Papal leaders here, aided by the whole influence of the Pope, and by a liberal supply of funds from Europe. The Jesuits in America, and those at Jerusalem and Constantinople, are working in concert, with one great common end in view—the universal re-establishment of the Papal authority, and a propagandism that shall rule the world. The efforts of the Catholic bishops, priests and Jesuits here, the intrigues in the Sultan's court, and the batteries at Sebastopol, have but one general significance, though distinct commercial interests are connected with the questions in the East. Nor should it be forgotten that the present revived and threatening aspect of the Roman Catholic Church is, according to the view of many intelligent students of prophecy, clearly foretold in the Word of God.

They find it stated, as they think, in the prophetic record, that previous to the final destruction of the Papal power, there will be formed a new combination of the western Latin nations in one new western Empire or confederacy, which shall give its full support to the authority of the Pope, as the Empire under Charlemagne once did, and that, possessed once more of the needful power, Rome will again seek to glut herself with Protestant blood. The tendency toward such a result in Europe is certainly sufficiently clear to arrest our earnest attention. Napoleon, we know, dreamed of the restoration of a Western Empire, and was crowned with the iron crown of Charlemagne. His ambition also took an eastern direction, and he meditated upon an eastern dominion, resting on the commerce of India.

Louis Napoleon is at least the heir of his uncle's ambition. France is at this moment the head and leader of the Latin (Catholic) Powers, and under her they are combined against the Greek Church and Russia in the East, and tending toward a confederacy in the West, which shall bear up the Papal throne. The influence of Russia over Austria, and her Sclavonic population, unfits her for a Catholic leader, and renders her position uncertain; while France, with her bayonets at Rome, her Jesuits at Constantinople, and her arms at Sebastopol, has prepared herself to be the head of Catholic Empire, while, at the same time, she stands in Africa with her eye upon the East.

Still another important aim of this new movement of the Roman Catholic Church is to retain its ascendency over the western portions of the Sclavonic race. The Bohemians, the Storraks, the Poles and Lithuanians (all Sclavonians), at their conversion to Christianity, attached themselves to the See of Rome; while the Servians, Bosnians, Bulgarians, and Russians, (all Sclavonians, also,) united themselves with

Constantinople and the Greek Church. The Russians and Poles are, therefore, of one race but different religions, and the hostility of the Poles to Russia is stimulated by Catholic influence, and were this withdrawn, the ties of race would gradually unite again these now separated branches of the same family. Hence the desire to wrest Poland from Russia, and prevent this union. Let it be remembered that if Poland is not controlled by Russia, she will be crushed by the worse despotism of the Papacy. Roman Catholic civilization curses whatever it touches.

Such being the state of Europe, and such the undeniable position, hopes, and efforts of the Romish Church, it certainly requires no far-seeing sagacity to understand the interests and dangers of the United States in this momentous struggle.

# CHAPTER XII.

## ENGLAND'S COURSE TOWARD RUSSIA IN REGARD TO THE EASTERN QUESTION AND THE CRIMEAN WAR.

The course of England towards Russia in regard to the Eastern Question and in the invasion of the Crimea, was so similar to her treatment of us, that the one explains the other, and at the risk of partial repetition in some points, it seems proper to present to Americans the main facts of that chapter in her history, in order that they may compare England then with England now, and learn that in her course towards us she is governed by the same policy which guided her then; that this is her national policy, to be applied to Russia or America, as the case may demand; and whether she strikes eastward at monarchy or westward at a republic, her general purpose is precisely the same. Particularly is it to be observed, that as France created a cause for war, and forced Russia into the conflict with her, so also England, on her part, sought an occasion for quarrel with Russia, and, notwithstanding all the denunciations of the British Press, it was England and not Russia who began the war.

England sought a war with Russia, and nearly the whole power of her Press was employed to cover this intention by the most violent accusations against Nicholas and his people, knowing all the while that the Czar desired more than all things else peace with England, in the same manner that the English Government stirred up the people to fury in the case of the Trent, with the charge that we desired to insult and declare war upon England, when at the same time they held in their hands official evidence that we were earnestly desirous of peace on any terms which would save our national honor.

That England was the aggressor in the war with Russia will be readily seen from the following facts and admissions by the English Press.

The Emperor Nicholas was England's guest in 1844, and while there he made certain propositions to the British Cabinet as to the manner in which the Turkish question should be settled upon the fall of that empire, an event that he declared must necessarily be near.

In regard to this matter, one of the most influential of the English periodicals used the following language soon after the death of the Emperor Nicholas:

"That it would have been most discreditable to England to have made such pact is generally admitted—far more to her indeed than to Nicholas, for the aggressive policy southward was the tradition of his race, and he spoke in the name of growing and expanding Russia. But we hardly saved our honor in the transaction as it was, *for the ministry listened smilingly, and the Times wrote leading articles on the sickness of Turkey.* Let this pass. We only meant to say that he (Nicholas) meant no harm to us, for we can not suppose that the Czar could have ruminated on the distant closing up of Russia on England, like the iron prison in its last fatal change on the victim of Italian revenge. There is no doubt that we have acted wisely, most wisely, in preferring the alliance of France to his, for France and England are doing each other good every day of their united lives; but still it is not fair that we should bear his memory any malice, FOR IT WAS WE AND NOT HE WHO STRUCK THE FIRST BLOW. He has done nothing to deserve at our hands unseemly caricatures, or that his death should have been applauded in an English theater."

In these few honest sentences there is much food for thought, and many reasons are found why Americans, at least, should hesitate to give credence to the specious declarations that England was *forced* into that war, in defense of civilization and humanity, statements which have been made merely to render the war popular, and to excite the people against Russia, a work which has been so thoroughly done that the English people disgraced themselves by savage cheering at the Emperor's death. England having possessed herself, by her maritime superiority, and by her conquest of India, of the commerce of the East, adopted the double public policy of securing to herself the advantages she had won, and of excluding if possible other nations from a participation in this lucrative trade.

It has been, therefore, one of her chief anxieties to establish, if possible, and hold for her own benefit, a monopoly of the East, and for this purpose her jealous care has been to prevent the re-opening of any of the old highways of that trade whereby it could be diverted from her own marts, or to gain possession of them herself. While the ocean route could remain the only or the main channel between India and Europe, by her ships and her possessions in Hindostan the monopoly of the trade would be hers, and she would rest content. But when the question of establishing other communications arose, England was almost omnipresent to secure herself against a rival. Hence her intrigues in Central America, and her establishment on the Mosquito shore, and her projects on the Isthmus of Panama, for ship canals, in order that she might gain possession of the American key to the Indies; hence, also, her fleet at the mouth of the Nile when Bonaparte was in Egypt threatening to re-open and hold for France the old Red Sea route to the East; which scheme, had it been successful, might have restored to the cities of the Mediterranean their ancient wealth and power; and hence, too, be it remembered, her anxieties for the fate of Constantinople.

Not sympathy for the Turk has ever moved the heart of England, but every movement in connection with Turkey has been made with anxious reference to her Eastern trade. It is because she has not been contented to share this commerce with the rest of the world. She has coveted a monopoly of its profits, and has been ready with her fleets and her armies to prevent any other Power of earth from building for itself a highway to India. She has endeavored to frustrate the United States in Central America; she succeeded in forcing the French army from Egypt—and she has also determined not only to prevent Russia from establishing herself at Constantinople, but to wrest from her the control of the Black Sea, and prevent her from occupying the old northern road to the East.

Let it not be forgotten here that it is not the conquest of British India at which Russia is aiming, or which she has ever proposed, but to open for herself a commerce with northern Asia by a route of her own; that she proposes not war on England, but an honorable competition for the trade of Asia; and this England opposed with a war whose object was to destroy forever all hope of maritime or commercial prosperity for Russia, which done, she would hold a complete monopoly of the richest commerce of the world, while at the same time the manufactures of Russia would be ruined, and she would again become dependent on Great Britain.

It is now easy to perceive the real policy of England in regard to the proposition made to the British Government while Nicholas was in London. He frankly informed England that the time was near when the Turkish Government must inevitably fall, without any external force, that it had no vitality, was in fact already seized by death, and that he desired some friendly understanding with England as to the course to be pursued when that event should come, that all of Europe might not then be embroiled, because other nations would be constrained to abide by the joint decision of England and Russia. It is understood that he proposed that England should occupy Egypt, while the control of Constantinople should be given to Russia.

*Simply as a bargain between Russia and England,* this

surely was not an ungenerous offer for Russia. The Czar offered to surrender to Great Britain the best of all the inland routes to India, the one which gave wealth and magnificence to Egypt, and Jerusalem, and Tyre, the one re-opened by the genius of Alexander, the one which she has long coveted, and to secure which she fought the battle of the Nile. It was a proposition which, to all appearance, would have made her supreme in the West, holding, as she does, Gibraltar, the Mediterranean key. Nor was it needful for her to be anxious in regard to the hostility of France, it would seem, with Russia for her ally. The holy indignation which England has so abundantly manifested at this proposition since war was determined on, was by no means aroused when it was first advanced; on the contrary, "THE MINISTRY RECEIVED IT SMILINGLY," then, and "THE 'TIMES' WROTE LEADING ARTICLES UPON THE SICKNESS OF TURKEY." The offer was taken into friendly consideration, and sympathy for Turkey was a rare virtue in England.

It is perfectly clear that the Czar had never received the slightest official intimation that his proposal had been unfavorably received, and that his confidential communications with Sir Hamilton Seymour were but the carrying out, on his part, of the design which he had been led to suppose was favorably received, and even virtually decided upon by the English Government. The Russian Emperor was frank and honorable in his dealings with England, and she, on the other hand, receiving his advances with marked favor, took them into long consideration, pondering in the mean time whether even a better bargain might not be effected in some other quarter, and so soon as she had decided upon a French alliance, endeavored to excite the world against Russia for proposing that "atrocious" partition of Turkey, which the hightoned honor of England had so decidedly rejected, though when presented, ministers had looked all smiles, and the TIMES had written leading articles to prove that Turkey was as good as dead, and it was time to determine England's share in the property. England at first was strongly inclined to favor and accept the proposition of Nicholas, and did not perceive its wickedness until the newly projected alliance with France.

Then the cry was opened upon "*barbarous Russia*," which was making war upon civilization, which had piratically proposed to divide Turkey, and whose advance must now be checked for the salvation of Europe. But this allusion to the smiles of ministers and leading articles in the TIMES is by no means the only evidence which shows that the English Government was merely playing a part in its affected horror at the proposition of Nicholas, and that so late as 1854, the Czar had every public assurance that his policy was approved, and would be defended by England. A few facts will render this point sufficiently clear, while they place the British Government in a most unenviable position, when compared with the straight-forward frankness of Nicholas.

Since 1844, England had been in possession of the proposal of the Russian Emperor, without a word of disapproval, tacitly consenting. In 1853, when the affairs of the East began to wear a threatening aspect, and when Russia was assuming a position which showed that she intended to resist the intrigues of France, Lord John Russell, on behalf of the Government, wrote as follows to the Czar:

> "Her Majesty's Government are persuaded that no course of policy can be adopted more wise, more disinterested, and more beneficial to Europe, than that which his Imperial Majesty has so long followed, and which will render his name more illustrious than that of the most famous sovereigns who have sought immortality by unprovoked conquest and ephemeral glory."

In another part of this dispatch are the following remarkable words: "The more the Turkish Government adopts "the rules of impartial law and equal administration, the "less will the Emperor of Russia find it necessary to apply "that exceptional *protection* which his Imperial Majesty has "found so burdensome and inconvenient, though no doubt "PRESCRIBED BY DUTY AND SANCTIONED BY TREATY."

The admission of Lord John Russell in regard to the correctness of the Russian interpretation of the treaty of Kainardji, does not stand unsupported even by English testimony. In a history of the Ottoman Empire, forming one of the series of the *Encyclopediæ Metropolitana*, published in 1854, is the following account of that treaty. "The most fatal condition to the Turkish dominion, and at "the same time the most honorable to Russia, was the re- "cognition of the latter Power as Protectress of the Mol- "davians, the Wallachians, and of the Christians generally "in the Sultans dominions.

At the time this sentence was penned, it is evident that the learned authors of that history believed that the claims of Russia were properly based upon treaty stipulations, although in a closing chapter, written *after the declaration of war*, Russia is denounced for adhering to such an interpretation of this treaty, though it was previously admitted to be just, even by themselves.

Here is the important concession made by a British minister in 1853, and by British historians, that Russia was not only right in her demands upon Turkey, but that this right was already secured by treaty, precisely as Russia declared, and as Turkey, instigated by France, directed—England then testified that the demands of Russia were just ones, and consequently she was not the aggressor in this war. She was unjustly attacked, through the influence of Papal France, and it is a war in defense of the rights, the territory, the faith, and homes of Russia. Nicholas, in his conferences with Sir George Seymour, in 1853, said, "We "must come to some understanding, and this we should do, "I am convinced, if I could hold but ten minutes' con- "versation with your ministers.

"And remember I do not ask for a treaty or a protocol, a general understanding is all I require—that, between gentlemen, is sufficient." The English Government replied through Lord Clarendon as follows, in March: "The gen-

"erous confidence exhibited by the Emperor entitles his "Imperial Majesty to the most cordial declaration of opinion "on the part of her Majesty's Government; who are fully "aware that *in the event* of any *understanding* with reference "to future contingencies being expedient, or indeed pos- "sible, the word of his Imperial Majesty would be *preferable* "to any convention that could be framed." After the British fleet had been ordered to the Bosphorus, Lord Clarendon informed the Russian minister that the "British "fleet had no hostile designs against Russia."

After the battle of Sinope, the British Government informed Russia, that "*measures will be taken for preventing* "*Turkish ships of war from making descents upon the coast of* "*Russia.*" In the opening debate of 1854, Lord Aberdeen declared "that he saw nothing to find fault with the memo- "randum (containing the proposal of Nicholas), and that he "looked upon it *with great satisfaction.*" Count Nesselrode, in a letter to the Russian minister, speaks of "*the late con-* "*fidential overtures which Sir H. Seymour has been instructed* "*to make to us,*" but in the publication of the dispatches by the British Government all this was sedulously concealed. The whole had been expunged.

In the light of such disclosures, how will England convince the world that she has not been guilty of treachery to Russia, while Nicholas was honorable keeping faith with her? And what shall be thought of her candor or her generosity when at the eleventh hour, while Russia was relying upon her declarations and her honor, having discovered, as she thought, that she might drive a still better bargain by an alliance with France, she deserted the Czar, called upon the world to admire the lofty honor that had rejected the proposals of Russia, and declared she was hastening to the defense of Turkey, and to protect civilization against the barbarism of the North.

The value of such pretenses can now be estimated at their proper worth, especially when we add to what has been stated already, the significant declaration of Lord Palmerston, that England had designs in this war *ulterior to the preservation of Turkey.* What potent argument in the way either of menace or of larger spoil was offered at this juncture by the French Government, that induced the change in English policy, lies hidden among the secrets of diplomacy; but that there was a sudden change, and that Russia was deserted and deceived, is too plain to admit of doubt.

But it may be asked, what explanation can be given of the course of England, except upon the supposition that she was sincerely indignant at the proposal of Russia, and that from truly lofty motives she had undertaken this war to defend weak and tottering Turkey against her powerful foe? First, it is quite clear that she was not indignant when the suggestion was made, nor until she had determined that an alliance with France would be more valuable than the friendship of Russia; and second, her policy is more fully explained by another suggestion. England proposes to herself to become the manufacturer for the world, and the chief factor of its commerce. The bearing which any settlement of the "Eastern question" may have upon this main purpose, is the important one in the opinion of English statesmen.

At first view the possession of Egypt, and the route to India by the Isthmus of Suez, would appear all that England could desire, controlling, as in that case she would, two main channels to the East. But then a second thought will show that with Russia holding the Black Sea and Constantinople, together with the mouths of the Danube, she might, with the eastern highway by the Caspian and the Aral, soon become a formidable rival both in the eastern and European markets; and there would be great danger that Constantinople would absorb much of the trade coming through the Red Sea. If, therefore, the power of Russia could be broken in the Euxine, if her influence at Constantinople could be destroyed, and Turkey, as a *nominally* independent Power, made by the free-trade system a mere dependency, a province of England, it would be far more advantageous than if she should gain Egypt, with Russia at Constantinople.

The interests of Turkey have been no more regarded in this whole transaction by England than by Russia. Both Powers have thought only of their own advancement. Another consideration seems to have influenced the English cabinet. France was evidently preparing herself for some new exhibition upon the theater of nations. She was providing herself with a truly formidable navy, and her military arrangements were upon a scale that were significant of anything rather than unbroken peace. England was made to feel her inferiority to her old foe, in military strength; her ablest commanders pointed out the insecurity of her position, should the French Emperor find it necessary to visit her shores in order to give employment to his army; and the probability of a French invasion was gravely discussed.

When, therefore, a French alliance became possible, it was evident that two important objects might be accomplished: that the fleet and army of Louis Napoleon might be drawn off from the English shores and their strength exhausted, or at least employed elsewhere, and that in addition to this securing herself at home, a rival might be crippled or crushed abroad. Although the secrets of cabinet councils are not disclosed, yet the *actions* of the British Government indicate that such were the ruling motives which led to the rejection of the proposal of Nicholas after it had been under consultation since 1844, and the acceptance of the alliance with France. A secondary reason for this choice may probably be found in the fact that France had already at great cost established herself in Africa, and might be disposed at some time, if not immediately, to dispute with her the possession of Egypt, while Russia at Constantinople would be comparatively secure within the closed gates of the Dardanelles.

The fear of the English Government, that France may hereafter seize Egypt and Syria, was clearly revealed in the debate in Parliament upon the Turkish loan.

The proposition which the Czar made to the English cabinet is a full disclosure of the main features of his policy. He was willing to surrender all claim to Egypt in behalf of England, and this of itself is conclusive upon one point, that he had no sinister designs upon western Europe, and that he desired simply a position from whence he could safely prosecute his favorite Eastern policy, and establish himself on the road to northern Asia. The right of Russia to execute her design is, to say the least, quite as clear as that of England to her acquisitions in India, or that of France to those provinces of Africa which she has violently wrested away. But Russia has not declared war upon Great Britain because she has spoiled the East Indian peninsula, nor upon France because of her conquest of Algiers; yet these, but lately mortal foes, allied themselves for an assault on Russia because she is pursuing a scheme of national aggrandizement, which, in its moral character, is certainly no worse than their own. No candid man will deny that the Russian Emperor was right when he spoke of the dissolution of the Turkish empire as an event not only certain, but near. Nor could any one doubt that when this should occur it would surely convulse all Europe, unless the whole question could be settled by some definite previous arrangement. It is difficult, therefore, to discover anything very atrocious in the frank and open manner in which Nicholas brought the subject to the attention of the British ministers; and in his subsequent conversations with Sir H. Seymour, England was certainly treated in an honorable manner, whatever may be said of the intention of either government in regard to Turkey.

But let it once be conceded that an unavoidable necessity of making some disposition of Turkish affairs was near at hand, and it will be difficult to show that the course of Nicholas was more open to censure than that of the other Powers who have made themselves parties to this conflict. If it be granted that a radical change was imminent in the Ottoman Empire, then it should be remembered that only about one-fourth of the inhabitants of that empire are

Turks, and that no less than twelve millions of them are members of the Greek Church, and therefore bound by religious affinities to Russia, and inclined toward her also by a common Oriental origin, while between these same Greek Christians and the Roman Catholic nations of the west, there is cherished an irreconcilable and mutual dislike.

To extend the dominion of Russia over the Turkish Empire, would be to incorporate twelve millions who are already in at least a partial sympathy with her, while with either French or English rule would be introduced a different race and a different religion—and with France a religion intensely hostile. These circumstances should all be taken into consideration in explanation of the demands and purposes of Russia. They will show that her pretensions in this Eastern question have at least as reasonable a foundation as those of her western rivals. The idea of a regeneration of the Ottoman Empire, with the Turkish element predominant, is, in the opinion of the best informed in Europe, a mere dream, contrary to every analogy in the history of the world, and in the nature of things impossible.

This will be dwelt upon more in detail hereafter. But, assuming here as true what will be proved in another chapter, that the dominion of the Turk is already virtually over, then the twelve millions of Greek Christians will at once be the predominant element in the population, and their natural affinities lead them to Russia, as the head and defender of the Greek Church. This certainly is the case with all but the higher clergy, who, from personal ambition, would dislike the control of Russia.

It may be safely asserted that an independent state on the present territory of Turkey, composed of Greek Christians, could not be maintained by all the power of western Europe. France, as a Catholic Power, could maintain no influence there except by force of arms—the influence of the conqueror over the conquered—and England, as the ally of a Papal Power, made herself obnoxious to the whole Greek Church, which regards this war as, in fact, a religious quarrel. The attempt to erect within the limits of

Turkey an independent Christian state, considering the elements that must compose it, would necessarily end either in its speedy incorporation with Russia or in a continual war, for the very same reasons which have originated the former struggle.

The single fact that fifty millions in the Russian Empire belong to the Greek rite, and that twelve millions in Turkey are of the same faith, is sufficient to show how the Eastern question will be finally settled. And to prove that the demands of Russia are by no means so preposterous and unjust as France and England would have the world believe, let it be supposed that twelve millions of evangelical Protestants, allied to the Americans by race and religious faith, were, for the present, held in subjection by five millions of Mexicans, and that this Mexican rule was weak and tottering—about to fall—would France or England be allowed to prevent these twelve millions from being incorporated with the United States? Would this Government permit these to be made an independent state even under French or English dictation, that it might be interposed between us and the West India islands and South America, hold us within such limits as they should prescribe, and so preserve here *the balance of power*?

It is quite evident that there could be but one settlement of such a question. The very existence of this Union would depend upon the continent being freed from any such foreign control. Every American would declare that the free development of the country should go on without let or hindrance from any others, whose only interest in the matter would be that of checking our too rapid advance, and keeping us to their own level of power.

This, in principle, is the very movement which we are called upon to meet in the French occupation of Mexico. The Emperor declares without reserve that he has seized it to interrupt and prevent the future growth of the Republic, and that this interference is in behalf of the Latin race, and we cannot safely forget that England declared herself to be in perfect accord with France in regard to American affairs, and that the French and English fleets were united in the expedition to Mexico. Louis Napoleon has explained his policy in words. Had English statesmen done the same the record in substance would have been this: "Our trans-"atlantic cousins are becoming too powerful, they must be "taken down. They are pressing hard on Mexico, having "already absorbed some of her finest provinces; and they "will soon wrest Cuba from Spain, and so obtain control of "the West Indian seas; and they are moreover construct-"ing a railway to the Pacific that may endanger our East-"ern trade, while at the same time they are building up a "manufacturing system which will render them independent "of our workshops, and enable them to meet us in the "markets of the world, and we must therefore sever this "Union or enable the rebels to do it; we must help the "Confederates to annihilate their commerce, force their "carrying trade into our own ships, and effectually cripple "their power." Thus the "Eastern Question" shows that it has a Western phase also, and the Alliance, as Lord Palmerston declared, had designs "ulterior to the preservation "of Turkey."

# CHAPTER XIII.

HAD THE ALLIES FULLY SUCCEEDED IN THE ATTACK ON RUSSIA THEY WOULD HAVE HELD TURKEY AS A COLONIAL DEPENDENCY, AS ENGLAND HOLDS INDIA, AND AS FRANCE INTENDS TO DEAL WITH MEXICO.

Only about one-fourth part of the population of the Ottoman Empire are Turks, and these, as masters, hold the remaining three-fourths in subjection, treating them as an inferior caste, just in proportion as they are not restrained by a fear of European Powers. A very large proportion of this subject class, perhaps fourteen millions, bear the Christian name. This fact alone would be sufficient to show that the days of Turkish dominion are numbered.

These millions of Christians could not be compelled much longer to endure the broken yoke of the Mussulman, and the Emperor of Russia only presented a most obvious fact to the English cabinet, when he intimated that it would be wise to make some proper provision for the approaching change. It was, however, urged, both in England and by those who sympathized with England here, that although the power of the Sultan may be annihilated, and Turkey proper disappear, still on the territory of the Porte a Christian State may be established, which, under the protection of the Western Powers, may give a Christian civilization to the East, while barbarism and oppression would be the result of the occupation of Russia. Thus it was declared that the war was one of Christian civilization against the barbarous fanaticism of the North. This opinion swayed many Christian minds in this country, who dreamed of free Christian states, perhaps republics, dotting all the East, under the protection of England.

It is not very difficult, certainly not impossible, to form an opinion of what the result of France and English dominion would be if extended over the East. Their position, and wants, together with their past conduct and present policy, surely afford the data for an accurate judgment of the future.

No one certainly is credulous enough to suppose that either of these Powers was carrying on war merely to deliver the oppressed, or to promote in any way the general welfare of mankind, unless at the same time their own interests were in some way to be advanced, or their own ambition to be gratified. To build upon Eastern soil such a nation or nations as France and England now are, rivals of themselves in wealth, civilization and power, to restore in short, to the East its old prosperity, and infuse an independent life into states to be erected there: this was not in all their thoughts.

Nay, more, such a result is not only contrary to every feature of their policy, but for no purpose would both England and France put their fleets and armies in motion sooner, than to forbid and prevent the interposition between themselves and eastern and northern Asia, of powerful and independent states. Such a nation as the United States, if one could arise there, would be attacked by the western Powers, for far more urgent reasons than have moved them to the war on Russia. In order to predict the results of French and English rule in these regions, it is only necessary to study these governments as they are, and in the light of their history.

In the very outset of such an investigation, a fact is presented whose importance settles all. Neither France nor

England can hold any territory outside of their present home limits except as *colonial dependencies*, and this determines of course the policy of the government in regard to them. Neither of these Powers desire, or would ever permit independent, self-developing communities in the East, but dependencies only, *in fact* if *not in form*, from which tribute could be in some manner gathered for the government and country at home. The object of these now Allied Powers is to manufacture for all other nations, and to control for themselves the commerce of the world. What they require then is raw material for their mills, and markets for their products.

Let it be remembered that the rule of France or England over the East must be essentially that of a foreign Power, whatever the relation might be. There are no affinities of race or religion which might produce or cement a union, but, on the contrary, there are violent antipathies, especially in regard to France, which are not to be removed, or even controlled, except by the arm of power. The connection between races thus politically united can be of one kind only—that of masters and dependents. In similar cases, then, what have been the results? What is the effect of English dominion upon the one hundred and fifty millions which she governs in the East already? Turkey and the adjacent regions may learn a lesson from British India. From the *Merchants' Magazine*, than which there is no better authority either here or in Europe, the following statistical information has been derived, which will show how India stands related to Great Britain, and how she is affected by her rule:

"During the last fifteen years, there has been accruing from this effeminate people the vast sum of £340,760,000, of which sum but £5,000,000 have been spent in public improvements. Its revenue in India is twenty-seven million pounds, of which but sixty thousand pounds are spent for the education of children. Its military expenditures, in 1839, were eight millions pounds; in 1852, twelve millions pounds, or about forty-six per cent. of the whole revenue. The taxes on the lands amount to twelve millions pounds annually, averaging from sixty to ninety per cent. of the whole production of the soil. *Wages of a laborer from six to eight cents a day.* Salt is not allowed to be manufactured, and every pound consumed pays *three-fourths of a penny, tax.*"

In addition to other articles, India can produce more opium than Europe consumes, and therefore England sends a fleet and army to China, and says, "You must buy from "me so much opium each year, or I shall lay your com-"mercial towns in ashes." China replied that this poison was ruining her subjects, body and soul, and that she had no need of opium, indeed, would be in every respect happier and more prosperous without it. England's answer was, "I must realize a certain sum from my opium; it can "not be done unless you buy, and buy you must. Here "am I, with shotted guns and matches lighted."

This is a sample of the colonial policy of England, and this is the prosperity and civilization which she confers upon her present possessions in the East. Such, modified only by circumstances, is her governmental scheme for colonies.

Colonial policy, as a whole, may be regarded as a system designed to convey to the coffers of the home or ruling country the largest possible amount of treasure, with the least possible expenditure. England needs colonies to raise her raw material and grain for her workmen, and for these she wishes to pay with her manufactured products, at prices secured by a monopoly of the trade.

This would be the governing principle of her policy, as well as of France, if they should gain control of Turkey, and the regions around the Euxine and the Caspian. It would be there, as in India, a system of oppression and exhausting demands. These countries would be allowed to produce nothing which could be supplied by the ruling race.

Turkey would possess neither manufactures nor an independent commerce, and consequently neither a high state of civilization nor wealth. She would be confined to agricultural labor, with wages at the minimum rate, to be paid for by inferior goods at such prices as can be maintained where competition is not allowed. Even now, England absorbs thirty-seven per cent. of the whole commerce of Turkey, and she derives from thence one-fourth part of all the grain that is imported for her operatives. Hence her anxiety concerning the occupancy of the Danubian provinces.

The term colonial policy is used here because, as has been stated already, whatever external political form the relation between the East and western Powers might assume, it would be *virtually* one of colonial dependency, because this is absolutely required by the commercial interests involved.

Lamartine has declared that England would sacrifice all Europe to her commerce, and the remark finds its reason in her history. If any are disposed to believe that India should not be cited as a fair example of her policy, let him consult our own colonial history, and observe the systematic and oppressive course pursued by the mother country to repress manufactures and commerce here, loading us with restrictions and prohibitions, and discouraging every description of industrial effort which looked either to independent existence, or to the production of anything which England could make or buy for us with her goods, and grasping the profits of our carrying trade by compelling a *re-shipment* in England of our exports to foreign countries. What an able writer has said in regard to France and her relations to the East, her designs upon Turkey, illustrates with entire accuracy the policy of the western Powers. Having stated that up to 1842 France desired the decay and dismemberment of Turkey, he proceeds:

"The question recurs, Why has she changed her policy, and why to-day does she help to rivet the chains by which twelve millions of Christians are made the slaves of a single Turk? We answer at once, it is not the holy principles of justice, honor, and right, but the desire of commercial supremacy, that leads her to attempt to stifle the cry of millions for the blessings of civilization, manufactures and commerce.

"To prove this, let us examine the nature of the trade with Turkey, and also its amount. By these tables (the details are omitted here) it will be seen at once that the trade of Turkey gives employment to a ninth part of the mercantile marine of France; that it consumes her manufactures to the amount of twenty-seven million francs, and above all, furnishes her with a raw commodity that is the basis of her manufactures, and upon the supply of which depends the prosperity of her cities and people. In addition to this, the increase of her manufactures is diminishing her capability of producing grain enough to feed them, and the failure of a single crop of grain might precipitate the nation into a revolution.

"The care of its present rulers, who are never too firmly seated, is to provide labor and food for the people. Now, the raw materials and provisions must come from countries where manufactures have no hold, and all are producers. Prior to 1830, and even to 1840, Russia was one of the nations which could supply her, and in all probability would for years to come, to any extent in case of emergency. *But Russia prohibited her manufactures in order to encourage her own*, and a single stroke of the Czar's pen could drive her peasants into rebellion."

Here, let it be remarked, is the true cause of this war, aside from its religious features and the Papal ambition. Russia had been to England and France only as a huge agricultural colony, supplying them with grain and raw commodities, and receiving in return their goods. Tired of this dependent life, which the Russian statesmen, and more especially the comprehensive mind of Nicholas saw, could never result in a real civilization, it was determined to build up for Russia a manufacturing and commercial system of her own.

If she succeeds, she will not only consume her own raw commodities and her grain at home, but with her manufactures she will meet France and England in the markets of the world. To prevent this independent growth, to repress the expanding life and civilization of a sister nation, France and England have taken up arms. It is a war whose design is to hold Russia in a dependent and semi-barbarous state, as a mere producer of raw commodities, and Russia is fighting for independence and the right of self-development; while Jesuitism has taken advantage of commercial interest to involve the world, and crush if possible the great rival of the Papacy.

The writer already quoted goes on to say: "Turkey "alone could be made to subserve her ends. She would "receive her manufactures at three per cent., and pay for "them in that raw commodity so necessary to France, and "then in addition to this, the rich fields of Moldavia and "Wallachia were loaded with grain waiting to be borne "to a hungry people. As Lamartine remarks, Turkey is a "necessity to the existence of France.

"Let civilization with its magic power once be felt upon her soil, and a Christian population would make the whole nation resound with the sound of industry and manufactures; she would become the consumer of her own products and raw material, and as a direct result, diminish the power of France." Speaking of the Crimean war he proceeds as follows—it would be well if every American would listen to his words:

"The war they (the Allies) are now waging is not to save Turkey, but to cripple and destroy the commercial prosperity of Russia. They have combined to set bounds to the progress of a nation that first opened to them and their merchant-fleets the whole commerce of the Black Sea, and which poured out the blood of her children like water in order to wring from the barbarous Turk that great boon

11

to trade and commerce. Both are leagued together that they may monopolize the commerce of Europe and destroy the commerce and manufactures of Russia. If they succeed in this case, to whom, let us inquire, will they next prescribe the limits of their possessions and the amount of their trade? Who appointed them to set limits to the progress of nations and the amount of their commerce? For we must never forget that if France and England possess the right to set bounds to the expansion of Russia, they possess also the same right in regard to us. Are we told that they are warring to preserve the integrity of an empire?

"Who but these Powers robbed Turkey of Greece, and threatened by force of arms to prevent Russia from aiding the Sultan from bringing Mohammed Ali under subjection, and thus save a flourishing state to the Empire? Hear the official order of the British Government upon this topic of the integrity of Turkey: 'To maintain the integrity of 'the Ottoman Empire in the sense sometimes attributed to 'the phrase can never be a political duty, for the simple 'reason that it is a political impossibility. Europe has been '*maintaining* this fabric for nearly a century; and how has 'it been maintained?

"'Half its dominions have been lost. Algiers, Egypt, Greece, the Archipelago, and Bessarabia, were once portion of the Ottoman Empire. To what governments do they pertain now? What *justice* did Turkey receive at the hands of Europe when the Porte was excluded from the provisions of 1815? when the Greek insurgents were protected by the Allies against their legitimate mother? when the Sultan was compelled by the five Powers not only to pardon a rebellious vassal that had threatened the very throne of Ottoman, but to confirm this rebel in the hereditary possession of his Pachalic? In every instance of intervention which has occurred since the decline of the Turkish Empire, the interposing States have enforced conclusions theoretically irreconcilable with the rights of an independent monarchy. Nor could it possibly be otherwise.

"'The plain truth is, that a dominion so universally ruinous and unnatural could not really be maintained in its integrity; nor can all the Powers of Europe do more than mitigate the successive symptoms of decay, and avert by *prudent concert the consequences of a violent catastrophe.*' Such is the testimony of an organ that controls the public opinion of England, and speaks the sentiments of its ministry."

This was its language while England was *considering* the proposition of Nicholas, ere it was thought that a more profitable connection could be formed with France, and while England thought equally with the Emperor of Russia, that the consequences of the sudden fall of Turkey ought to be averted by "*prudent concert,*" the very course Nicholas proposed.

"What," continues this writer, "was the declaration afterward? They asserted that they were sick of talking about upholding Turkey, and they were warring against Russia to prevent her from reaching the Bosphorus. Attempt to disguise the fact as we may, it is a war in behalf of barbarism, at the expense of civilization, and incited by a nation that has robbed India of every right she ever possessed, destroyed her manufactures, starved her people, and plundered her treasures; the other Power robbed Algiers from the Empire, obtained by means of fraud its ablest defender, and to crown their claim to honor, burned in caves the men who dared to defend their native soil.

"When France occupied Algiers, she said it was but a counterpoise to England's Malta. Now, the two Powers combine to forever exclude Russia from that sea to which she has the same right as they. The *entente cordiale* existing between them is dangerous to every commercial nation, for it is based upon an understanding that no nation that they consider capable of being their rival in commerce and trade shall extend its power beyond the limits they fix. To-day the United States may feel indifferent as to the result of the contest, but it affects our own security and prosperity as a commercial nation. Let us remember that for years England claimed the right to exclude *us* from the East India trade. But she then lacked allies. To-day we have obtained a foothold for our manufactures even in Persia, where she sends yearly a million pounds worth. If she can check Russia in her march to the ocean, then she can summon us to leave the Persian Gulf, for now she has an ally as grasping as herself.

"She can impress our seamen and search our vessels, for she has declared, by her agent, and that lately, since this war commenced, that while she assented to the declaration of Denmark's and Sweden's neutrality, she did not relinquish her *right* of search, nor retract her former definition as to the rights of neutrals. [These demands caused the war of 1812.] No American can be indifferent to the result of this war. It affects us as an expansive, acquiring and commercial people; it affects us as a liberty-loving and independent nation; for if it succeeds in drying up the streams of a mighty nation's manufactures and trade, it will check in it the development of civilization, the intelligence of the masses, and their approach to independence."

No more truthful words than these have been spoken in America, even, concerning that selfish and ungenerous war. How plain, in this light, appears Lord Clarendon's declaration, that the Alliance between France and England was intended to control the affairs of both hemispheres; how significant the threats borne occasionally from France and England that fleets shall winter in the West Indian seas, and that any vagaries of ours will be duly corrected, such as a disposition to possess ourselves of Cuba, or any other scheme not approved of by the self-appointed *regulating* Powers.

Before dismissing this part of the subject, it may not be amiss to add to what has already been said concerning the preservation of the Turkish Empire, the opinion of the

*Edinburgh Review*, in 1836, before opinions and policy had been warped by a French Alliance:

"Our fears and jealousies of Russia have been stimulated beyond the reasonable pitch, while in order to afford an imaginary counterpoise, we have been called upon to exert our utmost energies in preserving the Turkish Empire. To encourage us in so quixotic an enterprise, every effort has been made to paint the Turks as employed in throwing off the weight of centuries of bigotry and mismanagement, and ready to assist us ably and zealously by reforming their institutions.

"We can not hesitate to express our conviction that of all delusions, it is one of the greatest to expect that the Turkish Empire can or will be long maintained in its present shape, bolstered up, as it is, by foreign support."

Now, England calls on all the world to execrate the name and memory of Nicholas, because, in 1844, he made the same declaration to England, and invited her, as a matter of precaution, to provide for the result—a suggestion which she then received with smiles, and did not reject until 1853.

The *Review*, of 1836, proceeds as follows:

"History offers no one instance of an empire which, after its strength and sinews have moldered away, has recovered them again by the mere quiet process of internal improvement. Nor need we stop to show how absolute a barrier the Mohammedan religion presents between the Turks and European civilization; how utterly impossible it is for a state not Christian to enter on equal terms into the civil commonwealth of Christendom. But apart from such general considerations, no one who has seriously observed the national character and peculiar policy of the Turks, can imagine the possibility of an empire possessed of European strength and concentration, composed of them alone or in conjunction with subject nations.

"They do not build, but destroy, They show no wish to adorn the soil which they inhabit, or connect in any way the existence of the present generation with posterity. Their object in this world seems to be mere animal existence, as completely as that of the beasts of the field."

From what has been presented two conclusions seem to be inevitable: first, that the Turkish Empire, *as such*, can not be maintained, and that its preservation forms no part of the policy of the Allied Powers, except as a mere dependency of their own; and, second, that whatever change may occur in the *form* of the government, the settled policy of France and England requires that the lands of Turkey should form merely a vast plantation, worked for the benefit of its masters.

It may well be asked, therefore, and not without some anxiety, what benefits will the world at large receive, and how will the interests of the United States be affected, if the colonial policy of the Allied Powers is extended over Turkey, and if their fleets should control the Mediterranean and the Black Sea? If the yoke of the Ottoman Power could be broken off from the Christian population of the Empire, and they be not only permitted but encouraged to enter upon an independent career, and all the resources of that glorious land could be made available by the power of a true Christian civilization; then, indeed, there might be reason for rejoicing if the march of Russia could be arrested.

But in the present condition of Europe this can not be. England and France have chosen to terminate that arrangement by which the Porte might have tottered on yet longer in a state of merely nominal independence, and the only question now remaining is, by whom shall Turkey hereafter be exclusively controlled—by the East or the West? Another inquiry may be added: will it be better for other nations, and for Turkey, that it should become *virtually* a colony of the Western Powers, or that it should be incorporated with Russia? Between these two alternatives there seems now no middle ground.

Nothing is more certain than that France and England intend to apply the principles of the Russian policy to the western hemisphere, and they have seized upon the rebellion as the entering wedge in American affairs. Could they succeed, Mexico would first of all be shaped into a French colony in reality, whatever the *forms* of the government might be. Maximilian, if once seated there, would be simply a crowned puppet—the imperial overseer of a French plantation.

Texas would then be seized on the first pretext, and gradually the South, if nominally independent, would become merely a colony to raise cotton, sugar, &c., for the Allies, and the Pacific coast would if possible be wrested from our possession.

The policy of France and England contemplates all this, and all this we have good reason to believe was included in the original scheme of the Anglo-French Alliance. It was against America as well as Russia. It had, as English statesmen said, reference to both hemispheres.

Our great war for national independence is yet to come, and God is ridding us of our weakness, and bringing out our resources, and consolidating our strength, that we may be prepared. The question whether we are to be subjected to the dictation of European Powers is yet to be settled.

# CHAPTER XIV.

## FUTURE MOVEMENTS OF THE GREAT POWERS.

From this brief review of a portion of European history, it is thought that not only can the present attitude of France and England towards America be fully understood, but that the future relations of the great Powers to each other may also be foreseen.

The rebellion has shown us the deep-seated and now active hostility of some of the chief European nations, and we see clearly that this is the result of settled national policy. The sudden development of our military strength, and especially the rapidity with which we have created a navy among the most powerful in the world, will cause us now, far more than ever before, to arouse the jealousy of Europe. These things, with the movement of France upon Mexico, and the unfriendly temper of England, have brought us within the disturbed circle of European operations and policy, and henceforth we shall be compelled to act in reference to the movements of the great Powers that control the world, because their ambition and jealousies will no longer permit us to remain isolated and pursue an independent course. They seem determined to apply to America the European system of interference, in order to preserve "the balance of power," in other words they propose to combine to strike down every too prosperous nation. If by our intelligence, our action, enterprise and resources, we are in the estimation of France and England becoming too strong, they propose in some way to interfere and arrest our progress. This is not a sudden passing caprice, but a settled rule of national action, applicable to both hemispheres, as the English have declared; and the same spirit which made an English theatre ring with applause when it was announced that the Emperor of Russia was dead, caused the shouts of Englishmen on the sea when they saw the flame of our ships, fired by a pirate fitted out in their own harbors, and to congratulate each other upon the supposed ruin of the Great Republic.

It seems evident now, that the four nations which will control the destinies of the world in the immediate future, are France and England, Russia and America. The armies and the navies, the commerce, and the manufacturing power of the nations, are mostly in their hands. They wield the *forces* of the world, whether material or intellectual, moral or religious.

They represent three grand divisions of the human race, the Sclavonic, the Latin, and the Teutonic, and the three forms of religion by which Christendom is divided, the Greek Church, the Latin or Roman Catholic, and the Protestant.

These races are evidently drawing apart from each other and preparing for a separate career. The Sclavonian race tends to consolidate upon Russia, the Latins are drawing around France, and while the Protestants of Europe have as yet no recognized head, owing to the unnatural alliance of England with a Papal power, the United States is the Protestant head of the West.

These three forms of religion tend on all sides, not to union and friendship, but to divergence and hostility. The Papacy is incapable of alliance or true peace with any form of religion. Her claim is ever the same—to be the one only and exclusive Church, with the right and the duty to suppress every other whenever she has the power. As she has been, she will continue to be the active and uncompromising enemy both of the Greek Church and the Protestant.

Between the Protestant Church and the Greek or Russian, there is no hostility beyond that which has sprung from local and temporary causes. Still, probably, these will not coalesce, their mission and fields of action are different, and their work in the future will be apart, though there appears no reason at present why they should be rivals or enemies. Much will depend upon the future position of England. Were she the friend of Russia, then England, America and Russia, might together spread Christianity over the East.

The only safety, however, of this nation lies in acting in view of the present temper and policy of the leading powers of Europe. The causes that led to the attack on Russia, which leagued France and England in hostility to us, are not only in existence still. but they will work with greater intensity in the future.

Russia, at the head of the Greek Church, is more earnestly intent than ever upon carrying her government and her religion over the East. She is fully determined to gain back from the oppressing and usurping Turk the city of the Eastern Empire which he wrested from her mother church. Russia will not pause until another mighty effort has been made to establish herself upon the Dardanelles and the Mediterranean. Already, if the English Press is correct, she has a new fleet upon the Black Sea, and the Allies have done Russia a priceless service by compelling her to substitute a navy of modern ships for the worthless old "three-deckers" which were sunk at Sebastopol.

France is gathering to herself the nations which form the Papal Church, and aiming to restore throughout the world, west as well as East, the lost prestige of the Latin Church, and obtain the power and the glory of its political head. The United States aims to extend her political and religious life, the power of Protestantism, and of free institutions over this continent. She demands room and liberty to expand, unhindered by any power of Europe, over the whole field of her proper dominion; and while it is not necessary that she should conquer either north or south of her present territory, she will never permit, and cannot without peril to her life, a hostile monarchial power to be established on her border with the avowed purpose of checking her progress. It is somewhat more difficult to foresee the future position of England. Her policy is not controlled by attachment to a church or faith as Russia and the Latin nations are; the commercial idea is her pole star, and this fact alone deprives her of half her power, for no nation can be truly great whose chief motive of action is the making of money. In no case, however, is it safe for the United States to trust for a moment upon the friendship or even neutrality of England. She will cheer on every nation that may attack us, and aid them to the extent of her power, and this will be done for a long time to come in spite of the influence of the liberal party.

It is vain to suppose that England will ever be generous enough to feel willing that we should become greater than herself. Her desire to see us "taken down" will be stronger with her than any other feeling. The present monarchial, aristocratic England, cannot be the friend of the United States.

It seems at first sight not improbable, that so soon as France shall reveal somewhat more clearly her design of a grand combination of the Latin Powers which might be used against England, she might separate herself and seek alliance with Russia or America, or both, against France.

Will she dare to do this? France is at her doors with an army that she cannot match, and could either Russia or America help her with troops upon her own soil? Could they do this if disposed. Will not England find hereafter her only safety in favoring the designs of France precisely as she now does, and did in the Crimean war?

There is no safety for the United States, except to prepare herself to meet the hostility of France and England united. It may not for the present manifest itself in actual war; that will depend alone upon circumstances, but not far in the future the collision must come.

It is simply impossible that England and France, Russia and America, should pursue their several lines of national policy and not come into conflct. These, policies, on the other hand, cannot be abandoned; the national life is bound up in them. Russia must go forward, to pause is for the nation to die. France is urged on by the traditions, histories, and ambitions of a mighty race. England feels that her existence is at stake, and no man can doubt the future course of America in regard to foreign interference with this continent who sees the determination of the North in this war to maintain our nationality.

A great conflict then lies in the future. Let us carefully study the resources and power of these four nations, beginning with the only one that promises to be our friend, perhaps our ally—Russia. It behooves Americans now, if never before, to understand what Russia really is.

# CHAPTER XV.

## THERE SHOULD BE AN AMERICAN OPINION OF RUSSIA.

Although Russia has become the most powerful nation of Europe, she remains in great degree unknown. Her advance upon Europe and the East has been as steady, as resistless, as mysterious, as the descent of a glacier from the Alps. All the force of earth can neither turn the glacier backward, nor divert it from its course, nor even arrest its progress; nor can science fully explain the force that pushes forward the enormous mass. There remains, however, the fact, that year by year it encroaches more and more upon the valley below. Each summer melts off a little of its solid front, but still the icy boundary of to-day is beyond the line on which it rested a year ago.

So with Russia. Her colossal proportions are expanding still, her frontier line is moving on, plowing its way like the edge of the glacier through all obstacles, and though we hear continually of losses she incurs, and of defeats which she suffers, we find that notwithstanding all, she has been moving on, and has established herself in new possessions, at the very moment when the rest of Europe was rejoicing over her supposed discomfiture. Statesmen, political economists, even historians, give no adequate explanation of this overshadowing phenomenon, no satisfactory account of the interior life which is thus forcing the nations aside to make room for the growth of Russia. Europe sneers at the horde of northern barbarians, but then she saw the best appointed army and the ablest commander of modern times utterly crushed by them, and hurled in broken fragments over their frontier, and this, too, when up to the startling result, it was declared that Russia was beaten in every battle, that her capital was taken, and the Empire was ruined. At the commencement of the Crimean war, we were informed that Russia was exhausted by her disasters in the Caucasus, that a small tribe there was sufficient to hold her power at bay, that she had no money wherewith to prosecute a war, that her army was formidable only on paper, scattered through her vast territory in disconnected detachments, incapable of combined action; and many believed and asserted that Turkey alone was an overmatch for her foe; and yet a formidable English fleet spent two summers in the Baltic without daring to look upon Cronstadt, and the most formidable armament that the world perhaps ever saw, spent its force and exhausted its skill for two years in vain upon a single Russian outpost. England and France met not the unwieldy, stupid, almost helpless giant which they have loved to describe and call Russia, but the living power of a great nation, whose power has been wielded with a skill and energy at least equal to to their own.

Russia has made no great and sudden conquests in Europe; she has poured no living deluge abroad for the desolation of the world—a tide whose ebb follows quickly after the swell of the flood; but she is the more formidable for that very reason. *She grows.* Her progress follows the law of a life, and its development is after the model of a national idea. Herein lies her strength; and the power of this life, yet young and vigorous, will carry her far into the future.

Until recently, the Empire of the Czars has awakened

very little attention or sympathy in the American mind. Its remote position, and the channels through which we have obtained our scanty information, have prevented us from forming any correct and well-defined idea of its prospects, resources and policy. Most Americans have been led to think of Russia as a land of almost perpetual snow and frost, of interminable forests, or uninhabitable plains, and few perhaps have asked themselves, how in such frozen wastes and forest solitudes, seventy millions of people have not only contrived to exist, but have grown up into the most formidable nation of Europe. Again, thousands regard her as an assemblage of boisterous hordes, having no common life or bond, held together by the power of a military despotism, and ruled over by a half-savage tyrant. Few have been led to inquire how, upon such a supposition, we are to account for her rapid and steady advance to the foremost position of the eastern world. It would not be easy for a semi-barbarous people, with merely a military tyrant at their head, to reach so eminent a station by the very side of the civilization of western Europe, and in competition with such powers as England, France, and Austria. The national policy of Russia has been represented to Europe and America under the single idea of a perpetual longing to rush on Turkey, and seize upon Constantinople. Nearly all else has been vailed from view. The true character of this policy and its real objects have been but partially understood. Russia has, moreover, been viewed with dislike or indifference by Americans, because of the form of her government, and her supposed hatred of a liberal and republican policy. She has been regarded as the determined foe of the rights of man; as neither desiring for herself, nor willing to admit in others, any other form of civilization than such as may be produced by an absolute military despotism. It has been supposed that Russia and America are the true opposites and even antagonists of each other, the one representing a half-civilized oriental despotism, the other rational republicanism. The thought once scarce entered the American mind that a mutual regard might spring up between the two Powers, and that they may yet become the friendly representatives of the two leading ideas of the world.

It is quite evident that the popular opinion of the great Northern Power, does not correspond either with her past history or her present position. Her power and resources have been underrated even in Europe. France and England have miscalculated the strength of their antagonist. Europe has misjudged her, because the sources of her vitality are but imperfectly known. Yet it is manifest that she has interior springs, whose copious flow supplies a broad and steady stream of national life. Russia presents every external sign of a living organism—not merely an aggregation of tribes, of fragments bound into a mass by present circumstances, which in any important change may fall asunder. The resistance which, in 1812, she offered to western Europe, was that of an organized body, animated by a national life. There was a national heart beating with hot enthusiasm in the midst of her snows; there was a national feeling smarting under a national wound; there was unyielding resolution—ready to sacrifice all things for the preservation of their country, determined to make of that country a desert, if the invader could not be otherwise expelled; and it was the result of a living force that at last swept her foes away. It was not a subdued or dispirited people, not a people fired with no love of country, that pressed upon and bore down the retreating forces of Bonaparte. Since that period there has been a steady enlargement and increase of vigor, as by growth from a strong central life.

# CHAPTER XVI.

## THE ESSENTIAL ELEMENTS OF NATIONAL POWER.

In this age of the world, when civilization, instead of being confined to a single luminous point, is diffused over so large a portion of the world's surface, and a universal empire is no longer possible, there are certain conditions without which no great nation can come into existence—certain elements of strength necessary to procure for a people the first rank among the Powers of earth. The first of these conditions is an extensive territory. In the midst of the powerful kingdoms of modern times, no petty state, with limited domain, could exercise any important sway. Greece, placed on her ancient territorial footing, and possessed again of her former resources, would now be but a "little one" among the nations. Egypt could not now sway the world's sceptre from the valley of the Nile, nor could old Chaldea be in this age the "Lady of Kingdoms." Even if Rome should arise once more, possessed of all her Italian and Eastern power, leaving Russia, France, England, and the German states, as they now are, she would no longer be the mistress of the world. To hold rank among the present "great Powers" of Europe, a territory is required, capable of sustaining a population of at least thirty millions with the ordinary cultivation and modes of life, and therefore the "four great Powers" must remain at the head of affairs. But it is easy to see that if any one of these should possess a territory capable of supporting a population equal to that of France, England, and Austria, combined, without being more densely peopled than they now are, then, other things being equal, such a power would hold all Europe at her control, because all know that the other remaining nations could not be consolidated into a permanent union, though they may become allies in an hour of danger.

In estimating, therefore, the future position of the present powers of earth, extent of territory and capacity for population must be the basis of the calculation; for a state of thirty millions, of to-day, may, in a few years, stand in the presence of another with one hundred millions of people. But there must be not only extent of territory, but it must be so situated as to be easily and safely controlled by one central government. It is evident that India, Canada, and Australia add little to the effective strength of England. In proportion as they wax strong and prosperous will their sympathy with the home government be weakened; and therefore England, even with her great possessions, may be regarded as having reached the zenith of her power—because she can not construct from her separated dependencies one consolidated dominion. When it is said, however, that she has reached her culminating point, the meaning is not that she is now destined to an absolute decline; it is not necessary, even, to suppose that she will make no progress hereafter, but if another Power shall soon appear in Europe, with one hundred millions of people, with a common nationality, occupying one connected territory, and directed by one sufficiently strong central government; if, indeed, such an one has already taken its position on the theatre of Europe, then, not only England, but France and Austria, may be regarded as having passed the height of their influence, though their absolute power may yet continue to increase. Against such a Power, the balance could not long be preserved by any combination of western Europe. Moreover, to secure national greatness, based upon national independence, the territory of a people should stretch through so many degrees of latitude, and should embrace such a variety of position and climate as to procure within itself the main productions of the globe. In this respect, neither England, France, nor Austria, are so situated as to remain the very foremost nations of the world, though France and England, but especially the latter, have thus far been able to supply the deficiency by a command of the open commerce of the globe. But it is easy to perceive, that, in case of long-continued war, or if other states should adopt a restricted commercial policy, every nation incapable of extensive home production, would suffer severely, and perhaps be permanently crippled. A nation then, to become not only great, but independent and secure, must possess the means of a self-sustaining life, and this can only be when its territory stretches through several degrees of latitude.

Again, this territory must possess the means, natural or artificial, of free and extensive internal communication. Large lakes, or a chain of inland seas, and navigable rivers, will probably always afford the most important and cheapest channels for commercial exchanges, and a country thus furnished by the Creator will possess great advantages over one not thus favored; for, although modern science has put it in the power of any people to supply an adequate means of cheap and rapid transit, yet navigable rivers, and internal lakes and seas, are an additional advantage, conferring a superiority upon the nation possessing them. Any country may be traversed by rail roads, but when, in addition to these, God has scooped out the rivers and beds of navigable waters, there is a double system and a double advantage. Inasmuch, therefore, as God has designed the earth as the theater of national life, we are led to believe that those great divisions of its surface which are provided with adequate systems of lakes and navigable rivers, bringing all parts into connection with each other, were thus constructed in order to become the seats of national power; and even though such a territory may be now unoccupied, or but thinly inhabited, we are assured that the design of God will be accomplished. The future of America may, for this reason, be correctly inferred from the structure of its territory, although large portions of it are lying waste, without an inhabitant; and if we would form an opinion of the prospects of Russia, we must study her systems of rivers, and her general means of carrying on an interior trade, by which her remote provinces may be united by common interests, and bound to a common head.

Moreover, since modern skill and science have converted the seas into the great thoroughfares of the world, no nation with an interior position can hereafter hold the first rank among the powers of earth. The great nation of the future must have free access to the ocean—must not only hold free communication with the sea from all points, but must possess sufficient and convenient harbors as commercial marts, and depots of maritime power.

The admirable position of England, in the midst of the seas, has given free scope to the genius of her people, and enabled her to exert a controlling influence upon the affairs of nations; but should a nation arise in Europe, with a population many times greater than her own—equal in intelligence and skill—with a proportionate control of the ocean—in that case England, though still prosperous and advancing, would hold but a secondary position; and this would be equally true both of Austria and France. Whether there is a probability of the rise of such an empire, will be one of the questions to be discussed in these pages.

Again, a nation will be great and powerful, other things being equal, in proportion as its growth is the progress of a single race, instead of a mere aggregation of dissimilar communities, brought by conquest under the dominion of a single head. The one is a dead mass, tending ever to dissolution; the other is an animate body, unfolding a life, and tending toward maturity. Every mighty nation of earth has become great through the central life-power of one dominant race; and the growth of power has been steady so long as there was sufficient vitality in this center to mold and assimilate all foreign material. Another important question, then, connected with the prospects of the Russian Empire is, whether its population consists mainly of one race, which may supply a national life, and afford a true basis of national unity. If such a race exists, speaking a common language, bound together by the ties of common ancestry, national memories, interests, and hopes, creating a family pride and love of country; then it becomes important also to know whether this race possesses a clearly marked individuality, and if so, whether in these characteristics we are able to discover the elements of growth and greatness.

Still another element of national power exists, where a nation is knit together by the ties of a common religion, and when a deep religious sentiment pervades the public mind. There may be a profession of a common faith, in which the national heart feels little or no interest, where even the doctrines of Christianity are coldly admitted, more from the influence of tradition or early education than from a conviction wrought into the heart; such a belief can not be regarded as an element of strength, for the national soul can not be roused for its defense—it can kindle no enthusiasm. But when a great people are controlled by a religious system in which they have an undoubting faith, and which has power to excite and maintain a spirit of worship in the popular mind, such a people can be roused to the loftiest efforts of which man is capable, either for aggressive war, for the spread of a national faith, or in defense of their altars and their homes. In studying the characteristics of Russia, we should therefore not forget to inquire concerning her religious faith, and the warmth and strength of the religious sentiment among the millions of the empire, and whether there is a deep national feeling of belief and worship that can be roused in a common cause. Finally, all the elements of national power may lie through long periods without being combined for any lofty purpose; or a nation, even from the first, may seem to have some presentiment of its destiny, and works on through centuries perhaps, toward a distant end, dimly perceived even by itself, until some mighty mind arises that comprehends the capacities of his country, and institutes at once the proper methods of awakening the national energies, and directs them to a definite end. If then, upon investigation, we discover some or all of these elements of power in Russia, it will then be interesting to consider whether they are still lying like rude materials yet unshapen by the hand of the artist, or whether we find in the Emperor that greatness which has placed him at the head of an era in his country's history, a genius which has enabled him to mark out for his nation a noble career, to conceive a great scheme bearing a true relation to the capabilities of his empire, and then direct toward this high end the whole power of his people.

With these thoughts before us, let us proceed to the study of the great Northern Empire, and the policy and character of the Czar. This character and policy will be exhibited by presenting Russia as she is; for the Russia of to-day has been modelled according to the conception of the late emperor, a conception to whose grand proportions the empire will continue to shape itself in its future expansion. Nicholas formed the great idea of a Sclavonic civilization, with a territory for its theater stretching from ocean to ocean, with the Greek faith and worship for its religious basis, with a vast commercial and manufacturing system for its support, and expanding not so much by conquest as by growth from a central life.

# CHAPTER XVII.

## GEOGRAPHICAL CHARACTER OF RUSSIA.

In accordance with the suggestions made in the preceding chapter, let us now inquire whether Russia possesses a territory capable of sustaining a population that will give her a controlling influence in the affairs of Europe. It has been usual to speak of this empire under two great divisions, the one in Europe and the other in Asia, but we shall obtain a clearer idea of its vast dimensions by regarding it as one great whole. In fact, there is no great natural boundary to separate eastern from western Russia, the Ural mountains being little more than a long tract of elevated land, the loftiest portions rising only to the height of four thousand feet, the ascent and descent being so gradual where the great roads pass as to be almost imperceptible. We may then, without violence to any geographical feature, consider the Russian territory as one unbroken whole. Viewed thus, it stretches from the Baltic sea on the west, across the entire breadth of Europe and Asia to the sea of Okhotsk and to Behring's Straits, looking southward upon the entire northern frontier of Europe, Turkey, Tartary, and the Chinese empire. This territory contains no less than 6,750,000 square miles, or more than one-sixth part of all the land on our planet. It has been the custom of most to comprise the whole description of this immense possession within the sweeping remark that most of it is an inhospitable region of deserts and snows, incapable of sustaining human life, and altogether without any important resources which can contribute to the growth of a nation. The almost unequalled progress of the empire within the last century is quite sufficient to expose the absurdity of such views, and yet in the one of latest American work upon Russia is found the following: After speaking of the great extent of the Russian dominions, and stating that her territory is equal to two Europes, or the whole of North America, the author adds, "But by far the greatest "proportion of this prodigious superfices is almost unin- "habited, and seems to be destined to perpetual sterility; "a consequence partly of the extreme rigor of the climate, "in the provinces contiguous to the Arctic ocean, and "partly of almost all the great rivers by which they are "traversed having their *embouchure* on that ocean, and "being therefore inaccessible for either the whole or the "greater part of the year."

What could the uninformed reader infer from this description but that "by *far the greatest proportion*" of all Russia lies along the shores of the frozen ocean, and is therefore condemned to a "perpetual sterility?" But how does this idea accord with the fact that Russia, being somewhat less in extent than the North American continent, has already a population nearly double that of North America, and is surpassed by the United States alone in the rapidity of her progress.

Again the same author remarks, "The most distinguish- "ing feature of Russia is her vasts forests. Schnitzler, who "estimates the surface of European Russia at about four "hundred millions of deciatims (2 7-10 acres), supposes "that one hundred and fifty-six millions are occupied by "forests. They are so very prevalent in the governments "of Novgorod and Tver, between Petersburg and Moscow, "that it has been said a squirrel might travel from the one "city to the other without ever touching the ground. In "the government of Perm, on both sides of the Ural "mountains, containing eighteen millions of deciatims, no "fewer than seventeen millions are covered by forests! The "forests of Asiatic Russia are also of vast size." These may be facts, but facts thus presented without explanation, and in connection with the statements which have been mentioned concerning the sterile character of "by far the greatest proportion" of Russia, serve only to lead the mind of the inquirer astray. No long period has passed since the most "distinguishing feature" of North America, particularly of the United States, was the almost unbroken forest, and it was scarcely impossible one hundred years ago for a squirrel to have passed from the Atlantic to the Mississippi through one continuous wood; and yet on the very site of the old forest now stand our populous States, which indeed could not have sprung up with such marvellous growth had the forests been absent. These very forests constitute a most important portion of the wealth of Russia; they form a solid basis for her future progress, and an element of growth with which she could by no means safely dispense—as will be shown hereafter.

A fair comparison of the capabilities of the Russian Empire, so far as population is concerned, might be presented, could we make even an approximate estimate of the extent of territory within her limits, equal in productiveness to other portions of Europe, and then calculate what the number of her people would be if these lands were as densely settled as Europe now is. Sir Archibald Allison has attempted such a calculation, in which, as a basis, he rejects two-thirds of Asiatic Russia as sterile and unproductive. Having done this, he then proceeds to show that if Russia in Europe were peopled as Germany now is, it would contain 150,000,000 souls; if as dense as Great Britain, the number would be 311,000,000. He then adds, if that portion of Asiatic Russia which is capable of cultivation were peopled even as Scotland is, it would sustain 200,000,000 inhabitants; if as densely as the British Islands together, more than 500,000,000 people. If, then, the agricultural portion of Russia were populated only as Germany and Scotland now are, her numbers would be 350,000,000; if as densely as Great Britain, the population would be more than 800,000,000. This seems at first glance mere empty speculation. But let us consider that this would be the number of the multitudes of Russia, when she has only as many inhabitants to the square mile as Great Britain now has, and reckoning only the productive portion of her territory. The point to be observed here is, that with an equal number of inhabitants on the square mile, the population of Great Britain would be some 28,000,000, and that of Russia 800,000,000, and this without taking into account the sterile lands of the latter country. This, therefore, affords a fair comparison of the capacities of the two kingdoms, looking at this single point alone. Nor can it be said that it is impossible that the agricultural portions of Russia will ever support as many inhabitants on the square mile as are found in Great Britain now, for out of about 57,000,000 acres in the British Islands, 22,000,000 are waste lands. Besides, even the present ratio of increase in Russia will give her in the year 1900, 130,000,000 people; in 1950, the number will be 260,000,000; and one hundred and fifty years hence, with simply her present rate of progress, her population will be 520,000,000, and we have seen that her territory is abundantly sufficient to support even this enormous multitude—that even then she will not be overstocked with people, for the estimate is based upon her agricultural and productive lands alone, and facts would seem to indicate that this portion of her country is much larger in proportion to the whole than has been hitherto supposed. Indeed, in almost all our publications upon this subject, from the elementary books and geographies of our schools to the scientific lecture, we find only those sweeping generalities which are usually employed in the absence of definite ideas and accurate information.

It will be conceded by all that the territorial possessions

of Russia are sufficiently extensive to form the basis of an empire more powerful than any now on the globe—superior even to any nation of the past. But then we are at once reminded that most of this vast dominion lying under the frozen sky of the north is unfit for the habitation of man, and is doomed to eternal rigor and sterility. If this is indeed so, then western Europe has little to apprehend from the future growth of this northern Power, and the world at large little to hope from the civilization of the Sclavonic races. But it is better to study this subject in the light of admitted facts than to be guided by theories hastily constructed, and which, like false quotations from some ancient author, pass current for generations, sometimes without examination, and, consequently, without dispute. A few well established facts relating to position, climate, and productions, will enable us to form an accurate opinion upon the single point of the capacity of the Russian territory to sustain a dense population.

By far the largest proportion of the Russian Empire, whether in Europe or Asia, lies within the temperate zone, and this alone would furnish strong presumptive evidence, if not positive proof, that a small portion only of its lands are necessarily uninhabitable or barren, on account of the severity of the climate. Between the parallels of latitude that enclose entire Europe, Russia has a territory equal in extent to all the other European States, and from its southern limit, between the Black Sea and the Caspian, it stretches northward through about eighteen degrees of latitude, before it reaches the northern extremity of Great Britain, a distance equal to that from New Orleans to the center of Lake Superior—or in general terms, equal to the breadth of our country, from the Gulf of Mexico to British America.

This fact alone is quite sufficient to show that, so far as territory and climate are concerned, she possess the elements of national greatness almost immeasureably beyond any other single Power of Europe—holding a territory nearly equal to them all, which lies in the same latitude as their own, beside her more northern districts, and her immense possessions in Asia. The character of that portion of Russia in Europe which lies north of the latitude of Great Britain, and also that of her Asiatic dominions, may be understood by Americans, if compared with our own country. In this comparison, it must not be forgotten that the climate of Europe is milder than in the corresponding latitudes in America. The opening of the spring, the time of the autumnal frosts, and the beginning of winter, will furnish proper points for such a comparison. It would probably be very near the truth, if the average time for the opening of the navigation of the Hudson is fixed at or near the 1st of April. The ice in the Penobscot, as was stated, began to move this season (1855) on the 14th of April. At St. Paul, Minnesota, the navigation of the Mississippi opens from the 1st to the middle of April, and up to this time, also, the ice usually remains in the harbors of our western lakes. The period for the closing of these rivers and lakes, in the autumn, is from the middle of November to the first of December—the Hudson alone excepted, which often remains open until the last days of December. Throughout the Northern States, the time for planting Indian corn is between the first and 12th of May, and it reaches maturity, with a profitable yield, in regions so far north that the planting is delayed until June, while there, also, rye, oats, flax, barley, potatoes and other roots, as well as a great variety of fruits, grow in perfection. Now when it is considered that the most flourishing portion of our country is that where the commencement of spring ranges from the middle of April to the middle of May, and where the autumnal frosts begin about the 1st of October, it is surely a somewhat hasty conclusion that a country of Europe, possessing a similar climate, must be regarded as doomed to perpetual sterility, as a mere frozen waste. The ice on the Neva, at St. Petersburgh, is usually broken up about the 18th of April, while it again becomes stationary about the 1st of December. Vegetation commences by the 1st of May, and proceeds with a rapidity that outstrips the growth of more southern climes, and fully compensates for the later opening of spring. By an examination of the reports of various travelers, but especially the descriptions of the accurate and scientific German tourist, Erman, we learn that if we travel eastward from St. Petersburgh, through Russia in Europe, and Siberia, to the Pacific Ocean, we shall find that through all these immense regions, to within a short distance of the arctic circle, the climate corresponds in general with that of the northern portions of the United States, and the British American provinces; that the commencement of winter and the beginning of spring, and the range of the thermometer, are nearly the same on both the eastern and western continents. It would therefore be wrong to conclude that any portion of Russia, either in Europe or Asia, south of sixty-two degrees north latitude, may not support a dense population, when we have before our eyes New England, northern New York, Wisconsin, Minnesota, and Canada, with a climate essentially the same, yet evidently possessing all the elements of rapid growth and national greatness. In regard to the productiveness of the soil of Russia, our conclusions rest partly upon conceded facts, and partly upon inferences. Little need be said concerning the whole vast territory which lies opposite to the main portions of western Europe, embracing eighteen degrees of latitude, for although much has been said of the inhospitable and even uninhabitable steppes of the southern portion of this region, Americans have learned that a prairie land is capable of supporting an exceedingly dense population, and the "detestable *black dust*" mentioned by travelers in the Russian prairies, indicates, in a manner not to be mistaken, the fertile character of the soil. This region, then, lying side by side with western Europe, and almost equal in extent to that part of the United States which lies between the Atlantic and the Rocky Mountains, may, perhaps, be considered as equal in productiveness to the remainder of Europe. We have then to consider, in addition, the more northern portions of Russia, both in Europe and Asia. Here the winters are severe, and the summers are short; and, although the capabilities of the soil have scarcely been tested at all, it is probable that cultivation must cease at a point about one hundred miles south of the arctic circle. This opinion is founded chiefly upon the observations of Erman, who found that the grains of Europe had been brought to perfection within about this distance of the frigid zone, and even in places where the ground is perpetually frozen, a few feet below the surface. These northern regions, moreover, abound in immense forests, particularly of pine, and soil which is capable of supporting the growth of large forest trees will, by suitable culture, produce food for man. These forests form no inconsiderable portion of the wealth of Russia, and will materially contribute to her future growth; and the truth of this will readily appear when we remember that the snows of the winter, and the countless streams in the summer, furnish precisely the means of transport for lumber, which has been found so efficacious in America.

Some idea may be formed of the value of the forests of Russia, from the following statements which are found in Allison's History of Europe: "The cold and shivering "plains which stretch toward Archangel and the shores "of the White Sea, are covered with immense forests of "oak and fir, furnishing at once inexhaustible materials "for ship-building, and supplies of fuel, which for many "generations will supercede the necessity of searching in "the bowels of the earth for the purposes of warmth or "manufacture, for the inhabitants of the empire." He then quotes the following from "*Trans de l'Academie* "*Imperiale, de St. Petersburgh;* Maltė Brun and Bremner's "Russia":

"The extent of the forests in the northern provinces of Russia is almost inconceivable. From actual measurement it appears that in the three governments of Vologda, Archangel, and Olonitz alone, there are 216,000,000 acres of pine and fir, being about three times the whole surface of the British Islands, which contains 77,000,000. In one government alone there are 47,000,000 acres of forest.

It appears from M. Herman's calculations, that there are in thirty-one governments in the north of Russia, 8,195,295 firs well adapted to large masts, each being above thirty inches in diameter—a number more than sufficient for a long supply of all the fleets in the world, besides 86,869,000 fit for building houses. In twenty-two governments only, there are 374,804 large oaks, each more than twenty-six inches in diameter, and 229,570,000 of a smaller size." A country thus supplied with such magnificent forests of timber, for ship-building, the construction of dwellings, and all the purposes of the arts, and so abundantly furnished with the means of transport by her net-work of rivers, may not be carelessly described as a mere frozen, barren waste; for these forests when they disappear, as the population increases, and civilization advances, will be succeeded by grain fields, and orchards, and prosperous communities, in the same manner in which we have seen the change wrought on American soil. It is doubtless true, that there is much waste land even within the limits of what has been designated as the agricultural district of the Russian Empire, and the northern portions of her territory, even within the temperate zone, can not be considered productive when compared with the Danubian provinces, or with the valley of the Mississippi; but then it should be remembered what large tracts of land are found unfit for cultivation in every country. How large a portion of the whole surface, for instance, in New England, is occupied by mountains and rugged hills that the plow can not visit; yet these very mountains, covered with forests, sparkling with streams, and filled with mineral wealth, afford the means of supporting an exceedingly dense population. The capabilities of Russia have evidently been too hastily judged; her rapid growth, unequalled except by our own, would indicate that no unusual proportion of her territory is waste and sterile, and there are many proofs that the Russians are subduing a continent, expanding themselves on every side, and redeeming the wilderness, after the manner of the Americans here.

# CHAPTER XVIII.

## THE RELATIVE POSITION OF RUSSIA.

Whatever may be the extent of a nation's territory, or the productiveness of its soil, it can have no extended growth, or permanent greatness based on its own independent resources, if it is either hemmed in by other powerful nations, or excluded from adequate communication with the ocean. A nation thus situated can become great only by conquest or peaceful acquisition, thus securing to itself advantages which did not belong to its original domain. Russia has thus extended herself with astonishing rapidity; but this enlargement of her dominion has been not so much by overrunning contiguous countries as by the expansion of an internal life, which has sought space wherein to grow; and it is her present position, and what seems to be her immediate and inevitable future, that is presented for consideration here. Perhaps Americans may perceive in the picture enough of resemblance to our own position to awaken in them a new interest in regard to this *European America*, and to inquire whether two great nations now facing each other on the opposite shores of the Pacific, are not hereafter to be brought into more intimate association.

Like America Russia reaches from ocean to ocean, stretching across the whole breadth of Europe and Asia, and resting one wing on the Pacific and the other upon the Atlantic. She is thus placed, at either extremity of her empire, in communication with the commerce of the world. Through the Baltic she connects herself with Europe, and with the trade of the eastern coast of America, and eastward on the Pacific, there is opened to her the commerce of China, the East Indian Archipelago, and the Pacific slope of the American continent. From these two extremities the trade of the world may be drawn inward toward the heart of the empire. One acquisition has lately been made by Russia in the East, which will change the whole aspect of her eastern commerce, and will prove of the very highest importance in connection with the progress of our own population on the Pacific coast. This point will be made clear by the following quotation from Alison, and by the inspection of a good map: "The river Amoor, which flows "from the mountains of Mongolia into the ocean of Japan, "by a course twelve hundred miles in length, of which nine "hundred are navigable, in a deep channel, shut in on "either side by precipitous rocks, or shaded by noble forests, "is the real outlet of eastern Siberia; and though the Chi-"nese are still masters of this splendid stream, it is as in-"dispensible to Asiatic as the Volga is to European Russia, "and ere long it must fall under the dominion of the "Czar, and constitute the principal outlet of his immense "oriental provinces." Mr. Alison has underrated the size of the Amoor. It is twenty-two hundred miles in length, and navigable through a large portion of its whole extent. The upper portion of this stream lies within the Emperor's dominions, in the province of Irkoutsk, and with the Chinese in possession of its mouth, eastern Siberia is in a condition somewhat similar to that of the upper Mississippi valley before the Louisiana purchase. Russia has lately obtained the control of the valley of the Amoor to its mouth, and it will at once become the channel of an extensive commerce, not with the East alone, but with the

Pacific slope of America. Siberia is traversed from north to south by large navigable rivers, which empty, however, into the Arctic ocean; but so soon as the trade of these streams is carried on by steam vessels, changes will take place, such as have occurred on our western rivers, and these channels, united, as ultimately they will be, by railways pointing eastward and toward the valley of the Amoor, will pour into the sea of Japan, the mineral and other productions of southern and central Siberia, and the northern provinces of China, and bear back from other lands the means of comfort and civilization to the heart of northern Asia. On the shores of California and Oregon, and at the mouth of the Amoor, and in the harbors of the sea of Japan, Russians and Americans will meet for the exchanges of a mutual commerce, remote from the rest of Europe.

We shall scarcely overestimate the importance of the trade which, at no remote period, will flow to and from southern Siberia, and the adjacent provinces lately added to the Russian territory, if we may credit a distingushed English writer, who declares that the immense plains "which stretch to the eastward along the banks of the "Amoor, are capable of containing all the nations of "Christendom in comfort and affluence." Again, by her possessions upon the Black Sea, she is placed in direct communication with the commerce of the Mediterranean, and through the Mediterranean she has a third channel connecting her with the general trade of the world. In this calculation, no notice is taken of her long line of sea coast on the Arctic Ocean. In those frozen regions it possesses less commercial importance. A country so vast as Russia could scarcely touch the sea more advantageously than she does, resting in the east on the Pacific, lying in the west along the Atlantic, for the Baltic and the Gulf of Finland are to her as to the Atlantic sea coast, while along the southern frontier of her European territory stretches the Black Sea. It is apparent that nothing more is wanting but the possession of Constantinople and the control of the Dardanelles, to complete a territorial outline of the most imposing character that earth has ever seen in the possession of a single Power, and to which earth can afford no parallel, except in North America. He who studies aright the position, resources, and progress of Russia, will see at once that the possession of Constantinople is merely a question of time. The idea that the Powers of western Europe are able to check *permanently* the advance of Russia will not long be seriously entertained. The life of the Northern Empire lies beyond their reach, and she needs but to permit them to exhaust themselves upon her frontier positions, and quietly wait until they are forced backward by the resistless power of her growth. She is under no present necessity of possessing Constantinople; she requires only the power to control its owner, and shape for them a policy in accordance with her own, and the most splendid dreams of Muscovite greatness may then be realized, even while the Golden Horn remains in the possession of the Sultan.

It may not be uninteresting to the American reader to pause a moment here, in order to bestow a passing glance upon the general resemblance between the geographical position of Russia and North America, as well as a relationship of position—indicating, as it would seem, a closer connection between the two nations in their future career.

The comparison is instituted between Russia and North America because nothing in the future is more certain than that the North American continent, with its adjacent seas and islands, will be controlled by a single government. If the American Union continues, such a result will be reached by the inevitable law of national development. Russia and North America then are nearly equal in the extent of their possessions, and each is capable of supporting a population of a thousand millions, without overburthening its territory or exhausting its resources. They both stretch from ocean to ocean, each resting one broad wing upon the Atlantic and the other upon the Pacific; and together, the arms of their wide dominion reach round the globe. They face each other from the opposite shores of the Atlantic, for, as has been said, the Baltic and the Gulf of Finland form for Russia an Atlantic sea-coast. Again, the two nations lie fronting each other on the shores of the North Pacific—suggesting a future influence over the East Indian Archipelago, scarcely anticipated now: a control of the commerce of the East, which our Government is preparing for by her negotiations with Japan, and of which Russia is not unmindful, as was evident from the watchful presence of her fleet while our squadron was at Yeddo, and by her advancing to the valley of the Amoor. The eastern provinces of Russia on the Pacific, and the western territories of the United States on the same ocean, can furnish unlimited resources, either for a navy or a commercial marine, and therefore the trade of that "Exhaustless East" may yet flow along two new channels, running in opposite directions—one eastward, through the heart of North America, and the other westward, through the dominions of Russia. Such a change in the world's commerce is surely not altogether improbable; indeed the course of events already indicates such a result, and it requires no argument to demonstrate that, if it occurs, the Powers of western Europe will sink at once to a seeondary position, and yield up forever the control of the world. Such a view suggests the intimate relations which may hereafter be established between the United States and Russia; and the growing sympathy between the two nations may, perhaps, be regarded as a foreshadowing of the future. Again, these two countries resemble each other in their capacity for self-development and independent support. They both enjoy every variety of soil, climate, and production that can be found north of the southern limit of the temperate zone, and therefore, though they were shut out from all the world beside, each could still maintain a vigorous natural growth from their own domestic resources. Indeed, if it were possible for the Powers of Europe completely to blockade every seaport of Russia and America for the next fifty years, they would find, in the end, that so far from crushing the power of either nation, they had only, in each, nursed to maturity a compact and homogeneous power, self-balanced on its own resources, self-sustained by its own internal life, irresistible through its national unity and individuality of character. Each of these countries is capable of becoming a world within itself, independent of and even excluded from the rest of earth. Vast as is the foreign commerce of the United States, it is yet small when compared with our domestic trade, and the complete annihilation of our trade with foreign nations would not touch the sources of our national life, nor even permanently retard our progress. Russia and America are the only two Powers of earth that might become great nations if shut out from the rest of the world, and therefore the efforts of all other nations can not long or materially obstruct the growth of either. Both are impregnable on their own soil, and both may securely develope their exhaustless internal resources, without the possibility of being prevented by any. The two countries also present some points of general resemblance in the natural facilities which both possess for internal communication, as well as for the construction of artificial channels for travel and for trade. Russia can boast of no such magnificent chain of internal seas as those of North America, but she has the Caspian, eight hundred miles long, on the east—the Black Sea along the central portion of her southern frontier in Europe—and the Baltic, and the Gulf of Finland, affording her a long line of what may be called inland sea-coast, in the northwest, while her whole territory is covered, almost equally with the American continent, by a net-work of navigable rivers. In addition to these natural avenues of commerce, the nature of the country presents almost unrivalled facilities for the construction of artificial connections, whether canals or roads. Russia may be regarded as one vast plain, reaching from the Atlantic to the Pacific, and intersected by few mountain ranges, so that no obstacle is presented to the establishment of railways in any required direction, while the material for such structures exists in abundance. Both in the United States and Russia, therefore, are found unlimited resourees for a home growth, the cultivation of an individual and independent national life. In the external features and relative geographical position, then, of these two great nations, we perceive enough of general resemblance to suggest the inquiry whether they are not to be in some manner more closely associated than they have hitherto been—whether, in the new aspect of the world's affairs, now opening around us, they are not to act in concert, and possibly in united self-defense, against the Powers of western Europe. Especially may we suppose that this might occur if England and France should assume, as they now seem disposed to do, the office of *regulators* of the concerns of nations in both hemispheres, which, being interpreted, means simply that they propose to combine to repress the progress of any Power which, even in its legitimate growth, may overshadow their own. Russia and America have been prepared, as it were, in the wilderness, away from the great theater of European affairs. A little time since they were scarcely thought of, much less consulted, in the movements of nations; they have risen together to the position of great Powers on earth, and henceforth they can scarcely remain indifferent to each other's condition and policy. Unaccountable as it may appear, considering the different character of their political institutions, it is doubtless true that Russia regards America with more friendly feelings than she does any nation of Europe, and indications are not wanting that republican America will ere long strongly reciprocate this friendship of an absolute monarchy. It is believed to be quite impossible to estimate correctly, from any descriptions which have been given, the actual extent of internal navigation supplied by the rivers and lakes of Russia. The country has, as yet, to a great extent, been but imperfectly explored, unless by the government itself. Foreigners are acquainted only with the larger streams of the empire, and thousands of miles of river navigation may probably exist, altogether unknown to any who have visited Russia. The main streams which flow into the Baltic, those which empty into the Black Sea, and the Caspian, and the great rivers of Siberia, have been described in general terms, and we are informed that they are navigable to certain points. These descriptions have been given mostly by those who know little of river navigation as practised in America. Those who are accustomed to see American steamboats on our western rivers, carrying on a profitable traffic, with a depth of water from fifteen inches to eighteen inches only, will readily understand, from a map, that the Russian territory will yet be traversed, in all directions, by steamboats of light draught, such as now enliven the rivers of the west, and that such capacities for domestic traffic, and for reaching the seaboard, are ample for the development of the country's resources. A single statement, furnished by Ehrman throws, much light upon this interesting subject.

This author, in describing the mines of the Ural mountains, and the amount of iron annually produced, states the line of river navigation from the mining region to St. Petersburg, to be 3,350 miles. He also mentions that from the upper Volga, from 4000 to 6000 barges descend annually to St. Petersburg, by a canal connecting with the Neva; and when we consider that iron from the Ural, destined to European Russia, requires about 1000 boats annually, carrying each nearly one hundred tons at the commencement of the voyage, the cargo being increased at a certain point below, we may form an idea of the amount of the present internal commerce of Russia. Nor must we forget that this trade is yet almost entirely carried on in such rude boats as a few years since floated on the Mississippi and Ohio, and it is not therefore too much to anticipate that in the future progress of Russia, and in a period not remote, such a change may be wrought by the introduction of steam vessels upon her rivers, as we have already seen from this cause in the Mississippi valley. She has begun, and completed to Moscow, one of her great trunk lines of railway intended to concentrate upon her capital, and it is in progress and nearly finished to Odessa. Let but this be carried from Moscow, eastward to the valley of the Amoor, an enterprise only equal to our own Pacific Railway, and then a trunk line will connect Moscow with the East Indian seas, and from Moscow one branch will pass westward to St. Petersburg, and the other southward toward Constantinople, striking the Black Sea at Odessa. These lines would cross the whole system of the navigable rivers of the empire, and would be to Russian commerce, both foreign and domestic, what the Pacific road and its branches will be to the United States, passing the Ural and its boundless mineral wealth midway, as the American road will the Rocky mountains. No one doubts that the American railway will be completed at no distant period, and who that considers the past progress and present power of Russia shall say that she will not also construct a Pacific railway, aided by American skill and experience.

This, for Russia, would only be to construct the modern iron road, with steam carriages, along the old highway of her Eastern commerce, and certainly it would be an instructive sight to the boastful powers of western Europe if the two nations who have been the chief object of their ridicule, one as barbarian, and the other as composed of backwoodsmen, should ere long present them with one continuous line of railway and ocean steam navigation, reaching round the globe and turning the commerce of the East through the heart of America and Russia. Such a result is by no means impossible.

# CHAPTER XIX.

## RUSSIA EASILY GOVERNED FROM ONE CENTER.

It has already been remarked that no extent of territorial possession, however fertile its soil, or however dense its population, will afford a foundation for true national greatness, unless it is a contiguous territory, or can in some manner be bound into one whole, so that the remotest extremity will feel the influence of a central life. With such methods of communication only as the ancients possessed, no widely-extended government could long maintain itself united and secure; and with these examples of failure and dissolution before them, the wisest of the early American statesmen felt little inclination to enlarge our national domain; and only a few years since, the idea of retaining a united dominion over our present territory would have been rejected by many, perhaps by most, as absurd. But the steam vessel, the railway, and the telegraph, practically condense a continent into the space of a province, and all are now convinced that the magnitude of our country will never destroy the efficiency or unity of the government. That *alone* would not now prevent one central power from controlling the two Americas. In examining, therefore, the elements of power possessed by Russia, it is necessary to consider more particularly than we have hitherto done, the nature of these facilities for intercourse between different parts of her empire, which she now enjoys, or may probably create hereafter, in the regular and natural development of her resources. We shall then understand whether she is likely to remain a firmly-compacted whole, animate with a single life, or whether she must be regarded as a mass of heterogeneous materials loosely cohering even now, and soon to be separated entirely. A glance has been bestowed upon this point, in the brief comparison instituted between the United States and Russia, but the means of internal communication enjoyed by the latter demand a more particular description. This may properly commence with the rivers of the country. These may be separated into five groups, viz.: the Pacific, the Arctic Ocean, the Caspian, the Black Sea, and the Baltic. Beginning in the east with the river basins which stretch from the southern base of the Altai mountains, southeastward toward the Pacific, there is an extensive region of whose rivers little is known, except the Amoor, and even in regard to that our information is scanty and unsatisfactory, it having been until quite lately within the guarded Chinese dominions. It must henceforth be regarded as a Russian river, the natural and necessary outlet of the whole eastern portion of the empire. It is described as a "splendid stream," having a course of twenty-two hundred miles, for a large portion of which it is said to be navigable. Such a river must, of course, drain a territory proportionate to its own magnitude, and the glowing though indefinite accounts of the wide and fertile plains that lie along its banks, together with its actual magnitude and the distance for which it is navigable, remind one of the Mississippi and its valley, below St. Louis. Such a stream must also be sustained by many important affluents of which nothing definite is known to Europeans. Its whole course is through an attractive and productive region, and it requires but a slight effort of the imagination to present a picture of this great valley as it will be, when fleets of steamers shall cover the Amoor and its tributaries, not only bearing the production of the adjacent countries, but interchanging the commodities of Europe, Asia, and America.

This stream rises in the province of Irkoutsk in southern Siberia, and flowing in a southeasterly direction into the Sea of Japan, seems to have been formed with especial reference to the trade of Asiatic Russia, reaching from the Chinese seas to the head-streams of one of the largest rivers in Siberia that empties into the Arctic Ocean, and is thus prepared to receive the trade of the valley of the Lena—which reaches to the frozen shores of the Polar sea.

This extreme eastern portion then of Russia, is a vast and fertile river basin, stretching from the Sea of Japan north-westerly to south-eastern Siberia, traversed by a stream navigable for more than a thousand miles, according to estimates of river navigation made before American steamboats on our western rivers had shown how small a stream is capable of floating a profitable commerce. On the head-waters of the Amoor, that vast plain is reached which inclines slightly to the Arctic Sea, and across which flow some of the longest rivers of Asia. The traveler from the Pacific, following up the valley of the Amoor, would strike first in the province of Irkoutsk, the upper waters of the Lena, then passing far westward, he would reach the valley of the Yenisei, and finally at the eastern base of the Ural mountains, he would find a third broad river basin, that of the Obi. Each of these mighty streams is said to have a course of more than two thousand miles. Along these vast valleys, for about one-half their extent, the cereals of Europe come to maturity; and he who knows what success has crowned agricultural labor in Minnesota, and even much further north, where the range of the thermometer is much the same as in southern Siberia, will not hastily conclude that the latter must be regarded only as a frozen, desert waste.

The actual extent of arable land can not be estimated, with our present means of information; but the value of uncultivated lands in high northern latitudes, is almost universally underrated. Immense tracts of natural pasture spread over these great plains; heavy forests skirt the streams, even within the Arctic circle, furnishing exhaustless supplies of valuable timber, while the fisheries of the rivers, and the furs of the northern districts are of themselves the sources of a very important trade. On the western frontier of Siberia, and along the western edge of the valley of the Obi, rise the Ural mountains, embosoming a mineral wealth without a parallel on the globe, except in the great mountain ranges of America. These rivers and their tributaries are navigable for most of their course for about six months in the year, and considering the resources and extent of the country, it is easy to perceive what it may become with a railway crossing these valleys, from the head of steamboat navigation on the Amoor to the mineral regions in the Ural, from whence there is already a river navigation fitted for small steam vessels to the Caspian, the Black Sea, and the Baltic.

Before any one turns away from such statements, as idle and empty speculation, let him calmly consider the progress of the United States within the last twenty years, and the certainty that the whole breadth of our continent will very soon be spanned by a railway having one terminus on the Atlantic and the other on the Pacific, and then remember that in rapidity of growth and improvement, Russia stands next to America. Siberia then, traversed from north to south by rivers whose magnitude compares with those of North America, requires but a line of communication crossing them from east to west, such as a railway would supply, to develope her great resources, and put her in connection both with Asia and Europe. Her third system of rivers embraces those which fall into the Caspian Sea. Of these the Volga alone requires to be mentioned. This is the largest river of Europe, being two thousand miles in length, one and a quarter miles broad at its mouth, and navigable almost to its very source, or perhaps even, for steamboats like those of our western rivers, through its entire course, as it rises from a lake. It may be compared to the Mississippi, reckoning from the Falls of St. Anthony to the Gulf of Mexico. It receives numerous important affluents from the east and north-east, which connect the main stream by navigable waters, not only with important agricultural districts, but with the mining regions of the Ural. In the lower part of its course it approaches within about thirty miles of the Don, at a point where the nature of the country offers no impediment to the construction of a ship canal, which has been often projected, and even commenced, but not completed. By this comparatively small work, the whole valley of the Volga and the western slope of the Ural, would be connected directly with the Black Sea and the Mediterranean.

One of the tributaries of the Volga, coming from the northeast, has a course of one thousand miles, about equal to the Ohio from Pittsburgh to the Mississippi, and another, the Oka, on a branch of which is Moscow, is seven hundred miles long, and navigable almost to its source. The Volga is united by a canal with the Duna, which empties into the Gulf of Riga, and thus uninterrupted navigation is established between the Caspian Sea and the Baltic. Another canal connects a tributary of the Oka with the Don, and this opens an indirect communication between the Black Sea and the Caspian. Still another canal unites the Volga with the Dwina, which flows into the White Sea, and thus another navigable line is formed from the southern extremity of the empire, through its very heart, to Archangel and the Frozen Ocean. Yet another work opens a connection between the Volga and the Lake Onega, and St. Petersburg, and this city is also united with Moscow both by canal and railway. There are thus three main lines of water communication across the entire breadth of European Russia. One from the mineral region of the Ural to St. Petersburg and the Baltic; one from the Caspian northward to the Arctic Ocean, and one from the Caspian, and also from the Ural, through to the Duna, to the Baltic; and even yet another, by the way of the Oka and Moscow, to St. Petersburg by the canal. This is quite independent of that great number of smaller streams and shorter connections known only to the inhabitants of a country. Together, they present a perfect network of veins and arteries, along which the tides of internal commerce flow. Next are the rivers which flow into the Black Sea. Among these are: the Dnieper, which is twelve hundred miles long, a broad and deep stream, navigable for a large portion of its course; the Bog, or Boug, which is more than four hundred miles long, and navigable; and the Don, which is also a navigable stream, is about five hundred miles in length. The lower portion of this stream will be the channel of an immense trade so soon as the canal is finished between it and the Volga, a distance of about thirty miles; and, finally, the Kouban, a shallow stream coming from the Caucasus, and navigable only for boats of a light draught. Its length is about four hundred miles.

In addition to the rivers already mentioned, the Danube, having sixty navigable tributaries, falls into the Black Sea. Russia has obtained the control of the mouths of this important European stream, and her fortress of Ismail commands the commerce which passes by the northern or Kilia branch. If, as is said, the bar across the mouth of the Sulinah, or middle branch, is yearly increasing, the whole trade of the Danube may be thrown into the northern channel, and must pass under the guns of a Russian fortification. Russia owns the north shore of the Danube as far as Galatz, near which town it receives the Pruth, which, in a course of more than five hundred miles, flows along the province of Bessarabia. The fifth system of Russian rivers is connected with the Baltic. Its streams are smaller than those already described, but their importance is, nevertheless, great. The Neva, on which St. Petersburgh is built, has its source in the Lake Ladoga, which is one hundred and thirty miles long, while it averages seventy-five miles in breadth. The shores of the Ladoga, and the commerce of the streams which empty into this lake, some of which bring the productions of the Ural, make the Neva the channel of a very extensive trade. The Duna discharges itself into the Gulf of Riga, and being connected by a canal with the Volga, as has already been stated, it floats an extensive commerce. The Vistula is the chief river of Poland, and at Warsaw it is about seven hundred feet broad.

This completes a general, but by no means a full, survey of the facilities afforded by the Russian rivers for internal trade and travel. The government has already begun the establishment of lines of river steamers of the American build, and they are now running almost to the very base of the Ural mountains. No long time will elapse before these almost countless streams will present the aspect of our American rivers, and business and towns will spring up along their banks, as they have already done, by the use of similar means, in the Mississippi valley. The flat boat and the horse barges will disappear from Russian waters, as the broad-horns have from the Ohio and the Mississippi, and steam, both on the water and on the land, will convey the traffic of the empire.

As already stated, the country of the Czar can boast of no such connected chain of great lakes as are found in America. Still it is a land of lakes, and gulfs, and inland seas, which afford great facility for its commerce. On the west and northwest, almost countless gulfs and bays shoot inland from the Atlantic, giving long lines of interior sea-coast, and communicating with her navigable rivers. Lake Baikal, in Southern Siberia, is about the size of Lake Erie, and its valuable fisheries form the basis of an important commerce. The Caspian Sea is but an immense salt-lake, about eight hundred miles long; and the Black Sea, and the Baltic, may also be regarded as merely interior seas, of which Russia will ultimately retain the chief control, in spite of the combined efforts of western Europe. The lakes Ladoga and Onega are by no means inconsiderable bodies of water, the first having an area of more than six thousand square miles, and the latter being one hundred and thirty miles long and fifty miles in breadth. Smaller lakes, many of them large enough to become channels of trade, are scattered through both European and Asiatic

Russia. The largest of these are united either naturally or by canals, with the navigable rivers, and thus, when the progress of the country has covered these countless channels with steamboats, and when that system of railways, already begun on an enlightened scale, shall be completed, Russia will posssess more abundant means for intercourse and exchange, for the diffusion of one national life, and the preservation of national unity than any other country on earth enjoys unless it be our own. With a Pacific railway crossing Siberia, in addition to her natural advantages, and her system of roads in Europe already projected and partly finished she may extend her limits almost indefinitely, and yet not peril the unity of her government on account of her magnitude. Her position will be widely different from that of England, with possessions in the four quarters of the globe, that admit of no union; she will be one compact and living national body, growing and sustained by the power of one central life.

# CHAPTER XX.

## RUSSIA HAS FEW VULNERABLE POINTS.

Before entering upon this subject, it is well to remind the American reader of the utter worthlessness of many of the most popular accounts which have been given of the resources of Russia, and the character of her military defenses. The statements which travelers have made concerning the Empire of the Czars are only to be matched in absurdity or wanton misrepresentation by those which have emanated from similar quarters concerning the United States. Either a vitiated public sentiment, or a settled design to injure, has given rise to a systematic course of ridicule and misrepresentations, forming a distorted literary medium through which both countries have been seen only in caricature. Through this, western Europe has sneered at America and the Yankees, and through this also Americans have been greatly deluded in regard to Russia. Oliphant, whose opininions are quoted as reliable authority in this country, and whose statements were transfered to an elaborate American work, and sent forth to mold public opinion concerning Russia, with the remark that they are valuable because the result of recent observation, writes thus concerning Sebastopol, from personal survey, no longer ago than 1853, but a few months before the landing of the Allied army:

"Nothing can be more formidable than the appearance of Sebastopol from the seaward. Upon a future occasion we visited it in a steamer, and found that at one point we were commanded by twelve hundred pieces of artillery; fortunately for a hostile fleet, we afterwards heard, that they could not be discharged without bringing down the rotten batteries upon which they were placed, and which are so badly constructed that they look as if they had been done by contract. Four of these forts consist of three tiers of batteries. We were of course unable to do more than take a very general survey of these celebrated fortifications, and therefore can not vouch for the truth of the assertion, that the rooms in which the guns are worked are so narrow and ill-ventilated, that the artillerymen would be inevitably stifled in the attempt to discharge their guns and their duty; but of one fact there was no doubt, that however well fortified may be the approaches to Sebastopol by sea, there is nothing whatever to prevent any number of troops landing a few miles to the south of the town, in one of the six convenient bays with which the coast, as far as Cape Kherson, is indented, and marching down the main street, (provided they were strong enough to defeat any military force that might be opposed to them in the open field,) sack the town and burn the fleet."

Such absurdities as these are gravely sent forth from the English press, as the foundation of reliable opinions concerning Russia. Oliphant's work has gone through several London editions; it was republished in America, and its opinions were extracted and scattered abroad in American books. The siege of this fortification is a sufficient commentary upon the value of the book, and when the strength of a place that for months successfully resisted the most formidable attack which has been made in modern times is thus flippantly misrepresented, and when we remember that such impressions concerning Russia are, or have been, almost universal, and have been derived from similar sources, it ought at least to induce the American people to examine with more care the testimony upon which they are asked to make up an opinion of the resources, character, and policy of the most formidable power in Europe. The Allied forces tested the character of the fortifications at Sebastopol, and the same science and skill have been employed upon the other defenses of the Empire. Especially should we expect that those in the west, by which the approaches to St. Petersburgh are protected, and which guard her great naval depots, are at least equal to those in the remote province of the Crimea. It is sufficient proof of their supposed strength, that the Baltic fleet did not venture within reach of their guns.

The principal outlet for the Russian empire, on the west, is the Gulf of Finland, and here also are three of her great naval stations. As this is the only point where she can be approached from the Atlantic by a hostile fleet, it is well to observe how her fleets, navy yards, military stores, and capital are protected. At the entrance of the Gulf of Finland are two of the naval stations where she equips, and where also she guards her ships. The most important is Sweaborg, in the Bay of Helsingfors. This immense fortification is constructed upon several small islands, or rather rocks of granite, out of which the works have to a great extent been blasted and hewn, after the manner of Gibraltar, to which it is scarcely inferior in strength, and is denominated the Gibraltar of the North. Eight hundred pieces of artillery frown from its impregnable walls, and command the entrance to a magnificent harbor, which, to use the words of a late traveler, is "filled with ships of the "line and frigates," and in which they may safely ride free from the visits of a foe, unless the rock sides of Sweaborg can be scaled in the teeth of eight hundred cannon, and in spite of fifteen thousand men who man them. Here, too, the walls of the formidable batteries, being of solid granite, will not be likely to tumble down when the guns are fired, as was expected at Sebastopol. The fortress may be truly called impregnable. Within the harbor are not only the Russian fleets, but here, also, is one of the most extensive naval arsenals on the globe, and the chief recruiting station for the Emperor's navy. The province in which Sweaborg stands supplies the finest seamen of the North—those who are inured to hardship, and who gain experience and skill in the fisheries and trade of the Baltic—and here, too, are exhaustless supplies of the finest timber for the construction or repair of ships, as well as of pitch, tar, rosin, and other naval stores. Finland is intersected by numerous bays and lakes, communicating with each other in a manner which affords great facilities for the transport of these heavy materials; while, even in this high latitude, its agricultural capacities procured for it the name of the granary of Sweden, to which government it formerly belonged. Here, safe from all hostile visits, and surrounded by materials for unlimited construction, Russia may increase her navy, and accumulate her stores, restricted only by her necessities or the condition of her treasury. It is impossible, moreover, to cut her off from her supplies, for they all reach this point by interior communications, which a foreign force can not touch.

On the opposite shore of the entrance to the Gulf of Finland is Revel, another station for the Russian navy. Like Sweaborg, it is defended by extensive fortifications, whose strength Sir Charles Napier did not think proper to test with a fleet which many supposed would be able to annihilate the Russian power in the Baltic. Its roadstead is among sheltering islands, and the town itself enjoys considerable trade. In the Aland Archipelago, a cluster of islands at the entrance of the Gulf of Bothnia, is another naval station. Several of these islands are strongly fortified, but the principal establishment is at Aland, which has a harbor capable of sheltering the whole fleet of Russia, and a citadel where sixty thousand troops may be quartered. Here is kept a numerous flotilla, which forms a good nursery for Russian seamen. The vicinity of these islands to the coast of Sweden, some of them scarce thirty miles distant, forms perhaps their most important feature in a military point of view, for from them, at any time, a descent may easily be made upon the Swedish coast.

Cronstadt is, however, the most important Russian fortress in the Baltic, both as a naval station and as guarding the approach to St. Petersburgh. It is situated at the head of the Gulf of Finland, and only about sixteen miles from the Capital. The fortifications are constructed principally upon an island, on one side of which is a narrow channel, completely commanded not only by the long lines of guns upon the main island, but also by batteries placed upon various smaller islands and reefs, to say nothing of the powerful fleet always stationed in the harbors. Of these harbors there are three, or rather the harbor may be said to be separated into three divisions. The outer one is probably the most important naval station of the Empire. From thirty to forty ships of the line may float here, in addition to smaller vessels. The second division contains ship-yards, docks, arsenals, warehouses, and all the stores and machinery necessary not only for ship building, but for the equipment and repair of the main division of the Russian navy. The third harbor is devoted to trade, and can easily shelter a thousand merchantmen. The channel leading from the Gulf to the Neva is said to be so narrow that a single vessel only can pass at once, and this passage must be effected between lines of cannon that could annihilate in a few minutes any ship that floats. Besides this, ships drawing more than nine feet of water can not ascend beyond Cronstadt, so that St. Petersburgh is absolutely secure from the visit of a hostile vessel, and the impregnable Cronstadt must be annihilated before an enemy could occupy the head of the Gulf. The population of Cronstadt, including the garrison and the marine, is said to be about forty thousand.

The following very graphic description of Cronstadt, by an officer attached to the Baltic fleet, and written on the spot in 1854, and from personal survey of the works, will give the reader a correct idea of this celebrated fortress, and of the resources, science, and skill of the Power by whom these defenses have been constructed:

"The island of Cronstadt lies in a bight betwixt the two shores of the Gulf, and is nowhere distant more than about six miles from the mainland on either side; and even this, as a navigable distance, is so much straited by spits, shallows and mud-banks, that the actual passages are reduced to very confined limits. This is the case especially with the main channel, which runs betwixt the island and the south shore, and is so narrow and shallow that its navigation alone, except under experienced and skillful guidance, is a difficulty. It widens and deepens a little, however, toward the southeast end, into a tolerably convenient and spacious anchorage, and turning thence toward the south, ends in an inner harbor, well locked, and sheltered by a bend in the land, and partly protected by the Oranienbaum spit, which juts out toward it from the south shore, and which, being covered by only a few feet of water, offers an effectual barrier to the approach of ships, and is impracticable for the advance of troops. Two passages lead from this round the southeast side; but these are so intricate, so environed by shallows and patches, that they are navigable only by vessels of a small class, and afford no regular communication with the north channel, which is broader and deeper in the center than the other, though it also becomes very shallow at some distance from the shore. The island itself is about six miles long, and a mile and a half wide at the southeast, its broadest part. This part represents the root, and hangs on, like a square piece, to the Tongue, which shoots out narrow and narrower toward the tip, until it ends in a few broken rocks, over which the waves ripple. Slightly raised above the level of the sea, a little barren tract of rock and sand, it would scarcely afford sustenance for a family, or feed a flock of sheep, yet now, cut into docks, covered with barracks and storehouses, and surrounded by forts, it is a prize which mighty nations strive to win and to keep.

"Let us next see how art has so much enhanced the value of the spot we have been surveying. A first object in the design which sought to convert it into a naval arsenal was, of course, to find a suitable site for the docks, magazines and defenses, which must grow around the harbor and anchorage. The square end of the island was naturally adapted for this purpose. It had a sufficient and compact space for the building; it was surrounded by the sea on all sides, save where it was joined by a narrow neck of land to the promontory beyond, and would thus be protected by a complete line of circumvallation; and it offered, besides, a facility for digging immense basins on its south side, which might compensate for the smallness of the inner harbor, or Little Road, as it is called. There are three of these—the man-of-war, the middle, and the merchant harbor—all entered by regular locks from the Little Road. In the two former a great part of the Russian ships lie during the winter months, while their crews are transferred to the barracks on shore.

"The next step was to defend these harbors, and, as a consequence, the old-fashioned straggling fortress of Cronstadt arose. Then came Fort Peter; but, as time went on, it was deemed necessary that the Great Road, and even the entrance, should have their defenses. But the passage into the harbors was about mid-channel, and could not therefore be effectually commanded by forts on either shore. This was, however no obstacle, no difficulty to a system which has raised a city on a marsh; and straightway there sprang up a succession of gigantic island fortresses, commanding every approach, and threatening at many points a concentration of fire which must inevitably annihilate any attacking force.

"We must review these forts in the reverse order from their construction, and begin from the outside, as though we were advancing to the attack. Let us suppose, then, that we are making for their entrance. The first object which presents itself is the Tulbuken, a tall, solid, beacon-tower, stanking on a rock, connected probably by a reef with the island shore. We steamed onward, and on the right hand, or south side, Fort Risbank rises before us, the latest in construction, but not the least formidable of these extraordinary erections. Like all the others, it is built on a foundation formed by piles driven into the mud. It has two tiers of casemates, and on its top are guns mounted *en barbette.* The front facing the entrance obliquely, presents a curve springing from the center, with a short curtain on either side, which at the angles rounds off into towers. The number of guns in this fort is variously stated, but we could count fifty-six embrasures in this front beside the guns *en barbette,* and those which may be mounted on the rear face. In describing these fortifications, it is difficult to use the proper terms of art, as their peculiar construction and peculiar purposes required many and wide deviations from general principles. We must therefore try to be intelligible rather than scientific. A little farther on, on the left hand, or north side, Fort Alexander greets us, a huge round work, showing a semicircular front, bristling with four rows of guns, one row being *en barbette.* This fort is said to contain one hundred and thirty-two guns; they are of very large caliber, and their fire would effectually sweep the entrance of the channel, flanking and crossing that of Risbank. Passing Alexander, we are fairly in the Great Road, and come within range of Fort Peter, a low fortification, on the same side as Alexander but nearer to the island. Two low curtains, a large tower in the center, and smaller towers at either end, comprise the front of this work. It is not equal to the two others, either in dimensions or number of guns, but is still very formidable from its enfilading position. On the opposite side, just in front of the point of the Oranienbaum spit, and flanking the mouth of the inner harbor, Cronslott, or Cron Castle, threatens us. This the eldest of the series, the first demonstration of the scheme of defense which has since been extended and multiplied so vastly, is inferior to its successors in design ang elaborate workmanship. Though rather a crude effort it answered its first purpose, as a single fortress, well enough, and even now would play no mean part in the flanking and concentrating combination which forms the main principle in the defense. Last, but not least, either in size or importance, Fort Menschikoff rises, vast and glaring, towering above all the others with its four tiers and its massive walls. This was evidently meant to be the crowning stroke of the inner, as Risbank was of the outer defenses. Unlike its brethren, it stands on *terra firma*, and is built near the mole-head, at the south angle of the square end of the island. It is apparently a square, solid mass of masonry, constructed without any very elaborate or scientific plan, but presenting a front of casemated batteries which would flank Cronslott, and rake the approaches to the inner harbor with a tremendous fire. We might think that the achme of defense had been attained by such an aggregation of fortresses; so thought not the Russians, for they have moored some of the line-of-battle ships of their fleet between Menschikoff and Cronslott, thus effectually barring the entrance to the inner harbors, and forming an overwhelming increase to the force already concentrated for their protection. Beyond this barrier line, and behind Menschikoff, are the basins before spoken of, and behind them again are the great magazine, the dockyard and canal. More to the north are laid out the barracks and other public buildings. Such, and so defended, is the southern channel of Cronstadt. Such is the place which hair-brained theorists expected our fleet to attack and take. English hearts are stout—English ships are strong—English seamen are skillful; but the man who would lead them against such fearful odds would lead them to certain destruction, and leave the country to mourn over a catastrophe greater and sadder than has yet clouded her annals.

"Let us turn to the north side, and see what are there the characteristics of defense and the opportunities of attack. Passing round the Tulbuken, we trace a low glittering kind of rocks just rising above the waters; then a broader belt of red sand, slightly sprinkled with trees; then come houses, trees, and some glimpses of vegetation, until the eye rests at last on a large, well-designed earthwork, not yet finished, around and about the mounds of which workmen are still busy with pickax, spade and barrow. Tracking onward, we follow the long, low beach, along which are rows of houses, masses of buildings, churches with their gilded cupolas and spires, and all the varied objects which constitute the features of a town panorama; while behind and above all appear the tops of forts and masts of ships. Looking very closely and attentively, we can detect at intervals small batteries mounting a few guns, and carrying on a weak and broken line of defense, which terminates at the northeast extremity in a larger and more pretentious work.

"Nothing very formidable here as yet—nothing very obstructive, save the fact that large ships can not approach within a less distance than three miles; but gun-boats and small vessels might easily advance within fair range of town and arsenals. Yes, this had been foreseen and provided against by a novel and ingenious expedient. From the earthwork in the center of the island a barrier had been run out obliquely to a distance of three thousand yards, and then carried in a slightly deflecting line to the shore of the mainland, extending to a length of six or seven miles, and enclosing the passages opening from the north to the east and south sides of the island. The barrier consists of columns of piles placed at a distance of eighteen feet, and rising within two feet of the surface of the water. These columns are formed of several piles driven into the mud in a circle, the center being filled with rubble. This would sufficiently secure the shore from sudden assaults, or the town from the danger and annoyance of a distant fire; but the passages—the weak and vital points of the northern defense—could not be trusted to an obstacle so partial in its obstruction, and which a daring effort might destroy. Accordingly hulks, lightened for the purpose, were moored behind the barrier—in some parts within point-blank range

—effectually covering it through its whole extent, from the angle of the town to the main land. In rear of this, again, a fleet of gun-boats, under steam and sail, moved about ready to dash through the intervals and meet any assailant. Thus was a triple barrier raised—the first part merely obstructive, the second defensive, the third motive, and capable of being made aggressive."

It might have been expected, that a careless or inefficient government, without resources or military skill, or science, such as Russia has been represented to be, and relying upon the fact that the entrance to the Black Sea was closed by the fortresses of the Dardanelles, would have erected precisely such defenses as Oliphant would have the world believe those at Sebastopol were. In such a position, if anywhere, would be found the ill-constructed and neglected batteries, whose walls, ready to tumble with their own weight, could by no means stand the discharge of the guns. Here should have been found Russian officers without science or intelligence—here, admirals, such as Oliphant mentions, who lose their way between Odessa and Sebastopol, and flag-lieutenants, who propose to go ashore and inquire the way—instead of all which were fortifications before whose massive strength the combined fleets of France and England only made themselves ridiculous, and where the utmost efforts of these Powers, with all the appliances of modern warfare, were completely foiled.

The resources of the Russian Empire, in the East, require no labored description. Siberia and the valley of the Amoor contain exhaustless supplies of timber and other naval stores. The Siberian rivers supply abundant facilities for transportation, and with the commerce of the East Indian seas open to her, and with all materials at her disposal, in positions inaccessible to an enemy, what shall hinder her from establishing on the Pacific naval stations, a mercantile and an armed marine which shall rival those of the West? Such a work would be naturally expected from what she has already performed elsewhere: it accords with the general spirit and policy of the government.

The survey thus far made of the Northern Empire certainly presents it in a most imposing aspect, and exhibits the necessary foundations of a national power, which, other things being equal, would doubtless prove an overmatch for all the rest of Europe. Whether other fitting elements of strength and growth exist will be the subject of future inquiry. It is seen that her territory is capable of supporting a population of hundreds of millions, without being more densely peopled than the rest of Europe. This territory occupies a commanding position in the temperate zone, stretching between the Pacific and the Atlantic, open to the commerce of Asia and Europe, and forming indeed a great national highway between them, on one side of the globe, such as America presents on the other. These vast possessions are traversed from side to side by channels of intercommunication, remote from hostile attack, while her few exposed points, strong by nature, have been rendered seemingly impregnable by whatever military science can perform. Within these defenses, warlike preparations of every kind can be carried on secure from interruption, while her treasures of military stores, and even her fleets, if she chooses, are placed beyond the reach of an enemy. In addition to all this, if the seas are closed against her by a superior maritime power, a large foreign commerce is still open to her from the East through her own territory, and her domestic productions and home trade are so extensive as to make her, so far as any nation can be, independent of a foreign commerce.

# CHAPTER XXI.

## RUSSIA CONTROLLED BY ONE RACE—THIS GIVES HER A TRUE NATIONAL LIFE.

It is evident, that however extensive the territory of a nation may be, however productive its soil, or dense its population, there will still be no solid foundation for great and permanent national power if this population is composed of diverse races, bound together by the force of circumstances only, or forced into contact, not union, by external lashings of any kind. The moment the compressing bond is loosened in such a case, the discordant materials separate, and the whole mass of an imposing dynasty will suddenly crumble into fragments, which are scattered apart, because they are not the production of a common central life. Such has been the fate of most empires that have grown out of a succession of rapid conquests. Success has attended them, until the mass of material added could no longer be assimilated, until the national structure became a mere aggregation, not one living body, and the constituent parts instead of being united by mutual sympathies were hurled asunder by mutual repulsion. It has been fashionable to look upon Russia as occupying this precise position, and to represent the Czar as ruling over a rude mass of heterogeneous and discontented tribes, held in subjection merely by a cruel and relentless military despotism.

These views gave rise to the expectation, that in in any sudden calamity, or in case of the death of Nicholas, Russia would be separated into warring factions, and the Colossus of the North would vanish like the spectre of the Brocken. France and England pleased themselves, and calmed in part their fears, by picturing the inherent weakness of the Muscovite Empire. The general tone which prevailed may be seen by the following extracts from one of the ablest English Quarterlies, the *North British*, in November, 1854. The writer refers to a former article, in which was pointed out, as he says, "elements of "weakness in the Muscovite Empire which had never "hitherto been duly estimated." He goes on to say, "We "reminded our readers that the great conquests of Russia "had been effected by diplomacy and not by actual fighting, "and that these conquests were *annexed* merely—not assimi-"lated. All things considered, it is by no means unlikely "that if the present war continues, she may turn out to have "been a gigantic impostor—that when tried by the severi-"ties of a real struggle, she will prove weak, to a degree "which will astonish those whom she has so long duped "and dazzled; weak from her unwieldy magnitude—weak "from her barbarous tariffs and restrictive policy—weak "from the inherent inadequacy of her one-eyed despotism—"weak from the rottenness of her internal administration—"weak from the suppressed hatreds she has accumulated "round her—weak in everything save her consummate skill "in simulating strength." This was written in February, 1854; in November, 1854, the same *Review* says: "These "surmises, which at the time they were uttered were con-"sidered somewhat wild and rash, have been not only justi-"fied but surpassed by the event. The feebleness every-"where displayed by Russia, both in attack and defense, "have been matter of ceaseless astonishment. * * * As "soon as it was known that the expedition to the Crimea "was resolved upon, we took for granted that the Crimea "would be conquered, and that Sebastopol would ultimately "fall into our hands; but assuredly no one anticipated that "after months of notice, our armies would have been suf-"fered to land without the faintest attempt at opposition; "that our victory would have been so signal, so decisive, "and so rapid; or that the greatest fortified harbor of "Russia—probably the strongest in the world—would be "taken on such easy terms, and in so brief a period. Hence-"forth, the prestige of Russian military power is gone; "Europe need dread her arms no more. The Czar, hitherto "the great bugbear of Europe and of Asia, has been beaten "on all hands."

In a subsequent portion of the same article, the writer boasts and exults as follows, giving, as will be seen, also, a highly significant side-roar of the British lion at the Americans, who, after such English victories in the Black Sea, will, he thinks, be a "trifle less insolent and overbearing," when they remember that the Baltic fleet can winter in the Gulf of Mexico:

"But if Nicholas had been less rash or less stubborn we should never have been stirred into activity sufficient to afford the world the astounding spectacle it saw in April and May. In a few weeks time we sent forth the two largest and best-manned fleets that ever left our shores, and, beyond all parallel, the best equipped army that ever sailed from England on any expedition—both fleet and army provided with every new invention of science to which experience or judgment had given their sanction. * * The Baltic fleet alone consisted of forty-two ships, twenty-two hundred guns, sixteen thousand horse-power, and twenty-two thousand sailors and marines.

"In 1852 and 1853, there were doubts whether we had either ships or men sufficient to defend our own shores against a sudden descent. In 1854 we sent to our Ally both land and naval auxiliary forces, which have checkmated, conquered, and despoiled his colossal antagonist. All this, too, was done rapidly, silently, and easily; regiments were recruited, and ships were manned, without difficulty; volunteers flocked both to the militia and the navy; the moment there was a prospect of active service men were forthcoming in ample numbers, and neither conscription nor impressment had to be resorted to. This magnificent spectacle will not be lost either on Europe or America, or on ourselves. Already a great change of tone on all hands is observable. Our foes have had a forewarning with what sort of a people they will have to deal; *our transatlantic cousins will become a trifle less insolent and overbearing when they find that the fleet which summers in the Baltic can, without cost or effort, winter in the Gulf of Mexico.*"

In the summer, then, England proposed to amuse herself with demolishing Russia, and in the winter she would be occupied with checking the insolence of her "transatlantic cousins." This, moreover, agrees with the declaration of Lord Clarendon, with the corresponding semi-official statement of the French government of the far-reaching intentions of the English and French Alliance, viz: that it had reference to the western as well as the eastern hemisphere. The *Review* thus sums up the results of the first campaign, up to November, 1854:

"Russia, the great bugbear of Europe, and the great foe of free development, shorn of her prestige, baffled, beaten back, blockaded and despoiled—deprived, in a single year, of the conquests of half a century of intrigue and violence, not only thwarted and checked, but humbled and crippled, retreating across the Pruth in place of advancing beyond the Danube; and paying for the massacre of Sinope by the loss of Sebastopol and the Crimea. Such are the results of the first campaign."

Such was the language, not of some vain, flippant traveler, but of one of the gravest and stateliest Reviews of the British Empire, and when such a Quarterly as the *North British* will indulge itself in such transparent folly, we are led to believe that the British government really sent forth its fleets and armies in this same spirit, and with the same opinions of Russia. What a scorching commentary upon such an article subsequent events have given!

These things are not mentioned for the purpose of taunting or reproaching England, but as historical facts whose significance ought to be calmly considered by Americans. They show, first of all, the spirit of England in regard to Russia, and the worthlessness of most opinions and statements which have issued from the British press concerning their northern neighbors, and it should not be forgotten that these views, most derogatory to Russia, which are passing current in our country, have been derived from the representation of England. These facts show, moreover, the nature of the stake which the United States had in that Eastern war, an interest quite different from what many seem to suppose. They demonstrate a cherished purpose of England and France to interfere, not with Russia alone, but with the too rapid growth even of America.

The English *Review* pleases itself with a view of the internal weakness of Russia and her eminent danger of being rent asunder by domestic strife. Oliphant, writing in 1853, dilates largely, and with evident satisfaction, upon this same topic, and would have us believe that the whole power of the Czar is needed to protect his throne against the discontents and threatened uprisings of his own subjects:

"But the Russian Autocrat is also keenly alive to the critical position of matters at home. Before he decides upon prolonging indefinitely a hazardous contest, he will consider the present aspect of the internal condition of the empire as attentively as its external relations. He can not not forget that an extent of territory comprising one-half of what is now called Russia in Europe, has been annexed within the last sixty years—that, consequently, more than half of the European inhabitants of the empire, having been recently subjugated, are more or less disaffected; *that of these, sixteen millions, or about one-fourth of the entire population of Russia, do not profess the Greek faith;* that his Mohammedan subjects alone amount to two millions and a half; and that the protection of the Greek religion has been proclaimed as the ground upon which the present anti-Mohammedan crusade was commenced.

"Such is the present condition of those provinces which compose the European frontier of this vast empire. From the Baltic to the Black Sea—from the shores of the Danube to the banks of the Phasis—extends an indissoluble bond of common sympathy—a deep-rooted hatred of Russia, which nothing less than the dread of incurring the vengeance of a despotism almost omnipotent could have restrained so long; and when at last the auspicious time arrives for giving vent to this feeling, the flame will kindle wildly in the recently-acquired kingdom of Poland, for there the revolutionary spark has never been extinguished. It is true that in the southern provinces of the empire all hope of freedom has long disappeared, and terror and oppression have reigned so long that the inhabitants of the thinly-populated steppe have lost much of the energy of their Mongolian ancestors; but while they may hesitate to start at once into open rebellion, they will not fail to use measures of passive resistance, as a means of opposing the designs of Russia. Opportunities will not be wanting to insure some degree of success. When the presence of the allied fleets in the Black Sea denies to the Czar transport for his troops from the ports upon its margin, in any one direction, divisions of the Russian army will often be compelled to march across the inhospitable steppes of the south; and here, dependent for food and transport upon whatever a barren and thinly-populated country can supply, it is probable that they will find their wants altogether disregarded. The Tartars have only to remove their families and their cattle out of the line of march to render the onward progress of the army a matter of the utmost difficulty, if not altogether impossible; and thus they will be able to gratify at the same time their natural hatred to the Russians, and their no less natural desire of retaining possession of their own flocks and herds. Even this dejected race might be stimulated to more active measures by the presence upon their coasts of an overwhelming fleet hostile to Russia. It is impossible to foretell what the result may be of so novel a contingency. It rests with his Imperial Majesty to decide whether it will ever arise; but whatever weight he may attach to these considerations, and whatever may be the conclusion at which he may ultimately arrive, the facts, in so far as they illustrate the present internal condition of the empire, are important; for if, on the one hand, they combine to form any of the grounds upon which Russia may ever be induced to acquiesce in conditions proposed by the Allied Powers of Europe, a due appreciation of the difficulties by which he is surrounded, and which have compelled her to pursue a course so repugnant to Muscovite pride, must materially influence those upon whom the important task devolves of framing terms, the nature of which will depend in some measure upon the relative physical and moral condition of the hostile countries. But if, on the other hand, the attitude of Europe remains such that the Czar does not shrink from hazarding a war which must test the inmost resources of his empire, then it is well for the Powers who are engaged in the struggle to know what those resources are, lest, measuring them only by a standard provided by Russia, and judging of their value by reports which emanate from a source totally unworthy of credit, they forget that, when the different elements of which the nation is composed are incohesive as sand, the extent of a country which comprises scattered populations of various kindreds, differing in faith, habits, and interests, is really its weakness."

These quotations and statements may serve to show the spirit of those who have for the most part been our teachers in regard to the character and resources of Russia; they may aid in guarding ourselves against prejudices derived from such sources, and prepare us at least to do justice to

Russia by a calm, independent, and candid study of her actual condition and policy.

From what has already been stated, it is evident that the Muscovite empire must be one of immense strength, if in connection with its other advantages its destinies are in the hands of one dominant race, whose social affinities are strong enough to produce one compact national unity, and if this race possesses an individuality of character which will not prevent it from being absorbed by any contiguous families, but which forbids even any essential modification. The case will be all the stronger if such a race is found to possess a vigor that displaces that with which it comes in contact. The power which such a social unity imparts to a nation, the tenacity of that national life of which it is the source, is well illustrated by the example of the Jews, who not only preserved through fifteen hundred years a clearly-defined national individuality, but are still, after ages of dispersion and oppression, distinguished by their national characteristics. The unexampled prosperity of America, and the compactness and efficiency of her national power, are owing mainly to the fact that her population has sprung principally from a single root, which is covering the land with the vigorous shoots of one family tree, and the best guaranty for the future which our country now presents is the newly-awakened determination to preserve our national characteristics, and perpetuate our individual national life. Still the proportion of the population of the United States which has descended from a single race is much smaller than it is in Russia. For although the number of foreign-born may not exceed two and a half millions, there are many more than this who are not of Anglo-Saxon parentage.

The total population of Russia is differently estimated, even by those who are considered to be the best authorities. Mr. Hassel's tables give the number of inhabitants in 1823, as - - - - - - 59,263,700

Malte Brun believes this to be somewhat exaggerated, and estimates the number in 1827, at - - - - - - 59,000,000

| | |
|---|---|
| The *London Quarterly*, for April, 1854, states, upon what it declares to be good authority, the present population to be - - | 70,000,000 |
| Alison estimates it, in 1840, at - - - | 60,000,000 |
| and states the annual increase at near one million of souls, which would give now nearly - - - - - - - | 75,000,000 |
| If we take Hassel's tables as the basis, and reckon according to the conceded rate of increase, the present population of the empire will appear to be about - - - - | 93,000,000 |
| If we adopt Malte Brun's estimate, the present number would reach about - - - | 90,000,000 |

The calculation made by the English Reviewer is, it appears, very considerably below the estimates which other good authorities have supplied, and in the present condition of things, and the known temper of English writers in regard to Russia, we may safely assume the possibility at least of an under-estimate of the population of the empire. The mean of the four estimates given above is a little more than 80,000,000. But because the classification which is found in the tables of the *Quarterly* makes it convenient to follow them, they will be mainly adopted, though the evidence seems conclusive that the number of inhabitants is greater than the reviewer has stated, and the subject demands a further examination.

According to this English authority, of the seventy millions now in the Russian empire fifty-eight millions belong to the Sarmatian race, of which fifty-six millions are of the Sclavonic branch, and forty-nine millions of these are Russians.

Here, as is seen, are fifty-eight millions belonging to one race, fifty-six millions that have sprung from one branch of that race, and, as we learn from authority quite as good as the English Review, fifty millions bound together by all the ties of one family connection. Nowhere else in Christendom can be found such a mighty, compact national unity as this. We may well illustrate it by supposing the population of the United States to be seventy millions, composed of native Americans, fifty millions; of Englishmen, eight millions; and of all other races twelve millions. In such a case, it would at once be seen that the central dominant power would not only control but absorb the rest. The absurdity of all prophesies of the separation of such a nation on account of difference of race would at once appear.

But, in estimating this feature of the strength of Russia, another important circumstance should not be overlooked. The Russian race proper occupy, geographically, the heart of the country, while the tribes which belong to the other races are distributed along the frontier. They are, therefore, both from position and from character, incapable of a combination among themselves, and are, moreover, under the full influence of the assimilating power of the dominant race. By this influence, directed by the steady policy of Russia, the Finnish tribes have been almost completely transformed. Russia seeks everywhere not merely to annex, but to engraft and assimilate. She strives to diffuse everywhere the central Russian life, and to mold all that she gains into one homogeneous national body. That policy which now brings out so wide and hearty an approval from the American nation has been long and steadily pursued by Russia, and with marked success. She has strengthened, by all methods within reach, a Russian sentiment—an attachment to the soil and to the national religion, a national pride, a national ambition. The vigorous pulsations of the national heart are felt at the remotest extremity and the universal tendency is the substitution of the one Russian life for the individual life of the separate tribes of the frontiers, and there is a gradual melting of these individualities into the one national life.

The native Russian holds the same relation to the other inhabitants of the empire that the native Americans do to the other population of the United States. The active, energetic, "pushing" man everywhere in the country is the native Russian. For him others make room. The Russian may be properly called the Yankee of the East. By no means exhibiting now the lofty qualities of the Anglo-Saxon mind, there is yet in him a true life, whose power and destiny can not as yet be accurately measured. One might unite an American idiom with a Russian phrase, and say that the Russian is "bound" to "*find out something.*" The man whom the Americans call "shiftless" the Russians describe as "one who can find nothing out." This may be regarded as indicating a national characteristic, an unmistakable sign which points to future destiny. Fifty millions of people who are intent upon "finding something out" are not likely to play a secondary part in the affairs of Europe, while yet expanding with a vigorous life, and with an almost unlimited territory still unoccupied, abounding with the sources of national wealth and power.

It ill becomes any of the Powers of western Europe, and least of all, England, to predict a dissolution of the Russian empire because her population is composed of a variety of races, when a comparison is instituted between her situation and theirs. In Great Britain are only about nineteen millions of Englishmen out of thirty millions of inhabitants, and in France are but thirty-two millions of Frenchmen out of about thirty-six millions of inhabitants. Austria, it is said, has with her Germans some seventeen millions of Sclavonians, while in Russia are no less than fifty millions that present an almost complete family identity, nearly forty millions of whom speak exactly the same language, from the highest in society to the lowest. Such a social unity is presented in no other spot among civilized nations, and it forms an element of power, whether for defense or offensive war, which, with the aids of an appropriate civilization, would be perfectly irresistible. What the characteristics of Russian civilization really are, and what promise it gives for the future, is a question which will be considered hereafter.

This immense mass is not only bound together by family ties, not only speaks one language, but the uniformity of a single national household prevails in the manners and customs, including even dress, among nearly forty millions of the people, manifesting one great Russian nationality. To these interlacing bonds must be added another, stronger than them all, that of a common religion, which has a deep hold upon the national mind, because with the Russian people the age of faith has not yet passed away. The skepticism of western Europe has, as yet, exerted little influence upon Russia. The doctrines of the church are to the mass of the people solemn verities, and in the religious ceremonies there is to them, as yet, a solemn meaning. Bigotry and superstition doubtless, to a great extent prevail; but as an element of power, as well as a basis of national life, a deep, sincere, though misguided religious sentiment, is far superior to the infidelity of France or Germany: a skepticism indeed, which almost universally now underlies the forms of the Roman Catholic Church. As a bond of union, and as an exciting cause whereby to arouse a national enthusiasm, and knit a people into one firmly compacted body, the religion of Russia bears some resemblance to the Roman Catholic Church in the days of its strength and vigor. Russia is capable of being aroused and maddened for a religious war; and the course of the government now shows most clearly that it fully understands, and is prepared to use, this truly terrific power. Another tie which unites in one the great Russian family, is an attachment to the soil, or rather, as the distinction is properly made by Haxthausen, an ardent patriotism; and this idea perhaps, has never been so well expressed elsewhere, as by him in the following extract from his work:

"Their country, the country of their ancestors, the Holy Russia, the people fraternally united under the scepter of the Czar, the communion of faith, the ancient and sacred monuments of the realm, the tombs of their forefathers—all form a whole which excites and enraptures the mind of the Russian. They consider their country as a sort of kinsmanship, to which they address the terms of familiar endearment. God, the Czar, and the priest, are all called Father, the Church is their Mother, and the Empire is always called Holy Mother Russia. The Capital of the Empire is Holy Mother Moscow, and the Volga, Mother Volga. Even the high road from Moscow to Vladimir is called 'Our dear Mother the high road to Vladimir.' But above all, Moscow, the Holy Mother of the land, is the center of Russian history and tradition, to which all the inhabitants of the empire devote their love and veneration. Every Russian entertains all his life long the desire to visit one day the great City, to see the towers of its holy churches, and to pray on the tombs of the patron saints of Russia. Mother Moscow has always suffered and given her blood for Russia, as all the Russian people are ready to do for her."

If Baron Haxthausen, whose book is admitted to be the best extant on Russia, has not painted this picture in colors somewhat too warm, then the civilized world has cause to regard Russia with the liveliest interest. Fifty millions of people animated by such a spirit are capable either of blessing or cursing the world, to an extent to which history probably can furnish no parallel; because this tremendous power, thus treasured as it is in fifty millions of hearts—a spiritual force—has at its disposal all means of destruction or defense that are known to modern war. Such a people may not possess the impulsiveness of the French soldier, which hurls him like a shot on his foe; they may not be equal in individual prowess to the English, but there is a self-sustaining power of endurance that exhausts and wears out its enemy, that clings obstinately to its purposes, rising afresh from every defeat, prepared for, and undertaking or resisting a new attack. This patriotism, that suffers all things sooner than permit an invader to rest securely on their soil, this spirit that waits and watches, and suffers long, until its opportunity shall come, has been manifested too often to be doubted any longer. When Russia has been reported through all Europe as beaten continually, in battle after battle, when all the nations are summoned to exult over her ruins, then the issue has ever been the overthrow of her adversary. The Russians have thus far in the end shaken every invader from them, and made reprisals upon their foe.

The grand army of Napoleon fell before this inextinguishable love of country, which preferred the sacrifice of all rather than endure the presence, on their own soil, of foreign troops, and despisers of their religion; to which the ruins and ashes of Smolensko and Moscow were a less mournful sight than a hostile army trampling on their consecrated places and the graves of their fathers. It is perhaps consoling to French and English feelings to devise hard names for such a spirit, to call it fanaticism, bigotry, superstition, etc.; but it should not be forgotten that, notwithstanding this gift of hateful epithets, its qualities remain the same, its power is undiminished, and the soldiers stand as steadily to their guns, and throw their shot and shell with an aim as fatally accurate, as if they had applied to them terms of admiration and endearment. The characteristics of the Russian people, their determination to defend their country to the last, are not to be changed by bitter language, or by railing at the Czar as a bigot, or coward, or hypocrite, or fanatic, or unmanly rejoicing at the news of his death. Still another element which serves to produce a national unity in Russia, the influence of which is likely to extend far beyond the present limits of her dominions, is a national vanity and a world-wide ambition, which no one can approve of, and a traditionary belief that the Sclavonian race is yet to rule the world. Every Russian, it is said, high and low, entertains the undoubted opinion, that his race will yet control the destinies of the nations, and regards all events as only sweeping on toward this ultimate end. This may be condemned or ridiculed as mere vanity, as an absurdity, demanding no serious attention; and yet it is a fact, and in connection with other things it becomes an important fact, not to be disregarded in the calculation by which we would measure the power and determine the future of Russia. Though we may be disposed to reject the idea, that what individuals and nations perseveringly believe themselves capable of they do generally accomplish, this national characteristic must not be forgotten as a chief element of national power.

The misleading character of most of the statements concerning Russia is clearly seen in the light of these facts. Nothing could be further from the truth than to represent this empire as unwieldy and inefficient, as a mass of crude material cohering so slightly as to be in perpetual danger of falling into fragments, or of being rent asunder by internal dissension. Those who thus represent the Muscovite nation either know nothing of the real Russian, and are painting the creature of their dreams, or for special purposes they studiously misrepresent. The central homogeneous mass of Russia, its compact and vigorous nationality, as compared with the various tribes that skirt its wide frontier, may be regarded as a mighty continent with a fringe of islands scattered along its shores. This shows also how vain are all expectations that the death of a Czar will essentially modify the settled policy of the Empire, or endanger its peace. Russia has evidently entered upon a career which is the combined result of her geographical position, the nature of her resources, the condition of Europe, her national religion, and the genius of her people. These have prescribed for her. under the guidance of the God of nations, a national mission, which the west of Europe will not prevent her from executing. A national policy, with its general features very clearly defined, has become inwrought in the public mind of Russia, and that policy will not be suddenly changed, much less abandoned, because the characteristics of a great nation can not be at once obliterated. Although the character of him who wears the crown may accelerate or retard the progress of such a nation, it will, under any leader, still move onward toward its ultimate goal. Like a staunch and well-appointed ship, with a competent crew united in the determination to prosecute a definite voyage, that pauses not even though its commander dies, so the national career of fifty millions of united people belonging to one family will not be abandoned on account of the loss of any one leader. Her national unity is capable of being extended safely from the Atlantic to the Pacific, and the Powers of western Europe will not be able to arrest even her southward march by underrating her strength and resources, nor by sneers at her barbarism, her fanaticism, or her despotism. Her barbarism is found strangely connected with the very highest military science, her fanaticism appears very much like an enthusiasm for religion and country, and her despotism has not driven the people from an ardent support of the throne.

# CHAPTER XXII.

## CHARACTER OF THE RUSSIAN SOLDIER.

It will not, perhaps, be uninteresting to the American reader to look at a few short passages of history, in which the character of the Russian soldier may be studied on the field, and as it was almost half a century ago. It is probable that no portion of Russian history presents in a clearer manner the real character of the people, and the qualities which distinguish her army, whether soldiers or officers, than the record of the French expedition to Moscow. A study of that attack, its progress and results, will enable us to form an opinion as to the issue of any future assault by the Powers of western Europe, while, at the same time, the capabilities of Russia, and her national characteristics, will appear. Whether one regards the unrivalled qualities of the commander of that expedition, or of the army under his command, it will not be considered probable that the Northern Empire will again be compelled to meet upon her own soil so formidable a foe, while, at the same time, its power of resistance has been immensely increased since the invasion of Napoleon.

A glance at a few of the chief points in that memorable attempt at the subjugation of Russia, can not be without interest in the present crisis. In the first place, it is necessary, in order to understand what the Russians really accomplished, to consider the relative strength of the opposing Powers, at the commencement of the campaign. The total effective force with which Bonaparte entered the Russian territory, as quoted by Alison from the imperial muster rolls, was as follows:

| | |
|---|---|
| Total effective force which entered the Russian territory: Men, - | 647,158 |
| Horses, - - - - - - - - - | 187,111 |
| Total number of cannon, - - - - - - - | 1,372 |

To this force the Russians had opposed as follows:

| | Infantry. | Cavalry. | Artillery. | Cossacks. |
|---|---|---|---|---|
| First army of the west, - - | 111,194 | 20,434 | 12,985 | 9,000 |
| Second army of the west, - | 42,804 | 7,852 | 4,165 | 4,500 |
| Third army of the west, - - | 34,996 | 9,852 | 3,185 | 4,500 |
| Grand total, - | 188,994 | 38,138 | 20,335 | 18,000 |

SUMMARY.

| | |
|---|---|
| Infantry, - - - - - - | 188,994 |
| Cavalry, - - - - - | 38,138 |
| Artillery, - - - - - - | 20,335 |
| Cossacks, - - - - - - | 18,000 |
| Total, - - - - | 265,467 |

The immense disparity of the forces at the commencement of the campaign should be allowed to have its full weight with those who are accustomed to think of the Russians as being driven before the French onward to Moscow. The whole French army was 647,158, matched against a Russian force of 265,467—less than one-half the number of Napoleon's troops. The French cavalry amounted to 96,579, while this part of the Russian regular force was only 38,138, and, including the Cossacks, amounted to but 56,138. Such was the relative force of the combatants when the grand army entered the Russian territory, to which must be added the matchless ability and reputation of Napoleon himself. The state of the Russian people, in view of this overwhelming assault upon their country, is thus stated by Alison, on the authority of Boutourlieu: "The "intelligence of the invasion," and the addresses of the Emperor, "excited the utmost enthusiasm in the people "and the army. It was not mere military ardor, or the "passion for conquest, like that which animated the French "army, but a deep-rooted resolution of resistance, founded "on the feelings of patriotism and the spirit of devotion.

"Less buoyant at first, it was more powerful at last; founded on the contempt for life it remained unshaken by disaster, unsubdued by defeat. As the French army advanced, and the dangers of Russia increased, it augmented in strength; and while the ardor of the invaders was quenched by the difficulty of their enterprise, the spirit of the Russians rose with the sacrifices which their situation required." This may be regarded as describing a permanent characteristic of the Russian nation; from the earliest period of their history to the siege of Sebastopol, this long endurance and gradual but sure accumulation of strength to surmount an obstacle, has been conspicuous.

In the two first inconsiderable actions of this war of invasion, the French were defeated. In the attempt which followed to separate two divisions of the Russian army, Napoleon was out-maneuvered by the Russian generals, and failed to accomplish his purpose—he, however, charging the blame upon his brother Jerome. The first considerable battle was at Mohilow, a strong position held by the French Marshal Davoust with thirty thousand men, the difficult defiles of the forest being filled with artillery. This strong post was attacked by an inferior force of twenty thousand Russians, who fought for hours at the entrance of the defiles in a perfect storm of grape-shot and musket-balls, and then retreated in good order, and with "little molestation," the loss on both sides being nearly equal—about three thousand for either army. The object of Napoleon at this point was was to cut off Prince Bagration's forces from the other divisions of the Russian army, and, although he employed for this purpose two armies each of which was as powerful as the Russian division, he was foiled in the attempt The Russian general, Barclay, having assembled eighty-two thousand men at Witeysk, had resolved to wait the attack of Napoleon at the head of one hundred and eighty thousand, and Bonaparte felt himself sure of his foe. As he retired on the night of the expected battle, he said to Murat, "To-morrow, at five, the sun of Austerlitz." The two armies lay facing each other, their watch-fires shining on each other's camps. During the night the Russian general received intelligence that decided him to alter his plan, and retreat upon Smolensko.

The manner of effecting this retreat exhibited not only consummate skill, but the highest state of discipline in the Russian army. To break up a regular encampment of eighty thousand men is not a small matter under any circumstances, but to do it in the night, almost under the very eyes of a watchful enemy, and to do it so silently, and in such perfect order as not to awaken even a suspicion of what was being done, to accomplish the object so perfectly that at day-break when Murat went forward to reconnoiter, not a man, not a baggage-wagon, not a weapon, not a solitary straggler out of eighty thousand men, could be found; this evinced a skill and a military science which filled the French officers both with astonishment and mortification. There was in such movements thus executed no promise of easy victories. The advanced guard of the French army sent in pursuit were unable at the separation of the roads of St. Petersburg and Moscow to determine which an army of eighty thousand men had taken. At length, when the Russian rear-guard was discovered marching in perfect order across the plain toward Smolensko, it was attacked, but the assailing party was utterly destroyed.

The influence of the religious sentiment upon the Russian people is well exhibited by the reliance which was placed upon it by the Emperor, in rousing the nation for defense. The language of his address was, "The *national religion*, "the throne, the State, can only be preserved by the greatest "sacrifices." He added also to this an appeal to the love of *race:* "Holy clergy, by your prayers you have always "invoked the Divine blessing on the arms of Russia; "people, worthy descendants of the brave *Sclavonians*, often "have you broken the jaws of the lions which were opened "to devour you. Unite, then, with the *cross in your hearts*, "and the sword in your hands, and no human power shall "prevail against you." The result showed that the emperor knew his people. The population of Moscow voted a levy of ten men in the hundred; the merchants agreed to arm them at their own expense; they agreed to a *pro rata* tax for the public service, and then made an additional subscription of nearly one million of dollars.

The attempts which have been made by some European writers, to throw discredit upon this heroic spirit of the Russian people, exhibit neither truthfulness nor generosity. They have been represented as acting only through the influence of constraint and fear, as offering to make sacrifices because they knew that otherwise their property would be wrested from them by a relentless government. To an unprejudiced mind, one willing to do justice even to an adversary, every feature of the case presents an unqualified contradiction to such statements as these. Every step of the Russians under their alarming circumstances, shows not a cold reluctant support of the Emperor, but the spontaneous movement which springs from the glowing heart. The Czar appealed to his people both as a father and as the head of the State, and they responded with the affection of children, and the enthusiasm of patriots. No sacrifice appeared to them great or unreasonable, if by it their religion and country could be preserved. It reminds one of the spirit which pervaded our own country in the time of the Revolution. The whole power of the empire was brought to bear upon the execution of a single purpose to rid their soil at any cost of the presence of a foe. The religious character which was given to the war, the deep religious spirit everywhere excited among the people, of whatever rank, were made the subjects of mirth and ridicule in the infidel camp of the French, though not by Bonaparte. His knowledge of human nature was far too profound to treat with contempt a scene which excited both astonishment and apprehension. The next combat in this contest for power and conquest on the one hand, and for home, religion, and country on the other, was one in which twenty-five thousand Russians were opposed to twenty-seven

16

thousand French, and the French were defeated with a loss of four thousand men. An affair which soon after occurred while both armies were directing their march upon Smolensko, will show how little occasion there is for sneers at the valor of the Russian soldier. A small body of Russians consisting only of six thousand infantry and twelve hundred horse, which had been detached for a particular service from the main army, found themselves suddenly surrounded by eighteen thousand French cavalry, and cut off from all possibility of obtaining assistance. These troops were new levies, who had never been in action. The Russian general, Newerofskoi, determined not to surrender, even under such appalling circumstances. He formed his little company into a hollow square, and commenced his retreat across the plains, perfectly open as they were to the operations of cavalry, that hemmed him in on all sides by this dense squadron. With constantly-repeated charges, the French hurled themselves upon the bristling bayonets with a headlong valor equalled only by the steadiness of their foe; sometimes driven back by the constant rolling fire blazing on all sides of the square, and sometimes bursting through the closed ranks, dashing their horses into the centre of the living masses only to be slain or driven back, the ever-diminishing number of the Russians still moving on, and still closing up their ranks and presenting again an unbroken outer line of men and steel. *Forty times* during the day did the French cavalry charge that Russian square, and as many times were they driven back, until at nightfall Newerofskoi extricated himself entirely, though with the loss of more than a thousand men. The manner in which the choicest troops of Wellington withstood the repeated charges of the imperial guard at Waterloo has been the theme of many a warm and just eulogium, but it was fully equaled by the unflinching bravery of these Russian raw recruits, exposed through the whole day in the open plains to nearly three times their number of the veteran cavalry of France. It surely is unwise, to say the least, to speak slightingly of the military character of a people that can supply soldiers such as these. Such articles as within the year 1854 have appeared in some of the leading British Reviews and Journals, whose object is to disparage the Russian army, to represent the Russians as a nation of traders and mechanics, and essentially unwarlike, to prove that most of her distinguished generals are and have been foreigners, that the walls of her fortifications are ready to tumble down, that the Russian fleet is most unseaworthy, with other similar statements, are far more dishonorable to the English than the Russian name. The noblest and the best of England are superior to such studied detraction, but when writers—who are seeking both popularity and remuneration from the British public, pursue this course, the only rational inference is, that they believe that such sentiments will be agreeable to the public sentiment of England, that they will meet and gratify the wishes of the people. By a similar course toward America, as impolitic as it was unjust, England created in the American heart dislike and resentment which half a century has not removed. The wanton injury which English journalists are inflicting upon the feelings of the Russians will yet recoil upon her, it may be feared, in the hour of her great need. Had England, during the trials of our early career, shown toward the United States a magnanimous spirit, it would have bound us to her by ties of sympathy which would have made the two nations one. She chose instead to gratify her pride by scorn and ridicule, and she has already met her reward in the mortification and disappointment with which she perceives the lack of American sympathy.

The next great event in the march of the French army was the battle at Smolensko. The fortifications of this ancient city bore no resemblance to those modern defenses within which Russia has now entrenched herself. An old but massive wall surrounded it, but this had only the armament of fifty old guns, in bad condition, and without carriages. A citadel of modern construction was yet incapable of proper defense, having, like all the works of the town, been neglected in this interior spot, where no enemy had been expected. The town, indeed, was no longer of any consequence among the defenses of the modern empire, though it once occupied an important position. The first attack at Smolensko was by Marshal Ney upon the citadel, from which he was promptly repulsed with great loss. In the meantime, the main body of the Russian army hastened to the relief of the city, which at first was held by only nineteen thousand Russians. But after entering the city, it was resolved by the Russian general not to hazard a general battle, when a defeat might cut him off from supplies, and he began a retreat toward Moscow, leaving thirty thousand men as a rear guard to hold Smolensko, and thus cover his retreat. The Russian commander had placed a stream between himself and the main army of the French, which Napoleon in vain endeavored to ford when he saw the retiring columns, and then, as a last resource, ordered a general assault upon Smolensko. Napoleon here commanded in person. He had at his disposal about two hundred thousand men and five hundred pieces of cannon. Of these, seventy thousand were led against the walls defended by thirty thousand Russians, who had now placed two hundred pieces of heavy cannon upon the ramparts. The French army fought under the eye of Napoleon, with their accustomed enthusiasm. Preceded by a heavy artillery force, they advanced unwaveringly under the terrible fire from the ramparts, and were wrapped in the sheets of flame that burst from the walls. After an obstinate battle they forced themselves within the suburbs, and then one hundred and fifty pieces of artillery were brought to bear upon the walls at point blank range. But, notwithstanding, they were foiled in every effort, and at evening Bonaparte was obliged to draw off his troops with a loss of fifteen thousand men. The French howitzers had set fire to a part of the city during the day; the remaining portion was fired by the Russians in the night; the magazines were destroyed, and the Russian army, with its wounded and a great part of the inhabitants, withdrew before morning, leaving only ashes and ruin behind them—beginning a work that was completed at Moscow.

The two armies next met at Valentina, where was the rear guard of the Russian army, under Touczoff. A small stream divided the combatants who first engaged. The French first drove the Russians from their position, and forced them across the rivulet. But when they crossed in pursuit, they were themselves defeated, and driven back over the stream. In the course of the day thirty-five thousand French were opposed to twenty-five thousand Russians, and at the close of the battle the Russians remained masters of their position, and had lost six thousand men, while the French loss amounted to eight thousand. Such was the conduct of Russian armies up to the bloody battle of Borodino.

In the campaign, thus far, there is certainly little occasion for sneers at the Russian people as an unwarlike nation, or at the ability or conduct of their generals. Every strategical maneuver on the part of Napoleon was met by a promptitude and skill quite equal to his own, and history does not show a more admirable instance of the display of military science and discipline than was exhibited in the manner in which the Russian forces retreated towards Moscow. Every effort of the army was nobly seconded by the inhabitants. Cities, villages, mills, stores of provisions—whatever could, by any possibility, give aid or shelter to the invading host, was unhesitatingly destroyed. An enthusiastic attachment to their country which nothing could shake, which prepared them for any sacrifice and any effort—indignation at the presence of an enemy on their native soil—such feelings pervaded all ranks, and fired every heart.

Under these circumstances a marked national characteristic was exhibited. Thoroughly aroused, almost maddened, as the heart of Russia was, there were no rash counsels, no hasty, impetuous action. Instead of risking all in one great effort, when failure would have been ruin, the army of Napoleon was subjected to a long, slow, but certain process of exhaustion, by which it was wisely foreseen that his destruction, though longer delayed, would be certain and complete in the end. With this general policy decided upon impatience was restrained, and they watched and waited the time when the host of Bonaparte should be so reduced as no longer to be an overmatch for themselves. The name of Napoleon was a terror everywhere; it had of itself a power to overmatch thousands of men, and the Russian generals may well be excused for being even somewhat over-cautious in meeting such an enemy. But the Russian commander, after retreating as far as Borodino, felt that unless a blow should now be struck in defense of Moscow, that the spirit of the whole nation would be depressed, for Moscow was regarded as the Mother of the Empire, and every Russian heart beat with strong affection for the Holy City. Kutosoff felt that a defeat would be less disastrous than a refusal to meet the enemy.

The battle of Borodino was one of the most bloody, as well as among the most important conflicts of modern times, and exhibits the qualities of a Russian army when engaged on the grandest scale of modern war. It will serve to prepare us to estimate aright the defensive power of Russia. To all human wisdom, it seemed as if on the field of Borodino not only the fate of Russia but of Europe might be decided. The defeat of the Russians would open the road to Moscow, and once in the magnificent Capital of the Old Empire of Muscovy, Bonaparte supposed that he should be absolutely secure, and that the Emperor and his nation would be prostrate at his feet. The two armies were in numbers nearly of equal strength, each numbering about one hundred and thirty thousand men. But ten thousand of the Russian troops were fresh recruits who had never seen a battle, and seven thousand were Cossacks. The French force were therefore really superior; besides, they had thirty thousand cavalry, the finest in Europe, and this gave them an immense advantage. The Russians were superior in the number of their artillery by some fifty pieces, and they also occupied a strong position, and had the advantage of awaiting an attack.

This position may be made intelligible in its general features, if the reader conceives a strong redoubt in front of the center of the Russian lines, in the rear of this a second and much larger redoubt, called the Great Redoubt; then in the rear of this, crowning several eminences, stretched the long lines of the main army—all these heights as well as the redoubts being defended by artillery. Opposed to this Russian force was the greatest commander of his age, whose reputation alone had in it the power of an army, and at his command troops unsurpassed by any in Europe, in courage, experience and skill, led on by officers who had scarcely known defeat in any great battle. Whatever talent, reputation, science, skill, or courage could supply, the French army undoubtedly possessed, and these must be considered in estimating the results of the conflict.

Toward evening, on the day preceding the decisive struggle, an attack was made on the smaller redoubt in front, which was defended by ten thousand men and twelve pieces of artillery. This attack was led by Murat, at the head of a very heavy body of cavalry, attended by two divisions of infantry correspondingly strong. The French artillery as they advanced poured a storm of grape-shot into the redoubt, while the ranks of the assailing columns were momentarily thinned by the answering fire from the Russian guns, until the attacking party stood within sixty feet of the redoubt. There for a time each gave and received a destructive fire of musketry, till finally, by an impetuous charge, such as few but French soldiers are capable of, the Russians were driven from their intrenchment, and the redoubt was taken and partly filled with French troops. But in a moment more, the tide of battle rolled resistlessly back, those within the redoubt were utterly destroyed, and once more it was in the hands of the Russians. Another gallant charge and the Russians were hurled back again, and masses of the French once more filled the space within its low walls, but still again the returning Russians came like an avalanche and swept their foes away, and the eagles of the Czar waved once more above the bloody spot.

Three times thus that outpost was taken and retaken, until in the evening it remained in the hands of the French, and after this desperate struggle the first point was hardly won. On the following day the same skill, courage, and impetuosity in attack, and the same obstinate valor in defense was displayed by two hundred and sixty thousand men, with more than twelve hundred cannon. Whatever Napoleon could accomplish with troops worthy of such a commander was done; and as the result of one of the bloodiest fights the world has ever seen in civilized war, the French army had twelve thousand killed, and thirty-eight thousand wounded—fifty thousand in all; while the Russians had fifteen thousand killed, and thirty thousand wounded—forty-five thousand in all—and two thousand more had been taken prisoners.

At the close of the action the Russian army was entrenched in a new position, stronger than that from which the French had driven them, and Napoleon drew off his forces from the battle-field. Neither army was in a condition to renew the battle, and the Russian commander deemed it prudent to sacrifice Moscow rather than risk another engagement before receiving reinforcements. Bonaparte entered Moscow only to see a city of three hundred thousand inhabitants, first utterly deserted and silent as a city of the dead, and then blazing, as the funeral pyre of his hopes, then ashes and ruin, as his hopes were doomed to be. Kutosoff threw his army between Moscow and all supplies, while, from the rich provinces in his rear his own troops were refreshed, and from all sides reinforcements were continually pouring in.

It is needless to pursue the history of this campaign. The object for which these few incidents have been introduced is accomplished. In a few weeks more the grand army was annihilated, and scarce an individual of that mighty invading host remained on the soil of Russia. Such a vengeance had been taken as causes men's ears even now to tingle with the recital. The facts here presented have been mainly derived from the most reliable sources of information, such as the most candid of English historians, so far as Russia is concerned, deemed to be authentic. They present a picture of the character of Russian soldiers which it would be well for any nation, however powerful, to consider, before entertaining high hopes of crushing a Russian army with ease, under any circumstances whatever. They should bring a blush to the cheek of any man who utters a scoff at Russian courage or efficiency. In all the history of the world there is not a story of a more enthusiastic devotion to country, or of a more heroic defense, nor of one more skillfully conducted. The Russian conduct of the campaign was in the main admirably suited to their circumstances, and its ultimate and complete success justifies the foresight with which it was planned, and adds lustre to the skill with which it was conducted.

Such an army, whether we consider its numbers, its equipments, its experience, its commander, or its general officers, can not now be led against Russia by her present antagonists, while she, according to the conceded rate of her growth, must have increased her population since 1812 by at least two-thirds of what it then was, while, at the same time, she has been perfecting herself in the science of war, as the fatal superiority of her artillery at Sebastopol has abundantly proved. These facts, taken in connection with the events of the Crimean war, are quite sufficient to indicate the probable results of any invasion of the soil of Russia. The combat with a Russian army, and especially a conflict with the empire, as a whole, has ever been a deceitful one. The manner of resistance which is assumed, partly by the force of the national characteristics, and partly because they rely much upon the aid which the nature of the country affords them, wears the appearance in the first stages of the conflict of inaction or timidity, sometimes even of continued defeat. Bonaparte seemed to be driving the Russian forces like sheep before him on his march to Moscow, and yet he could never break the perfect order of their retreat, even with the matchless cavalry which he commanded, nor could he succeed, in a single maneuver, by which to separate the divisions of their army or prevent a junction, or to cut them off from supplies. On the other hand, he found himself imprisoned and starving in Moscow, and then not only compelled to retreat, but to march back along the very desert that his army had made in its advance, and thus, and by successive actions, where either nothing was gained or victory was purchased at too great a cost, his army was annihilated, and he transformed into a solitary fugitive fleeing for life.

In like manner we heard of uninterrupted successes both by the Turks and the Allies at the commencement of the Crimean war. The Allied troops could hardly obtain an opportunity to show their valor, the enemy was so easily, even disgracefully beaten, and the English people were busying themselves with the question what should be done with Sebastopol and the Crimea—how this Russian possession and the other should be disposed of—soberly making a new map of Europe, and declaring what they would and would not accept or offer as terms of peace, and endeavoring to decide how much humiliation Russia would safely bear, when at once they find the whole force of France, England and Turkey, arrested effectually before a single fortress, around which most of those splendid troops that originally landed in the Crimea are now lying in their graves. The most extravagant accounts of the new engines of destruction carried out by the French and English armies were sent round the world. It was expected that a hostile fleet would be almost instantaneously destroyed at a distance that would preclude a return shot, and Lancaster guns were in like manner to batter down fortifications, themselves entirely out of the reach of the cannon of the fortress.

Instead of all this, it has been stated by English writers that the first siege batteries opened by the French were silenced by the Russian guns in three hours, and their whole artillery proved itself superior, both in construction and in the manner in which the guns were served. A resistance which sustains itself indefinitely, which becomes more formidable as a campaign advances, and which wears out its foe and overwhelms him in the end, is the characteristic of Russian war when their own soil is invaded. The world, however, is informed that the sudden setting in of winter and the destruction of Moscow were the causes of the ruin of Napoleon's army, that frost and snow, and not Russian skill or weapons, were its destroyers. But a candid examination, not of partizan statements or of elaborate eulogies of Bonaparte, will show that his destruction in Russia was inevitable aside from these causes. The people that burned Moscow were equally prepared for any other similar sacrifice, and Napoleon was expelled from Russia because the nation was resolved that cost what it might, he should be forced back across their frontier or be destroyed.

The following observation of the elegant English historian who has had the courage and magnanimity to present facts in regard to Russia will exhibit this matter in its true light. When Bonaparte commenced his retreat, the Russian commander first by a most skillful maneuver forced him back along the path which he had made a desert in his advance, while at the same time the Russian army pursued him *not in the rear*, but on a *parallel line of march*, through a district abounding with supplies. Upon this Alison remarks as follows :

"Justice requires that due credit should be given to the Russian mode of pursuit, by a parallel march, a measure which was unquestionably one of the greatest military achievements of the last age. Had Kutosoff pursued by the same road as the French, his army, moving in a line wasted by the triple curse of three previous marches, would have melted away more rapidly than his enemy's. Had he hazarded a serious engagement before the French were completely broken by their sufferings, his own loss would have probably been so severe as to have disabled him from taking advantage of theirs. Despair rapidly restores the courage of an army; a disorderly crowd of stragglers often resume the strictest military order, and are capable of the greatest efforts when the animation of a battle is at hand.

"The passage of the Beresina, the battle of Corunna, the victory of Hanan, are not required to demonstrate this important truth. Well knowing that a continued retreat would of itself weaken his enemies, the Russian general maneuvered in such a manner as with hardly any loss to himself to make prisoners of above half their army, and that at a time when the storms of winter were making as great ravages in his own troops as in those of his antagonists. Had he not pursued at all, Napoleon would have halted at Smolensko, and soon repaired his disasters; had he fought a pitched battle with him on the road, his army, already grievously weakened by the cold, would have probably been rendered incapable of pursuing him to the frontier.

"By acting a bolder part he might have gained a more brilliant, but he could not have secured such everlasting success; he would have risked the fate of the empire, which hung on the preservation of his army; he might have acquired the title of conqueror of Napoleon, but he would not have deserved that of savior of his country. But it would have been in vain that all these advantages lay within the reach of Russia, had their constancy and firmness not enabled her people to grasp them. Justice has not hitherto been done to the heroism of their conduct. We admire the Athenians who refused to treat with Xerxes after the sack of their city, and the Romans who sent troops to Spain after the Battle of Connæ; what then shall we say of the general who, while his army was yet reeking with the slaughter of Borodino, formed the project of enveloping the invader in the capital which he had conquered? what of the citizens who fired their palaces and their temples lest they should furnish even a temporary refuge to the invader? and what of the Sovereign who, undismayed by the fires of

Moscow, announced to his people in the moment of their greatest agony his resolution never to submit; and foretold the approaching deliverance of his country and the world? Time, the great sanctifier of events, has not yet lent its halo to these sacrifices; separate interest have arisen; the terror of Russia has come in place of the jealousy of Napoleon, and those who have gained most by the heroism of their Allies are too much influenced by momentary considerations to acknowledge it. But when these fears and jealouses shall have passed away, and the pageant of Russian, like that of French ascendancy, shall have disappeared, the impartial voice of posterity will pronounce that the history of the world does not afford an example of equal moral grandeur."

There is one remark in the foregoing extract which is worthy of special attention; that those who have gained most by the heroism of Russia in breaking the power of Bonaparte, have been since unwilling to acknowledge it. Had Napoleon not been checked in Russia, that threatened French invasion of England might long since have become to her a very sorrowful reality, and it ill becomes her now to speak in terms of scorn and disparagement of that gallant people, who at such a fearful cost interposed itself between Bonaparte and the rest of Europe.

But it is insisted by English writers, that however formidable Russia may be at home, aided by the defenses of her climate and country, she is incapable of maintaining an army abroad, and of carrying on successfully an offensive war. We are told of the total inefficiency of her commissariat, and of the immense losses which her armies sustain, and we are pointed to the campaigns in the Caucasus, and latterly to the unsuccessful siege of Silistria, as proofs of inefficiency and unskillfulness. More than one point here is worthy of consideration. In the first place, will the operations of the Russian army abroad compare unfavorably with those of England herself, even when England has the command of the sea, and the means of transport. Has a

Russian army often suffered more from the want of order, skill, and efficiency in every department, than the English army in the Crimea, if their own witnesses are to be credited? Has any campaign in the Caucasus been more disastrous or ineffectual than the efforts of the Allied troops? Russia need not shrink from a comparison with those who affect to despise her.

But again, if the whole time of the foreign operations of Russia is considered, where has she been successfully and permanently driven back? On all sides, her frontier has been continually extended, and at what point has she failed to maintain herself? She has been driven back, it is triumphantly said, from the principalities, across the Danube, across the Pruth. But the end is not yet. Will she *remain* there? A question which her past history perhaps will answer more correctly than present temporary appearances.

Again, it is not in accordance with the genius or policy of Russia to make aggressive war for the sake of extensive and sudden conquest. It is by no means necessary for her to do this in order to become a great military Power. She need not attempt to march her armies over the prostrate thrones of Europe after the manner of Bonaparte; this is not her mission—not thus is her ultimate position to be won. It is only necessary for her to possess and wield with skill sufficient military power to defend herself against the combined assault of western Europe, and then, under God, her future is secure. She requires only the means of protecting her natural growth. Within certain limits she intends to displace or control all. It is in this point of view, and with this purpose of hers before the mind, that the military capacities of that great Empire are to be studied. She is not to be extended simply or mainly by conquest alone, by the direct application of military power to the acquisition of territory. Her vast military resources are demanded to protect her growth, to shield her from foreign aggression. As an attacking force pushes its columns forward, under the cover of its guns, so Russia *grows out* on *every* side with continuous enlargement, under the cover of her military power. Behind her fortifications, and the lines of her army, within her impregnable home, she cherishes and makes strong her interior life, that swells ever outward by a resistless vigor.

# CHAPTER XXIII.

## THE ARMY AND NAVY OF RUSSIA.

Having in the preceding chapter presented some facts and statements which show the real character and capabilities of the soldiers of the Northern Empire, it becomes important to inquire how many such soldiers a Russian Emperor can command for offensive or defensive war. Certainly her military power must be regarded as of the most imposing character, if the number of effective soldiers is in the usual proportion to the population of the country; if they are well armed and disciplined; if the munitions of war are abundant, and of suitable quality; and if stores and troops can be readily transported, and accumulated at points where they are required. These points will be the subjects of investigation in the present chapter, to which will be added also an account of the size, position, and condition of the Russian Navy. It is by no means an easy matter to ascertain, even with an approximation to accuracy, the actual military force of the Muscovite nation. While, on her part, national pride and ambition would lead her to present to the world an imposing array, on the contrary, those who fear or dislike her find their interest, as they think, in reducing as far as possible by all manner of deductions, the published statements of the condition of her military establishment, and after reducing thus her armies within reasonable limits they proceed to show, either that it can not be supported in the field, or that its different corps are so widely separated that they can not be concentrated upon any single point; and again, that the vast extent of territory to be defended absorbs in its protection a large part of the available force of the empire. It is also asserted that the state of the country is such as to render the transport of large bodies of troops from point to point exceedingly difficult—indeed, almost impossible.

These statements are founded rather on the past than the present condition of the Russian Empire, and, though not wholly without foundation, must be received with due caution, when we remember under what strong temptations those who control the press of western Europe now are to underrate the power of their formidable antagonist, and to vail somewhat from the people the actual condition of things. By a comparison of the various estimates of the population of Russia, it would appear that her numbers are nearly or not quite equal to those of France, England, and Austria.

So far, then, as mere numbers are concerned, she should be able to present a military array nearly or quite as formidable as the three combined. What the power of Russia was in 1812, when the immense army of Bonaparte was swept away, not alone by frost or the fires of Smolensko and Moscow, but equally by the courage and skill of the defenders of their country, is now a matter of history, and well known to the world. Since that period she has spared neither effort nor money in augmenting her strength, and giving to it all the efficiency which can be derived both from science and discipline. She has brought to her aid both European and American skill and experience, and has been steadily and silently perfecting her army, her fortifications, and her navy.

Within the last quarter of a century, no state in Europe has augmented its forces in numbers proportionate to the increase of Russia, nor has any other Power so much improved the quality of its troops. During his long reign, Nicholas applied himself with unremitting ardor to perfect the whole military organization of the empire. Both his capacity and his resources proved fully equal to the task, and, while we heard only of the poverty of Russia, of her barbarism, of the inefficiency of every department of the public service, of the corruption of her officials, and the system of peculation and fraud everywhere established, she has built and equipped a navy which places her in the foremost rank of naval powers, equalled by England, France, and America, alone; she has established arsenals and depots of wood and other military stores, unsurpassed, to say the least, by any; her fortifications show the perfection of military science; her military schools have no parallel anywhere, and her army is, beyond all comparison, the most formidable in Europe, taking into consideration its numbers, its discipline, and the resources from which its losses may be repaired.

The support of such a vast military establishment must press heavily upon the general industry of the nation beyond all doubt; military despotism, and the necessary hardships of a soldier's life, are constantly doing their cruel work, but whether this burthen presses *disproportionately* upon Russia, as compared with the establishments of other nations of Europe, does not yet appear. The magnitude of her army is scarcely beyond the due proportion of her population, as compared with other military Powers, while she can maintain her troops at home at less expense than any other nation of Europe. The cost of maintaining a foot soldier in the different armies of Europe has been estimated as follows:*

| | | £. | s. |
|---|---|---|---|
| Cost of a foot soldier for a year in Russia, | - | 5 | 00 |
| " " " Austria, | - | 9 | 8 |
| " " " Prussia, | - | 10 | 00 |
| " " " France, | - | 14 | 6 |
| " " " England, | - | 21 | 14 |

* Marmont's Voyages.

This shows an immense difference in favor of Russia, and much of this is owing to the fact that the food of the common people, and consequently of the soldier, is abundant and cheap. A late German writer, Haxthausen, describes the Russian peasantry as physically a fine race of men, generally, indeed, eating meat only once a week, but having a variety of other food, and well contented with it, comfortably and even expensively clothed. This proves that the small cost at which the Russian army is maintained is owing, not to their being ill-fed and scantily clothed, but because the means of supporting life with comfort are easily obtained. The vast extent of the empire, and the difficulty which is always experienced in moving large bodies of troops by land from point to point, led the Emperor Nicholas to the adoption of two very important measures, one of which is completed, and the other is urged forward as rapidly as circumstances allow. The first was the arrangement of the whole army into different corps, stationed according to the geographical character of the country, and where they would be needed either for attack or defense.

The English and French governments would probably have avoided their mortifications in the Crimea, had they possessed themselves of reliable information concerning the actual strength of Russia, the character of her defenses, and the condition of her army. By stationing it at the different points of the empire where it will be needed most in case of attack, Nicholas obviated to a great extent the sudden movements of large bodies of troops when the late war began. His force was ready to enter the Principalities, ready to defend Sebastopol, and equally prepared to cover St. Petersburg and support the garrison at Cronstadt.

But a measure far more important than the one already mentioned, having a bearing upon the internal commerce and general development of the country's resources, as well as upon the transport of armies, is the construction of a system of railways already begun, and which, when finished, will greatly increase the military efficiency of Russia. A grand trunk line is already in operation from St.

Petersburgh to Moscow, about four hundred miles, and from Moscow to Odessa the work is in progress, and now nearly finished. These two lines alone through the heart of the empire, crossing, as they do, so many navigable streams on which steam navigation is already begun, will enable Russia to transport troops, munitions of war, and supplies of all sorts, with great facility from the Baltic to the Black Sea, and between her southern frontier and the extreme north. These two railways, as any one will see at a glance by consulting a map, would, by their connections with a network of navigable rivers and uniting canals, command almost all the resources of the Empire, either for the Black Sea or the Baltic. Indeed, with fleets of light steamers on all her navigable streams, she possesses means of transport from and through every portion of her country, even without railways, such as no other country on the eastern continent can boast; and those who believe that she will yet fail from inability to place troops and supplies at any threatened point will be sorely disappointed.

But the world is constantly reminded of the poverty of Russia, of her limited revenue, and her exhausted treasury, and that therefore she can not maintain her military establishment in an efficient position. Those who favor us with such statements forget that the achievement of the Czar show as yet no evidence of want. He has expended money on the most enlarged scale upon every public project, and everything has been done in a manner which France and England may imitate with advantage. Take the admitted fact that for a hundred years no country has made so rapid a progress in all that constitutes a great nation as Russia; that her population doubles in about fifty years, that this is not caused by immigration, but is mainly caused by the natural increase of the people; and add to this that in the meantime Moscow has been rebuilt, the ravages caused by the invasion of more than six hundred thousand men repaired, one of the most magnificent capitals in Europe has been created, an army of more than a million completely organized and fully armed, not with the arms of barbarism, but with the most formidable weapons of destruction known to modern war, that a first-class navy has been produced, and fortifications erected which have defied the utmost strength of the two great nations of western Europe, that at the same time long lines of railway are constructed, schools start into being, manufactures increase, and agriculture is improved, and it must be allowed by all who are capable of a candid judgment, that we behold on all sides evidences of prosperity rather than of ruin. One important fact should not be forgotten in this connection. It has been the steady policy of the government to foster to the utmost its own industry, and to render the nation independent by a self-sustaining power.

Of the actual strength and resources of such a country it is difficult to judge, and they are generally underrated, and especially by such a commercial people as the English. The North American colonies made but an insignificant figure in the world's tables of wealth and power when each farmer of New England manufactured for himself his clothing from materials raised on his own farm, and when his food was produced in a similar manner; but when England thought to crush them she was met by a power that did not appear in statistical tables, and there was a solid and available wealth in our country that commerce could take no note of, and which was sufficient for successful defense. There is in Russia a vast amount of home manufacture, of home strength and resources, which can not be expressed by figures, and which does not appear in official reports. In such a state of society there is power which does not lie on the surface. The condition of Russia can be more readily understood by an American than by most Europeans, for a similar process in reclaiming wild lands, and filling up a new country, and carrying forward improvements, is going on there as here, though our national character and our free institutions have imparted greater vigor and velocity to our movement. The descriptions of the log-houses, the lines of unbroken forests, the log, or "*corduroy*" roads, forcibly remind the American reader of home scenes.

It has cost *our* "transatlantic cousins" some painful experiments before they could be convinced that a vigorous national life, a substantial and most formidable national power, could clothe itself in such rude forms, having only the aspect of poverty and discomfort. It was necessary for them to receive lessons from the broadsides of our "fir-built frigates," and from behind earth walls and cotton-bags, before they could comprehend how a country of forests and cabins, and log-roads, and mud-roads, could possibly be a powerful country; how troops could be mustered, or fed, or clothed, or paid, or transported. Similar mistakes are evidently made in regard to Russia, and they may be corrected in a similar manner.

Again, those who are disposed to amuse themselves with the poverty of the Northern Empire, should not forget that the gold-mines of the Ural are for Russia what California is to the United States—what Australia is to Great Britain, and that the produce of these mines is to a great extent under the control of the government, which has a deposit of treasure of its own, whose amount is known to the chief officers of the realm alone.

A country capable of performing such things, and at the same time preserving a rate of advance beyond that of her neighbors, and which has had her whole military establishment on the war footing since 1848, was not likely to sink suddenly from exhaustion, with only that same army to support, as before, on her own soil. Besides, if Russia was so soon to suffer national collapse, with but a slight addition to her armies, and with her fleets lying in her docks, what should be said of France and England, with their common expenditures vastly increased, maintaining immense fleets in foreign seas which afforded them no supplies, and vast armies, far from home, on a spot where nothing could be obtained for man or beast—armies whose diminished ranks were to be constantly filled up by fresh drains on the population at home.

These statements of the wretched condition of the Russian army, of the sufferings and privations of the troops, of the terrible ravages of disease, of the inability of the government to sustain its establishment on a respectable footing, which have filled English and French books, Quarterlies and newspapers, have been shown to have originated either in utter ignorance of the facts, or in the vain hope of increasing the chances of success by a deliberate system of detraction.

The Turkish Empire, withering under the curse of God, tottering near the goal where the unerring word of prophecy declares that it must fall, was exhibited to wondering Europe and America as a nation freshly set out on a new career of civilization, having in itself a recuperative vital energy, which would place it alongside of western nations, and which might be able soon to cope single-handed with Russia, if a little help were offered it by the Allies, while the Russian forces were represented as flying before the victorious Turks without the courage or skill to meet an enemy anywhere, and the only complaint was that victory was too cheaply won, and then these journalists sat down to a revision of the map of Europe as confidently as to the carving of a turkey for their dinner. The folly of such proceedings was most satisfactorily shown, in a manner which England and France will have cause to remember through long years. It is now evident that the retreat of the Russian forces from the Principalities was decided upon before the failure of the siege of Silistria, and was determined by this event; that the Russian officers foresaw in due season the real plan of the campaign decided upon by the Allies, and their troops were therefore withdrawn, and placed in a position to be within reach of Sebastopol.

The course of the Russian army there was in perfect keeping with the well-known national characteristics. Their enemies were constantly shouting victory and progress, but at the same time they were being exhausted, and fresh supplies of troops, ammunition, guns, and warlike stores of all kinds were constantly demanded from home.

The Muscovite empire exhibited its ancient and proverbial power of resistance, united with a science, skill, and fertility of invention and resources, not displayed in previous wars, and this is shown by the testimony of those before the walls of Sebastopol. The result, if it brings no lesson of wisdom to European writers, should at least teach Americans to be exceedingly cautious in regard to testimony thus furnished against Russia. She shows by her course, that she is expanding by a vigorous life, and the character of this life, and the relations which America may sustain to its future developments, should become for us a matter of earnest consideration. Giving due weight to the most reliable testimony in the case, it seems but a fair conclusion that the statements which exhibit the Russian army as numbering about one million, are open only to such common reductions as would be made in estimating the military strength of any other European Power, and that in determining her *relative* power a force of a million may be taken as a standard nearly correct.

# CHAPTER XXIV.

## THE NATIONAL SENTIMENT OF RUSSIA AS AFFECTING NATIONAL POLICY AND DESTINY.

One of the most suggestive facts taught by history is, that very often individuals who have reached positions of commanding influence have early felt a consciousness of their powers, and have apprehended the general features of their allotted task; a fact which, perhaps, gave rise to the remark of a distinguished English writer, that, in general, a man's aspirations may be taken as the measure of his capabilities. The remark has doubtless truth for its foundation, though it must be received only with important qualifications. The same thing is true of some nations which have held a sovereign's place among the kingdoms of the world. It appears that in some manner, none, perhaps, can tell how, a national sentiment has arisen pointing to some specific ultimate destiny. Its beginnings and its progress seem removed from all ordinary causes, till a well-defined public opinion pervades all classes—becomes, as it were, the national soul, and shapes the national policy. And, whatever extravagance human pride may attach to such popular convictions, there is often a most remarkable *general* resemblance between such national anticipations and the results actually reached. When once such a sentiment has been established, and become inwoven with the national faith—when it has been handed down as a traditional belief from the fathers—it is readily seen that its power is almost resistless. It shapes all national action, because the national mind is ever reaching out for the accomplishment of destiny. It prompts ever to effort, at the same time that it gives to power a definite direction. It sustains the courage of a nation under the severest reverses, because it believes that a superior power has already determined its ultimate success. It is national faith which, as in the individual, prompts to effort, and goes far to make achievement sure.

The doctrine of "manifest destiny" may not be dismissed with a sneer. Faith in her destiny has given a specific direction to the national energies of Great Britain, and has made her so long mistress both of the seas and of the commerce of the world. Faith in destiny rolled the fiery, bloody deluge of Mohammedanism into Europe. Faith in manifest destiny established the Western Empire, under Charlemagne; it had made Rome before; and it has upheld the Anglo-Saxon race in all its wondrous career. The American mind expands with a vast idea—its "manifest destiny." Thousands condemn, and thousands ridicule, and yet the conception has its origin in the circumstances of national position, and in national character; it has shaped itself to existing wants, and even existing probabilities, and its very existence is the herald and guaranty of future accomplishment.

The fact that such an idea may possess the mind of a nation, and may become a reality in the course of its progress, does by no means determine its moral character, or prove that the steps are justifiable in themselves by which a great national end is finally reached. God causes the wrath of man to praise him, and national sins will no less be punished because committed in working out a previously appointed destiny. Connected with this subject another fact should be remembered. No nation, probably, has been conscious of the hour when it passed its culminating point, and when its mission was accomplished, but, on the contrary, retains in the decay and infirmity of old age the brightest anticipations of its youth, and all the pride of its day of vigor and of power. It refuses to perceive that the scepter has passed into other hands, and still pompously commands the obedience of the world. It is not generally difficult to determine whether such a national sentiment is connected with a youthful and expanding life, or whether it belongs to the empty and powerless vanity of old age.

If now, with these facts in view we turn to Russia, we find all travelers testifying to the existence of two national opinions, which may be said to be universal with the fifty millions of the Russian race. One opinion is, that they are to possess Constantinople, and the other, that they are destined to become the most powerful nation of the world, and to control all Europe, at least, if not the world. Upon fifty millions of minds the impression seems to have been made, whether true or false, whether pointing to a reality in the future or not, that Russia is entrusted with a great mission in the social regeneration of the world. Whence this impression has arisen who shall pretend to say; that it will find no corresponding reality in the future who will venture with confidence to declare? That the national, or it may also be called the traditional, policy of the empire is founded upon these ideas, is now known probably to all. That fact alone is worthy of attentive consideration, because it shows that the course of Russia is the result of a national impulse, and that no change of rulers can essentially alter the policy to which the nation has committed itself, and may admonish the Powers of western Europe that it is no easy matter, even by severe reverses, completely to annihilate the pride and the hopes of fifty millions of people, subvert an all-pervading national sentiment, and compel a great empire to a new line of policy.

In estimating the influence of these sentiments as elements of power in a national movement, it must not be forgotten that they are found not alone in the breasts of the Emperor and the nobles, or a few restless and ambitious men, but they are cherished and firmly believed in by the lowest of the peasantry, and made the basis of a truly national anticipation—they are but the expression of a national thought, and the determination of a whole people; and when to this is added the fact that this hope stands inseparably connected with the spread of their national religion, it becomes evident that this idea of "manifest destiny" is the source of a power whose importance can scarcely be overrated. It renders Russia most mighty for the accomplishment either of good or evil. The following is an extract from a late American writer, who regards everything Russian with a somewhat unfavorable eye, and presents his opinion of the character of that race upon whom the national sentiment alluded to is working with greatest power.

"The great Russian lives to an extreme old age, longer, upon an average, than the man of another country. His generative power is remarkable. In central Russia the increase of the population is beyond all former precedent in Europe; while the natives of the conquered provinces are diminishing with fearful rapidity, the population of the whole empire, refreshed from this exhaustless source, counts every year another million among its multitudes. Thousands and tens of thousands, in a perpetual stream, flow from this fountain head into the vast regions of the north, south, east, and west. In every country, and among every people beneath the scepter of the Czar, the Weliki Russian will be found, asserting the supremacy of his race, and showing his skill and cunning. All the tribes with whom he comes in contact yield to his activity, and dwindle in significance before the progress of his encroachments. He even penetrates beyond the frontiers of the empire. While he profits as a merchant, he is often the secret agent of the government. His advance precedes the march of armies, and his aggression pave the way to conquest."

When the idea of a definite national mission or destiny has taken full possession of such a race, it is very likely to produce important results. The portrait drawn by this author can scarcely fail to remind one of many of the characteristics of the American race; and when he adds that these Russians are ignorant and dishonest, it should be borne in mind that the Yankees have by no means escaped imputations of this kind, and yet New England is the work of Yankees. And if, as the author affirms, the Russian in his superstition imagines that a great work has been committed to his country, in the social regeneration of the world, it must be confessed that a similar superstition has seized also on the minds of Americans. It would perhaps be interesting to study the present prevailing national sentiment in the prominent nations, and inquire how far these presentiments may shadow forth the actual future. The following is probably near the truth. Russia and America are full of boundless hope, and even confidence of ruling, each over half a world. They think of nothing less than expansion on every side, and progress reaching far into the future. France hopes to head a combination of western States. England is filled with apprehension, and no definite future opens before her. The preservation of what she possesses is probably the prominent thought. Austria and Prussia are nearly in the same position, while Turkey is oppressed with a sense of approaching ruin. Will not these sentiments be very likely to produce a corresponding reality?

Certain it is that England is no longer the head of western Europe. She follows in the train of Catholic France, and we are led anxiously to inquire to what extent she may yet put on the Papal yoke, when such a man as Lord John Russell, with his suite and family, attends high mass with all signs of sincere devotion. When those who are at the head of the affairs of England stand in such relations to the Papal power, and she deliberately allies herself with the Latin Church, choosing as she declared, a western combination in favor of the Roman Catholic Church, rather than the progress of Russia and the Greek Christianity, American Protestantism may well find cause to rejoice in the traditional sentiment of the Muscovite Empire, which has placed it as the present sole bulwark in Europe against this new advance of the Papacy.

The world may well hope that both Russia and the United States may attain unto what they consider their manifest destiny, because they are the only great Powers of the world now, which can be fully relied upon in the present struggle with Rome. With the religious aspect of the Eastern war fully and clearly before her, England has espoused the quarrel of the Pope, and with this evidence of her spirit presented to the world, who shall say that in the terrible struggle for principle, and for faith, upon which the nations have apparently entered, she will again ally herself to the right.

# CHAPTER XXV.

## THE EDUCATIONAL INSTITUTIONS OF RUSSIA.

The Crimean war was declared by England and France to be a war of civilization against barbarism. The *London Quarterly* for April, 1854, holds the following language, in which is expressed the sentiment that England is industriously striving to spread abroad: "If this contest is to be "waged between the forces of civilization and liberty against "those of a *semi-barbarous empire*, aspiring to crush the inde- "pendence of Europe, we neither doubt nor dread the issue "of the war in which England and France have been *com- "pelled* to engage." How will this appear when impartial history shall show that Russia, so far from being aggressor in that war, was compelled by the meddling intrigues of French Jesuitism either to yield to the pretensions of Rome or defend her own equal rights by arms? How the charge of barbarism which rings out from the English Press, and which a portion of the American Press is disposed to echo, will stand by the side of facts which will soon be presented, the reader will judge.

The *North British Review*, for November, 1854, in describing what the consequences of success, then considered certain, would be, says: "Europe would be for generations, if not for centuries and forever, liberated from the dangers of a *semi-oriental barbarism*, and England and France, differing in the forms, but yet harmonious in the tendencies of their civilization, *might go to rest in each others arms.* It seems indeed not unlikely that Protestant England will lie down in the arms of Catholic France, but whether she will awake and find herself still *Protestant* England admits at least of question. "Semi-oriental barbarism" is the phrase applied by this religious journal to Russia. "A war of "civilization against barbarism, of liberty against depot-"ism," and on this ground an appeal was made by England and France to the sympathies of the world, and especially of Republican America.

That the Crimean war was in no sense a war of liberty against despotism will be made to appear, and we shall be enabled to judge of the barbarism of Russia, and of the spirit and tendency of her institutions, by a glance at her educational systems. We shall be able to decide from these whether Russia presents a stationary barbarism, without internal life or vigor, or whether she exhibits the spectacle of a nation rapidly assuming the forms of a superior civilization, and with vigorous step advancing in the career of solid improvement, aiming in all her institutions to cultivate and develope her own individual national life. We only deceive ourselves when we seize upon phrases such as liberty and despotism, civilization and barbarism, and use them in describing Russia, without a careful study of her position and character.

In studying even an imperfect sketch of the educational system of the empire of the Czar, it should be borne in mind that the popular conception seems to be, that whatever improvement has been made in Russia is due to foreigners alone. Her army, it is said, is officered by foreigners; by them her ships have been built, her fortifications have been constructed; by them her cannon have been cast, and by them her schools are taught. But another conception of this nation is of a people earnest, active, and capable of availing themselves freely of the world's science, experience and skill, to aid them in their work of national elevation. It will be found that the latter idea alone can explain the character of her educational system. The military schools, as the most prominent, first demand attention. The *exact* condition of these schools now is not known, but insomuch as they have received the constant and most zealous attention of the government, it is to be presumed that the cause of education keeps pace with the improvements and discoveries of modern science, and that the number of pupils increases in proportion to the growth of the empire. Some years since, the number of pupils at the military schools was reported as follows:

| | |
|---|---|
| Pupils at Military Schools under Grand Duke Michael, - - - - - | 8,733 |
| Pupils at Navy Board Schools, - - | 2,224 |
| Total, - - - - | 10,957 |

The above are principally, if not entirely, from the best families of the empire, and are subjected to the most thorough scientific and military training, a course which, for completeness and finish, is not exceeded by any schools of the world. By common consent of all who know their character, they are admitted to have no superior. Some details will hereafter be given. These eleven thousand supply the officers for the army and navy. In addition to these there were at the same time in the schools under the direction of the Minister of War one hundred and sixty-nine thousand pupils, making in all nearly one hundred and eighty thousand of the very flower of the Russian youth, a number which, with the increase of the population, may now be reckoned at two hundred thousand, who are receiving at the hands of the government the most complete military education that the science of the world is capable of supplying.

This fact bears with great force upon the question of the military power of Russia, and might be profitably considered by those who insist that the army of the empire is incapable of becoming efficient. The world beside, exhibits no such spectacle, no such scientific preparation for war, and the fortresses, the armament and gunnery, bear ample testimony to the proficiency of these scholars.

Although for convenience sake, reference has been made to the estimate made by the *London Quarterly* of the population of the Empire, yet the preponderance of evidence would seem to show that the number stated is too small, and that eighty millions is now nearer the truth. This indeed is the estimate of a writer lately quoted in another English Review; while the calculations of Malte Brun would swell the present population beyond even this. But admitting the existence of eighty millions on Russian soil, having a formidable, active, united race, as the central life and power of the mighty mass, it is an important question, not for Europe alone, but for Americans to study, what is to be the influence of such a power upon the world's destiny, when directed by the flower of the Empire, with the most thorough military education? Let those who suppose that the power of this great empire is to be suddenly checked, or even ultimately repressed, until its national mission is accomplished, study the influence of the schools attentively, and they will find good cause to review their opinions.

Let Americans consider the effect which our one small military school has produced upon our army, and even upon the whole nation, and then estimate if they can, the power created by the constant education of ten or twelve thousand such young men for the control of the Russian armies, and of the regular training of one hundred thousand more in the acquisition of the arts of war. No system of detraction, however skillful or deliberate, or perseveringly maintained, will prevent such institutions from working out their legitimate results; and France and England have been compelled reluctantly to admit that they met in the Crimea a military science, particularly in engineering, more excellent than their own. This skill, which baffled the allied armies before Sebastopol, and which devised and directed the terrible artillery that hurled defiance and death from its walls, has been acquired in these military schools; and when it is remembered that many of these most efficient guns are taken from the ships in the harbor, it may awaken some reflections as to what the gunnery of the Russian navy may yet accomplish. Some idea of the completeness of the education in these schools may be obtained from a few facts.

The system of Russian fortifications by which the empire is defended, is separated into ten distinct divisions. In the old Michaeloff palace, now the School of Engineers, in St. Petersburgh, a separate hall is allotted to each of these divisions, in which is collected whatever can illustrate the character of the district which the hall represents, and the fortifications which it contains. Here, for inspection and study, are plans general and in detail, of all the fortifications of the empire, arranged according to their territorial divisions, and not only of all the fortresses, but of all that have been projected and are yet unfinished, and each particular fortress has a department by itself, in which are collected specimens of the materials used or to be employed in its construction, including bricks and kinds of earth, and descriptions of stone which can be found in the neighborhood, so that each pupil has in this way a local education in addition to his general scientific training. Here also, as subjects for study, are accurate models in wood and clay of every fortification in Russia, presenting each with perfect exactness, so that not a single object, even to a tree, is omitted. By such means, the study of the defenses of each fortification, and the manner in which it might be attacked, may be conned on as perfectly as if on the spot, and every cadet, when he graduates, is prepared for any post in the country, understanding beforehand all the local characteristics of the station to which he is appointed.

It is strongly significant of the traditional policy and prevailing feelings of the nation, that here also is a perfect and most minute plan of the fortifications of Constantinople; the castles of the Dardanelles, with every feature, are presented, together with the aspect and character of the Straits, so that every young Russian officer studies the nature of an attack on Constantinople in addition to his general preparation for war. A single fact is sufficient to show the practical character of the instruction in the naval schools—the senior class of cadets annually take in pieces and rebuild a large model of an American frigate. The instruction in these schools embraces the higher mathematics, and their application to military and naval architecture, and navigation, drawing in all its departments, both the theory and practice of the construction of fortresses and ships, with modern languages, history, and general literature.

The children of soldiers, and especially the orphan children, are particularly cared for by the government, placed in schools, and educated for the army. At St. Petersburgh there is the Miner's School. It occupies a magnificent building, in which more than three hundred pupils are constantly studying under competent professors, with every facility for obtaining an education having great breadth and thoroughness. In this institution the pupil spends eight years, and then, with as perfect a training as science can impart, he is sent to superintend the government mines in the Ural; and this school and the number of its pupils is enough to indicate the importance of that portion of the resources of Russia.

Attached to this important school is an immense and very complete collection of whatever can illustrate the sciences of geology and mineralogy, but particularly that of Russia. These several museums, rich, it is said, beyond comparison with any similar collections elsewhere, contain minerals, geological specimens, and fossils, from the most interesting localities, not only in Russia but from other parts of the world, and here also are collected models of machinery, and implements, and even models of mines themselves. The completeness of the education which the government bestows upon its servants, and the enlightened character of its policy, may be seen in the expenses incurred and the pains which have been taken to prepare those who are to have the care of the public mines and the imperial mint.

In addition to what has been already described, artificial mines of various kinds have been constructed by the actual excavation of subterranean galleries, such as are found in the real mine, and a *fac simile* of a mine in the Ural is produced, with the real earth, rocks, and imbedded ores and minerals, precisely as they are found in the distant mountains. Here the Geological student beholds the iron, the copper, the coal, the precious stones, and the gold, in their natural position, and precisely as he will meet them in his future operations in the actual mines. Certainly no more admirable device could be found for preparing the students of this school for the duties of real life. Is there any government in the world which has undertaken the developement of its mineral resources on so magnificent a scale, and in a manner so thoroughly scientific and at the same time so practical?

The Academy of Fine Arts is a building four hundred feet long and seventy feet high, in which is not only a magnificent picture gallery, but a school of Art, in which three hundred pupils are supported and educated. A school of the Arts is also maintained by the government, in which two hundred students, the sons of tradesmen, receive not only a general education, but also special instruction in the mechanical arts, and who are sent for the general improvement of the country by directing its various branches of labor. There is a Normal School of importance; the University, with five hundred students and fifty-eight professors; a Medical College, with five hundred pupils; a Female Institute, in which four hundred young ladies are gratuitously educated; and there are also theological, commercial, and other schools of various character.

Among these the Agricultural School deserves particular mention. A farm of seven hundred acres has been laid out, under the direction of the government, and on the premises, an agricultural school has been established, where both the theory and the practice of agriculture are taught to two hundred young peasants. An extensive museum is attached to this farm containing whatever relates to the occupation of a farmer, including all descriptions of agricultural implements, even to the latest improvements known in America. Here also the finest breeds of cattle are collected, and model cottages are introduced, with the design of improving the architecture of the Russian farmers, which resembles very much the log-cabins of our own "*backwoods.*" Each province is allowed to send annually a certain number to this school, and each year fifty graduates are distributed through the country, bearing abroad the skill and science which they have obtained in a four-years' course.

The pupils are also taught here the various trades which may be either useful to a farmer remote from markets, or which can be followed as a business by the pupils. Blacksmiths' and carpenters' work, cooperage, the construction of agricultural implements, tailoring, shoemaking, and cabinet making, are included in the course of instruction, and connected with the school is a foundry, a brick-yard, a pottery, a tan-yard, and a wind-mill.

As by the testimony of candid travelers this establishment is well conducted, its influence must be extensively felt in the development of the agricultural resources of the country. Great care is taken in this school for farmers to show how the principles of agricultural science shall be applied to particular localities, so that the education of the pupils becomes eminently practical and available. At the conclusion of the course each graduate is presented with a farm and one thousand roubles to stock it, and the government encourages them to become, by theory and practice, the teachers of the neighborhood in which they are located.

Baron Haxthausen, whose notes on Russia are among the most reliable sources of information, made a close examination of one of these farms, and describes it as in a good state of cultivation, and as having exercised a marked influence upon the adjoining country. He found the farm house "comfortable and *scrupulously clean*"—there were books indoors and flowers without, and all the furniture of the house, as well as the farming tools and machinery, had been made by those who occupied the farms.

A second government school of this description, on a very extensive scale, is now in a flourishing condition at Lipezk, in south Russia, and, in addition to this, a horticultural school has also been established by the emperor, and placed in charge of some German teachers. Separate from these schools for special purposes, is a school system for the empire, yet in its youth, but which promises great results for the future, and is indeed already exerting a transforming power upon the character of the nation.

The whole of Russia is divided into university districts, with a district university in each with subordinate schools attached, and at the head of them all is the National Univerity at Moscow. All the schools of each district are under the charge of the district university. It is a completely organized national system, which when fully carried out, will make the means of education universal in Russia.

The following statements, condensed by the *London Quarterly* from the "Notes" of Baron Haxthausen, will be found interesting, as affording accurate information concerning the schools, and some of the institutions of Moscow, and throwing light upon the spirit and aims of the government:

"Few capitals can boast so many educational institutions as now exist at Moscow under the crown patronage. Beginning with the University, the Baron speaks of the upper professors as fully acquainted with all that has been written in other countries on their respective subjects, nor is he less pleased with the state of the numerous schools subordinate to this University. Other schools are, those of commerce (partly supported by the Merchants of Moscow), of drawing, for soldiers' orphans, and for cadets; but the greatest of all seems to be the Imperial House of Education, founded by Catharine II. It has at least twenty-six thousand children belonging to it, either within its walls or put out to nurse in the country—all of them orphans of officers, or foundlings. Of the children in the house, the boys are brought up to be schoolmasters or to be sent to the University;

the girls to be governesses—learning German, French, drawing, dancing, history, geometry, and music, besides sewing, knitting, etc. Places are found for them, by-and-bye, but not in either of the capitals, which are thought unsafe for "unprotected females." They are watched for six years, and if marriage comes in their way proper inquiries are made about the swain. Attached to the institution is a school of Arts, the pupils of which are thoroughly trained in the practice of some one of the different trades that figure on the list, and which are in number *seventeen.*"

Among the educational institutions of Russia, the public libraries of St. Petersburgh should not be omitted. The Imperial Library is one of the largest in the world. It contains four hundred thousand volumes, and fifteen thousand manuscripts. It is open daily for the use of the public. It is a curious fact that some of the most valuable of the state documents of France are now found in the Russian Imperial Library. During the French revolution, these treasures of the French government were seized by the populace and sold to the highest bidder, who proved to be a Russian, and by whom they were forwarded to St. Petersburgh. There has been gathered here—partly by purchase, partly by presents, and also by the spoils of war—one of the very best collections of oriental works to be found in the world. The library of the Academy of Science contains one hundred thousand volumes, and that of the Hermitage has one hundred and twenty thousand.

The present condition of Russian literature, and the activity of the public mind, may be shown from the fact that in the ten years next preceding 1843, seven millions of volumes of Russian books were printed, and nearly five millions of volumes of foreign works were imported. In a single year of this period, eight hundred and eighty works were printed and published within the Russian empire, and only seventy of these were translations from foreign tongues. The whole subject of education is committed to one of the great departments of state, at the head of which is the Minister of Public Instruction.

This is necessarily an imperfect sketch of the educational institutions, in which many details are necessarily omitted, but enough has been exhibited to enable the reader to judge of the justice of the epithet "barbarian," so constantly applied to the empire of the Czars. No one will fail to perceive that these are only different parts of one grand and harmonious system. There is an admirable compactness and unity in the whole design, and two main ideas have evidently both originated and shaped the whole—first, as most important, the defense of the empire, and, secondly, the development of the national resources and the encouragement of domestic manufactures. In regard to the first of these many an invective has been hurled at Russia, because, as is charged, she consumes her strength in the equipment and support of an immense military force wherewith to threaten or overrun all western Europe; whereas instead, as is maintained, she should have devoted herself to the arts of peace and of internal growth. But a candid observer of the condition and progress of Europe from the time of the French revolution, will perhaps be inclined to admit that Russia has neither gone too fast nor too far in her military preparations, and that her policy has not only been a prudent but a necessary one. The invasion of 1812 was an admonition not soon to be forgotten, and Nicholas was too keen and too intelligent an observer of passing events not to foresee that a second attack on his nation was certain to be made, sooner or later, either by the infidel democracy of Europe, or if the republican movement should fail, then from the western Powers, directed by the Roman Catholic Church.

The control of the Black Sea is essential to the growth and even safety of Russia, and no Russian statesman has been ignorant how restive both England and France have been at the predominance of the power of the Emperor there. Under these circumstance Russia certainly showed a true sagacity in holding herself prepared, and the event justified the wisdom of her policy. What would have been the fate of the nation now, unless western Europe had found her with her harness on awaiting their approach.?

Russia can not preserve her nationality, her existence, far less execute the mission which she believes has been entrusted to her, unless she maintains a military force capable of resisting the combined power of western Europe, or at the very least, as the event has shown, the united strength of England and France. She maintains her immense force to secure herself from successful attack, not for foreign conquest. Instead of sacrificing internal development to the support of an army and navy, she maintains them in order that within their circling lines and guns the works of peace may make secure progress in the heart of the empire. France and England have intruded themselves where they have no right to interfere with the growth of Russia, which has been more legitimate, more reputable, and marked with less injustice to the weak, than the progress of either of her adversaries. As has been well observed by an English writer, France made more aggressions upon neighboring nations in the space of ten years than Russia has done in as many centuries; and when England complains of Russia let her think of her East Indian exploits. These things do not lessen the guilt of Russian aggressions, but they ought to silence these her special and busy accusers, who arraign her at the tribunal of public opinion, as if they alone were innocent of ambition, or oppression, or robbery.

After the safety of the nation has been cared for, the government turns its next care to internal national development; and certainly no nation in the world can boast of a more enlightened, thorough, or scientific system of instruction than Russia herself has established. The great sources of her national strength, and from which she derives her vitality, are agriculture, her mines, and her manufactures. Constructing as a basis of educational operations a complete national sytem, which is extending itself regularly with the progress of the country, she has then provided schools of the most magnificent character, to give the minds of the Russian youth that special direction which is demanded by the character and policy of the country; and from these schools, as centers, an influence is diffused through the whole nation by which the resources of the empire are sought out and developed by a combination of science with mechanical skill.

It is doubtful whether any other nation of the world has studied its own resources more carefully, or instituted a more effectual method for making them available. A nation capable of such designs, and of executing them on a scale of such grandeur, deserves not the name barbarian.

# CHAPTER XXVI.

## THE CHARACTER OF THE RUSSIAN INTELLECT.

Having made a partial exhibition of the elements of greatness which belong to the Russian Empire, it may be well to pause before the introduction of additional statements on these points, and bestow some attention upon the mental characteristics of the race in whose hands these resources and advantages have been placed in the providence of God. This, perhaps, will enable us to determine the probable character of Russian civilization, and its future influence upon the destiny of Europe and America. Two interesting questions here present themselves. Will Russia assume a form of civilization, individual and national—a Russian or Sclavonic civilization—and if so, what will be its distinctive characteristics? It is a common remark of French and English writers, that Russia produces nothing original, that she is destitute of the creative power of genius, and possesses only the imitative character of some of the oriental nations, and is therefore doomed like them to the inferior life of a mere copyist of western Europe. She is represented as wearing the garments of civilization after the manner of a savage; a European exterior, which can not conceal the barbarian. No intelligent opinion can be formed of the future of this great empire, until we decide whether such representations are true or false. In the very beginning of such an investigation it should be remembered that even the highest forms of genius must operate with materials already in existence, that strictly speaking it creates nothing, and that its most signal triumphs are won by presenting familiar things in a new light, and throwing them into original combinations.

Every modern nation to a great extent is necessarily an imitator. Our age is the heir of the past, and has come into possession of the treasures of thought and art accumulated by preceding generations, and the only question which remains is, whether from this stock of material, common to all Christendom now, a nation can rear a social, political, and religious structure, which shall exhibit a distinctive and individual character? The nations of the modern world are all the inheritors of the mingled Greek and Roman civilization, and these forms of national life have been developed, in western Europe, from the materials thus supplied—the Latin, the German, and the Anglo-Saxon. These, however, are being now mingled, and the original individuality by which they were distinguished is disappearing, and a constantly increasing intercourse is sweeping away the peculiarities of each. It would appear impossible, under present circumstances, for any one of the nations of western Europe to work out hereafter a separate and individual destiny, or to pursue a strictly national policy. Each is molding each, and society must become the resultant of conflicting forces. Europe can neither be English, nor French, nor German, nor can either nation retain the sharp distinctness of its own original outline.

It remains to be seen what excellencies these mingled elements may exhibit as they combine. Still Germany, France, and England, stamping their own characteristics upon the materials furnished by the ancient world, have each produced a national form of civilization, a form which France shares with the other branches of the Latin family. In the same manner the Roman forms received the impress of the Grecian mind, and thus Greece herself softened and adorned the stately gigantic grandeur of Egypt. Nor will it be easy to discover any nation this side the deluge that has originated, strictly speaking, its modes of thought and expression, and its form of national life. Wherever we search we find something still due to the past; a former age has bequeathed its legacy of wisdom and experience.

If, then, Russia is able to avail herself of the materials which the age affords her, and can construct from them a national edifice which shall bear the impress of a distinct national character, the world must then admit that she possesses an originating power, and can produce a Russian civilization which, in the end perhaps, will assume the more definite, as well as more comprehensive name, Sclavonian. This she may do, although the style of her architecture and dress, her manufactures, tools, weapons, etc., have the European form. America presents an example of what is here intended. Through forms which, with the exception of the political structure, are essentially European, there appears an individual, an American life, which, with each succeeding year, will become more distinct and dominant, till the ultimate result is reached, not an Anglo-Saxon, but an *American* civilization, separate and peculiar.

The people of the United States are continually reminded that they are mere blind imitators of what others perform, that they have no literature, or art, or science, of their own, or independent national life or character. Doubtless this is to a great extent true, or rather it has been true. Still it should have been remembered, that nothing less than a miracle on the most extended scale could have enabled an English colony, with the task of subduing a continent on their hands, to present at once all the phenomena of an independent national existence. The question should rather have been, whether a germ had been planted here, which, in its maturity should have not only a territory but a name, a character, a history of its own.

Such considerations should not be lost sight of in forming an estimate of the present condition and prospects of

Russia. For although, if we adopt the mere reckoning of years, Russia may be considered old, yet her true national career dates back not more than a hundred years; and indeed it was not until the reign of Catharine II., that she first appeared as a great nation upon the theater of Europe. At the time of the landing of the Pilgrims at Plymouth the population of the Empire was about twelve millions, at the death of Peter the Great, in 1725, about twenty millions, and at the ascension of Catharine II., in 1763, about twenty-five millions. One hundred years, then, is quite as long a time as can reasonably be assigned as the true national life of the Muscovite nation, for the impulse given to the nation's growth by Peter the Great was subsequently lost in a great degree, and the attempt to improve the country was made in a new direction. It is then quite too soon to charge Russia with a want of original power; the capabilities of the Sclavonic race are yet but in the germ.

In studying the future of this nation, we should regard not so much the Russia which now is, as that which is so rapidly forming itself from the mass of accumulated material. Travelers have deceived themselves and misled others by dwelling upon and magnifying the fact of the existence of many races within the limits of the empire, describing it as a mere aggregation which must soon fall asunder. They forget that there has been a rapid acquisition of territory and population, and that sufficient time has not yet elapsed to secure a complete consolidation of the mass. But had they looked a little beyond the external aspect of things, and studied with some care the actual movement of the forces which shape the course of the nation, they would have discovered a central life power which, with an almost unexampled energy, is diffusing itself through the whole national mass, assimilating or displacing whatever it touches, and aided in its operations by the settled policy of the government. They would have discovered one dominant race, compacted by every tie that can bind a people together, inspired by common hopes and a common ambition, wielding a power before which all else disappears, either by incorporation or removal, and which, unless arrested by the providence of God, will inevitably fill the vast territory of Russia with one single family, with one language, one literature, one government, and one religion.

Of the mental characteristics of this race, then, we should gain, if possible, a distinct idea, in order to estimate the future—because the future will be the work of their hands. There are three methods of estimating the mental characteristics of a people. They may be studied, as exhibited in individuals, or in those public manifestations which are the expressions of national thought, or in the characters of those great men who sometimes stand forth as the exponents of their age, an individual expression of the characteristics of a nation. The true Russian possesses in an eminent degree energy, activity, and fertility of resource. He is found in every part of the empire, as a merchant, a mechanic, a pedlar, a speculator, and in all society his is the ruling spirit; he is the shrewd, successful man, to whom others give place—removed from his path by superior skill, or force, or fraud, as circumstances seem to demand. Society receives from him its impulse—new schemes are hatched in his brain—he drives the sharpest bargain—and, like other sharp men, he overreaches and deceives. Some travelers speak of him in terms that might have been borrowed from the descriptions given by southern men of the pedlars and clock-sellers from New England. The Russian universally thinks or says *he can.* His disposition is to surmount obstacles, or sweep them from his path. He endures the toil, and labors hopefully on.

De Custine, who was filled with true French disgust every moment while in Russia, who saw almost nothing that he could approve, has, nevertheless, recorded this national characteristic as a noble trait. He says, "One of the most "attractive traits in their character, at least in my opinion, "is their dislike to objections; they refuse to recognise "either difficulties or obstacles. With his hatchet in his "hand, which he never lays aside, a Russian peasant "triumphs over accidents and predicaments which would "altogetner stop the villagers of our own provinces, and he "answers 'yes' to everything that is demanded of him." In such a character there are at least the elements of power, and a capacity for progress. The native force of the mind may, in the uncultivated and unregenerate man, break forth in acts of unkindness and cruelty, but this same strength, if properly directed, might also be employed in creating a national power that would bless the world.

His versatility of talent and power of imitation render the Russian a most successful scholar, and he makes rapid progress in whatever he undertakes. The raw recruit is transformed, in an incredibly short period, into one performing correctly the evolutions of the regular soldier, and assumes with great facility the air of the camp. He is capable of being metamorphosed as suddenly into a tradesman, a mechanic, or a pedlar. He is crafty, and to a remarkable degree insinuating in his address, and without being distinguished for muscular strength, is capable of great endurance.

The Russian can scarcely be considered as possessing the military spirit in the ordinary acceptance of that phrase. His nature does not prompt him to arm himself and sally forth in quest of adventure and conquest. He is neither a sea king, to rove the seas for booty, nor a knight errant, fighting for renown and the mere love of battle. He plans no revolutionary uprisings for the rights of universal humanity. He is more inclined to the peaceful arts of agriculture, manufactures and trade, wherein his skill and cunning can be exercised, and where success is obtained by superior activity and address rather than by blows. As a fighter he is distinguished more by resistance than aggression. His enemy shouts as victor in the first onset, but is generally exhausted by victory, and in the end destroyed. He conquers not in the assault, but in his defense.

The Russian army, therefore, has heretofore been far more formidable at home than abroad. For although the Russian prefers peace to battle, he defends his property and his country to the last extremity. No candid man will fail to perceive that a race possessing the qualifications which observers attribute to the true Russian, is capable of a higher form of civilization than the nation yet has reached. Fifty millions of people, with these characteristics, can not fail to make an impression upon the world. And, although the highest forms of genius have not yet been manifested, there are germs of intellectual power, whose future expansion may surpass the present expectations of the world. Russia needs the development which another century will give her, before her capabilities can be correctly estimated. The progress of the nation for the last hundred years corresponds, in a remarkable degree, to the course of the individual Russian. What he is to individuals of other races, Russia has been, and is, to the nations on her frontier. She has made an aggressive progress, and without direct wars of conquest, has continued to absorb one portion of territory after another, till she has swallowed up the contiguous countries, or important portions of their domain.

Another method of determining the mental qualities of a people is by observing the public manifestations of thought, in which the general mind of a people will embody itself, such as their public works and institutions, their national policy, the national structure which becomes the exponent of the popular thought. Such productions are often ascribed to the genius of the individual mind, and a nation is often regarded as the creation of its great men, molded by them as clay in the hands of the potter. But this idea should be received with important qualifications. The man of genius, in whatever department he moves, is in a great degree the exponent of national thought, which through him obtains expression, and he becomes a national favorite because each one beholds at least a partial revelation of himself. When a great poet arises, it is as if the hitherto dumb nation had found its speech. Similar thoughts had long been floating chaotically through the popular mind—thousands of hearts had been stirred with similar feelings, and at last all are delighted to find them so well expressed. The national soul has found its interpreter. Even when the poet, like Shakspeare, addresses himself to universal humanity, his work still bears the individual impress of his nation. Shakspeare is the poet of the race, but his poem is English still. There was a basis in the English mind for such a production as his. Burns gave an articulate expression to the thoughts and feelings of the Scottish peasantry, and wherever we direct inquiry an individual national mind is found, which, by the aid of genius, finds expression in national works and institutions.

The wondrous creations which made glorious the valley of the Nile, are not to be regarded as simply the conceptions of individual artists, but as expressions of national thought. The grandeur has clothed itself in Egyptian forms, the enormous structures enshrining the vastness and elegance of Egyptian thought. They exhibited the individuality of the national mind. So also the poets, the orators, the statesmen, the philosophers, the artists of Greece, were all formed after a Grecian intellectual model; there was a national Grecian soul that molded the genius of the individual. If we study a nation as a whole, in all its productions, in all its actions, in the character and direction of its public efforts, we behold in them all combined but the legitimate out-growth of the national mind, the outward forms in which the thought of the nation has expressed itself—even as a plant unfolds itself from its germs.

Russia, when judged by this standard, will neither appear like a mere barbarian nor as only the servile imitator of the rest of Europe. In the national structure which she is erecting there are already individual features, and a largeness of conception, that give promise of a future greatness which shall be known as her own, bearing the impress of the Russian mind. Her territorial idea, which she is so rapidly working out, is the grandest conception of the kind of modern times—perhaps of any age. Bonaparte himself, unless in some of his day-dreams of an eastern empire, with its capital at Alexandria or Constantinople, never conceived of such a kingdom as that whose image fills the national mind of Russia as a definite object of pursuit, and toward which she has thus far made a steady advance. There is much more of folly than of wisdom in sneering at a nation which proposes for itself an empire that rests one broad wing on the Atlantic, and the other on the Pacific, with one capital controlling the Baltic and the adjacent seas, and the other on the Dardanelles—and which has so nearly converted her original conception, vast as it is, into a historic reality. There is grandeur even in the thought of such a dominion, and we may well marvel how it could have originated with a people that was hemmed in on every side by surrounding nations more powerful than themselves, without a ship, or even a sea-port; but when we behold that secluded race expanding itself on every side, swelling out to the proportions of its great idea, devising the means by which it has wrought successfully on toward its ultimate purpose, until it seems now to have nearly reached its goal, in spite of the opposition of Europe, it is far wiser to study such a fact than to turn away with a scoff at the "barbarians."

It is simply absurd to deny that the successful working out of such an idea is a task which can be executed only by a people capable of greatness. The morality of Russian progress is no more to be admired or defended than are the national acts of the other Powers of Europe, or even the method of our own growth, but viewed as a creation of human intellect, and, throwing out of sight the means employed, Russia, as she is, may well challenge the respect of the world. The morality of her national acts will scarcely suffer in comparison with that of her *civilized* neighbors. The treachery, fraud, oppression and cruelty of others do not, of course, justify her own similar acts, but England, France, and even America, might well shed some penitential tears over portions of their own territory before they sit in judgment upon Russia.

Again, the conception of her plan of national defense, and her execution of the work, is an exhibition of the character of the Russian mind. She has not only created a powerful navy, but she has constructed for this navy places of security, where the two great maritime Powers of the world have not as yet, in two campaigns, been able to touch an important prize. She holds still her naval treasures safe for her future need. Her great fortifications have been built on a scale of grandeur, and have been equipped with a science which baffles as yet the military skill of Europe, and these, too, are exponents of the national mind, and are proofs of its capacity. The same vastness of idea characterizes the whole military establishment of the country, and is also stamped upon the schools, and indeed upon every department of the government. There is not seen as yet, perhaps, a perfect adaptation of part to part in the great machine, but there is a largeness of idea that gives promise of a most imposing future.

The idea so often insisted upon, that all this is the work of foreigners, is as puerile as that with which England pleased herself so long, that our naval victories were won by the valor of English sailors on board our ships. Russia is doubtless largely indebted to foreign science and skill, and so also is America. But this foreign aid has only served, in both countries, to assist the growth of the native mind, and the foreign effort has been shaped by the national model. With all the assistance which has been rendered, Russia is not a foreign nation, and America is American still. The diplomacy of a nation also affords a criterion whereby to judge of national capabilities. Russian intellect has long been tested in the councils of Europe in its encounter with the most cultivated and distinguished men of the surrounding nations, and no one has yet pretended that the diplomatic agents of the Czar have been deficient in talent or skill, or that they have been wanting in success.

On the contrary, Russia has enlarged and enriched herself more by her skill in negotiation than by the conquests of her armies. She is, it is true, largely accused of duplicity, and even fraud and bribery, but until the hands of other Powers have been somewhat cleansed, such charges may be regarded, perhaps, as an expression of those who have been losers in a game where all parties alike were endeavoring to play with marked cards and loaded dice. Had Russia possessed no capacity but such as manifests itself in treachery and cunning, a lofty and unspotted integrity on the part of the other Powers might have baffled her long ago; but there is much reason for believing that the Czar and his ministers have merely foiled the neighboring cabinets in the use of their own weapons. Russian diplomacy, it must be confessed, is not distinguished for frankness and integrity, but it certainly evinces great sagacity and consummate skill, while it is not easy to show that in her political morality she has fallen below the standard of her cotemporaries. The vast conception of an empire which she holds steadily before her mind, and which by gigantic effort she has well-nigh realized, her immense military system, with the resources she has accumulated, the science and skill evinced in her admirable schools and other governmental institutions, the style of her one modern city, and the success of her diplomacy, are all so many witnesses that indicate the power and the characteristics of Russian mind.

The Russian empire, as it now is, huge, imposing, impregnable as it seems as yet to be, is the production of Russian thought, as truly as was the Egyptian or Grecian civilization the proper out-growth of the national mind. The national idea is one of grand proportions; it has taken full possession of the public thought, and it lies clearly defined even before the mind of the Russian peasant. It has shaped itself into a settled public policy, and this policy is the expression of the desires, and hopes, and determinations of the great Russian family. Russia gravitates by a law of her national life toward Constantinople; her never-ceasing endeavor is to realize the national conception of the empire, and in all her operations she has exhibited a capacity for enlarged thought, a power of extensive combination, and a skillful adaptation of means to ends, not second to any Power in Europe. If she is still to be considered only as a barbarian nation, then, in some important branches, civilization may well become the pupil of barbarism.

Another method of determining ths characteristics of a race, and of measuring its capabilities, is by studying its great men. A truly great man is the exponent of his age and nation. He combines in himself the chief qualities of his race. In the youth of a nation a great man is in himself a prediction and guaranty of national greatness; in its manhood he represents his country as she is; in its decay he is but a proud memorial of the past. Thus Hildebrand was the true prophet of the Roman Catholic Church. He first conceived and clearly defined the great idea which has since been the center of its life, and shape, and growth. Charlemagne was the individual expression of his age. Alexander was the true exponent of the Macedonian thought. Louis XIV. was the embodied France of that age, and Chatham exhibited England in her proudest hour; and the men of the American Revolution were predictions of the American future. In the same manner Nicholas may be regarded as the true exponent of Russia as she is, and the earnest of what she will become. He was not only thoroughly Russian in feeling and aims, but he so combined in himself the chief qualities of Russian character as to be a true representative of his nation, and Russia may be properly studied in him. He was more thoroughly Russian than any other man in the empire, though his family was in part of German origin.

But the future of Russia will be shaped not alone by *Russians*, but by the combined power of the great Sclavonic race, organized around a common center, and working out the problem of a common national life.

# CHAPTER XXVII.

## TERRITORIAL PROGRESS OF RUSSIA.

In connection with these observations upon the characteristics of Russian mind, it is interesting to consider the actual progress of the Empire, and observe whether it corresponds to these supposed capabilities of the race, and in what direction the national effort has been made. It will be seen that the policy of the nation has been steadily shaped toward certain definite aims, that have not been lost sight of at least for a hundred years, while Nicholas has been the first to conceive a truly national scheme fittted to accomplish the national purpose. This purpose embraced several distinct points, viz: general territorial enlargement, the control of the Baltic and the adjacent seas, the control of the Black Sea and the Dardanelles, an outlet for her Siberian possessions on the Pacific, and a station there for a great eastern naval depot for a Pacific fleet and the East Indian commerce. In 1452, at the time of the fall of the Greek Empire, the territory of Russia was estimated at a little more than two hundred thousand square miles, not quite equal to four States the size of Illinois, and its population was only about six millions. It had not a single seaport, nor any independent method of communication with the commerce of the world. At the accession of Peter the Great, in 1689, the territory had been increased to nearly four millions of square miles, while the population was still but fifteen millions. At the present time her territory is considered to be equal to about seven millions square miles, and her population is variously estimated from seventy millions to eighty millions. The following account of the steps of Russian progress is taken from Alison's History of Europe:

1721.—The battle of Pultowa and the treaty of Neustadt gave the Russians the province of Livonia, and the site where Cronstadt and St. Petersburgh now stand.

1772.—The frontier of the Empire, on the side of Poland, was brought down to the Dwina and the Dnieper.

1774.—By the treaty of Kainardji, the Muscovite standard was brought down to the Crimea and the Sea of Azoff. At about the same time acquisitions from Tartary were made, larger than the whole German Empire.

1783.—The Russian sway was extended over the Crimea, and the vast plains which stretch between the Euxine and the Caspian, as far as the foot of the Caucasus.

1792.—The treaty of Jassy advanced the frontier to the Dniester, and Odessa was brought beneath their rule.

1793.—In this year they obtained command of Lithuania.

1794.—The Russians extended their frontier to the Vistula, and nearly half of the old kingdom of Poland was obtained. The peace of Tilsit rounded their eastern frontier by a considerable province.

1809.—Russia attained the whole of Finland, as far as the Gulf of Bothnia.

1812.—Her southern frontier was extended to the Pruth, and she gained partial possession of the mouths of the Danube.

1800 to 1814.—Many conquests were made from the Persians and Circassians, and Georgia obtained.

1815.—The Grand Duchy of Warsaw was added to the Empire.

1828.—The Araxes became the southern frontier of their Asiatic territories.

1834.—The Dardanelles were closed to armed vessels, and the Black Sea was open only to her ships of war; and whether France and England will succeed in holding open the gates of the Euxine, or whether they will be closed forever against them, remains yet to be seen.

Since the above dates, additional territory has been obtained in Poland; a province has been gained from China, on the Pacific, which gives Russia the command of the river Amoor, navigable in the direction of south-eastern Siberia, for more than two thousand miles, and affording a most important naval station at its mouth.

Such has been the actual progress of Russia, and such is her present position. With her position, resources, and means of defense sufficient to arrest the combined power of France and England at one of her outposts, it is difficult to understand how a reasonable man can entertain the idea that Russia can now be persuaded or compelled to abandon the settled policy which is interwoven with the thoughts and desires of the whole nation, surrender those advantages which it has cost the labor of a century, and an immense expenditure of life and treasure to obtain, and give up the very purposes for which the Russian government exists.

Russia has too strong a faith in her national mission, to be easily checked in her career, or to be turned permanently aside from the line of her nation's march. The demands which the Allies made upon her, required a complete revolution in her national policy, the surrender of her settled scheme of Empire. They asked, indeed, that modern Russia should cease to exist, and that the Empire should be rolled back a hundred years in policy and position, and should return to its former state of seclusion. France and England virtually demanded that Russia should retire from the field of Europe, and yield the control of the world to them; and it may be safely predicted, that the Muscovite will never do this while he has people and arms.

# CHAPTER XXVIII.

## RUSSIA AIMS AT A CIVILIZATION DISTINCT FROM THAT OF WESTERN EUROPE.

The popular opinion concerning Russia may, perhaps, be expressed in a single sentence—her government is a horrible despotism, and she is the determined foe of liberty, the chief barrier to European progress. This assumption underlies all the attempts which have been made, both in Europe and America, to arouse against her the indignation of the world. Another outcry was popular on both sides of the Atlantic, that the ferocious Northern Bear was about to seize and devour the Lamb of Turkey, and an armed world was bound to rush to the rescue. If this were disinterested benevolence, if those who raised the cry were not so anxious to be the guardians of the lamb for the sake of the fleece, or to appropriate it entirely to their own use, it would be entitled to more respect. But if the lion wars against the bear merely because he desires the prey himself, it is not needful, on this account, that American sympathies should be strongly excited. Another English charge against Russia is made more particularly for home consumption. It is that Russia will not consent to adopt the free trade system, and render herself, on that account, a huge dependency of England, but insists on protecting her own industry, and applies herself to the steady development of her own resources. Russia thus threatens to become the competitor of England in the markets of the world, and so England sends forth her fleets and armies in the name of progress and liberty to cripple and arrest her too rapid growth.

The charge that Russia is a cold-hearted despotism, and that she is the chief opponent of European civilization, should be studied in the light of some facts which seem to have received little attention from many of those who are striving to stir up the human race against her. She is shaping a civilization of her own, distinct from that of western Europe, based on a separate idea, and intended for a separate race, and in connection with a distinct form of religion. The value of this, her national conception, can only be estimated by studying carefully the genius of her own people, and also the condition of the rest of Europe, and the character of the influences by which the western nations are controlled. The system of Russia is intended for a separate and peculiar race; her national idea is not only Sclavonic in its origin, but it is Sclavonic also in its design. It is a home system, a family institution on a great scale, which she wishes to conduct upon a model of her own; and before she is utterly condemned, it would be well to take a calm survey of the actual state of affairs of Europe. Three distinct forms of civilization are at this moment struggling for pre-eminence on the field of western Europe—the Papal, which allies itself to civil despotism; the infidel democratic; and the Protestant, which connects itself with the idea of constitutional liberty. These three systems are quite distinct from each other in theory, and are separate as actual movements, though the friends of each are not yet drawn into separate communities.

It is necessary to study the character of each of these forces, now contending for the mastery in western Europe, before we can be prepared to form an accurate opinion of the policy of Russia. The central idea of the Papacy, upon which the whole system is based, is this: the Roman Catholic Church is the one only true church of the world—that out of her pale there neither is nor can be salvation—that to her, as the one true church, belongs the supreme power of the world, vested in her head, the Pope—and that he, reigning in the stead, and by the authority of Jesus Christ himself, is the rightful king of kings, and that he, at his pleasure, may plant or subvert all civil power, as subservient to the proper authority of the church; and that it is his duty to overthrow every government which rejects the Roman Catholic communion, because it is heretical. Infallible in doctrine, she claims it to be her duty to prescribe a faith for all men, and she considers the mission of the Romish Church to be to stretch its scepter over all the earth, to embrace all the kingdoms of the world in one universal monarchy, of which she, by the appointment of God himself, is the rightful head. This may be called the "Bill of Rights" of the Catholic Church, the Magna Charta which she has granted to the nations—the right to be governed in all things, temporal and spiritual, by the Pope, the heaven-appointed head of the one true church.

A right granted to all kings to receive their crowns at his hands, and from all men in authority to derive their authority from him, and the right to be punished as heretics if they assert the right of private judgment or of independent government. This is the one unchangeable idea of the Papacy—the essential nucleus of her system, the center of its life—to reign supreme over all the world, as the true representative of Jesus Christ, ruling in his stead, and wielding his authority as lord of lords and king of kings. This idea, from the time it was first proclaimed by Hildebrand, has never been abandoned, never lost sight of in her darkest hours, never despaired of amid her sorest defeats. This scheme, which seems worthy both of the intellect and pride of the lost archangel himself, is pressed at this time, with fresh activity and zeal, upon the attention of the world; and it presents a very grave subject of thought that, in this nineteenth century, when, according to the boast of some, the world has passed so far beyond the reach of every form of superstition, the renewal of the most absurd pretension of the Catholic Church, instead of repelling all men from her, is adding to her popularity and strength. It has not been without a profound knowledge of human character, that the leaders of the Papacy have put forth the new dogma of the Immaculate Conception. It is not the offspring of a mere puerile conceit, but of a clear-seeing sagacity, which, knowing the weakness of men, uses it for its own purposes, and which understands perfectly that no mere intellectual progress, no influence of what we call modern improvement can, of themselves, save men from the grossest superstition, or secure them against the vilest imposture of a religious character.

So far as mere worldly policy is concerned, the Roman Catholic Church is wise in assuming the loftiest ground of Hildebrand, and the Innocents. The very loftiness of her demands, bordering even upon absurdity, will secure the respect and belief of thousands. The same world that scoffs at moderate pretensions is inclined to worship the man that resolutely persists in declaring himself a god. In reviving, therefore, the most preposterous demand of their church in the middle ages, and in adding thereto the new dogma of the Immacnlate Conception, the leaders of the Papacy are really playing a safer game with the credulity of the world than if they had moderated their pretensions. The Romish Church, as a mere religious denomination, one church among many, is simply a contemptible juggler, that could not command the respect of the lowest; but that same church, expanded to the gigantic proportions of the rightful ruler of the world, walking in queenly robes, and wearing the triple crown, demanding homage and obedience as the vicegerent of the Lord Jesus, will excite wonder and fear, and even the spirit of worship, though in the nineteenth century, and amid railroads, and printing-presses, and telegraphs.

A church that proposes to stoop to the level of human reason, and make herself and her doctrines fully understood by the unregenerate mind, will obtain such measure of regard as the rationalist is willing to bestow—no more. But a church that throws itself above reason, that commands the obedience of reason, in the name of God, will make even the philosopher tremble. For this reason, we often behold some proud and lofty intellect rejecting the truths of salvation as taught by the Protestant Church, yielding itself to the pretensions of Romanism, or mastered by a pride and audacity superior to its own. To abate one tittle of her proudest claims would be fatal to the Romish Church.

The strong reactionary movement of the Roman Catholic Church throughout Christendom is one of the most significant facts of the present time. A short time since, it seemed as if her power was broken forever. She appeared to be not only at the mercy of the people, but to be rejected by them and doomed to destruction. The Pope fled before the revolutionary wave, and most perhaps supposed that the long-predicted overthrow of the Papacy had finally come. It seemed altogether improbable that its influence could be again restored, and many looked for the speedy triumph of Protestantism in Europe. Now, that Papal power has not only arisen from its apparent defeat, but is wielding at this moment the controlling influence of western Europe; scorning all companionship with the world that attacked her, she re-asserts all the proudest claims of the church in the hour when monarchs bowed before her, and has made a great and skillful effort for the recovery of her supremacy over the nations. Once more her Jesuits are busy in embroiling the world. In Jerusalem, at Constantinople, in the court of France, they fan the fires of strife, and direct the western Powers upon Russia. The jealousy, ambition, and pride of England, are successfully played upon, until she marches her armies under the guidance of a Papal flag, while every effort is made to win the nation as a whole back to the support of the Pope.

In the United States a well concerted and persevering attack is made upon the very life of American Protestant institutions; the money of Europe is freely used for our overthrow; the strife of parties is employed to weaken the national sentiment; the same spirit which has directed the armies of France and England upon Russia, is excited in regard to our own country, and there wants but the fitting opportunity, and we may expect an armed attack originating in the same motives which gave rise to the war on Russia. The Papal power is in the ascendancy in the councils of western Europe, and all influences tend swiftly to a combination of the Latin nations, with France to lead them, on which new union of these civil Powers the Papal throne will rest once more, for a time at least, securely. This is one of the forms of civilization which are now in conflict with each other in Europe. Its ambition is as wide as the globe, it aims at nothing less than the supreme dominion over all nations. History records the means which it has been accustomed to employ to secure its ends, and these same methods it will use again when occasion offers, with whatever new instrumentalities the modern world is able to supply. What this power can do for the world is already known.

The condition of society where the Papacy has had undisputed sway is too clearly marked to admit of a mistake. The sickening monuments of her misrule stand thick upon the earth. Liberty has been crushed, public and private morality has been destroyed, industry has been crippled, and thought has been repressed. Yet, inexplicable as it may appear, upon any theory of the supposed advance which the human mind has made in these days of light and philosophy, the nations are rallying once more, in an unexpected manner, around the Papal throne. There may be much which is merely political in the movement, but there is nothing in the moral or mental condition of Europe which forbids the idea that the Papacy may yet bind the people of the west of Europe by an earnest faith in her pretensions. The science, and steam, and railroads, and printing presses of the nineteenth century have not lifted men above the influence of superstition or religious imposture. On the contray, just in proportion as man recedes from the true light and God, in his liability to embrace false religion, and there is but a step between the present

20

infidelity of Europe and the blindest superstitions of the Roman Catholic Church.

Against the Papal form of civilization Russia would be strongly and watchfully opposed, from two principal considerations: first, since the separation of the original church into the Latin and Greek churches, the Papal power has waged constant warfare upon the Greek church, and has left no measure untried to move or force it into subjection to the Papal scepter. The quarrel between the two churches has been carried on for almost a thousand years; it is bitter and irreconcileable. Russia, as the present head or representative of the Greek church, is the inheritor of this ancient religious war, and of course, would regard with watchful jealousy any movement of the ancient enemy of her ancient mother church, and now equally an enemy to herself. More especially would the Russian government guard itself against the power of the Roman Catholic church in the latter portion of the reign of Nicholas, when the movement among the Latin nations in favor of the Papacy has been so marked, and when a disposition has been growing in England unfriendly to Russia, and a tendency to unite with the Papal Powers against her. The Roman Catholic church is not only the most bitter foe of Russia, as head of the Greek church, but she has been busy in arraying western Europe for the overthrow of the power of the Czar. Russia stands in opposition to the Papacy from the necessity of self-preservation.

The very same feeling which has roused the American mind in regard to the Papal Power and its designs and aggressions, has excited the Russian nation also, and with far more reason, for the attacks upon Russia have been more palpable and open: it was but too evident that Rome was aiming at the prosperity and even the life of Russia, and therefore Nicholas was on his guard. The sense of danger, and the necessity of uniting his people for self-defense by the power of one national faith, induced Nicholas to separate some Russian communities from a union with the Roman Catholic church, and this has been denounced as bigotry and intolerance. The *Edinburgh Review*, for April 1855, says: "He gave a persecuting character to the Russian church, and waged a war of a sanguinary character against the Roman Catholic faith in "Poland." If a man is justified in defending his home from the intrigues of a spy, or the meditated violence of an enemy, then is the Russian government not to be blamed for repelling everywhere in its dominions the influence of the Papacy.

The Czar was not blind to the character or designs of the Papal church, nor of the obvious tendency of affairs in Europe, and one necessary preparation for the blow which has been at last struck at Russia, was to exclude as far as possible Catholic influences from his dominions. There was no other safe course left for him to pursue. As a sovereign and protector of the interests of a vast country, he was bound to protect her against the presence and machinations of his country's hereditary, most active, and most bitter foe. If he performed his duty with severity or cruelty, for this he should be held responsible; but Americans, who are themselves awaking to a sense of the necessity of destroying the influence of the Papacy in the United States, or run the risk of destruction at its hands, will never join in an outcry against the Czar, because he was not disposed to permit the Papal Power to provide the means of annoyance or injury within his own dominions. Nicholas knew full well that no art of Jesuitism would be left untried to excite the spirit of dissatisfaction and to stir up revolt among his Polish subjects, and with the enemy nourished and sheltered in the bosom of Poland, how could he be prepared for that attack which he knew sooner or later would come from western Europe. With a strong Papal influence in Poland, where would now be the security of Russia in that portion of her territory, and how soon the Allied Powers would be able to kindle there the fires of insurrection.

A sound and justifiable policy dictated the exclusion of all Papal influence from the dominions of Russia, and

Americans, instead of condemning the Czar for the use of any proper measures for obtaining security from Jesuitical schemes, would show a statesman-like wisdom if they should look more narrowly than ever at the intrigues and designs of the Papacy here.

A second phase of civilization in Europe is the form aimed at by the revolutionary movement—that which seeks the establishment of Democratic institutions. To this, doubtless, Nicholas was inflexibly opposed, and therefore he is denounced as the foe to progress, and the enemy of freedom. To favor this idea, England and France are guilty of the mockery of inscribing Liberty on their banners when they march against the Muscovite. However strongly the Czar may be opposed to Republican institutions, he is fully matched in this opposition by Louis Napoleon and the English nobility, while the hatred of the latter of any rule of the people, any form of truly popular institutions, is more cordial than that of the Czar himself. Let the candid American reader once place himself in the position of the Emperor of Russia, let him look out on the revolutionary spirit of Europe from his point of view, and then he will be able better to understand, if he does not approve, the motives of the Czar in opposing the democratic movement, as earnestly as he does the power of the Roman Catholic Church. In the first place, it should be considered that an American starts with a deceitful assumption in regard to the democratic movement in Europe. He very naturally looks upon those engaged in it as he would upon so many Americans seeking a rational liberty embodied in republican forms, such as that for which our fathers toiled and died. But American Protestant republicanism is a widely different theory from that of European democracy. Let this difference be borne in mind, and let it be remembered also, that while Russia has steadily opposed European democracy she has been as uniformly the friend of America, and perhaps the motives of the Emperor may then be better understood. A firm, undoubting religious faith, and a regard for properly constituted authority, are among the controling ideas of the Russian mind. This faith is doubtless obscured by superstition, but still it is faith, though blindfolded and led astray, a faith strong enough to form one of the mightiest elements of national power. The respect for authority is also allied to a blind reverence even for despotism, but then every Christian mind will acknowledge that without these elements, viz: a religious faith, and a regard for proper authority, there can not be a State. The foundations of government are wanting where these are absent. How then would a man like Nicholas, educated in the forms and theories of his national church, cherishing as an individual an undoubting faith, and observant of the forms of worship, and referring all earthly authority, even his own, to God, regarding it as resting upon the Divine sanction, how would he look upon the democratic theories of modern Europe? He, in common with the rest of the world, would regard the whole movement as the direct fruit of the French revolution, and that would stand inseparably connected in his mind with the invasion of his country and the burning of Moscow. He, and every other Russian, would from these associations be led to look upon everything savoring of French opinions with extreme suspicion, or even with disgust.

It is not necessary, therefore, to regard the feelings and policy of Russia concerning the republican spirit of Europe, as arising *merely* from a love of tyranny or a hatred of constitutional forms of government. The Czar may well be excused if he should cherish strong feelings of distrust, and even dislike, of that spirit which, receiving its birth in France, rushed forth for the overthrow of all the constituted forms of society, which regarded nothing as sound, and from which nothing was safe, which swept over his own native land like a storm, and wrapped in flames some of the chief cities of his empire.

Again, the emperor of Russia from the very necessities of his education and belief, as well as the facts in the case, would look upon the democratic spirit of Europe as the spirit of atheism. It would be considered by him as an impious attempt to establish a government independent of the authority of God. To him it was a proposition to subvert the whole structure of society, to banish from the world morality and religion, to create a State, and institute a society, which should lie without the jurisdiction of God. Looking at the theory of the French philosophers of the revolution, at the results actually reached in reducing that theory to practice, how could a Russian prince regard it but as the spirit of atheism arrayed against every form of belief and worship, the spirit of lawlessness bent upon the leveling of all distinctions and the overthrow of every description of authority. Nor was the Russian emperor singular in such opinions. The most candid and judicious everywhere, while thankful for such good as was accomplished by the wild outbreak among the nations, headed by France, have regarded atheism as the central idea and moving power of that bloody era. It was not so much an attempt to obtain a rational freedom as the annihilation of every form of authority, and the removal of all restraint from the individual man. It was an effort to live without God in the world, upon the assumption that the authority of a government rests upon human compacts, and not upon God himself, thus annihilating the moral power of a State, and substituting instead the mere will of a present majority, with no recognition of the eternal right and wrong, nor of God as the ultimate Judge and Supreme Legislator. Nor can it be denied that this is the character and scope of the radical democratic movement of Europe even now. Doubtless there are many good and true men who sympathize with the disposition to overthrow both the civil and ecclesiastical despotism of the Continent, and who desire for the people a freedom based upon a Protestant faith, but this is not characteristic of the modern revolutionary spirit as a whole. In its essential principles it is the antagonism of religion as well as of monarchical forms of government. It abjures a Protestant faith as decidedly as the belief in the supremacy of the Pope. It rejects the cross as scornfully as the worship of saints. It places the Bible among the inventions of a priesthood, and the legends of monks. It substitutes a holiday for the Sabbath, and the theater, the saloon, and the club-house, for the worship of the sanctuary. Such is this movement in Europe in its most radical forms, such was its spirit as manifested in the French revolution, and such do we behold it in thousands who have made our own country their home.

European democracy must not be mistaken for, nor confounded with American republicanism. They have more points of antagonism than resemblance. The type of the one must be sought in the atheistic movement which was originated by the French philosophers of the Revolution, while the true model of the other is to be found in American society as it existed in the colonies and in the era of our Revolution. It separates man from his God, and recognizes no higher rule for human action than the present will of the present majority. This is the form of civilization which Red Republicanism would establish in Europe, and this also is the movement to which Russia has stood inflexibly opposed. That she has met it with the watchful spirit of despotic power is doubtless true. That she has been jealous of every movement in favor of popular liberty in Europe is also true—but it is also a fact, that the movements of the people have partaken of the infidel democratic spirit, with the single exception of Hungary, and how far that should form an exception we are not now prepared to judge. Had that revolution, however, became a general one, embracing Italy, Germany, and France, its character would have been that which has just been described, for such is the type of European democracy as a whole.

The interference of Russia in Hungary, unjustifiable as it was by any moral rule, was not a crusade against liberty, but a stroke of policy to secure Austria against that hour of need which now has come. Its sagacity as a measure of State policy, is sufficiently shown by the late negotiations, and the present position of Austria. Let it then be considered exactly what is meant by most European writers when they charge the Russian government with being the foe of liberty. It means that the whole spirit of the country is as strongly opposed as the Emperor himself to the idea of an infidel democracy, and that the Czar has shut his country up, as far as possible, against such influences, and discouraged and repressed it elsewhere, according to his power. It would be difficult to show how Europe would be improved by another French revolution—not local, but general in its character—ending, as it inevitably would, in the re-establishment of military despotisms. It certainly remains to be shown that even Russia would be improved, and the condition of the people ameliorated, by any form of freedom which rejects as its basis a Protestant faith. Russia has not directed her intrigues or her armies against American liberties, nor shown herself in any way unfriendly to our government or our progress.

The United States have been twice compelled to meet England in arms in order to preserve their liberties, and French and English intrigues have been full often arrayed against our interests even on this continent; and both these Powers have shown a constant desire to become the self-constituted "regulators" of American affairs, while Austria and the other Papal states have sought to overthrow the Republic by the influence of the Roman Catholic church; in short, there is no Power of Europe that has evinced so constant and consistent a friendship for this country as Russia. This so-called foe of liberty and progress has shown a steadfast regard for that people among whom liberty and progress are the two national ideas—the chief forces by which society is controlled. Americans, then, should certainly pause before they echo the clamor against Russia which has been raised by the Papal Powers and England, for the purpose of vailing their own designs, and to justify the Crimean war. It does not necessarily convict Russia of being the enemy of mankind, to prove that she excludes her most bitter foe from any influence in her affairs, or that she guards her interests and people from the intrigues of the Jesuits, or even that she does not favor a second edition of the scenes of the French Revolution.

She may do all this, and yet the government may have some scheme of its own for the elevation of humanity—some policy fitted for the advancement of the Russian people, different both from Red Republicanism, and from the civilization which is proposed for the world by the Roman Catholic Church. The exact character of the Russian government can not be understood from either French or English descriptions. Their writers observe and narrate with previously formed opinions to which Russia is made to conform, and their testimony is strongly colored by interest and prejudice. Such men visit Russia in order to see and describe the barbarous foe of liberty and civilization. They mark and paint in vivid colors whatever is objectionable in Russian society, or the general condition of the country, but feel no sympathy with a people struggling with heroic spirit against the difficulties that beset them, and endeavoring to work out a national destiny.

Another form of civilization which is striving to establish itself in Russia, is that which is the proper outgrowth of a Protestant faith. Its influence upon the destinies of the eastern world is probably less, so far as national councils are concerned, than at any time since the Reformation. The Papal influence is the ascendant power in the affairs of western Europe, and England declares that she prefers the reaction in favor of the Papacy, with the French nation to lead it, to the further advance of Russia. She is willing to see the Roman Catholic Church again lording it over the nations, if only Russia can be humbled. The influence which Protestantism now exerts in Europe is by the indirect and silent power of truth, and not by any great Protestant nation standing up in noble defense of the principles of the Reformation, as England has done in former times. America is at this moment the great Protestant Power of the world—as such she is watched, hated and plotted against by the Papacy, and as such, God is preparing her to execute her mission. But Russia is charged with hostility to Protestantism. The English journals declare that the Russian Church is as strongly opposed to a Protestant faith as

Romanism itself. The assertion is an unfounded one. The Russian Church is not intolerant in its nature, and has not one essential element of the Papacy. In the character of the church itself, there are no more reasons for hatred of Protestantism than are found in the Church of England against dissenters. The Russian Church is simply a national establishment, with the Greek form of worship.

The Romish Church is by theory, in spirit and practice, the changeless foe all that dissent from her dogmas and that refuse her communion. The tolerant spirit of the Russian Church, its tendency to affiliate with Protestants, was clearly shown in the reign of Alexander, when the government united its efforts with those of Protestant churches for the circulation of the Bible, and for the evangelizing the world. But now this policy, it has been said, has been abandoned, and Russia no longer co-operates even in the circulation of the Bible. This is true, but then the circumstances of this case are worthy of consideration. In the reign of Alexander, England was the ally of Russia against France. Alexander was sincerely desirous of elevating and refining his people; he wished to enter in earnest upon the career of national civilization, and he was disposed to regard with favor the English example of Protestant constitutional liberty, and as a basis of the work which he hoped to perform, he engaged in the circulation of the Bible, and encouraged the British Bible Society within his dominions.

But Nicholas was placed in entirely different circumstances. He found himself compelled to prepare for the approaching hostility of western Europe, including even Protestant England, notwithstanding her professions. He saw the Papacy and Protestantism, in the person of its chief champion, arraying themselves against his dominions, and with a far more comprehensive and clear-seeing mind than Alexander, he perceived that the future greatness and even safety of his country depended not upon giving to Russia the impress of western Europe, but upon the cultivation of a true Russian nationality. When, therefore, Protestantism, as represented by England, was gradually changing from an ally to the enemy of his throne, it was perfectly natural that he should think it needful to repress the growth of Protestant influences within his dominions. It is altogether unjust, in such circumstances, to accuse the Russian government of hostility to a Protestant faith. England has not always been so pure and disinterested in her policy as to scorn the idea of using even a religious influence for state purposes, and what American statesmen would desire that even the English church should obtain a wide influence in this country, while the government of England was not only showing unfriendly feelings but even making preparations for war, and allying herself with a Papal Power against us.

That Nicholas, under such circumstances as these, should discourage the spread of Protestantism in Russia, is surely not a very decided proof that he hated its principles; but it shows most conclusively that he was aware of the dangers that were gathering round him, and that he had the sagacity to perceive the most effectual method of defense, by strengthening the national sentiment and the attachment of the people to their national church. Discerning the real purposes of England through the veil of her diplomacy, it would have been suicidal in him to have adopted a different course. English Protestantism, in the hands of the *government*, is not a perfectly harmless thing, and what perplexities would now surround the Russian Court if a strong English religious influence had been permitted to establish itself in the country. In distinction from the three forms of society just mentioned—the Papal, the infidel democratic, and the Protestant as represented by England—Russia has been aiming at a civilization which shall be the joint result of the national religion, and the cultivation of an independent national life, a civilization not European, but, Russian—a political, social and religious structure, fitted to the genius of Sclavonians. These considerations, though they may not justify the policy of Russia in all respects, serve to explain her course, and to relieve her from the charge of mere wanton intolerance and bigotry, which has been argued against her. Candor should induce us to give her the full benefit of such explanations, and not to present a mere carricature of her faults.

The rapid progress which has been made by Russia within the last hundred years is conclusive proof that her system has in it the germ of a true life. Seventy millions of human beings can not be permanently ruled by a mere show and cheat, much less can they thus be taught to make swift advances in what elevates and refines the race. Nor can they long be crushed by a mere heartless despotism which has in it no element of good, which affords no protection to the people, and bestows no blessing, and where society exists for the benefit of a single man and his court. Such a system has no perpetual lease of life, even among a barbarous people. But Russia presents the spectacle of an enduring and an improving life. Individuals have been often hurled from the throne, but the system itself has remained unshaken, still constantly accepted by the people, and tending also continually towards the adoption of more liberal forms. These facts give evidence of the existence of a true life, of a system which has been called into being by the actual wants of a people, and which continue, because with all its faults those wants are at least in some degree supplied. The system is endurable, and therefore it remains. Upon investigation a very important fact is revealed. The germ from which the Sclavonic civilization is unfolding consists of two principles, which are identical with the central ideas of Protestantism, viz: a strong religious sentiment, based on a creed which in its essential features is orthodox, and the idea that the State, however represented, derives its authority only from the higher sanction of God, and therefore that to a properly constituted human authority obedience is rightly due. This theory derives the right of government from God himself, and not from human compact or the mere will of a present majority. While, therefore, the government may properly demand the obedience of the subject, when in the proper exercise of its authority, because wielding a power derived from God, it is under the most solemn obligation to conform its acts to the principles of the Supreme Law of God as revealed in the Holy Scriptures, nor can the subject be rightfully called upon to obey that order of the human government which contravenes the statute that has been enacted by the Supreme Legislator himself.

The difference between this and the Papal theory is essential and apparent. The Pope also rests his authority upon that of God, claiming a divine sanction for his acts, but then he assumes to be himself the sole and infallible judge of the character of these actions, and thus leaving no liberty, or right of judgment or conscience, to the governed, stands in the place of God himself, allowing no question, and no right of appeal. The Protestant principle secures to the citizen the rights of conscience and of private judgment of the character of acts of the ruler. The one secures a rational liberty, and the other is a crushing despotism.

The Russian or Sclavonic civilization, then, in its infancy now, and though it dimly discovers truth as yet, seeing "men as trees walking" in its imperfect vision, does, nevertheless, embody a true life, resting upon truthful principles, distinct from the essential and changeless despotism of the Papacy on the one hand, and from an infidel movement on the other, and beyond comparison better than either. True, the religious sentiment is now perverted and clouded with much of folly and superstition, yet the Russian mind is in the attitude of faith ; it sincerely believes in the truths and rites of the national religion, and may therefore be regarded with hope. Authority, too, is used in a despotic manner; cruelties and abuses there are many. Still, instead of gathering up all evidences of present wrong, the true question should be whether Russia is capable of a better future, and whether she is earnestly and successfully endeavoring to rise to a more elevating position in the scale of civilization. While the mind of the nation is bound to a religious faith which presents the actual plan of salvation, and while governmental authority is respected as emanating from God, Russia may be regarded as possessing not only the elements or national greatness, but as holding to principles from which rational liberty yet may spring. And this, perhaps, will more clearly appear, if we consider the peculiar form which all society in Russia has assumed, a form to which there is nothing in the rest of Europe, or at least outside of the Sclavonian tribes, that bears a resemblance. The patriarchal idea pervades the whole social and political structure, from the father of a family upward through all the gradations to the Czar, the father of the nation, and to God the Heavenly Father of all. In theory, this is not only beautiful but true, and could it be *properly* realized in practice, Russia, even though an empire, might become a model State. In practice these Russian fathers are, doubtless, often stern, exacting, and cruel; such fathers as some of the Czars have been, have conferred no special blessings on their millions of children; still the beautiful theory itself remains a witness against those who abuse it, to be itself, perhaps, completely vindicated and reduced to practice at some future day.

Covered, as this theory may now be, by the rubbish of a despotic government, or by the superstitious observances of a corrupt Church, it is still a great truth, and as such it will survive, and in spite of all obstacles it will, in the end, clothe itself in a body of fitting institutions. Aside from Protestantism, there is no theory of social life and government in Europe so likely to win for itself a noble future as that which prevails in Russia. There is evidently no possible hope for Europe through the Papacy. It is utterly incapable of conferring any benefit upon the human race. It may persecute and degrade, and destroy, but to elevate or to save is no longer within its power. The atheistic movement is doomed to destruction because the Almighty God watches and reigns in heaven. Protestant and Russian civilization *may* yet affiliate, and the goverment of the North be liberalized, not by association with an infidel democracy, but by the spirit of Protestant freedom. If the power of England could now be thrown in favor of the right, how mighty the influence she might exert in favor of constitutional liberty. But every shot she fired in the Crimea was in favor of Papal aggression, and tended to hinder or defeat a noble experiment in civilization, whose success might open a new era for the world, and especially for the wasted East. It would be wise for those among us who desire that the influence of Russia may be destroyed, to inquire what will take its place in Europe; what power will be in the ascendant, if Russia falls. The choice seems to be between the Papacy and Atheism; a thought worthy the serious attention of Americans, and especially of American Christians. Protestant England, even if she remains Protestant, can not now rule Europe. She holds, and must continue to hold, with her present policy, only a secondary position. She has shaken hands with the Papacy, and she must eat the fruits of her bargain. A Sclavonic civilization, Atheism and the Papacy, are the real contending powers in Europe. With which should America sympathize?

The aggressive intermeddling policy of England, by which she attempted to repress the growth of all other nations in order to aggrandize herself, and compel them to buy and sell only as she should dictate, a policy which explains alike the Crimean war and the earnest support she has given to our own rebellion, has been lately exposed and rebuked by Mr. Cobden and Mr. Bright, in a debate upon the relations of the British Government to China.

England is endeavoring to conquer China, as she has attempted to cripple Russia, and the United States, in order to force her to purchase from and sell to her alone.

Mr. Cobden first showed by statistics that the intervention of the Government had nearly destroyed the trade with China, and then continued as follows:

"This is the moral—that it is not by blood and violence that you are to extend your commerce. That is the way to destroy trade, and not the way to create it. I hope that after all this expecrience we shall none of us again advocatè any violent measures with the view of extending our trade either in China or elsewhere. The noble lord told us truly that there is one-third of the human race—that is 350,000,000 or 400,000,000 of human beings—in China. They are but very small customers, but look at it in another way. If you are to follow that policy which is peculiarly the noble lord's (Palmerstone's), if you are to break into the country, hold it, and be its police; if you are to make another Turkey in China, and if, in addition to meeting Russia and France, you are to meet the United States at Pekin; if you are to trouble yourselves and future generations with governing and controlling, and intriguing in China, recollect that you have a country of vast extent and prodigious population to govern, and that you ought well to consider whether it is worth your while to incur all these risks, and enter upon this policy, with the proofs that you have that you are not likely to do more trade with that country than you are with Brazil or Egypt."

The insolent spirit of England, which leads her to meddle with the affairs of all nations, and attempt to control them all, was thus rebuked by Mr. Bright:

"Here we are, a small island on the opposite side of the globe, with a population so limited that we are told we have not an army that we could transport to Denmark [hear, hear], yet still we are somehow to take within our great ambition this vast empire of three or four hundred millions of persons; we are to influence the dynasty that shall sit on its throne; and in point of fact, we are to direct the whole affairs of the country, just as we should those of some small neighbor close to our shores. I do not know how such an idea ever got into any man's head, but having once entered in, and having taken absolute possession of the noble viscount, I suppose at his time of life he cannot get rid of it."

The time is not far distant, when England will receive the just retribution for the insults and wrongs which she has wantonly heaped on the nations. She has reached the limit of her aggressions, and henceforth Russia and the United States will both stand across her path.

# CHAPTER XXIX.

## THE NATIONAL IDEA OF RUSSIA.

THE life of a nation resembles that of an individual. Its early portion is spent in mere growth and preparation, which has, perhaps, no definite aims. There is enlargement of parts, a husbanding of strength, a discipline of faculties, with no distinct perception of the purpose which is to be attained. But the period at length comes when the object for which the man is to live and act presents itself clearly to the mind, and the individual perceives his task, his mission in life is revealed, and thenceforth his effort is to shape his actual life according to the idea which he has formed. So also with great nations. There is a preparatory period in which there is no consciousness of a special national destiny. Like the boy at school, a nation in childhood forms no settled plan for the future; but, in the progress of its growth, there is gradually shadowed forth—no one can explain how—a conception of what the national purpose should be, and this in time shapes itself to a clearly-defined idea, and becomes the object of national existence and effort. This may be called the national idea, and when truly so, it shapes the whole policy of a government, and directs upon itself the whole energy of a people. As with an individual, so with a nation, the actual achievement will bear some proportion to the grandeur of the conception and the loftiness of the aims, for, in the arrangement of the universe, there seems to be some correspondence between desire and capacity.

Russia, as it would seem, has now so far emerged from her years of childhood as to have formed a distinct and individual national idea, upon which she has shaped a well-defined national policy, and to this all her efforts tend. This, then, must be the key to all her movements, and until we obtain a clear view of her national idea, Russia will remain an enigma, and we shall hear only of despotism and barbarism. This policy will, perhaps, be best understood by presenting, as preliminary, some negative statements. And first among these, it may be truly affirmed that the conquest of Western Europe is no part of the policy of Russia. The oft-repeated cry that the Crimean war was undertaken for the purpose of preventing the Czar from overrunning Europe, and that, therefore, it was a contest of civilization against barbarism, has no foundation in fact. There is not a single proof that Russia has ever entertained the idea of using her military power for the conquest of England, France, Germany, or any of the larger nations of Europe. Her designs in this direction have been confined to a control of the Baltic and the adjacent sea. The Russian Court has never been seized with such a madness for conquest. The Russian statesman knows full well that if all these Western crowns could be laid at the feet of the Emperor, the gift, if accepted, would be fatal to his country. The incorporation of such masses of heterogeneous material into her state, is no part of the Russian scheme. On the contrary, such an idea is the exact opposite of the one which really rules her. She is much more likely to draw around her a *cordon* of armies to keep Europe out and away, than to use them to conquer and incorporate the Western nations. In fact, this is precisely the signification of her military system, so far as Europe is concerned. Her fortifications are intended to keep Europe away, while within her bristling lines of artillery she pursues her national work. Russia would never attack Western Europe unless in self-defense, to ward off a clearly-meditated blow. Whatever has been written in regard to the peril of England or France from the arms of Russia, has been either in ignorance of her real and obvious policy, or with the direct design to cover the true character and objects of the war. That hereafter she may seek to cripple these powers, whenever she has the ability, may perhaps be expected.

France and England have made an issue not to be misunderstood or evaded. Their utmost strength was employed to humble Russia, and will be while a hope of success remains. Necessity will compel her to a similar course toward them. She has been taught, in a manner which she will never forget, that she has nothing to hope except from their inability to injure. The idea of the conquest and incorporation of the Western nations, Papal and Protestant, is clearly an absurdity too palpable to be entertained. It is not, by any means, a universal dominion of this sort to which Russian ambition aspires. The associating of all animals of different natures in one harmonious family, and within one cage, is a trivial feat compared with bringing into peaceful relationship, under one government, the different races and religions of Europe. The thing is impossible, even were there adequate physical power, until the people shall be all righteous—in short, until the millennial age.

But, possible or impossible, it is not a purpose which the rulers of Russia have ever seriously entertained. Whoever will glance at the map of Europe will perceive at once, that, so far from its being demanded by any interest of Russia that she should absorb the German states, she greatly needs them precisely where they are. They constitute her southern frontier defense, and help to render her impregnable, by standing between her and her more formidable Western foes. Not conquest and incorporation of Germany, but influence over its policy, is what Russia both requires and seeks; this, through the Sclavonic race, she will be very likely to attain. Of this, the course and position of Austria and Prussia afford sufficient proof. Instead of meditating aggressive war upon France and England,

Russia merely desires to be free from assault herself, that she may pursue unhindered her own separate career; and by what means will the influence of Russia over Austria be prevented, when seventeen millions of the population of Austria are Sclavonians? This fact of the alliance of races is the true key to the policy of Austria.

Neither does the policy of Russia contemplate aggressive war as the mere propagandist of despotic principles and forms of government. She abhors the theories of the atheistical movement; they shock the deep religious sentiment which pervades the Russian mind. The late Czar began his reign with the necessity of crushing a conspiracy which originated in French influence, and he detested a spirit which he regarded not as the spirit of freedom, but of lawlessness, which sought to trample all authority under its feet, and reproduce, even in his own empire, the scenes of the reign of terror in France. To prove that Russia opposes the infidel democratic tendencies of a portion of Europe is not necessarily to show that she is the determined foe of human liberty. There are millions in England, and millions in republican America, who regard the atheistical movement on the continent as hostile to the best interests of humanity, and tending to enslave, not to liberate, the race. There are millions of the firm and devoted friends of freedom and progress who would much prefer to have every throne in Europe remain, to the triumph of that lawless spirit which scoffs at and rejects all authority, both divine and human, and claims to be a lawgiver and a god unto itself. No man, of course, will attempt to prove that Russia was not a despotic government, both in spirit and in practice, but it does not prove her love of despotism to show that she opposes *such* a democracy as has once convulsed Europe only to the destruction of popular rights. To such a miscalled liberty as many seek to establish in Europe, the vast majority of Americans are as steadfastly opposed as the Czar himself. Let, at least, this justice be done to Russia. Has she ever sought to overthrow the constitutional liberties of England? Has she ever shown herself hostile to the republican liberty which has embodied itself in our own institutions? She should have all the benefit of a clear discrimination between a rational liberty, based upon a religious faith and a due recognition of the authority of God, and a mere desire to sweep all authority and restraint away, and enthrone the individual will, or human reason, or the bare decision of a majority, in the place of God himself. Has Russia shown a settled hostility to any movement for the elevation of the race, except the infidel one of Europe?

This question should be fairly answered before she is condemned, and Americans should be careful to distinguish between the theory of our Protestant republicanism and that false theory of freedom which, discarding religion, would begin with bloodshed, and end in the most hopeless forms of despotism.

Neither the conquest of Western Europe, nor a propagandism of despotic principles, nor the arresting of human progress, nor the destruction of human rights, are the purposes which shape the national policy of the Northern Empire. What, then, it may be asked, is the true national idea of Russia? Her *territorial idea* is of a kingdom which shall include the Baltic on the west, which on the south-east shall cover the Black Sea, the Caspian, and Constantinople, with a floating eastern frontier advancing toward India, while on the north-east her possessions already lie along the Pacific, including the mouth and valley of the magnificent Amoor. This is the Russian conception of territorial limits, and it is one whose grandeur stands unequaled by any idea of empire, whether of ancient or modern times, except by the American thought, which embraces the twin continents of the West. Rome herself, in the hight of her pride and power, was but as a third-rate power compared with what Russia would be, could she once realize her vast conception. It is one of the most splendid ambitions that has ever stirred the human heart. Let those who so lavishly heap the epithets barbarous, and ignorant, and rude, upon Russia, take a map, and sit calmly down and study this national idea of territorial greatness. In extent and position, in variety and amount of resources, in every element of prosperity and power, such an empire would be foremost in all the history of earth thus far; and instead of its being a mere empty vision—a day-dream, to muse over—Europe awakes now, with a start, to find this whole scheme so nearly accomplished as to render it doubtful whether the combined strength of the Western nations can offer any effectual resistance. These vast regions she proposes to populate mainly with *Russians*, or at least Sclavonians, and to extend over it all the influence of a single race, and, if possible, a single religion. Lastly, by these means she intends to restore to its ancient channels the commerce of the East. These, it must be conceded by all, are vast conceptions, and they form together what may be regarded in general as the national idea of the great Northern Power—the scheme which shapes her policy. That she has been, or will be, scrupulous in the choice of means for the accomplishment of her purposes, will not be pretended; but, judged by the moral rules which have governed the policy of other nations, she will not be found a sinner beyond them all; and there is something truly ludicrous in the present position of England, which has never scrupled to seize and appropriate where she could, in all the regions of earth, priding herself now upon her spotless and irreproachable integrity for refusing an offer of the Czar, for the partition of Turkey, because it did not suit her interests, and after it had been virtually approved. She who has swallowed half of India, and still declares herself insatiate, is shocked and cut to the heart that Russia should enlarge her territory. Treachery, force, injustice, and oppression have marked the progress of every great nation of earth, Russia included, but her virtue is fully equal to that of those who are accusing her so loudly; and, of all nations, England is least fitted to teach others the commandment, " Thou shalt not steal."

To work out this great idea, and produce the corresponding reality, is undoubtedly the main ambition of Russia.

To the acquisition of this territory, to establish this unity of race on the firm basis of a common religion, to direct toward herself the riches of the commerce of the enriching East, she bends her energies with a steadfastness and strength of will that would seem to be the earnest of success. It is not a policy which depends upon an individual or a party. It belongs to the nation, and Czars may be deposed, or assassinated, or die in the midst of their schemes, still the course of the empire is toward Constantinople and the East. It will be seen, therefore, that the real national idea of Russia is to become a great commercial state—the great commercial power of the world; and her military array, vast as it is, was never intended for conquest, but for self-protection, for an hour like this, when Papal hatred and commercial jealousy are seeking to cripple her power, to arrest her progress, and to prevent her from restoring the Eastern Empire and the Greek Christianity on the Sclavonic basis, to far more than their original power and splendor. The reader, perhaps, will now be prepared to study with increased interest, and more in detail, the means which Russia has chosen, and the facilities which she possesses for executing her designs.

# CHAPTER XXX.

## RUSSIA, LIKE AMERICA, AIMS TO GROW BY THE DEVELOPMENT OF HER OWN RESOURCES.

ONE of the leading ideas of the policy of this government undoubtedly is to render itself independent, as far as possible, of all other nations, and hence its steady adherence, under great difficulties, to a system of self-culture and the endeavor to stretch its dominion over a territory which would afford within her own limits the means of independent support. Peter the Great undertook the impossible task of civilizing his country by forcing it into the mold of Europe. He put Russia into foreign costume, and declared that the nation was civilized. His successors perceived dimly the mistake, and did what in them lay, though little, to apply the remedy; but Nicholas first saw clearly that Russia could be made great only by being expanded from a national living center of her own, and that the individual Russian character must be the basis of the empire. He therefore adopted a thoroughly national system, too exclusive, doubtless, in some of its features, but intended to accomplish a purpose worthy of a great man and a great nation—the complete development of the resources of his empire. Much had been done, indeed, before his reign, but he alone had the comprehensive mind which enabled him to form the fragmentary designs of his predecessors into one compact and clearly-defined system, embracing all the great interests of his kingdom, stimulating, guiding, and protecting its industry, and opening up its hidden resources. His far-reaching sagacity foresaw the coming collision with the West, and he addressed himself to the task of rendering his country independent of others.

The sound statesmanship which dictated this policy is now abundantly evident to the world. Russia was not only able to bear the shock of Western Europe, but such was her financial condition, that, in the very midst of the conflict, the rates of exchange threatened to remove the bullion from the Bank of England to St. Petersburg, and against every effort made to prostrate her credit, it stood firm and unimpaired, and her stocks commanded a better price and market than any of our first-rate American securities, though we were at peace, and with no external causes to impede our prosperity. England, at the commencement of the Crimean War, took occasion to sneer at the weakness of Russia, occasioned, as she declared, by her "barbarous tariff," as she has now sneered at and raged over our Morrill tariff; but this same barbarous Russian system, by which home production and manufactures have been stimulated and improved, proved, in her hour of peril, the salvation of the empire. England and France might blockade every port of Russia for fifty years, and, instead of crippling her power or diminishing her resources, they would only exhaust themselves, while she grows strong within. They might, in this way, for a time, hinder her external progress, but she would thereby daily become more formidable from the concentration of her strength, from the increasing power of her central life, and, in the end, she would burst all barriers away, and sweep far and wide with resistless flow. Such is already the variety and extent of her resources and manufactures, that her progress would still be steady, even though it were possible to cut off altogether her European trade, for she could soon produce for herself whatever she purchases in the West, and she has an extensive Asiatic trade, which can not be interrupted. But her European trade can not be cut off by any blockade that would be tolerated by the rest of the world. After the Baltic fleets had blockaded the Russian ports through one season, it was discovered that the exports of Russia were still as large as before. All articles had found their way to the markets of the world by having first been conveyed to neutral ports. Had the Czar been deluded with the policy of England, had he allowed Great Britain to become his merchant and manufacturer, suffering meanwhile his own resources to remain untouched, and using up the product of his Ural gold mines yearly to settle his account for English goods, he would have been completely at the mercy of the Western powers, compelled either to submit to their every demand, or to see himself humbled, crippled, exhausted even in a single campaign. England seems to have so far convinced herself, by her own false reasoning, concerning the doctrine of free-trade, as to be incapable of believing that Russia could make progress under her "barbarous tariff," and, at the beginning of the war, was really ignorant of the condition and strength of her foe.

As in our own revolutionary war England refused to believe that her soldiers, duly provided with "pig-tails," and each one properly "pipe-clayed," and understanding, too, all the mysteries of drill, could, by any possibility, be beaten by men in "tow frocks," who knew nothing of "pig-tail," or "pipe-clay," or "drill," so with England now it has been deemed a sufficient answer to all suggestions of the strength of Russia to say she is weak, even bankrupt, because of her "barbarous tariff." But when the Muscovite was found full of vigorous life, well-nigh or quite impregnable in his positions, England could no more solve the enigma than she could understand the battle of Bunker Hill, when the Americans knew no more of the proprieties of war than to slaughter and defeat regularly-drilled soldiers in "pipe-clay and pig-tails." The Czar was too barbarous to comprehend how his state would be enriched by digging and coining gold wherewith to purchase abroad what he had every facility of producing at home; and so he concluded to manufacture for himself what he needed, inasmuch as his people had both time and material, and then he would lay up the produce of his gold mines against a day of need, or he would at least keep it in circulation at home. At the same time he employed a liberal portion of this newly-created wealth and newly-developed activity and skill in strengthening and multiplying the defenses of the empire; and in this, with liberal hand, he has, it appears, exhausted the power of modern science; and thus, when the Western Powers assailed him, instead of finding a needy bankrupt, ruined by his "barbarous tariff," it was discovered that he had more bullion in his coffers than the Bank of England, and they dashed themselves against fortifications that defied their utmost effort, and which can only be captured, if at all, by a most shocking sacrifice of treasure and of life.

It is quite clear that Russia, under the influence of her home system, had reached a degree of power, of an independent interior strength, of which the Allies had no adequate idea, and for which they were evidently unprepared. Under the walls of Sebastopol they learned the art of war from an enemy they had affected to despise; and the present aspect of Russia before the world conveys the most impressive lesson in political economy that has been taught in modern times. She now presents a practical argument in favor of self-development which can neither be evaded nor answered. She stands mighty and self-balanced, and therefore calm, self-reliant, and hopeful, reaping the fruits of a wise attention to the culture of her own national life. She presents an example well worthy the study of American statesmen, of what may be accomplished, even under great disadvantages, by a protection of home interests.

The system which the government has adopted is one which embraces in its design the leading interests of a nation. It has given no more prominence to the military department than was demanded by a prudent regard for the condition and purposes of the great powers of Europe. Her preparations to meet the assault of the Western Powers were neither too rapid nor too extensive. The formidable character of the Crimean conflict, and the spirit in which it was conducted, showed conclusively that Russia has not overrated the means needed for her defense. It must not be forgotten that the policy which now controls the empire is of recent origin, and owes its present form and efficiency to the statesmanship of Nicholas and his son. It has, therefore, had too little time as yet to work out completed results. There, as in the United States, society is still in the transition state, and the Russians, like ourselves, are struggling forward in the career of improvement, under all the disadvantages which are found in a country where resources, though abundant, are yet in great measure unused, and to a great extent, perhaps, unknown. Peter the Great undertook to force upon his country a system of life copied wholly from the West, for which his people were unprepared, and which was in measure unsuited to their genius; and though he awoke Russia to a new life, yet it wore more of the appearance of a masquerade than of a real life. Alexander, on the other hand, proposes to himself to create a civilization for his empire which shall be a proper outgrowth of Russian mind, and be based upon the home resources of the country. England is disposed to discourage and sneer at these efforts, for obvious reasons, precisely as she derided the early attempts at manufacturing in the United States. The folly and ruinous consequences of cherishing home production was duly pointed out, the rudeness of our machinery, the unskillfulness of our workmen, the impossibility of competing with English establishments, the inferior character of our fabrics, were all most clearly shown; and yet, with the fostering care of government only capriciously extended, and as capriciously withdrawn, and in spite of much adverse legislation, American manufactures have grown up to their present importance. The efforts of Russia are being crowned with an earlier success, because the Imperial Government has extended to this home policy its full support. Still the nation has but just entered into this new career, and what it has already accomplished may be regarded only as the earnest of a more glorious future. The adoption of this policy has placed the national life of Russia beyond the reach of the rest of Europe. Her outworks may be, perhaps, destroyed, but the process of destruction will be more costly to France and England than their erection was to Russia, or than their reconstruction will be. The Allies can not afford to demolish many such fortresses as Sebastopol; while Russia, if she adheres to her present policy, will each year be able to construct such defenses with greater facility.

This system, as has been said, embraces all the great interests of a state, although as yet it is not equally developed, nor working in perfection anywhere. But great results have already been reached, and the promise for the future is abundant, and enough has been done to render this future secure. The leading idea is to secure for Russia the control of the native race, to fill the territory of the empire mainly with the native population. For this reason, foreign influences and foreign control are guarded against with a watchful care; and the exclusive policy, which has brought such showers of reproaches upon Russia, is one whose necessity the native American population is beginning to feel even here, and when we consider the policy which circumstances are forcing upon this nation, we shall at least be better able to comprehend the motives of Russia. She pursues her course, it may be, in a manner which the liberal might condemn, and which she, even now, is modifying; but, on the other hand, Americans now perceive that in their extreme liberality to foreigners, they have been unjust to themselves, have put in jeopardy the republic, and have even prejudiced the best interests of the foreign population themselves. Russian statesmen are resolved that the native race shall control their country, and believe that this is the essential idea of a true national life.

Then, as next in importance, both for purposes of trade and for preserving the national unity, great attention has been paid to a system of internal communications. This has been conceived and executed on a scale proportionate to the extent of the country. The most distant points of the empire are already connected with each other by lines of river and canal navigation, and these are so located in the interior that it is scarcely possible that the domestic trade of the country should be affected by foreign war.

These communications are becoming every day more important and valuable to the inhabitants, on account of the introduction of river steamboats, by which, as with us in America, the transit of passengers and merchandise is yearly rendered more cheap, more rapid, and more certain. The navigable rivers are connected by numerous interlacing canals; and, by means of both, the Caspian, the Euxine, the White Sea, and the Baltic, have all communications with each other, running through the heart of the empire, affording almost unequaled facilities for the transportation of the various commodities which are required by seventy millions of people.

These works, begun by Peter the Great, have been constantly extended and improved since his reign by his successors, as an important feature of national policy; and, in addition to these, the late Czar projected a system of railroads on a scale equally extensive, two important trunk lines of which are nearly completed.

The government schools, already mentioned, are a most important feature in this scheme of national policy. They look equally to the protection of the country and to the rapid and scientific development of its agricultural, mineral, and manufacturing resources. In these schools thousands of scholars are scientifically trained in mining, in agriculture, and in the mechanical and manufacturing arts, and then they are scattered through the country to become the practical teachers of the communities in which they reside. Results of the most important national character have already been reached in the mining and manufacturing operations, which are far more extensive and complete than most, either in Europe or America, suppose. This fact, perhaps, can not be more clearly shown than by the following quotation from an article lately translated from the French for the MERCHANTS' MAGAZINE:

"At the same time, Russia attempts to naturalize in her provinces all the industrial arts of the West, and has made a real progress, which is easy to be proved, and of which Europe makes too little account. The Czars, in their haughty pride, do not wish to be obliged to ask any thing from the rest of the world, and, profiting by the different climates united in their vast empire, endeavor to cultivate the productions of every clime. They have no colonies for the production of sugar, but the provinces of Orel and Sacolef are covered with immense plantations of beets, from which sugar is manufactured. Their southern provinces furnish wheat for part of the West. In 1850 the exportation was enormous. The northern provinces produce prodigious quantities of flax and hemp.

"Cotton is cultivated in Georgia and the country taken from Persia. Since 1845 indigo has been introduced into the Caucasian provinces, merino sheep by hundreds of thousands are all around Moscow, toward the Baltic, and on the shores of the Black Sea. They prosper everywhere, and produce abundantly. Silk is produced in the southern provinces, and, in 1833, the Emperor Nicholas caused four millions of shoots of the mulberry-tree to be planted. The gold mines of Asiatic Russia are very productive, and furnish annually one hundred millions of francs to the treasury.

"Finally, the Czars wished to have their wine independently of France, and the Crimea is covered with vineyards. We look with astonishment, and almost with fear, at the rapid and powerful development of Russian activity; for the genius which has given and still gives impulse to this great movement of Oriental slavism is not the friend of liberal institutions, or the tendency of the people toward political or religious emancipation. Any nation whatever that rises and marches onward in grandeur and prosperity has a claim to our respect and to our sympathies; but in Russia it is not the *people* that rise, it is the Autocrat."

Here is presented, and apparently in an authentic form,

some most valuable information concerning the condition and progress of Russia, but one can not avoid being amazed both at the narrow spirit in which the article is written and the conclusion which the writer has reached. It proves how impossible it is for France to form a candid judgment of Russia.

It is certainly difficult to perceive why a desire to avail themselves of the great natural advantages of their territory, even to the utmost, should be stigmatized in the Czars as a haughty pride. How much more worthy of reproach or contempt would they be if they had either overlooked these advantages, or, knowing them, had suffered them to remain unused! It has generally been considered as evidence of wise statesmanship where a government understands and earnestly avails itself of its own resources, and, by a course of honest industry, increases the amount and variety of its productions, until, if possible, it can obtain an independent support from its own industrial pursuits.

But it seems that Russia can not appropriate her lands to such productions as soil and climate indicate, without being charged with a haughty desire to become independent of surrounding nations. This desire, coupled with protection to her own industry, is denounced as an evidence of barbarism by England and France. If Russia would consent to confine herself to the raising of such raw material as England and France require, sell it to them at prices established by themselves, and purchase from them all her supplies of manufactured goods, at their prices also, and settle by specie the yearly balances, thus making herself a huge and helpless dependency of the West, then she would be admitted to the rank of highly-civilized nations, and the loud cry against Russian despotism would be heard no more, at least from England. Russia, converted to the wisdom of free-trade, would be lauded and caressed.

The Czars of the North see in the free-trade scheme only an effectual plan for sending the gold and silver of the Ural district to the Bank of England, and they are barbarous enough to desire to hold it in deposit at home, and employ it for the general advancement and defense of their country. England and France are sore amazed at this uncivilized want of discernment on the part of Russia, and therefore endeavored to enlighten her with cannon-shot and twenty-two-inch shells, under General Pellissier, the *Arabic Professor* of Christian civilization, who, in a most enlightened and highly-civilized manner, suffocated, in their rock fortress, the brave Arabs whom he could not conquer in an honorable battle.

Russia barbarously enacts a tariff and cherishes her own native industry, and avails herself of all the aids of modern art, as found among her neighbors. Haughty Russia! exclaims France; too proud to be dependent. Barbarous Russia! replies England; she enacts a protective tariff, and manufactures for herself, despising the wisdom of free-trade and dependence. Why should not the hill-sides of the Crimea be covered with vineyards as well as those of France? Why should not Russia exclaim, O haughty France! that seeks to drink wine independently of my Crimean vineyards?

Why should not merino sheep feed on the hills of Russia as well as on the mountains of Spain? And why should not Russians, if they have the skill, be allowed to spin and weave their fleeces? Why is it not as reputable to raise beets as sugar-cane? Is it a better proof of high civilization to take forcible possession of some tropical island or province, and obtain sugar therefrom by compulsory labor, than to grow beets at home?

The writer of the article from which the quotation has been made, after presenting a picture that shows most clearly the vigorous life which pervades the empire on account of its industrial activity, reaches two sad conclusions: first, that the tendency is not toward political or religious emancipation; and second, that the Czar alone is rising, not the people. It is doubtless true that the tendency of Russian civilization is not toward such a political or religious emancipation as France has gained, and it is no less true, that no sane, Christian well-wisher to humanity would desire such a result. Russia neither desires a Papal despotism nor an infidel liberalism, nor such a republic as France has established. Few, however, out of France, will consider this a just cause of reproach.

It would, perhaps, open up a new chapter in political economy, if some philosopher would explain how, with this general and rapid progress of the nation, the Czar alone is rising. It has been heretofore supposed that when a nation is making swift and permanent progress in agriculture, education, commerce, and the manufacturing arts, by which new sources of wealth are continually opened, roads are laid out, canals are dug, and railways are built, that the *people* are thus inevitably elevated and refined. It has been thought that these are the means by which modern nations are advancing; and it is not clear how Russia can be an exception, nor how one man, the Czar, can reap all the advantage of this general movement of the nation. Such statements, of course, show either an invincible prejudice, or a determination to wrest plain facts to a wrong conclusion. Russia is, doubtless, carrying forward her system for the stimulation of her home industry with a rapidity and success which have astonished and alarmed both France and England, and this writer attributes to Russia a hatred and jealousy of England, which certainly has never manifested itself by sending her fleets and armies to blockade her ports, to destroy her commerce, and to burn her towns and batter down her fortifications.

It is the successful prosecution of the protective policy by which she has grown so rapidly into a great and independent nation, the foremost power of Europe, able to cope, single-handed, with her two mighty foes, that so aroused the fears and jealousies of England as to lead her, goaded on by France, with other ends in view, into that disastrous war—disastrous to all parties, whatever its termination might be—for it could not materially and permanently check the growth of Russia, while all parties engaged might consume upon it the earnings of half a century.

That policy which Russia adopted for the purpose of cherishing her own industry, and to render available her own great and varied resources—a system which England denounces as barbarous and injurious to her prosperity—is the best possible proof of political wisdom, showing that Russian statesmen have discovered the only method by which their country can attain unto a true civilization. She has been reproached with being simply a semi-barbarous military despotism, having neither commerce, nor manufactures, nor literature—as contributing nothing to the general stock of wealth or knowledge—as producing little, originating nothing, and worthy of no respect, except such as may be given to the strength of her armies. Then when she adopts a course whose object is to create a wealth and power of another description, a greatness based on the more ennobling pursuits of a higher civilization, she is accused of barbarous exclusiveness and savage ignorance, because she is not converted to the free-trade philosophy of England.

Simply as a producer of raw materials, no country, however productive its soil may be, can reach the highest stages of civilization. The intellectual stimulus and culture are wanting, by which alone true national greatness can be created. Without commerce or manufactures, Russia would be a nation of agriculturists, miners, fur-hunters, and soldiers. Such a nation would consume all the earnings of its industry upon food and those coarse, cheap goods which manufacturing nations can supply with the greatest possible advantage to themselves, and with all the profit derived from machinery.

It would be the unequal contest between unskilled manual labor on the one hand, and the power of capital, skill, machinery, and steam on the other, resulting inevitably in a low state of civilization, dependence, and poverty for Russia—in wealth and power for those who might supply her wants. There would be for her no basis on which to rear the highest forms of civilization, and she would remain equally without the means of independence or defense. It has been long perceived by the Russian government, that, without an extended commerce, the idea of holding a first position among nations must be abandoned, but no profitable foreign commerce could be maintained without a manufacturing system of her own. The materials for almost every variety of manufacture were known to abound within her own territory, not excepting exhaustless deposits of the precious metals, and a net-work of navigable rivers and lakes offered, throughout all her vast dominions, the means of easy transport; and it was resolved, therefore, to create, maintain, and perfect, if possible, a system of home manufactures, which should not only render her, in a measure, independent of foreign production, but which should also open to her a participation in the commerce of the East.

But how could this be accomplished without that "barbarous tariff," which has drawn forth such loud complaints from England. The manufactures of Great Britain are more effectually protected, by far, than those of Russia can be for a quarter of a century, by all the fostering care of the government. The capital and skill of England have fenced round her interests more strongly than a tariff of prohibition. Her policy aims steadily at a complete protection of every branch of her own industry, and from this course she has never deviated for a single moment. Her free-trade means simply freedom for all nations to sell to her their raw material to the extent of her wants, and freedom to purchase from her all manufactured articles in return. She throws no branch of her trade open until she is certain that she can defy all competition.

The only possible course then open to Russia was to grant such a protection to her infant manufactures as should shelter them from a ruinous competition from abroad. But it is said that, by this course, the cost of her manufactured articles is far greater than it would be if she should procure them from England and the west of Europe, and thus the tax upon her imports is laid really upon the consumers at home. But is not this an entirely inadequate view of the whole subject? It is necessary to observe the general result upon the nation at large; it is necessary to compare the Russia of to-day with the empire one hundred years ago; or, we may observe only the change which has been wrought in a quarter of a century by the influence of this very system which free-trade condemns. If it be conceded, for argument's sake, that the tax imposed upon foreign goods has been paid by the inhabitants of Russia, has there been rendered to them and the country at large no equivalent for this money?

A new life has been infused into all parts of the empire, an increased activity marks every department of society; roads have been opened, canals have been dug, railroads have been constructed, steamboats have been placed on rivers; factories have been built, villages have sprung up, and local markets have been opened for the productions of the soil. The establishment of one principal manufacture has called into existence a host of dependent but connected branches, and countless new modes of industry, and new sources of wealth, have been discovered by the inhabitants. By such means new desires spring up, new wants are created, and ingenuity seeks the method of supply. Thus mind is stimulated to effort, the intellectual power of the country is increased and guided to profitable action.

Capital accumulates, and is expended upon the refining arts of life; a higher taste is cultivated in architecture, dress, and furniture; a love for the beautiful is created, the fine arts are cherished, and a literature appears. These are the processes by which civilization advances toward perfection; upon such a career Russia has entered, and the aspect which she has presented in the terrible conflict that tested her powers, is proof conclusive of the efficacy of that system in creating the elements of national strength, while the extent of her present eastern commerce reveals the rapid progress she is making. If a mighty system of national industry, which lays its quickening hand upon the multitudinous resources of the land, creating wealth and sending it through the empire by ten thousand new channels, can be produced simply by the tax on imports, certainly it is a most profitable expenditure for the nation, yielding dollars in return for cents invested.

Nothing, however, is clearer than that the active competition of the home-workers speedily brings down the cost of the domestic article to the price at which the foreign goods could be purchased if the trade were free to the foreign rival; and the protection granted to the manufacturer, instead of becoming a tax upon industry, provides new and more profitable employment to labor, multiplies the comforts of the industrial classes—who are, in consequence, better fed, better clothed and educated—while the general awakening and stimulus of thought leads, in the end, to mechanical invention, discoveries in science and art, and the higher creations of genius.

The rapid advance of the Northern State, and the new career upon which she has entered, have awakened the jealousy of England, and aroused her fears; and, lest her own commercial supremacy should be endangered, she sends forth fleets and armies to extinguish, if possible, this new light of civilization which is dawning upon the world; and in order to protect, in this manner, her own monied interests, she is willing that millions of lives should be sacrificed, and that the Papal despotism should, through France, be re-established in Europe. But it will prove an abortive effort. Sclavonic civilization has become a mighty fact—its march is eastward, and the Euxine and the Hellespont must yet be the center of its life.

# CHAPTER XXXI.

## THE RUSSIAN CHURCH.

IN a religious point of view, the contest in the East lay between the Russian Church on the one hand, and the Roman Catholic on the other. The two leading powers in the conflict head these two great divisions of nominal, if not real Christianity. Protestantism, as a religious interest, did not enter into the war.

England armed for national aggrandizement, or, to speak with greater precision, to prevent what she deemed the undue expansion of a rival power, which might lessen her comparative importance, and perhaps diminish her actual strength. She did not wage war to establish the Protestant religion in the East, much less the American type of Protestantism. If she gains her commercial ends, she will rest content. The character of the Russian Church then becomes an exceedingly interesting subject of inquiry.

Without understanding the nature of that religion which is the faith of fifty millions of Russians, we can form no correct judgment upon the influence which Russia would exert upon Turkey and the East should she gain the ascendancy there. If the world is called upon to choose between the Papacy and the Russian Church as a ruler of the East, we ought to understand the distinctive features of each. As has been already remarked, the Russian Church, though adopting the Greek rite, and constituting indeed the Greek Church of modern times, must not be confounded either with the Greek Church in Turkey or in Greece.

The latter have shown a persecuting spirit which the Russian Church has not manifested. The three divisions doubtless sympathize with each other to a certain degree; but the Church of Russia will eventually control and give character to the others, unless the Allies succeed in forcing her back and repressing her growth. Many—perhaps most in America—confounding the Greek with the Russian Church, charge upon the latter the spirit of persecution which assailed our missionaries in Turkey and Greece, and are therefore led to suppose that the Papal Church and that of Russia are of similar character; and thousands unjustly imagine that both are equally bigoted, persecuting, and corrupt. England endeavors to persuade the world that civilization has less to fear from the Papacy than from the Church of Russia. This opinion most certainly has no foundation in truth, but yet it is often expressed.

It is important, therefore, for Americans to make themselves acquainted with the facts connected with this question, and form for themselves an independent judgment. With the character of the Roman Catholic Church, its spirit, its aims, and its doctrines, the United States have been made familiar; and a nation that has been goaded to an almost universal uprising against its insolent demands, and its plots against Republican liberty, will have very little confidence that liberty will be promoted through its influence either in Europe or the East. Indeed, one of the most cogent reasons why the Americans were sparing of sympathy with the Allies in the character and aims of that war, was, that just in proportion as success attended them, would the Papacy be strengthened, and in that exact ratio, also, must the cause of human freedom be weakened in Europe, for the Papacy and despotism are natural and inseparable friends and supporters of each other.

The characteristics of the Russian Church are less known to the people of the United States. Russia has not emptied her population by millions upon our shores, nor sought to colonize our territories for religious ends; and no bands of priests or Jesuits have been ordered on from St. Petersburg as spies upon our proceedings, and to subvert, if possible, our institutions. We lack, then, those means of judging Russia which are unfortunately so abundant in the case of Rome. Still the doctrines of the Church of Russia are sufficiently well known, and her practice, history has recorded. It will be found that, in essential doctrines, there are almost no points of comparison with the errors of Romanism. As a religious system, the distinction between it and the Papacy is broad and palpable, as a comparative exhibition of their theories will show; and, from this comparison, what the nations have to fear from each may be clearly seen.

The Roman Catholic claims to be the one only true Church—the one *universal* Church, whose dominion, of right, and by the authority of God, extends over all the world, that there neither is, nor can be, salvation for any without her pale, and that all who reject her authority and refuse her ordinances, are heretics, to be punished whenever and wherever she has the power, and are to be regarded as in rebellion against God. Nor is this a claim to spiritual dominion, or in matters of faith only. She claims, as the vicegerent of Jesus Christ on earth, to wield in his name supreme power in all things, and to exercise a rightful control over all governments and rulers of the earth.

This involves not only the right, but the duty, to suppress all Protestant or other States, whether republics or monarchies, that refuse submission to her will, and this supposed duty she has constantly endeavored to perform, either by force or intrigue, and hence her unwearied efforts to subvert the government of the United States, her war upon the Bible, her assault upon our schools, her efforts to control the ballot-box. Hence, also, her intrigues at

Jerusalem and Constantinople, and the war with Russia, her mighty European antagonist.

These claims are among the essential ones of the Papacy, never abandoned, never even abated. Religious toleration is with her a thing unknown. She *endures* where she must, and *crushes* where she can. To establish these claims, to compel the nations to acknowledge her authority as supreme over all things on earth, she has slain fifty millions of people in war, at the stake, in the dungeons of the Inquisition, and by every variety of outrage and torture. Between such a church, claiming the right of universal dominion, and a mere national establishment like the Church of England, local only in its character and claims, its jurisdiction confined within its territorial limits, there is a distinction broad and *essential*. The one demands the obedience of the world, of all nations—threatening eternal damnation to all who refuse, and interposing everywhere, and by all means, to enforce its claims, and disturbing thereby the peace of earth. The authority of the other extends over a single people only, and asserts no right to interfere with the conscience or worship of sister States, and no commission from God to subdue to its own faith the surrounding nations.

The English Church does not pretend that it may rightfully interfere with religious worship in the United States in order to establish here its own rights, even if it had the power. But the Papal Church not only asserts the right, but endeavors to obtain the power, and declares that it only waits until the power is gained, and that then religious liberty shall be put down in this country, and the people be compelled to adopt her forms and creed, or be punished at her pleasure as heretics. The Russian Church is simply a national establishment like the English Church; like that, it is local only, claiming no jurisdiction beyond its own territories—no commission from God to exercise *universal* dominion, and to go forth to bring all nations into subjection to itself, and in the name of God. It claims no right to be the troubler of the world, no authority over governments; it pretends not to be the ruler of princes, the governor of kingdoms.

The claim of the Russian Church is national only; that of Rome is universal, and the comparative danger to the world from each is therefore easily estimated. The Russian Church will simply be co-extensive with the Empire. It will not rule the world, unless Russia should conquer all nations—a result which no one apprehends. Again, the Romish Church claims absolute infallibility, claims to speak and decide with the unerring wisdom of God himself, in the language of the Scriptures, "showing" herself "to be God." Such a Church, from the necessity of its nature and demands, must be a persecuting Church.

Persecution—the putting down of error—with such a hierarchy, assumes the form of duty, and heretics are destroyed for the glory of God and the safety of the world. The Russian Church makes no such claim, and asserts no such power; it is simply the national religion of Russia, holding its due position in connection with the civil powers.

The Russian Church wields no such instrument of power and corruption as the Romish Confessional. No more subtle or efficient engine of despotism was ever contrived by wicked ingenuity, than this has proved to be in the hands of the Roman Catholic Priesthood.

Possessing themselves by this means, not only of the history of human actions, but even of the unuttered thought or desire, and pronouncing judgment upon all in the name of God, it lays the immortal soul bound, helpless, and exposed, even to the heart's most secret chambers, at the feet of a fellow-creature who has usurped the prerogatives of God. The Church of Rome has, in this manner, subverted the virtue of thousands, who, but for her priests, might have remained innocent, has destroyed the purity and peace of households, trampling in secret upon the holiest domestic ties, and has managed to guide the policy of Courts by its knowledge of State secrets obtained at the confessional. It has furnished a power almost sufficient of itself for the control of every nation where it has been established, and is essential to a perfect spiritual despotism. The Church of Russia teaches the duty of confession, but then this confession may be either specific or *general*, at the option of the one who confesses; and, consequently, a practice which, as conducted by Rome, is almost omnipotent for evil, is, in Russia, incapable of being thus perverted, and can neither be used for purposes of corruption or oppression.

The Church of Rome has, in all places and time, opposed with her utmost strength the circulation of the Scriptures among the people, knowing well that despotism is secure only in proportion to the ignorance of those whom it oppresses. Hence its persevering attacks upon the Bible and the free-schools of America. Russia permits the circulation of the Word of God among her people, and such was the affinity of the Russian Church for Protestant principles and effort, that in the reign of Alexander a Russian Bible Society co-operated with the British Association for the printing and distribution of the Scriptures.

Nicholas, whose policy was more exclusively national, and who seemed to foresee from afar the gathering of that storm of hostility in England and France which burst with such fury before his death on Russia, evidently feared an influence which he well knew might be used for political purposes, and therefore discouraged and broke off the connection with the British Bible Society, and suspended altogether the work which had been begun. To ascribe this to the intolerant spirit of the Russian Church seems altogether a mistake, nor is there any evidence that it originated in any hostility to the circulation of the Scriptures, which has always been allowed. Nicholas was a keen and most sagacious observer of the tendency of the affairs of Europe.

He felt the necessity of protecting his country at all points, and he was not willing to expose himself to any peril which might arise from a foreign influence of any sort established within his dominions, and by which the power of the national Church might be diminished. Doubtless he intended to use this national Church for State purposes; and viewed merely in the light of worldy policy, his sagacity has been clearly shown by the result. He was enabled to concentrate the whole religious sentiment of the empire upon the defense of the nation the moment he was attacked. Russia's breastwork of united hearts burning with religious enthusiasm are more impregnable than her granite walls, her frowning artillery, or her sparkling lines of bayonets.

A Church that favors the circulation of the Bible, however it may be entangled in superstitious observances, holds, nevertheless, within it a living germ, and there is reasonable hope of its recovery. Again, the Russian Church does not believe in purgatory, nor in the sale of indulgences, and consequently does not possess one of the chief means of robbery and delusion so freely and profitably employed by the Church of Rome. Nor does it prescribe celibacy for the clergy, and this of itself presents a feature, which, in comparison with the Roman Catholic Church, should commend it to the world's favorable regard. Language is incapable of describing the wretchedness and sin and delusion which have been caused in the Papal Church by "forbidding to marry." It is a mournful characteristic of her apostasy.

The Russian Church is not entirely free from the error, but, compared with Rome, it is of small importance. The lower orders of the clergy are all married, while the bishops and the highest officers of the Church remain in a state of celibacy. These superior ecclesiastics are derived from the *one only* order of monks existing in Russia, which might rather be called the cloistered clergy.

The system of monasteries and convents has little or no influence in the Russian State, for they have no rich endowments, and are merely establishments supported by a revenue from the government; consequently there can be no such pious robbery, no such accumulation of land, or hoarding of millions of treasure, as has been accomplished by the similar establishments in countries governed by Rome. The industry and wealth of the country are not devoured in Russia by swarms of monks, friars, and priests.

There are in the Russian Church two orders of the clergy—one constituting the only order of monks in the empire, from whose ranks the higher dignitaries of the Church are taken; but these and their establishments, being without independent ecclesiastical revenues, have no means of oppressing the people or of making their power formidable.

Women are not allowed to enter nunneries until they are forty years of age; the men may become monks at the age of thirty; and thus the Russian Church has wisely guarded against the corruptions which have stained all the history of Romanism.

The intolerance of the Papacy is not found in the Church of Russia. The Russian clergy will officiate in Protestant houses for worship, and will also permit their own churches to be used by Protestant ministers. They are tolerant toward all other denominations, and do not pretend to confine salvation to their own Church. They do not refuse to administer the consolations of religion to dying Protestants, and they permit Protestants to be buried in their cemeteries.

Attempts have been made to represent the Emperor of Russia as only an Eastern Pope, to be as truly feared and shunned as the Pope himself at Rome. It would be equally reasonable to excite similar prejudices against the sovereign of England, who is the head of the English Church, as the Czar is the head of the Church of Russia. Such are the main features which distinguish the Russian from the Roman Catholic Church.

The difference is radical and essential. In principle, they are utterly unlike. One aims at a despotism universal and exclusive. For the attainment of such an end, the whole system has been most cunningly devised, and adhered to with a constancy which has almost insured its success. Its steadfast aim is to rule the world—to subject all nations to its control. Therefore, its interference is everywhere felt, its tools and spies are in every land, the disturbers of the world's peace.

The Church of Russia, on the contrary, is the Church of a single nation, having, however, twelve millions in Turkey, and some also in Greece, who are in sympathy with its worship; and while it is clogged, debased, and hindered by a thousand frivolous and superstitious observances, it has, nevertheless, not one essential element of a spiritual despotism, and it rejects every great distinctive error of the Roman Catholic Church. With a creed orthodox in its essential teachings, and with the Word of God circulated among the people, it can not be regarded as beyond the reach of reformation.

It has a deep, strong hold on the affections of the Russian nation, and, as a body rising rapidly to a prominent position among nations through the swift progress and expansion of the mighty state of which it is the religious basis and life, it is worthy of a careful study and candid judgment. It would reflect no credit upon the generosity or independence of the American people, if, in regard to the Russian Church, we either become the mere echo of English prejudices or interested statements, or if we fail to make the proper distinction between the Greek Church in Turkey, from which our missionaries have suffered, and the Church of the Russian Empire.

A country where the Word of God is circulated, where a tract distribution is carried regularly on, by which *four million* tracts have been already distributed, should not be treated by Protestants with cold suspicion, much less should American Christians permit the "*war interest*" in England to excite in them a spirit of hostility against its Church, which evidently might be largely influenced by American friendship.

The following extracts from STANLEY'S GREEK CHURCH will show what one of the most distinguished scholars of England thinks of the importance of the Russian Church, its influence over the people, and what it may yet accomplish for civilization and Christianity in the East:

"Western ecclesiastical history would lose more than half its charms, if it had not for its subject the great national Churches of Europe. And, in like manner, Eastern ecclesiastical history must fail of its purpose, unless it can find some field in which we can trace from century to century, and in their full-blown development, those principles and practices of the Oriental Church which have been already unfolded in general terms.

"This field is presented in the Russian Church. In it alone we trace a growth and progress analogous to that which Western or Latin Christianity found in the Teutonic tribes of Europe. And, although the Northern and Sclavonic elements form the basis of the Church and Empire of Russia, yet, by its situation, by its origin, and by the singular powers of imitation with which its members are gifted, it is essentially Asiatic and Oriental. And, further, through the gradual incorporation of Russia into the commonwealth of Western nations, the Eastern Church has acquired a voice or speech which it has lost, or has never gained, elsewhere. The feeling which the native Russians entertain toward the Western world is a likeness of the feeling which we ourselves entertain toward the Eastern world. The Russian word for a foreigner, but especially for a German, is 'the dumb,' 'the speechless;' and it has happened, within the experience of an English traveler, that Russian peasants, passing by and seeing a conversation going on in a foreign language, have exclaimed, in astonishment: 'Look at those people; they are making a noise, and yet they can not speak!' Very similar to this is the way in which, as a general rule, we regard, almost of necessity, the Eastern Churches generally. To us, with whatever merits of their own, they are dumb. Their languages, their customs, their feelings are unknown to us. We pass by and see them doing or saying something wholly unintelligible to us, and we say: 'Look at those people; they are making a noise, and yet they can not speak!' In a great measure this difficulty severs us from the Russian Church, as well as from the other branches of Oriental

Christendom. Still, in Russia, if anywhere in the East, we can from time to time listen and understand with advantage. The Sclavonic power of imitation opens a door which elsewhere is closed. The Western influences which, from the age of Peter, have streamed into Russia, though they have often undermined the national character, have yet, where this is not the case, given to it the power, not only of expressing itself in Western languages, but of understanding Western ideas, and adapting itself to Western minds. A Russian alone presents, amidst whatever defects and drawbacks, this singular interest: that he is an Asiatic, but with the sensibility and intelligence of a European; that he is, if we will, a barbarian, but with the speech and communications of civilization.

"Another peculiarity of the history of the Church of Russia is, that it enables us, within a short compass, to go through the whole field of ecclesiastical history, which, in the West, while familiar to us in detail, is too vast to be comprehended in any one survey. With many differences, produced by diverse causes of climate, of theology, of race, the history of the Russian Empire and Church presents a parallel to the history of the whole European Church from first to last, not merely fanciful and arbitrary, but resulting from its passage through similar phases, in which the likenesses are more strongly brought out by the broad differences just mentioned. The conversion of the Sclavonic races was to the Church of Constantinople what the conversion of the Teutonic races was to the Church of Rome. The Papacy and the Empire of Charlemagne had, as we shall see, their dim reflection on the throne of Moscow. Russia, as well as Europe, had its Middle Ages, though, as might be expected from its later start in the race of civilization, extending for a longer period. The Church of Russia, as well as the Church of Europe, has had its reformation, almost its revolution, its internal parties, and its countless sects.

"The events are few; the characters are simple; but we shall read in them again and again, as in a parable, our own shortcomings, our own controversies, our own losses. The parts of the drama are differently cast. The Eastern element comes in to modify and qualify principles which we have here carried out to their full length, and beyond it; but it is this very inversion of familiar objects and watchwords which is so useful a result of the study of ecclesiastical history, and which is best learned where the course of events is at once so unlike and so like to our own, as in the Church of Russia.

"In Russian history the religious aspect, on which our thoughts must be fixed in these lectures, is, on the one hand, that part of it which is the least known, and yet, on the other hand, is full of interest, and not beyond our apprehension. It has been sometimes maintained by writers on political philosophy, that, however important in the formation of individual life and character, religion can not be reckoned among the leading elements of European progress and civilization. I do not enter into the general discussion; but the great empire of which we are speaking, if it has not been civilized, has unquestionably been kept alive by its religious spirit. As in all the Eastern nations, so in Russia, the national and the religious elements have been identified far more closely than in the West, and this identification has been continued, at least outwardly, in a more unbroken form. Its religious festivals are still national; its national festivals are still religious. Probably the last great historical event which in any European state has externally assumed a religious, almost an ecclesiastical form, is nearly the only event familiar to most of us in Russian history, namely, the expulsion of the French from Moscow. From the moment when Napoleon, according to the popular belief, was struck to the ground with awe at the sight of the thousand towers of the Holy City, as they burst upon his view when he stood on the Hill of Salutation, to the moment when the tidings came of the final retreat 'of the Gauls and of the thirty nations,' as they are called, the whole atmosphere of the Russian resistance is religious as much as it is patriotic. The sojourn of the French in the Kremlin is already interwoven with religious legends, as if it had been an event of the Middle Ages. A magnificent cathedral has been added to the countless churches already existing in Moscow to commemorate the deliverance. 'God with us,' is the motto which adorns its gateway, as it was the watchword of the armies of the Czar.

"The services of Christmas-day are almost obscured by those which celebrate the retreat of the invaders on that same day, the 25th of December, 1812, from the Russian soil; the last of that long succession of national thanksgivings, which begin with the victory of the Don and the flight of Tamerlane, and end with the victory of the Beresina and the flight of Napoleon. 'How art thou fallen from heaven, O Lucifer, son of the morning!' This is the lesson appointed for the services of that day. 'There shall be signs in the sun, and in the moon, and in the stars, and upon the earth distress of nations with perplexity. Look up and lift up your heads, for your redemption draweth nigh.' This is the Gospel of the day. 'Who through faith subdued kingdoms, waxed valiant in fight, turned to flight the armies of the aliens.' This is the epistle.

"I have dwelt on the religious aspect of this crisis, both because it may serve to remind us that there is at least one event in the history of the Eastern Church with which we are all acquainted; and also because, coming as it does at the end of a series of similar deliverances and celebrations, it brings before us one special interest which the Russian ecclesiastical history possesses, namely, its relation, both by way of likeness and illustration, to the history of the Jewish Church of old. Hardly in any European nation shall we so well understand the identity of the religious and national life in the ancient theocracy as through the struggles of the Russian people against their several invaders. The keenness with which they appropriate the history of the old dispensation is but the natural result of their (in many respects) analogous situation. In the sculptures of the cathedral of which I have just spoken as the monument of the deliverance of Moscow, it is the execution of one and the same idea when the groups from Russian history alternate with scenes from the story of Joshua's entrance into Palestine, of Deborah encouraging Barak, of David returning from the slaughter of Goliath, of the coronation and the grandeur of Solomon."

The religious character of the Czar of Russia is thus described by Mr. Stanley:

"First is the Czar. In the West, as well as in the East, the frame-work of all religious and civil institutions was molded on the idea of a Holy Roman Empire succeeding to the Pagan Roman Empire of former times. But in the West this institution has signally failed, as in the East it has signally succeeded. Charlemagne was a much greater man than any of the Russian potentates before the time of Peter. His coronation by Leo was a much more striking coronation than any that has fallen to the lot even of the greatest Russian emperors. The theory of his empire was defended by Dante with far more genius and zeal than ever was the theory of the White Czar by any poet or philosopher of Russia. But, nevertheless, the Holy Roman Empire has faded away, while 'the new Cæsar of the Empire of Orthodoxy' still stands. In part, this difference is owing to the fundamental diversity of the Eastern and Western characters. In part, however, it was fostered by the peculiar circumstances of the Russian history, and obtained an importance in the Russian Church and Empire beyond what may be ascribed to the same tendency in other regions of the East. The very slowness of the growth of the institution indicates the depth of its roots in the national character and history. The transformation of the Grand Princes of Kieff, Vladimir, and Novgorod into the Czar of Muscovy, and of the Czar of Muscovy into the Emperor of all the Russias, was not the work of a day or a century; it was the necessity of the long-sustained wars with Tartars, Poles, and Swedes; it was the craving for union among the several princes; it was the inheritance of the ceremonial of the Byzantine Empire, through the intermarriage of Ivan III with the daughter of the last Palæologus; it was the earnest desire for peace under one head, after the long wars of the Pretenders; it was the homogeneousness of the vast empire, uniting itself under one common ruler. The political position of the Czar or Emperor is not within our province, but his religious or ecclesiastical position transpires through the whole history of his Church. He is the father of the whole patriarchal community. The veneration for him was in the Middle Ages almost, it is said, as if he were Christ himself. The line of Grecian emperors, so it was said even by Orientals, had been stained with heresy and iconoclasm: never the line of the Orthodox Czars of Muscovy. 'He who blasphemes his Maker meets with forgiveness among men, but he who reviles the emperor is sure to lose his head.' 'God and the Prince will it; God and the Prince know it,' were the two arguments, moral and intellectual, against which there was no appeal. 'So live your Imperial Majesty, here is my head;' 'I have seen the laughing eyes of the Czar'—these were the usual expressions of loyalty. He was the keeper of the keys and the body-servant of God. His coronation, even at the present time, is not a mere ceremony, but a historical event and solemn consecration. It is preceded by fasting and seclusion, and takes place in the most sacred church in Russia; the emperor, not as in the corresponding forms of European investiture, a passive recipient, but himself the principal figure in the whole scene; himself reciting aloud the confession of the orthodox faith; himself alone on his knees, amid the assembled multitude, offering up the prayer of intercession for the empire; himself placing his own crown with his own hands on his own head; himself entering through the sacred doors of the innermost sanctuary, and taking from the altar the elements of the bread and wine, of which then and there, in virtue of his consecration, he communicates with bishops, priests, and deacons. In every considerable church is placed a throne in front of the altar, as if in constant expectation of the sudden apparition of the sovereign. In every meeting, council, or college, is placed the sacred triangular 'mirror,' 'the mirror of conscience,' as it is called, which represents the imperial presence, and solemnizes, as if by an actual consecration, the business to be transacted."

It is evident that a nation, whose religious and political life are so intimately blended, are capable of being profoundly moved, either for defense of their "sacred soil," or to recover the lost possessions of their Mother Church. Seventy millions of people thus penetrated by a deep religious sentiment, and directed by one who is at the same time their political and religious head, can not be permanently checked by any power in Europe.

Mr. Stanley's closing reflections upon the possible future of the Russian Church may well be pondered by Americans now:

"I have thus glanced at some of the leading characters of the modern Church of Russia, and of its existing tendencies. They will be enough to show that its inherent life has neither been choked by its own tenacity of ancient forms, nor strangled by the violence of Peter's changes. But what its future will be, who shall venture to conjecture? Will it be able now, in these its latter days, to cease from foreign imitations, Eastern or Western, and develop an original genius and spirit of its own? Will it venture, still retaining its elaborate forms of ritual, to use them as vehicles of true spiritual and moral edification for its people? Will it aspire, preserving the religious energy of its national faith, to turn that energy into the channel of practical social life, so as to cleanse, with overwhelming force, the corruption and vice of its higher ranks, the deceit and rude intemperance of its middle and lower classes?

The Russian clergy, as they recite the Nicene Creed in the communion, embrace each other with a fraternal kiss, in order to remind themselves and the congregation that the orthodox faith is never to be disjoined from apostolical charity. Is there a hope that this noble thought may be more adequately represented in their ecclesiastical development than it has been in ours? Will Russia exhibit to the world the sight of a Church and people understanding, receiving, fostering the progress of new ideas, foreign learning, free inquiry, not as the destruction, but as the fulfillment, of religious belief and devotion? Will the Churches of the West find that, in the greatest national Church now existing in the world, there is still a principle of life at work, at once more steadfast, more liberal, and more pacific than has hitherto been produced either by the uniformity of Rome or the sects of Protestantism?

"On the answer to these questions will depend the future history, not only of the Russian Church and Empire, but of Eastern Christendom, and, in a considerable measure, of Western Christendom also. The last word of Peter, struggling between life and death, was, as has been already described, *Hereafter*. What more awful sense the word may have expressed to him, we know not. Yet it is not beneath the solemnity of that hour to imagine that even then his thoughts leaped forward into the unknown future of his beloved Russia. And to us, however curious its past history, a far deeper interest is bound up in that one word, which we may, without fear, transfer from the expiring Emperor to the Empire and the Church which he had renewed—'HEREAFTER.'"

# CHAPTER XXXII.

## THE RUSSIAN CHURCH MAY RECOVER THE EAST.

THE observations which have been made upon the Roman Catholic and Russian Churches will naturally suggest the inquiry, what would be the character of the religious influence which Russia would exert upon the East should her power be established there? Before attempting a direct reply to this question, there are some preliminary considerations which deserve attention.

Americans are yet in a position to weigh candidly the character and claims of Russia, and they can not fail to perceive that if she were fitted, *in a religious point of view*, to give Christianity to the regions around and to the east of the Hellespont, the Euxine, and the Caspian, *then, in other respects*, she is better prepared for this mission than any nation of Europe; and, unless some great change should occur in European politics, America is the only nation that could co-operate with her in that work.

In the religious aspect of this question it can not be denied that Russia has, beyond comparison, a larger interest in the population of the East than any other power, and that she wields over them already an influence greatly surpassing that of any other nation. Twelve millions of Greek Christians in Turkey sympathize with her in her faith and general policy, and regard her as their head. The population of Greece is similarly situated, though, from position, largely under European control.

Russia has stretched the lines of her attachments to the foot of the Caucasus, and fastens them upon a Christian population there. She has commercial relations and political influence through all Persia and even beyond, in China and Northern Asia in general. Her facilities for spreading a Christian civilization through all these vast regions are greater already than those of all the earth besides. She is the only power of earth that can, by expansion, *incorporate* these territories under one government. They would become merely colonial dependencies of France and England, not integral parts of their home governments. Not so with Russia.

These provinces, if annexed to her dominions, would become incorporated with her, a part of herself, as the Louisiana Purchase and Texas are now integral parts of the United States. Those countries, now ruled by a few millions of Turkish masters, treating the Christian population as a degraded caste, would then be as much a part of Russia as the provinces around Moscow, and one social, political, and religious structure would be extended over the whole. There are, as has been said, twelve millions of Greek Christians in Turkey, and only one million of Roman Catholics.

Allowing both Churches to be on an equal footing in purity and spiritual life, (which they are not), which is, then, in the most favorable position for spreading Christianity in the East? France, with her one million of Catholics, and twelve millions of Greeks, who hate and would oppose her; or Russia, with twelve millions to sympathize with and assist her? This, of course, is upon the supposition that they could be spiritually prepared to spread the Gospel of Christ. The Oriental character of the Russian nation, and the religious affinities which connect her with the Christian population of the East, designate her as the proper agent for recovering that now-wasted land, and making it once more what it was during the best days of the Eastern Empire. That the breaches are to be restored, the old highways rebuilt, and prosperity and the Gospel once more revisit Western Asia to the expulsion of Mohammedanism and its wasting misrule, the student of prophesy can scarcely doubt; but opinions differ widely as to the agencies which God will probably employ in producing the glorious result.

American Christians have fondly hoped that this work has been committed to the American, or at least to Protestant missions. Doubtless they have accomplished much. What has been thus done in the heroic spirit of self-sacrifice and Christian enterprise will not be swept entirely away, whatever changes may occur, and whoever may rule at Constantinople.

Still, in any event that now seems possible, Protestantism must enter the East as a protected and not as a ruling element, because French or Russian influence will predominate, and between these two, as controlling powers, the choice of the world must lie.

If, therefore, some power should hold the East that would tolerate the presence and efforts of Protestant Christians, it is the utmost that could be expected while political affairs remain unchanged. We know that the Roman Catholic Church knows nothing of toleration, and from France and the Pope there is absolutely nothing to hope. If, therefore, Protestant efforts are to be tolerated at all in these regions hereafter, it must be through the friendship of Russia, while by her the main religious influence will be exerted, whether it be good or evil.

It has been already shown that the Russian Church has yet a living germ—has a little strength. The distinctive errors of the Papacy do not attach to her. She is not what most Protestants believe the Papal Church to be—an apostate and anti-Christian body. On the other hand, she is far from being what she should be. Her spiritual life and power are overborne and well-nigh smothered by idle or superstitious ceremonies; there is a lack of apprehension of spiritual truth, and ceremony is in great degree substituted for the religion of the heart. But let it be supposed that England, instead of sending against her fleets and armies, instead of joining a Papal crusade, had striven to maintain the friendly spirit which existed in the time of Alexander, when even the government co-operated with the British Bible Society, might we not have seen, ere this, a spiritual revolution begun in Russia?

Might there not have been an arousing of that Eastern Church by a contact with the life of Protestantism, and a casting aside of dead forms to assume the garments of a living holiness? A tract publication and distribution is even now going on quite actively in Russia; and these tracts, and the books published and circulated, are of a character to elevate the tone of piety, and quicken and strengthen the spiritual life. There seems to be no bar to the introduction of Protestant Christian literature of this description, for it is said that the censorship of the government is exercised in a candid and liberal spirit in regard to this religious effort. Who shall say that important changes might not thus have been wrought ere this in Russia?

Could she not thus have been enlightened, liberalized, advanced in civilization, and prepared, by the reception of a new life herself, to spread the Gospel of Jesus throughout the East? Such a Christian intercourse might have led to a harmonious and righteous settlement of those questions which have since plunged Europe into a terrible conflict, whose results were evil only. And if England, by her policy, has lost this opportunity of doing good to a sister state, and of conferring a precious boon on Europe and the East, why should not America endeavor to cultivate with her a friendly alliance; and, as the foremost Protestant nation of earth, strive to infuse, by the help of God, a new life and a new spirit into that mighty people of the North? Then, should Russia succeed in establishing herself in Turkey, the American Churches may help to prepare her to Christianize the East, and share with her the labor and the honor of the work. Invectives of the most bitter kind were heaped upon Nicholas because of the proposition which he made to England. Would there have been more dishonor in accepting that offer, and thereby securing the peace of Europe, than in engaging in a bloody war, in order, not to save, but, in conjunction with France, to obtain the exclusive control of Turkey?

Leaving the question of right, of moral principle, to be discussed elsewhere, let it be supposed that England had accepted the offer of the Emperor of Russia, and that even now the fall of the Turkish Empire were passed, the Czar ruling over Constantinople, and England instead of France established in Egypt, with her railroad or ship-canal, or both, across the Isthmus of Suez, opening to Europe once more this old highway to India. At the same time, let it be imagined that Russia had perfected one eastward route, by railroad, through Siberia, across her vast mineral regions, to the head of navigation on the Amoor, thus uniting St. Petersburg and Moscow with the Pacific; and another Asiatic highway, by the Caspian, the Aral, and the connecting waters—would Europe and the world suffer more from this arrangement than from a sanguinary war for much more questionable ends? Could Russia, by friendly association with such a Protestant power as either England or America, be made to sympathize with the spirit of evangelical religion, she could effect more for the recovery of the East than all Christendom besides.

Such an opportunity as was never presented before is now offered to the American government and American Churches to cultivate with that power friendly relations, not as against others, but such as are proper to establish with all. Would not this advance the general cause of liberty and religion more than estrangement and a causeless hostility?

# CHAPTER XXXIII.

## STRUCTURE AND WORKING OF THE RUSSIAN GOVERNMENT.

At the commencement of the Crimean war, unwearied pains were taken to spread throughout the civilized world the idea that the government of Russia is merely a heartless, crushing, military despotism, with no redeeming quality, no element of progress, cherishing no regard for the people, and no desire for their advancement; and, therefore, the war was declared to be one of civilization against barbarism—of humanity against the one great foe of liberty and man.

This accusation is certainly a very grave one, and deserves our serious regard. If such is the character of Russia, and if her growth is but a prolonged crusade against human rights and happiness and hopes; if, moreover, the powers which assaulted her are the firm friends of popular freedom, and took up arms to establish it, then have they a right to expect American sympathy, and it ought to be freely bestowed. But they who remember how our own country has been vilified in the same quarter, will be disposed to regard with some suspicion similar charges against Russia; while the idea that the Allies engaged in a contest for the defense of popular rights is already abandoned by most. Again, nothing can be more ungenerous, not to say absurd, than to rake up from the records of other ages, whatever can be discovered there, of ignorance, barbarity, or tyranny, and present it as a picture of Russia as she is at present. The true question is, Whether Russia, in spite of all crimes of the past, or errors in her government and general policy, is sincerely endeavoring, and with good hope of success, to establish a form of civilization by which the Sclavonic races may be elevated.

Let it be granted that the Emperor of Russia possesses unlimited power. That does not of itself demonstrate that the government is despotic and cruel, regardless of the welfare of its subjects. The true question is, How is this power actually employed? Is the Czar only a tyrant, crushing the proper energies of his people merely that he may rule supreme? Or, is he the exponent of the nation's will, the representative of a national sentiment, the recognized defender of a nation's faith, the guardian of a nation's resources and honor, a chieftain to direct a nation's power?

Doubtless the truth lies between these two suppositions; but, then, all the reliable evidence in the case shows that it coincides far more nearly with the last supposition than with the first. Nothing is more deceitful than names. A monarchy may be liberal; a democracy may be a despotism of the most hateful character; and even in a constitutional monarchy, intelligence and merit may be constantly trampled under foot by a hereditary and incompetent nobility, absorbing both the honor and wealth of a country.

Notwithstanding all the aspersions which have been cast upon the Northern Empire, it is nevertheless true that there is no state in Europe where talent is so certainly recognized and employed; where the ablest man so surely fills the most important post; where the road to preferment is so freely opened to merit, as in Russia; and that government is not, in the proper sense, a despotism, where an unimpeded ascent is opened from the very lowest to the highest positions in society. The candid and philosophic Erman presents the following view of the structure and working of the Russian system, which should be carefully studied by those who have been led to think of it only as an engine of tyranny:

"If we were to endeavor to classify the inhabitants of the capital, according to those circumstances of life which are pervading and essential, we certainly should not adopt the official distribution of the population into fifteen classes. The nation, in truth, fall naturally into a few leading groups, which remind us of the division of organic bodies in natural history, into artificial systems and natural families. Grouped in this manner, the inhabitants of the capital come under the following heads:

"1. The numerous class of persons engaged in the service of the state, and enjoying, consequently, high privileges, and who, collectively and exclusively, are entitled and bound to wear the state uniform (Mundir).

"2. Individuals who enjoy high privileges, not for their own services, but owing to their relationship or connection with the first class. Considerable estates and a sort of hereditary nobility distinguish this class, which is not, however, very numerous.

"3. Foreigners, chiefly merchants, who, from a sentiment of hospitality, converted into a maxim of state, are treated with more consideration than is strictly due, according to the popular mode of thinking, to their occupations and employments.

"4. Russian merchants and handicraftsmen, partly free, partly in servitude.

"5. Russians engaged in trades and manual arts, at their own choice and on their own account, or in the service of others, and who have the lowest amount of privilege. These, also, are either freemen or serfs; but this circumstance is here, as in the case of the fourth class, of little outward value, and is hardly to be detected in the actual relations of life. The clergy do not constitute a particular group; but, according to circumstances, belong either to the official class or to the people, and seem to form a mean between both.

"In the modern language of St. Petersburg, one constantly hears a distinction of the greatest importance conveyed in the inquiry which is habitually made respecting individuals of the educated class: Is he a plain coat or a uniform? However one may be surprised and shocked at first at the unusual value thus set on an outward decoration, and at the abrupt line which severs the members of the same community, yet the system grows more comprehensible, and less offensive, when we fix our attention on its actual working.

"In truth, though the Russian official is sharply and completely separated from the rest of the people by his uniform, yet the aristocracy thus created is, possibly, less odious than that of other countries; for its internal organization is extremely simple; all who belong to the order are on a perfectly equal footing. In the privileged class there is no peculiarly favored caste.

"Again, within this wide circle of privileged equals, personal ability and agreeableness of manners are duly appreciated. The way in which the interests of the individual are involved with the public service gives rise to an '*esprit du corps*,' and, besides, entrance into the most favored class in the nation seems to be as easy as it is desirable; thus the public servants in Russia form, in truth, a class of nobility which may be called an order of merit, which has maintained itself in greater purity here than in other states, because Peter I bestowed the offices and employments which had formerly been held for personal services to the autocrat only as rewards for faithful service to the state.

"Every kind of public service carries with it some personal immunities, and only a certain advancement in official rank is required to make them hereditary. Thus, for example, the acquisition of landed property, and of serfs attached to it, is reserved for a certain rank, (the eighth of the artificial classes); but, as hereditary succession is inseparable from these, there thus arises hereditary nobility. It is a remarkable fact, that in society in St. Petersburg, where there is a constant rivalry between the official and hereditary nobles, the former always have the upper hand. Here the love of rank or office is spoken of always as a peculiar and noble passion; while one not actuated by the thirst for honors is described by the word *Nedorosl* (undeveloped), a term applied in old times to those who, from immaturity or bodily defect, were unfit to bear arms.

"The mutual relation of the official and the hereditary ranks in St. Petersburg seems to be very distinctly marked, if it be only admitted that a foreigner here can really get an insight into the social system. But the stranger is sure to feel immediately the cautious reserve with which the natives converse with him; and he soon discovers that the prompt attention and civility which he experiences in society must be ascribed to the desire to conceal the repugnance felt toward every thing foreign, which it would be inhospitable to avow. Among themselves, the Russians of the upper classes are bound together by a feeling of kindred, in consequence of which they never feel quite at ease but in purely national circles.

"These peculiarities must not be ascribed to the influence of despotism, nor to any wish to conceal from strangers the backwardness of the country. They originate in a positive homogeneousness of disposition, which unites the Russians as one people, and makes them involuntarily shrink from contact with a foreigner as from something heterogeneous. It can not be doubted that, in feeling and moral sentiments, the Russians differ fundamentally from the people of Western Europe; and they themselves say that a stranger must *obrusyety*—that is, become *Russified*—before he can properly appreciate their national character.

"With respect to the intellectual cultivation of the class here referred to, it is impossible to make a general estimate of it, or to describe it in terms universally applicable, for in this very respect are found the widest differences in the same rank of life. Naval officers, civilians engaged in the administration of state, and philosophers by profession, members of the academy and other public institutions, all belong to the privileged class, and meet together as equals. It were more to the purpose, and more capable of being done briefly, to explain what they understand by social refinement. Here the national circle is characterized by an unusual degree of dexterity in the manifold arts of society, by a correct and practiced sense of outward propriety, and an extraordinary faculty of quick comprehension, and of lively repartee, often combined with great felicity of expression. On this point previous travelers all agreed, though they differ most unaccountably on many others. They are obviously in the wrong, however, when they ascribe these social gifts to the influence of French manners. The social refinement of the Russians is altogether of home growth, founded in the moral temperament of the nation, and plainly indicated in the structure of the language."

Russia, then, under the external forms of its imperial government, cherishes a true and most important democratic element, and has succeeded, in a degree surpassing any other state in Europe, in making merit the basis of rank and the condition of power. The same result is aimed at as in free America—to place in office the ablest man; and if the system is liable to abuse through the almost unrestrained will of one man, it must also be remembered that the popular mind makes many and most egregious mistakes in the selection of its office-bearers.

Russia depends not upon a hereditary and imbecile aristocracy for the operations of her government, but draws continually fresh life and power from the people at large, regarding not birth or wealth in its selection, but elevating merit only, and having constantly at its disposal the intellectual strength of the nation. The stimulus which is thus infused into the whole mass of Russian society, reaching to even the lowest circles, may thus be readily conceived. An order of merit, an aristocracy of talent, is thus established, to counteract the paralyzing influence of the hereditary nobility; and though the man who wins rank by merit retains it as hereditary in his family, yet that family is in turn open to the free competition of those who continually rise from below.

A man may hold rank as an empty title, but office and power are bestowed upon those alone who are thought to possess fitness and capacity. The liberalizing influence of such a feature as a nobility of merit can scarcely be estimated, because of the degree to which that word "*despotism*" has blinded the judgment to the actual facts.

If that government is really the most democratic which opens freely the door of preferment to actual merit; if that is most liberal which selects widely from the people those who appear most capable, and allows among its officers only that official distinction which has been honestly won by service performed, then Russia is far more liberal and democratic than England, which so bitterly condemns her as despotic and barbarous. The Emperor of Russia need not hesitate to compare his system with that of England, and let them both be judged by their fruits. England and Russia confronted each other at Sebastopol, and there the world has had a fair opportunity of observing the efficiency of the two governments as they appear in action, and the sympathy of each with merit, aside from birth and rank.

Russia, in her hour of peril, sought for her ablest man. The government asked not how many epaulets were on his shoulders, or how many stars shone on his bosom, but whether he had courage, skill, daring, invention—in short, whether he could defend Sebastopol. Such a man was found in a mere captain of engineers, and over the heads of all titled and noble ones he was placed in command of the defensive works of the beleaguered fortress; and in two weeks a barrier was erected that France and England could neither cross nor force, and the whole aspect of modern war was changed. Nor was this the single example of the operation of the system. The whole defense, by the reluctant confession of the Allies themselves, had exhibited not the forced working of mere human machines which had been anticipated, but the most intense intellectual activity, that has manifested itself in a fertility of resource, a novelty of invention, a skill in the use of means, and a judgment to direct the right thing at the right time, which has never been surpassed.

It demonstrates the efficiency of that scheme which avails itself of capacity wherever found, even in the ranks, and elevates it to the fitting position, and bestows the proper reward. Such a government reaches democratic results under the forms of an empire. England, on the contrary, boasts of her constitutional liberty, of a government regarding the welfare of the people; and calls upon the world to aid in crippling the tyranny of Russia, and invokes the sympathy of the nations on behalf of these down-trodden millions. England called for her men of rank, of titles, epaulets, and stars; she placed *men* in the ranks, and *kept them there*, whatever their merit. She put *nobles* in office, whatever their incapacity, and one titled imbecile was only displaced to make room for another equally helpless; and so incapacity and mismanagement marked every fatal step of her enterprise, and under it the finest army that England ever equipped miserably and fruitlessly perished.

Which, then, of these two systems should be denominated a despotism: that which by intrusting the conduct of affairs to the ablest men wherever they can be found, which excites and brings into requisition the whole talent of a country, forming a noble order based upon merit only, or that which represses and crushes all merit under a weight of titled shams and decorated imbecilities? In true democracy; in opening paths by which the people may rise; in her appreciation and reward of real merit, however humble its position; in her disregard of baubles on a man's coat, or the names of his ancestors, Russia is far in advance of England, and approximates in this respect the spirit and practice of America. It is not entirely a misnomer to call Russia a democracy, governed by an emperor—England a constitutional monarchy, under the despotism of an aristocracy.

Another liberalizing influence in the Russian system, of a most important character, tending strongly to the elevation of the people, is that municipal system which embraces so large a portion of the rural population. Sheltered within these small municipalities, the germs of national freedom are planted thick throughout the empire, and they contain the safeguard of the present, and the promise for the future. This system must be studied in order to understand the condition of the Russian peasantry, which has been so widely and utterly misrepresented. The attention of the reader is invited to the following accounts of these rural communities, the first condensed by the LONDON QUARTERLY from Baron Haxthausen's "Notes:"

"The great feature of the rural system is, that every head of a peasant family is a member of a *commune*, and as such has a right to a portion of land. These village communities, which are found in their most perfect state on the domains of the crown, have a very regular though complicated organization. At the head of each village is the *starosta*, who presides over a council called the *ten*—because, says the Baron, every ten families are entitled to nominate a councilor; but we think it more likely, both from the distinctness of the title and its application, and from the fluctuating number of members which must have attended such a system as the Baron supposes, that the council itself consisted originally of ten persons, and no more. These officers are all elected annually by the peasants. Their duty is to divide the obrok, which is levied upon the community collectively, among the individual members, according to their ability; and to distribute any lands which may escheat to them by the death of the occupiers. They also form a court for the settlement of local disputes and the punishment of minor offenses; in short, there is perfect self-government as regards internal matters. Several of these villages form a district, under an officer styled a *starchina*, who, with assessors, holds a superior court and levies the recruits required for the army. He is elected by deputies sent from the villages within his jurisdiction. A number of these starchinates again form a *volost*, under a functionary, also elective, who, with his assessors, presides over a court possessing higher as well as wider authority. We think it is impossible not at once to be struck with the resemblance of this system to that of frankpledge, commonly said to have been founded by Alfred. Our old *tithing* was generally coextensive with the modern parish, and is said to have been so called as containing ten freeholders. Whether this is exactly correct or not may be doubtful; but certain it is that here, as in Russia, the number ten had something to do with the arrangement; and the persons, whether ten in fact, or more or fewer, were sureties or free-pledges to the king for the good behavior of each other. They annually elected a president, called the tithing-man or headborough, who therefore answered to the Russian starosta. Ten of these tithings formed a hundred under its bailiff, who, like the starchina, held his hundred-court for the trial of causes. Many of these hundreds together formed a shire, having, like the volost, its higher or county court under the Shirereeve, who was formerly, as mentioned in a statute of Edward the First's reign, (and exactly as now in Russia), chosen by the inhabitants.

"The condition of the crown peasants has been very much improved, under Nicholas, by the establishment of the *ministry of domains*—the Russian 'Woods and Forests'—but said to be more economical in its stewardship than ours—a question too delicate for journalistic decision. Its duty embraces a rigid care of all the imperial estates, but more especially the protection of the poor from the extortion of the employees; and this function certainly seems to be so discharged that the crown villages are everywhere the envy of those belonging to private persons. All the peasants are free to go where they like; and any man leaving his village to exercise a trade pays no higher tribute than his share would have been at home as an unskilled laborer; whereas the nobles generally charge the out-living mechanic according to their estimate of his earnings. Meantime, the ministry of domains has a sort of museum of geology, agriculture, and manufactures, at its office in each province; and in many villages it has established elementary schools for the peasants. The 'Autocrat's' hand is everywhere felt indeed—or, at least, everywhere wished for. By stringent laws—whereon no man in that region dares to exercise his talent for quibbling, or any other tricks of evasion—he has prevented the manufacturers from exercising over their people that tyranny which the Manchester school have imported with their cotton from the latitude of Louisiana. The sanitary condition of the workshops is matter of most strict surveillance—the truck system forbidden—and every master forced to provide a hospital, a physician, and a school.

"In some parts the soil is cultivated by quite a different class from any we have hitherto spoken of: they go by the name of Polowniki, are perfectly free, and seem to stand to the owners of the land in nearly the same relation that our tenant-farmers do. Their existence as a distinct class may be traced to a very remote period—some antiquaries say even so far back as the eleventh century. An ukase, in 1725, declared that, not being serfs, they might go where they liked, subject to certain regulations; and their condition was further regulated by an order of the Minister of the Interior, in 1827. Their present tenure seems to be nearly as follows: The rent consists of half the harvest—the tenant finding the stock, as also the labor in the erection of farm-buildings, for which the landlord provides the materials. The length of the leases varies from six to twenty years, but either party contemplating an actual dissolution of the connection must give a year's notice before the expiration of the expressed period."

The English reviewer finds a parallel to this system, as

is seen, in the rural institutions of England in the time of Alfred, which were the germs of the British constitution; and why, therefore, do they not contain also a guarantee of the future of Russia? The American reader will at once perceive a strong resemblance in these "*communes*" to those New England municipalities, the townships, which were the nurseries of our intelligence and our liberties. The elevating principle of self-government is imbedded in both, and that is a principle not only of life but of power.

The second extract is from a writer in HARPER'S MAGAZINE, professing to give the very words of an intelligent Russian, explaining the process by which emancipation was going swiftly forward in 1854. The speaker is describing the dawn of freedom for the serfs, which, since he wrote, they have obtained:

"A reaction commenced at the beginning of the present century; and, since that time, a system of emancipation has been silently operating in Russia, to which the world can show no parallel. In the first year of the century, Alexander made it a fundamental law of the empire that no more grants of serfs should be made to any individual whatever. In the mean time, the extravagance and profligacy of the nobles had passed all bounds. They became popularly known as *Velmoje*—'those who say and it is done.' Their expenditures outran their income, and they were forced to mortgage their estates. Institutions were established by the emperor for lending money to these spendthrifts, at a high rate of interest, secured by mortgages upon their lands and the serfs pertaining to them. As these mortgages ran out, the crown took possession of the estates, and the serfs became peasants of the crown. In the fifteen years just past, the numbers of the peasants of the crown has increased by a million and a half, notwithstanding the numerous emancipations that have taken place, while the number of serfs has increased but half a million. The two classes are now just about equal in numbers; but it is estimated that fully half of the serfs are mortgaged to the state beyond the hope of redemption. These must all, within a few years, fall into the possession of the crown.

"But will they gain any thing by the transfer? Will they not still be serfs? They will gain much. Instead of being subjected to the caprice of individuals, their condition is fixed by general laws and principles, which, in intention at least, operate in their favor. The best evidence that can be offered of the superior condition of the crown peasants is the eagerness of the serfs to pass into their number. It happens not unfrequently that when the government offers for an estate a price less than the proprietors are willing to accept, the serfs join together and pay the difference, in order that they may pass into the hands of the state. Even if the system of emancipation goes on without acceleration, the serfs will be wholly absorbed by the state within the space of two or three generations.

"The crown peasants are grouped into communities of two or three thousand souls. The use of the soil belongs to these communities as a mass, the fee-simple of it being nominally vested in the crown, and each peasant is charged an annual *obrok*, or rent, of ten or twelve rubles. The whole community is chargeable with the payment of the obrok and capitation tax of each of its members. Each commune has a sort of elective assembly, presided over by the *starishina*, or mayor, which meets at regular periods, and has charge of all the internal affairs of the body. It apportions to each family its due proportion of the land, collects the taxes, has charge of the distribution of the recruits among the several families, punishes all petty offenses, and has jurisdiction over all disputes arising among the members of the commune. In a word, there is probably no body of people who have so entire a control of all their local affairs, with so little interference from the superior authorities, as do the Russian peasants of the crown. It is true, that in the general affairs of the empire they have no voice; but in all that concerns their every-day life they are untrammeled. The government exercises no control over the movements of the peasants. Any one of them who wishes to leave the place of his birth can do so by obtaining permission of the commune; and this can not be refused if he is able to make provision for the performance of his communal duties. Provided with a certificate from his commune, the whole empire is open before him without let or hindrance. It is from this class chiefly that the artisans who flock in such numbers every summer to St. Petersburg and Moscow are drawn. They carry on the whole of the extensive interior commerce of the empire, and find ample space for the exercise of their wonderful mechanical faculty.

"Thus, within certain narrow limits, the Russian crown peasant is an absolute freeman. He is, to be sure, subject to many extortions from rapacious and unprincipled government employees; but the occasions upon which he comes in contact with these are so few, compared with those in which the serf of the noble is exposed to the exactions of his owner and overseers, that his condition is looked upon with desire by the serfs. This is not the hopeless longing with which the slave contemplates the state of his master, or the poor laborer of other lands regards the lot of those above him. No impassable barrier separates the two classes. The serf knows that in the natural course of things he or his children will pass into the class of the peasants of the crown; and the crown peasant knows that it is the Czar that has raised him from the condition of the serf." That Czar has now liberated them all.

These statements will enable us to form a more accurate judgment concerning what is called "Russian despotism," and all may see who will that a noble future is already opening before her.

Another powerful agency in liberalizing the spirit of the Russian government is found in that system of manufactures and commerce which she is so assiduously endeavoring to establish, and which France and England are as earnestly striving to repress and destroy, and, thus far, are making war upon civilization themselves. A barbarous despotism would be quite unlikely, in the first place, to conceive such a system, nor could it long exist beneath its influence when once in successful operation. A commercial and manufacturing state becomes of necessity a highly civilized one, and intelligence and wealth sweep away at last the despotic features of the throne.

Just in proportion as the empire succeeds in its new career will the influence of the people in the government increase. Nicholas himself shaped the whole policy of his reign toward the liberalizing of his institutions and the elevation of his people, and he died regretting that he had been unable to accomplish more. The emancipation of twenty millions of government serfs, which the late emperor had so far accomplished that they considered themselves virtually free, was a vast step toward a complete change in the condition of the lower peasantry, and that change has now been nobly wrought by his noble son.

The following account of the criminal system of Russia was condensed by the LONDON QUARTERLY REVIEW, from "Haxthausen's Notes on Russia," and was published before the Crimean war:

"Political offenders, who are merely to be kept under surveillance, live, to all appearances, in the ease of freedom, at Wologda; those whose sins are of a deeper dye become *exiles*—that is, go to Siberia. The exiles are removed to their destination in convoys of one hundred or two hundred, under charge of an escort; and, until the number is complete, they are kept in a comfortable prison, well lighted and warmed. While *en route*, they experience much kindness from the Russian peasants, who send them presents of their best food at every resting-place; and, in large towns, the excess of such contributions over what they can consume is so great that it is sold to buy them better clothing. Before starting, the convicts are inspected by a surgeon, and those who are unable to walk are put in carriages; of the others, every two men carry a chain of four or five pounds weight. They only walk fifteen miles a day, and every third day they rest. Wives are allowed, and expected, to accompany their husbands. The journey lasts seven months. In the Asiatic part of it the comforts are not on the same scale, and there is often great mortality; between 1823 and 1832 it amounted to about one-fifth, and the average number of exiles was ten thousand a year. On arrival, the worst subjects are sent to the mines; and, in former times, they hardly ever again saw daylight; but, by the present emperor's regulation, they are not kept underground more than eight hours a day, and on Sunday all have undisturbed freedom. Those of a less heinous stamp are employed on public works for some time, and then allowed to become colonists. The least serious offenders are at once settled as colonists in Southern Siberia, and thenceforth may be considered as quite free, except that they can not quit their location. In such a soil and climate, with industry, they may, within two or three years, find themselves established in good houses of their own, amid fields supplying every want of a rising family. It is asserted that the young people reared in these abodes turn out, on the whole, of most respectable character, and are associated with, accordingly, on the kindest terms by neighbors of other classes—especially the peasants of native Siberian race, who, by the way, are all entirely free, and many of them very rich. The only drawback to this paradise arises from the recent and rapidly-increasing production of gold, which is said to have already done considerable harm to morals. Let us hope that the Arcadian simplicity of Van Diemen's Land will escape the similar pollution threatened it by the vicinity of Port Philip.

"A model prison at Odessa is described as greatly more successful than any we know of nearer home. It contains, we are told, seven hundred criminals, who all work at different trades, their earnings being either applied to promoting their comfort while in durance, or given them to start in an honest life with, on their emancipation. On entering the prison they wear a chain; but, on good behavior—very generally within three months—they walk the streets without it. They are allowed to go out to work for private individuals, under the direction of one of the best-conducted prisoners, and are constantly employed to put out fires, yet have scarcely ever been accused of stealing on such occasions. After ten years a full pardon is very often granted; in fact, not one-tenth of the whole number are detained beyond that period, and, on its expiry, many obtain small offices under government."

This is abundantly confirmed by the statements of Erman, as the following quotation will show:

"Among the various tales circulated in Western Europe respecting Siberia, may be reckoned the statement that the exiles of this or some other description are obliged to hunt the sable or other fur animals. But, in truth, it is only in the Uralian mines and those of Nerchinsk, and in certain manufactories, that persons condemned to forced labor are ever seen; and several of the rioters whom we saw here in Beresov had already served a year of punishment in Nerchinsk. All the rest, and the great majority of the Russian delinquents, are condemned only to settle abroad; and, if they belong to the laboring classes, to support themselves—yet, with this consolation, that, instead of being serfs as heretofore, they become in all respects as free as the peasants of Western Europe. Political offenders, however, who belong, in Russia as elsewhere, generally to the upper classes, or those not used to manual labor, are allowed to settle only in the towns of Siberia, because the support allowed them by the government can thus reach them more easily.

"I have often heard Russians, who were intelligent and reflecting men, mention as a paradox which hardly admits of an explanation, that the peasants condemned to become settlers, all, without exception, and in a very short time, change their habits, and lead an exemplary life; yet it is certain that the sense of the benefit conferred on them by the gift of personal freedom is the sole cause of this conversion. Banishment, subservient to colonization, instead of close imprisonment, is, indeed, an excellent feature in the Russian code; and though the substitution of forced labor in mines for the punishment of death may be traced back to Grecian examples, yet the improving of the offender's condition, by bestowing on him personal freedom, is an original as well as an admirable addition of a Russian legislator."

The authority of these statements is not to be disputed, and they show conclusively that whatever the condition of Russia once was, her criminal system, under the enlightened direction of Nicholas, was so modified as to compare favorably with that of any other state of Europe, and perhaps surpasses any in the number which it reforms and restores to society and to usefulness.

# CHAPTER XXXIV.

## RUSSIA AS SHE NOW IS, AND HER PROBABLE FUTURE.

It is hoped that Americans will not feel that too much time and space are here occupied with the character, resources, and policy of the great Northern Empire, and the treatment which it has received from those "Allies" who have lately undertaken to settle our American affairs. Russia, among all the powers of earth, has remained true to us in our hour of trial. For many years her friendship for us has been increasing; she felt deeply, and is still grateful for American sympathy in her own great struggle with France and England; and, because of common perils from a common enemy, and from many points of resemblance in our national resources, capabilities, and policy, the Great Empire of the East and the Great Republic of the West are very likely to be not only friendly, but allied powers in the not remote future.

The causes which have brought Russia and America into sympathy are not events which pass and leave no trace behind. The drawing together of these two nations is one of the mighty movements whose influence sweeps over centuries. The Russian fleet anchored in our harbors, the enthusiastic welcome given to its officers, the time of this significant meeting, the joy with which it thrilled all Russia, these things are solemn prophesies of the future.

Those who have regarded this as an empty "flirtation," while America, as they think, longs only for an alliance with England, mistake both the temper of our own people and the signs of the times.

The United States desire peace with England, if she will do us justice; but Americans have been forced, by her own conduct, into a position where they regard her good opinion far less than ever before.

They know her power, and yet they do not fear her, and are by no means, at present, in a mood to court her favor. Great Britain must wipe out not only the stain, but the memory of her conduct in this rebellion, before the United States will seek her favor. But there are no wounds to heal which Russia has made; there is no bitterness in the memories of the past. The friendship first formed has been growing stronger from the beginning, and events indicate that it will reach far into the future; and, whether we look at Russia as she now is, or consider what she soon will be, we may be thankful that we may count upon the friendship of such a power, both in our present conflict and in the severe struggles which apparently await us in almost the immediate future.

Russia stands now before the world with every element from which to construct the most powerful empire that has yet arisen on earth, not even excepting Rome, for her civilization springs from the nobler and intenser life of Christianity; and possessing already the mightiest political and religious organizations of the world, she is just starting upon a new career, with every advantage gained from modern progress. She is the head and representative of the great Sclavonic race, which, even in Poland, would rally to her, were not the people held back by the aristocracy, very much as the people of the South have, by the slaveholders, been brought into a war with the Government. She is the sole life-power in that Sclavonic civilization in which is bound up the destiny of a hundred millions of people.

Her national Church is the grand life-center of almost a hundred millions bearing the Christian name, and these can be brought to the true Christian life only through the instrumentality of Russia. They must all be reheaded under her, if the fragments are ever gathered. Beyond any other nation, Russia is penetrated by the religious life. Whatever we may think of the spirituality of that religion, it is the controlling power of the State; it is, indeed, the soul of the political body.

The Czar is reverenced, not so much as a political officer, a mere emperor, as the religious head and father of the people. He rules rather as the head of the Church than as the governor of the State; and this fact alone may show us what measureless power there is in a nation numbering seventy or eighty millions, bound, by religious enthusiasm, to one personal leader.

Russia presents, too, the noblest moral spectacle of modern times. Foremost among all nations, she, who has been denounced as the barbarian despotism, steps forth the champion of human rights, investing, at once, some twenty-five millions of serfs with all the ennobling rights and responsibilities of citizenship, and then changing an absolute monarchy into a constitutional kingdom; and it proves both the strength and the value of the government, that these vast changes have been wrought without bloodshed or serious commotion. These two great acts inaugurate for Russia a new era; they prove that, in truly liberal ideas, in measures intended to elevate the working people, she is in advance of every nation in Europe, not even excepting England; that a spirit pervades her like that which is liberating our own laborers, and that a new-born life, energy, and enterprise are quickening the whole mass of the Russian nation—a life in character, activity, and aims, closely resembling our own.

The emancipation act and the new constitution are the sure prophesies of her magnificent future. Russia and America are both passing through a revolution which will place the future greatness of both on the same basis, and that an immovable one—a working population of landholders. The change which is being effected in the South by the breaking up of the great estates, and placing them in the hands of the laborers, and the operation of our homestead law, are doing for America precisely what the emancipation of the serfs is doing for Russia. In both nations the workers will own the land to a far greater extent than in any other country of the world, and will make them true democracies, whatever the name of the government may be.

The new freemen of Russia are already purchasing small farms, all over the empire, and the government assists them by loaning them money, and cherishes, in all ways, the new national life. The increased value of the lands of the Russian Empire is already beyond calculation, and improvements are rapidly going forward on all sides. The new wants of the people are giving a new impulse to manufactures and internal trade, steamboats are multiplying on her net-work of rivers, and the whole nation feels the throb of an intenser life. Her nobles, who formerly spent their time and money abroad, are now living on their estates, anxious to assist in the general improvement of their country.

Before emancipation, such a thing as a day-school was scarcely known among the peasants; but since, in the short space of two years, more than eight thousand have been established, and this shows how quickly educational institutions of all grades will be established throughout the land. Their eagerness to learn is like that of our own freedmen, and, as there is no prejudice of color or race to overcome, the serfs being Russians, it is easy to see, that, in a short time, all traces of former condition will disappear, and, in every sense, the population of Russia will be a homogeneous body, animated by one national life. The New Testament is being circulated among the people at twelve cents per copy, and it is intended that the religious life of Russia shall keep pace with her material development.

This robust, expansive Sclavonic life is applying its energies to a territory that, in Europe, stretches from the Baltic to the Black Sea, with an eastern frontier which is floating on toward India, and with a valley, on the north of China, nearly equal to that of the Mississippi, opening upon the Pacific, and traversed by a navigable river more than two thousand miles long; a position which, in spite of Western Europe, will give her a controlling influence over China, Japan, and the whole East Indian Archipelago. Her past history, her present irrepressible aspirations, her Asiatic character, her relations to the Greek Church, all point steadily to the occupation of Constantinople, the removal of Mohammedanism from the line of her march, and then, with her navy on the Baltic, on the Euxine and Dardanelles, and the Pacific, with her boundless resources, her hundred millions of people elevated by free institutions, and quickened by friendly contact with our American life, with a national Church coextensive with her territory, and that Church giving already signs of spiritual resurrection, why should not Russia recover that Eastern empire, and become the regenerator of Asia?

Such is the nation which proposes to join hands with our Republic, and walk with us into the nobler future which is opening before the nations. Her firm friendship has helped to save us from foreign intervention, and common sympathies and common dangers may bind us still more closely hereafter.

# CHAPTER XXXV.

## ENGLAND—HER PRESENT CONDITION, POWER, AND PROSPECTS.

THE statements which have been presented, drawn from sources with which the mass of the people are probably not familiar, will enable them to form more accurate opinions than have hitherto prevailed in regard to the great nation which alone, among all European powers, is likely to remain our friend, and, perhaps, become our ally in the stormy future upon which the world is entering.

It is equally important that Americans should be able to measure accurately the condition, power, and resources of those who have combined to hinder our progress, and cripple our power; who have striven, by all means short of actual war, to make the rebellion a success, and thereby ruin the Republic here, and the cause of free institutions in Europe. We ought to know what ability France and England have for attack, in order to compare with it our own power for offensive or defensive war. For this purpose it is proposed, first, to study the condition of England.

Great Britain must be judged, not alone by her present position and power, but by her elements of permanent prosperity, be they few or many, which may enable her to maintain her present supremacy in competition with other nations, and especially with Russia and America, in the new career upon which these are entering now. England will probably find, when too late, that, in attacking Russia and the United States, she has provoked a struggle from which neither party can recede, until it is determined whether she, with France, can dictate to the world; and, if she discovers that the conflict involves either a change in her institutions, or a surrender of her national life, she must remember that the issue is one which she made up and presented herself. It has not been forced upon her either by Russia or America.

What, then, are the elements of her power and sources of her life, and what does her present condition indicate for the future? The first essential element of enduring national greatness is a home territory sufficient for the support of the population of a first-class power. Where this is wanting there can not be a great *independent* nation; there can not be one mighty homogeneous body of population, whose life and power of growth are derived from a common center, and from which center continuous lines of attachment and interlacing bonds spread over the whole nation, like the nerves and veins of the living body. This requires one undivided theater of national growth and activity, broad enough to bear up the social and political structure. There may be, without these, a greatness derived from separated colonial territories, a manufacturing and commercial greatness and power, enduring or temporary, according to circumstances; but the territory of a nation, its extent and quality, must, in the end, be the measure of its power.

Of course, territory alone can not insure national power; but, if one nation has a domain which will support a home population of twenty-five millions only, and another holds land enough to maintain one hundred millions, and is equal in all other advantages, the latter has elements of power four times greater than the former, nor would distant colonial possessions make up the deficiency of territory at home.

These colonies, while they can be held simply as tributaries, may increase the wealth and power of the home government through its manufactures and commerce; but, in the end, prosperous colonies throw off the yoke of bondage, and new nations spring up to compete for the commerce of the world.

What, then, is the condition and prospect of England in regard to this point? What are the foundations of her national structure, and what are her prospects in rivalry with, or hostility to, Russia and America, for the next quarter of a century?

England, Wales, Ireland, and Scotland, together, have a territory of about one hundred and twelve thousand square miles. This constitutes the whole home territory of Great Britain. It is less than that occupied by our three States of Ohio, Indiana, and Illinois, and less than half the size of Texas. England, alone, is not quite as large as the single State of Alabama.

The arable land of England is estimated at only twenty-eight millions of acres, which is less than the estimated arable land in the single State of Illinois. While the home territory of Great Britain is about one hundred and twelve thousand square miles, that of the United States is about three millions of square miles, all in one body, and which, by navigable rivers, lakes, railways, and coast-line navigation, can be controlled by one people and one central government.

These numbers form the proper basis of comparison between the United States and England which reach into the future, though they are by no means indications of their present relative strength. But such comparisons will be truthful guides in the future, because the time is not distant when Great Britain will lose the control of every one of her principal colonies, and our present war is consolidating our people into one American nation, whose life is vigorous enough to extend over a continent. England, at no very distant period, must rest her power upon the resources of her home empire, competing as she may with the rest of the world for the trade of her present colonies.

England is almost a miracle of energy and power; she is the most wonderful product, thus far, of modern civilization, and no American should desire to diminish aught of her proper glory; but, when she proposes to interfere with our private affairs, when she seems to desire our ruin, and gives her sympathies to our bitterest enemies, and forms alliances to hinder our progress, and holds herself in a threatening attitude, it will do us no harm to remember that, ere this century closes, she will see here a hundred millions of people, who will be at least her equal in every thing pertaining either to peace or war, and outnumbering her nearly three to one.

On this territory of one hundred and twelve thousand square miles, Great Britain has twenty-nine millions of inhabitants, averaging, for the whole surface, two hundred and fifty-eight persons. It is evident, therefore, if we regard the land as a basis, the British Empire has reached the limit of growth, and, indeed, has passed that limit, unless her great estates are divided, for one-third of her population is, even now, fed from foreign countries. Her power to maintain her present rank among nations, and even her ability to keep her population from starving, depend upon her being able to supply the markets of the world with her fabrics, and retain her position as the chief factor of the world's commerce. Should other nations succeed in competing with her on this, her chosen field, her political supremacy would at once be stricken down. Hence her extreme anxiety in regard to the progress of Russia and America, and her attempts to put them down by force, when she fears that they will not only manufacture for themselves, instead of buying from her, but will become her rivals in the great markets of the world.

The London Quarterly, for July, 1861, thus sets forth those fears which were the real motives for the attack on Russia, and for the hostile attitude of England toward the United States:

"The policy which the Czar has marked out for himself appears for the present to be the consolidation of his empire and the encouragement of foreign trade, as forming the basis of that maritime greatness which is a traditional object of Russian ambition. Whenever the mercantile and maritime development of Russia shall be in any degree proportioned to its colossal empire, it is impossible that such a country should not become an object of apprehension to all independent States.

"England has immense interests at stake in the maintenance of her commercial ascendency in the East; and if Russia should ever acquire the power to control British trade, or become a successful competitor for the supply of the principal markets of Asia, a heavy blow will have been struck at our political greatness."

The leading article in the NORTH BRITISH, for May, 1863, reveals very clearly what gigantic specters are terrifying the people of England—one in the East and the other in the West. The writer turns, first, to Russia, with intense alarm, with visions of Cossacks quartered in the capitals of Europe, but comforts himself with the prediction that the Russian Empire can not long be held together; she will, undoubtedly, he says, be disintegrated, and Europe will be relieved from terror.

He then turns to the Republican specter of the West. English thinkers have just begun to get glimpses of the real significance of this war, and the revolution through which we are passing. They begin to perceive that this rebellion forms the transition stage from a Confederacy of States to a true American Nationality. They see that the people are determined to form, now, one consolidated American Nation. This vision of an American Nation has frightened England from her propriety. This, above all things, she dreads, and, to prevent it, she hastens with all aid and sympathy to the side of the Rebels; hastens to send fleets with Enfield muskets, rifled cannon, and mans, and arms, and sends forth piratical ships, under the Rebel flag, to plunder and burn our ships. An American Nation controlling this American continent is a thing not to be endured.

The writer in the NORTH BRITISH comforts himself, and quiets his fears, first of all, by declaring that such a thing can not be.

"Fully may it be granted, and religiously may it be believed, that large purposes in the world's future are, in the divine intention, to be accomplished *for* and *by* the nations of the North American continent. Nor need the boldest speculations on this ample field be restricted or suppressed. But when this liberty of speculation has been granted—sobriety barely listened to—then there comes in a question of momentous import, which may thus be worded: Shall the destinies of the North American nations be accomplished, and the divine purposes thereto relating fulfilled, by the means of a one all-grasping, all-absorbing empire, doing its ruthless pleasure from the Mexican Gulf to the Arctic regions—from the sea-board of the Atlantic to the sea-board of the Pacific Ocean?—shall it, indeed, be *thus* that the same Hand which long ago scattered the nations from the plains of Babylon and Nineveh, will be seen favoring an enterprise *of the same quality*, in these last times? A negative answer to a question of this sort must, we think, commend itself to all calm minds, on whatever grounds it is argued—whether the *religious* aspect of the question be regarded, or that of political or philosophical speculation. It shall not be that the destinies of the nations of the North American continent will be worked out under the administrative hand of a Nebuchadnezzar."

He then goes on, prophetically, to declare "the inevitable and not remote disintegration of the hitherto United States." Not quite satisfied that he has laid this specter yet, he proceeds to say: "It is nothing but a dream, after all. We might stop short of formal prediction, and might affirm, on the premises given us, that this gigantic North American Empire which haunts the dreams of loyal Americans is a *dream*, and can never be a reality."

He then kindly invites us to "*disintegrate*" for the benefit of the world, and England in particular, and intimates that, if we do not, God will probably "come down" and destroy us, as he overthrew Babel, the city and tower of old.

"Disintegration, gracefully accepted, timely submitted to, and wisely turned to account, is the call of Providence audibly addressed to the people of the United States at this moment. We say it is the call of Providence; and this phrase brings with it a train of thought which we do not propose to pursue; or thus far only to follow it. On all grounds of secular calculation, the gorgeous phantom of an empire, stretched from ocean to ocean, which now rules the American mind as a frenzy, is, as we think, demonstrably an absurdity: no such mad scheme shall ever be realized. But turn now to another side of the subject. If at all the ways of God toward the human family, so far as these are known to history, may be understood and interpreted—and if there be a visible overruling of human affairs—this intervention of Heaven, this 'coming down of the Lord to see the city and the tower,' has been repeated from age to age—in Asia, in Europe—in the most remote times, in times quite recent; and always it has occurred at moments when some vast conception of boundless empire and irresistible despotism has been proclaimed, and boasted of, and has seemed near to be realized. At such critical moments a voice from on high has been heard, 'It shall not be.' The instances need not here be named; but, among all these instances, not one can be mentioned that carries upon its front, as this latest instance does, the character of a national delirium."

These English terrors, these fits of shivering apprehension at the growth of Russia and America, afford a completely satisfactory clue to the meaning of the Alliance, the invasion of the Crimea, and the present hostility to the United States—the *hitherto* United States, as the North British delights to call us.

These things show at once the fears and perils of England. She knows that, if Russia and America become great manufacturing nations, with a commercial marine and navy proportioned to their power in other respects, her own supremacy will be gone. She will be tempted to make desperate efforts before she will yield her present place of pride, and hence our own continual danger. She will watch for our overthrow. She will ruin us if she can. Let us, then, turn again to the study of her condition and resources.

Russia and America are both pursuing a true democratic policy in regard to their lands. They are putting them, as rapidly as possible, into the hands of the people. The Russian freedmen are rapidly buying them homes, the government loaning them money for the purpose, while our homestead law gives every man who wishes it a farm. America and Russia are being occupied by a land-owning yeomanry, the true basis of national power, stability, and growth. England is pursuing the exactly opposite policy. She is depriving her people everywhere of land, and forcing them downward to the condition of serfs, from which her agricultural laborers are, even now, but a step removed.

Alison, writing thirty-one years ago, says there were then four millions of land proprietors in France, while there were not three hundred thousand in Great Britain and Ireland. In France, he says, "the proprietors are as numerous as the other members of the State; in England they hardly amount to one-tenth part of their number."

This was thirty-one years ago. Investigations made since, show that even this estimate of Mr. Alison is much too high.

In the Rev. H. Worsley's Essay on Juvenile Depravity, quoted by Kay in his Social Condition of the English People, it is stated, that all the lands of England are in the hands of thirty-two thousand proprietors. This one amazing fact, all the lands of England in the hands of only thirty-two thousand men, is quite sufficient to account for the perfect sympathy between the English aristocracy and the Southern slaveholders, and also for the shocking condition of the English laborers, as described by Mr. Kay. England, alone, contains some eighteen millions of people, only thirty-two thousand of whom own a foot of land; and the destructive process of diminishing the number of estates, of bringing the land into still fewer hands, is yet going swiftly forward.

The English system, then, is precisely that of the slaveholding South, which brings all the lands, and all the other wealth of the country, into the hands of a few, and reduces the laborers to slaves, or a condition but little better than slavery, even in England, as her own writers have fully shown.

The EDINBURGH REVIEW, for January, 1860, in an article on British Taxation, states, that *at least* three-fourths of the population of the United Kingdom belong to the working classes; that is, to those who live *by wages*. By working classes in England is not meant those who are working, as in America, on their own farms, but who are *hired* in some form to capital—who live by wages.

The present condition of these laborers, the *people* of England, is set forth by Joseph Kay, Esq., who was commissioned by the Senate of Cambridge University, England, to travel through Western Europe, to examine the comparative social condition of the poorer classes of the different countries.

His chapters on England have lately been published by Harper & Brothers, and his statements will show us the condition of the *people* of England, and from this it is easy to understand both the strength and the weakness of Great Britain, and know the real nature of that haughty power whose hostility we are compelled to meet. Of her twenty-nine millions of inhabitants, nearly twenty-two millions are hired laborers, and one appointed to investigate the subject has given us the results of his inquiry.

The first facts relate to the rapid decrease of small farms, the increase of the large estates, and the effect which this produces upon the laboring classes. Mr. Kay says:

"I was in Westmoreland for some time, during the autumn of 1849, and I took great pains to discover the present condition of the last survivors of these small proprietors. I can not describe it better than by giving the words of a gentleman of great intelligence and of conservative principles, who is engaged in the management of some of the largest estates in Westmoreland and Cumberland. He resides in that part of the country, and is interested in opposing the system of peasant proprietors. There are obvious reasons why I can not mention this gentleman's name. He said to me:

"'The greater proprietors in this part of the country are buying up all the land they can get hold of, and including it in their settlements. Whenever one of the small estates is put up for sale, the great proprietors outbid the peasants, and purchase it at all costs. The consequence is, that, for some time past, the number of the small estates held by the peasants has been rapidly diminishing in all parts of the country. In a short time none of them will remain, but all will be merged in the great estates. While this has been going on, the great landowners have been also increasing very considerably the size of the farms. The smaller farms have been united, in order to form great farms out of them. So that, not only is it becoming more and more difficult every day for a peasant to *buy* land in this part of the country, but it is also gradually becoming impossible for him to obtain even a leasehold farm. The consequence is, that the peasant's position, instead of being what it once was, one of hope, is gradually becoming one of despair. Unless a peasant emigrates, there is now no chance for him. It is impossible for him to rise above the peasant class.

"'All this I believe to be a great evil. I have lived all my life among these people, and I believe that the old system of small estates was one which did the greatest possible good to the peasants. It stimulated them to exertion, self-denial, and sobriety, by affording them a chance of obtaining a farm of their own; and, when they had obtained one, it made them interested in the careful cultivation of the soil, in the preservation of public order, and in the general prosperity of the country.

"'Besides all this, the situation and duties of a small landowner were in themselves an excellent education to the small proprietor. He had many things to do and think of, with reference to county rates, poor rates, police, markets, agriculture, the effects of national proceedings on prices and on taxation, and the seasons. All this was as interesting to the peasants, and as improving to them, as it is to our country gentlemen, and it made up, in great measure, for the want of good schools and good instruction. But all the effect of this education of circumstance is now being done away. The situation of the peasant is becoming one void of hope, and of all improving influences whatever.'

"As the Rev. Henry Worsley says: 'The laborer's hope of rising in the world is a forlorn one. There is no graduated ascent up which the hardy aspirant may toil step by step with patient drudgery. Several rounds in the ladder are broken away and gone. A farm of some hundred acres, requiring for their due cultivation a large capital, would be a day-dream too gaudy ever to mix itself with the visions of the most ambitious laborer, earning, on an average, probably less than nine shillings a week. The agricultural workman's horizon is bounded by the high red-brick walls of the union-house: his virtual marriage settlement can only point to such a refuge if troubles arise: his old age may there have to seek its last shelter.'*

"What is the effect of all this? Why, that the millions in England and Wales fancy that they have nothing to lose and every thing to gain by political changes, and that, instead of our institutions being based upon the conservatism of the masses, they are only based upon the conservatism of the few. So that we have really much more reason than any other country to dread the growth of democracy.

"Besides the depressing and demoralizing effect of our system of monopoly of land upon the peasants, another

* Essay on Juvenile Depravity, p. 54.

great evil which results from our English system of great and few farms, and great and few estates, is, that it drives vast numbers of the young peasants, and of the younger sons of farmers, into the manufacturing towns, and, by overstocking their labor markets, renders it more and more difficult every year for the small shopkeepers and laborers of these towns to make a livelihood amid the ever-increasing competition around them.

"Let us look this evil more fully in the face. An active and enterprising son of a farmer sees that there is no chance of his ever getting a farm in his native parish, or of his ever purchasing or even renting a small plot of land, or of his ever rising above the rank of a farm laborer, earning eight or nine shillings a week. The only opening left for such a young man, if he would climb above the lowest rank in the social scale—the peasant's position—is, either to go and seek his fortune in one of our colonies, or in one of our towns. There are many such young men, who can not persuade themselves to break off the ties of home and kindred, and to leave their native country, but who feel compelled to leave their native villages. All such crowd to the great manufacturing towns of England. The peasants go, to seek labor as operatives or artisans; the sons of the farmers go, to endeavor to establish shops or taverns. What is the result? The labor market in the manufacturing towns is constantly overstocked; the laborers and shopkeepers find new and eager competitors constantly added to the list; competition in the towns is rendered unnaturally intense, profits and wages are both unnaturally reduced; the town work-houses and the town jails are crowded with inmates; the inhabitants are overburdened with rates, and the towns swarm with paupers and misery.

"I know not what others may think, but to me it is a sad and grievous spectacle, to see the enormous amount of vice and degraded misery which our towns exhibit, and then to think that we are doing all we can to foster and stimulate the growth and extension of this state of things by that system of laws which drives so many of the peasants of both England and Ireland to the towns, and increases the already vast mass of misery by so doing.

"I speak with deliberation when I say, that I know no spectacle so degraded, and, if I may be allowed to use a strong word, so horrible, as the back streets and suburbs of English and Irish towns, with their filthy inhabitants; with their crowds of half-clad, filthy, and degraded children, playing in the dirty kennels; with their numerous gin-palaces, filled with people, whose hands and faces show how their flesh is, so to speak, impregnated with spirituous liquors—the only solaces, poor creatures, that they have!—and with poor young girls, whom a want of religious training in their infancy, and misery, has driven to the most degraded and pitiful of all pursuits."

The first result of such a state of affairs is sufficiently startling. In England and Wales alone, exclusive of Ireland, there are two millions of paupers, and this number is continually increasing. The number of paupers in England and Wales is about one in eight of the whole population.

Of the whole population of Great Britain and Ireland, about three millions are said to be paupers, or on the verge of pauperism. Certainly, it would seem that a country whose political system is reducing its laborers to the condition of serfs and paupers, can not have a perpetual lease of national existence in its present form. Its prosperity rests not on the welfare of the masses, but in the wealth of a class, whose riches have been wrung from the earnings of the many.

The reader should bear in mind that the statements which follow are the results of a widely-extended official inquiry, and that they relate not to isolated cases, but to whole classes of laborers, and in all parts of the country, and presented, as they have been, from a great number of independent witnesses, may be received as representing correctly the *general* condition of the working classes of Great Britain; and it is hoped that the laboring people of this country will earnestly study this subject, and ponder these facts, and thus learn to value more than ever the free institutions of our land, by which those who produce the wealth of the state are duly rewarded, instructed, and elevated, instead of being forced down by an aristocracy, as in England, to the condition of paupers and serfs, while bearing the empty name of freemen. The first question which it is proposed to consider is,

### ARE THE LABORERS OF GREAT BRITAIN EDUCATED?

This question is thus answered, by the latest investigations of Englishmen themselves, in statements copied from Mr. Kay's Report, who gives the authorities upon which he relies.

"I will give a short summary of the present state of primary education in England and Wales, as collected from the reports of Her Majesty's Inspectors, of the Commissioners of Inquiry in Wales, of the National Society, of the Statistical Society, and of the city mission; from Mr. Redgrave's reports from some very able articles in the NORTH BRITISH REVIEW, and from numerous personal inquiries in various parts of England and Wales:

"1. It has been calculated that there are, at the present day, in England and Wales, nearly 8,000,000 persons who can not read and write.

"2. Of all the children in England and Wales, between the ages of five and fourteen, more than the half are not attending any school.

"3. Even of the class of the farmers, there are great numbers who can not read and write.

"4. Even of those children of the poor who have received some instruction, very few know any thing of geography, history, science, music, or drawing. Their instruction in the village schools has hitherto generally consisted of nothing more than a little practice in reading, writing, and Scripture history.

"5. Of the teachers who are officiating in many of the village schools, there are many who can not read and write correctly, and who know very little of the Bible, which they profess to explain to their scholars.

"6. A very great part of our present village and town-schools are managed by poor and miserably-instructed dames, who thus seek to make a livelihood, and who literally do no good to the children, except it be keeping them, for a certain number of hours in the day, out of the dirt and out of worse society.

"7. Many of these dame-schools are so wretchedly managed, as to do the children a very great deal more harm than good—by uniting miserable associations with the sacred writings, and with the subjects of the wretched instruction given in these schools.

"8. Very many of our town-schools are held in small and unventilated cellars or garrets, where the health of the children is seriously impaired.

"9. If we except only the *worst* part of the dame-schools, we have not even then *one-half* as many school-buildings as we require for the *present* numbers of our population.

"10. By far the greatest part of our school-buildings have only *one* room, in which all the classes are instructed together, in the midst of noise and foul air.

"11. Many of our present school-rooms have no forms and no parallel desks—both of which are to be found in every school-room throughout Western Europe; and in all such schools the children are kept standing the whole day.

"12. Very few of our school-rooms are properly supplied with maps, books, or school-apparatus.

"13. The majority of our town-schools have no playgrounds; and, in all these cases, the children are turned out into the streets during the hours of recreation.

"14. Scarcely any schools throughout the country have more than *two* class-rooms; the classification of the children is, therefore, very deficient, and the instruction is thereby much impaired.

"15. Very few schools have more than one teacher.

"16. Great numbers of parishes and districts throughout England and Wales have no school-room at all, and no place in which their children can be instructed.

"17. Of these latter districts, many are too poor or too careless to raise any thing toward the erection of school-buildings; and in none of these cases does the Committee of Council give any assistance.

"18. In many other districts, the inhabitants are so divided in religious opinions, that they find it impossible to act in concert in providing for the education of their children; and in these cases the Committee of Council renders no assistance.

"19. In most of our schools it is necessary, in order to provide salaries for the teacher and funds for the support of the school, to charge from 2*d.* to 4*d.* a week per head for the instruction of scholars. This absolutely excludes the children of all paupers, and of all poor persons, who can not afford to pay so much out of their small earnings; while, throughout the greatest part of Western Europe, the education afforded in the primary schools is quite gratuitous.

"20. There is no public provision for the proper payment and maintenance of our teachers, and these latter are, therefore, generally placed in so very humiliating and dependent a position, as in many cases virtually to prevent any man of ability and education from accepting such an office.

"21. A great part of our village teachers are only poor, uneducated women, or poor men who are not fit for any other office or employment, and who are themselves miserably educated.

"22. In proportion to our population, we have scarcely one-fourth part as many colleges for the instruction of teachers as any of the countries of Western Europe, and not one-fourth part as many as are necessary for the education of a sufficient number of teachers for our poor.

"23. In nearly all the few colleges we have established

for the instruction of teachers, the education is very limited and meager in its character, as these colleges depend upon voluntary aid, and can not afford to give the students more than a year's or eighteen months' training; while throughout Western Europe the teachers receive *three years'* training in the teachers' colleges at the expense of the government.

"24. The colleges we have established are so poor that they can not afford to support nearly so large and complete a staff of teachers and professors as are to be found in almost all the teachers' colleges throughout Western Europe.

"25. A great part of our schools and teachers are never visited by any public inspector, or by any private person, or committee of persons, from the year's beginning to the year's end. In many of these cases, bad teachers are left to do great injury to their scholars, unchecked and unheard of; and, in many other cases, good and able teachers are left, without encouragement or advice, to labor on—unknown, disheartened, and alone.

"26. In most of our schools, owing to the teacher either not having been trained at all, or not having been educated for a long enough time in a college, the methods of teaching are miserable and ridiculous. The noise in the school-rooms is often so great that it is with difficulty that any individual can make himself heard. The children are often kept standing the greater part of the day, and are wearied beyond endurance, so that the lessons, and all the associations connected with the subjects of instruction, are rendered hateful ever afterward. The highest religious subjects are thus often made odious to the children, who, during their after life, avoid as much as possible recurring to what awakens so many disagreeable recollections. In most of our schools there is little or no attempt to interest the children in their studies, or to teach them to think or reason. The instruction is mere parrot work. They are taught by rote, and forget again almost as soon as they have left the school.

"27. Great numbers of the school-buildings in the more remote country districts are of the most wretched and miserable character.

"An idea of some of these may be formed from the following descriptions, selected from the able report of Mr. Lingen on the state of education in South Wales, published in 1848. These are fair specimens of schools which may be found throughout England and Wales.

"Mr. Lingen says: There was no room for making furniture and apparatus separate considerations in most of the schools throughout the remoter districts, exhibiting, as they did, every form of squalid destitution. I subjoin a few instances out of many others perhaps more striking.

"Of one school, he says:

"'The furniture consisted of one desk for the master, two longer ones for the pupils, and a few benches—all in a wretched state of repair. The room was not ceiled. In one corner was a heap of spars, the property of the master, for the purpose of thatching his house; in another place was a heap of culm, emptied out on the floor. The floor was boarded, but all the middle of it was in holes.'

"Of another, he says:

"'The school was held in a miserable room over the stable; it was lighted by two small glazed windows, and was very low; in one corner were a broken bench, some sacks, and a worn-out basket; another corner was boarded off for storing tiles and mortar belonging to the chapel. The furniture consisted of three small square tables—one for the master, two larger ones for the children—and a few benches—all in a wretched state of repair. There were several panes of glass broken in the windows; in one place paper served the place of glass, and in another a slate, to keep out wind and rain; the door was also in a very dilapidated condition. On the beams which crossed the room were a ladder and two large poles.'

"Of another, he says:

"'The school was held in a room built in a corner of the churchyard; it was an open-roofed room; the floor was of the bare earth, and very uneven; the room was lighted by two small glazed windows, one-third of each of which was patched up with boards. The furniture consisted of a small square table for the master, one square table for the pupils, and seven or eight benches, some of which were in good repair, and others very bad. The biers belonging to the church were placed on the beams which ran across the room. At one end of the room was a heap of coal and some rubbish and a worn-out basket, and on one side was a new door leaning against the wall, and intended for the stable belonging to the church. The door of the school-room was in a very bad condition, there being large holes in it, through which cold currents of air were continually flowing.'

"Of another, he says:

"'This school is held in a dark, miserable den under the town-hall; the furniture comprised only a few old benches and tables; in the corner was a litter of broken cups and a bottle; there was a starling of the master's loose in the room which, by flying about, greatly disturbed the children during my visit.'

"Of another, he says:

"'In one corner was a heap of culm, in another a bench or two piled against the wall, and various litter; at the bottom of the room lay a gravestone, on which the master had been chalking the letters which the village mason was to cut as an inscription; on the table lay a jug and pipe.'

"I might quote endless instances to prove the miserable character and ill effects of the present school-buildings in Carmarthenshire and Pembrokeshire. Indeed, report after report is too often only a wearisome repetition of such particulars. It will suffice for me to subjoin a few instances, by way of illustration, taking them almost at hazard.

Of another school, he says:

"'The school was held in a room, part of a dwelling-house; the room was so small that a great many of the scholars were obliged to go into the room above, which they reached by means of a ladder through a hole in the loft; the room was lighted by one small glazed window, half of which was patched up with boards; it was altogether a wretched place. The furniture consisted of one table, in a miserable condition, and a few broken benches; the floor was in a very bad state, there being several large holes in it, some of them nearly half a foot deep; the room was so dark that the few children whom I heard read were obliged to go to the door and open it, to have sufficient light.'

"Of another, he says:

"'This school is held in the mistress's house. I never shall forget the hot, sickening smell which struck me on opening the door of that low, dark room, in which thirty girls and twenty boys were huddled together. It more nearly resembled the smell of the engine on board a steamer, such as it is felt by a sea-sick voyager on passing near the funnel. Exaggerated as this may appear, I am writing on the evening of the same day on which I visited the school, and I will vouch for the accuracy of what I state. Every thing in the room (*i. e.*, a few benches of various hights and sizes, and a couple of tables) was hidden under and overlaid with children.'

"Of another, he says:

"'This school is held in a ruinous hovel of the most squalid and miserable character; the floor is of bare earth, full of deep holes; the windows are all broken; a tattered partition of lath and plaster divides it into two unequal portions; in the larger were a few wretched benches, and a small desk for the master in one corner; in the lesser was an old door, with the hasp still upon it, laid crossways upon two benches, about half a yard high, to serve for a writing-desk! Such of the scholars as write retire in pairs to this part of the room, and kneel on the ground while they write. On the floor was a heap of loose coal and a litter of straw, paper, and all kinds of rubbish. The vicar's son informed me that he had seen eighty children in this hut. In summer, the heat of it is said to be suffocating; and no wonder.'

"Of another, he says:

"'In the school-room which, at six square feet per child, is calculated to hold twenty-eight scholars, I found fifty-nine present, and seventy-four on the books: some of the children are drafted off into the master's dwelling-house.'

"Of another, he says:

"'The school is held in a room over a stable, which is a very small one. The children were much crowded. There was a very comfortable fire in the room on the day of my visit. Some ten or twelve of the senior boys were obliged to sit in the adjoining chapel, on account of the smallness of the room. The chapel had no fire in it, and was very cold and uncomfortable.'

"Of another, he says:

"'The school-room is part of a dwelling-house, on the ground-floor, and the smell arising from so many children being crammed in such a small room was quite overpowering. There was a large fire in the grate at the time. The window was a small one, and was kept closed. The floor, walls, and the room altogether, were in bad repair. I observed, after the scholars went out at noon, (for there were no seeing any thing but children while they were in the room), one square table for the master, two long tables for the writers and cipherers, five benches, and one chair.'

"Of another, he says:

"'This school is kept up stairs in two rooms of the master's house. There is a door to each room from the landing at the top of the stairs, but the master can not see all the scholars from one room while they are in the other. He generally sits with the elementary classes.'

"Of another, he says:

"'The floor was of the bare earth, very uneven and rather damp. There was a fire in an iron stove placed in the middle of the room. The steam which arose from it was quite insufferable, so much so that I was obliged to keep both door and window open to enable me to breathe.

The master remarked that it was "bad to a stranger, but nothing to those who were used to it."'

"Of another, he says:

"'This school is held in the church. I found the master and four little children ensconced in the chancel amidst a number of old tables, benches, and desks, round a three-legged grate full of burning sticks, with no sort of funnel or chimney for the smoke to escape. It made my eyes smart till I was nearly blinded, and kept covering with ashes the paper on which I was writing. How the master and children bore it with so little apparent inconvenience, I can not tell.'

"Of another, he says:

"'The day-school (which used to be held in private houses) is now held in an old Independent chapel, no longer used for religious purposes, and rented by the master. There was a raised hearth of brick in the room, with a grate on the top, but no chimney. There was a fire of culm burning on it; the heat and vapor made the room almost insufferable to one coming from the fresh air.'

"Of another, he says:

"'The floor of the chapel was of earth and lime, very uneven and broken; it contained a few pews, a pulpit, a table, and a couple of desks, with a few benches in use, others being heaped together at one end of the chapel; there was a grate full of culm* in the middle of the chapel, but no chimney.'

"Of another, he says:

"'The room in which this school is held is a most miserable hut, not fit to shelter cattle in, as the thatched roof would be any thing but proof against bad weather. The master said that he often suffered from the rain; and there were large quantities of straw inside the roof to shelter in some degree himself and pupils.'

* This is the name of the common fuel in Wales, which is anthracite coal made up into balls with clay. It burns without smoke, but with a glowing vapor, like charcoal.

"Of another, he says:

"'The boys' free-school was held in a most miserable hovel, lighted by four small windows. The floor was of the bare earth, and excessively damp. The door was in a very dilapidated state, and the rain was coming through the thatch when I was in the school-room.'

"Of others, he says:

"'I am about to enter on one of the most painful subjects of my inquiry. It is a disgusting fact that, out of 692 schools, I found 364, or 52.6 per cent., utterly unprovided with privies.'

"These are not isolated instances. I could quote hundreds of such descriptions of schools situated in all parts of England and Wales. I have myself seen many which are held in cellars, garrets, chapels, and kitchens, badly warmed, wretchedly ventilated, dirty, unfurnished, dark, damp, and unhealthy. Are the miserable hours spent in these miserable places likely to leave good impressions afterward? Are they likely to create happy, moral, and healthy ideas and associations in the minds of the children? Are they likely to make the children love what they learned in such scenes and places, and remember it with reverence and with a desire to act upon it afterward? Are they not much rather likely to make the children hate and shun every thing which would remind them of the school and the miserable school-day?

"28. By far the greatest majority of the criminals who are convicted every year in England and Wales are persons *who have never been educated at all.* Very few persons who have received even a tolerable education are found among the great numbers annually committed.

"29. While throughout the agricultural districts of Western Europe, the children remain in school until they have completed their fourteenth year, and very often until they have completed their sixteenth year, very few even of those children who go to school at all in our agricultural districts continue to attend school beyond their ninth year, while very many do not continue to attend them beyond their eighth year. So that of the children of the poor who do go to school in England and Wales, the greatest number discontinue their attendance long before they have received any thing worthy the name of education.

"30. The present system is bearing very unfairly and very oppressively upon many conscientious and benevolent clergymen in the remote rural districts.

"The nation is entirely ignorant of the almost marvelous efforts which some of the clergy are making in the remote rural districts to provide schools for the poor.

"Many poor clergymen, with not £150 of annual income, are, out of that small stipend, supporting their schools and teachers themselves, wholly unaided either by the public or by their neighbors. How they can do it, God only knows; but that many of them, in all parts of the country, do effect this prodigy of self-denial, all the inspectors unanimously attest. These good men receive and expect no public praise as their reward. They are laboring, unheard-of and unknown by their fellows, and are looking for their reward to Heaven alone.

"But what a disgrace to us, as a nation, to impose such a burden upon any of our clergy! What a shame it is that the small stipend of a religious and benevolent man should be made still smaller by forcing him to pay what ought to be borne by the nation at large! And what a precarious means of support for these schools! It is not reasonable to expect that each succeeding incumbent can or will be equally self-denying; and when one fails to give the accustomed support, such a school must necessarily be closed.

"Such is a short summary of the state of education of the poor in England and Wales, as attested by the inspectors of schools, by the government, and by the clergy. While foreign countries, by the aid of the central authority, have established such perfect systems, and have accomplished such magnificent results, the system of leaving the education of a nation dependent upon the efforts of charitable individuals finds us, in 1849, in the situation which I have described.

"I have shown, in Chap. IX of this work, that, notwithstanding the very large size of the primary schools in the towns of Germany and Switzerland, (many of them containing as many as *ten* class-rooms and *ten* teachers, and scarcely containing fewer than *four* class-rooms), there were:

"*In Prussia:*

1 primary school for every 653 inhabitants.
1 teacher for every 522 "
1 normal college for every 377,360 "

"*In Saxony:*

1 primary school for every 900 inhabitants.
1 teacher for every 588 "
1 normal college for every 214,975 "

"*In Bavaria:*

1 primary school for 508 inhabitants.
1 teacher for every 603 "
1 normal college for every 550,000 "

"*In the Duchy of Baden:*

1 primary school for every 700 inhabitants.
1 normal college for every 500,000 "

"*In Switzerland:*

1 teacher for every 480 inhabitants.
1 normal college for every 176,923 "

"*In France:*

1 primary school for every 568 inhabitants.
1 teacher for ever 446 "
1 normal college for every 356,564 inhabitants."

Such are the educational privileges of the working-classes of England and Wales. So far is England behind even Continental Europe, according to the testimony of Englishmen who were specially appointed to investigate and compare. These statements will surprise the American people; and they would be beyond all belief were they not presented by England's own witnesses. It seems incredible that the mass of English workers, the English *people*, can be in this state of degradation and ignorance. It is amazing to learn how small a number of the inhabitants of Great Britain are educated at all. England, at the time of the Crimean war, called on Europe and America for aid or sympathy in her effort to prevent the *barbarism* of Russia from spreading over Christendom. Within two years, more than eight thousand schools have been established among the Russian peasants, while such is the wretched condition of the English laborers under a system which is constantly sinking them lower still.

Let our American people ponder these facts, and compare the state of England with the condition of the free North, with its free schools, its high schools, its normal schools and colleges, covering all the land. Let them inquire, and see how many among those born in the Free States are unable to read and write, and let them turn a moment to the Southern Slave States, and consider the ignorance and degradation of the laborers there, where, as in England, the land has all been in the hands of an aristocracy, and they will thank God more fervently than ever before for our free schools, our free institutions, our cheap lands, our homestead law, and our millions of landowners.

England is swiftly approaching the point where reform will be impossible; indeed, in the opinion of many of her own thinkers, she has passed it already, and the only choice now is between her ruin of her people, or a revolution which, as in France, shall sweep her aristocracy away, and distribute her lands among the laborers. Such a revolution our rebellion is working with the aristocracy and lands of the South.

The next subject presented by Mr. Kay is,

### The Dwellings of the Agricultural People of England and Wales.

It will be seen that the investigations have covered the whole field, and there can be no mistake. Americans can now understand how the laborers are housed on the lands of England. The writer has hesitated in regard to the sad and most revolting facts which the official witnesses of Great Britain have collected and presented in regard to the cottages of the English peasantry. Ought they to be laid before the American reader? In deciding to make somewhat copious extracts from these reports, omitting the most offensive portions, the writer has been guided by two considerations: First, England has united with a powerful nation in hostility to us and our institutions, and that hostile policy will continue; she must necessarily remain our enemy until her own social and political system is reformed or revolutionized; and it is, therefore, wise for Americans to study the condition of her people, for they are the real sources of her national power; and the actual state of her laborers can only be learned from such facts connected with their homes and daily life as are stated here.

Second, Much is said in regard to the assumed fact that the *people* of England sympathize with the North in this war, and it is well for us to know the character and influence of this people of England, that we may judge what influence they are likely to exert upon the course of the government.

Third, The American people should know the condition of the laborers of England, that they may prize the more the blessings of our own free institutions.

Mr. Kay, after describing the habitations of the poor of the towns, proceeds as follows:

"But miserable as the habitations of a great part of the poor of our towns are, the cottages and the cottage life of the peasants in our villages are still worse; and, what is more, they have been for some time past, and are still, rapidly deteriorating. The majority of the cottages are wretchedly built, often in very unhealthy sites; they are miserably small, and crowded to excess; they are very low, seldom drained, and badly roofed; and they scarcely ever have any cellar or space under the floor of the lower rooms. The floors are formed either of flags, which rest upon the cold, undrained ground, or, as is often the case, of nothing but a mixture of clay and lime. The ground receives, day after day, and year after year, between the crevices of the flags, or in the composition of clay and lime, water and droppings of all kinds, and gives back from them and from its own moisture combined, pestilential vapors, injurious to the health and happiness of the inmates of the cottage.

"The cottages are fit abodes for a peasantry pauperized and demoralized by the utter hopelessness of their situation.

"They may be classified as follows:

"1. Small cottages built of brick, of only one story in hight, with a thatched roof, and without any cellar, so that the bricks or flags of the room rest immediately on the earth; with two small rooms between seven and eight feet in hight—one used as the day-room and cooking-room, the other as the bed-room, where husband and wife, young men and young women, boys and girls, and very often a married son and his wife, all sleep together; without any garden, and with only a very small yard at the back, in which the privy stands almost close to the back door, pouring its gases into the house at all hours. This species of cottage is to be found in all parts of England and Wales. In some counties they are very numerous, as in Cambridgeshire, and especially in that part called the Isle of Ely, in Hertfordshire, in Leicestershire, in Dorsetshire, Devonshire, Somersetshire, Cornwall, Surrey, Sussex, Kent, Essex, Bedfordshire, Buckinghamshire, Berkshire, the northern counties, and in Wales.

"2. Cottages which have two stories, with one small kitchen-room on the ground floor, and with another small room above on the first floor, in which the whole family—father, mother, and children of both sexes—sleep together. These houses have generally no garden, and only a small yard behind, in which the privy stands close to the back door. This class is very numerous throughout the country.

"3. The third class of cottages are those which have two stories—the ground floor, where there is a day-room and a little scullery, and the upper floor, on which there are *two* bed-rooms, in one of which the parents sleep, and in the other of which the children—boys and girls—and young men and young women, all sleep together. In many parts of England and Wales this class of cottages is very rare.

"The accounts we receive from all parts of the country show that these miserable cottages are crowded to an extreme, and that the crowding is progressively increasing. People of both sexes, and of all ages, both married and unmarried—parents, brothers, sisters, and strangers—sleep in the same rooms and often in the same beds. One gentleman tells us of six people, of different sexes and ages, two of whom were man and wife, sleeping in the same bed—three with their heads at the top and three with their heads at the foot of the bed. Another tells us of adult uncles and nieces sleeping in the same room close to each other; another, of the uncles and nieces sleeping in the same bed together; another, of adult brothers and sisters sleeping in the same room with a brother and his wife just married; many tell us of adult brothers and sisters sleeping in the same beds; another tells us of rooms so filled with beds that there is no space between them, but that brothers, sisters, and parents crawl over each other, half naked, in order to get to their respective resting-places; another, of its being common for men and women, not being relations, to undress together in the same room, without any feeling of its being indelicate. Nor are these solitary instances, but similar reports are given by gentlemen writing in ALL parts of the country.

"The miserable character of the houses of our peasantry is, of itself, and independently of the causes which have made the houses so wretched, degrading and demoralizing the poor of our rural districts in a fearful manner. It stimulates the unhealthy and unnatural increase of population. The young peasants, from their earliest years, are accustomed to sleep in the same bed-rooms with people of both sexes, and with both married and unmarried persons. They, therefore, lose all sense of the indelicacy of such a life. They know, too, that they can gain nothing by deferring their marriages and by saving; that it is impossible for them to obtain better houses by so doing; and that, in many cases, they must wait many years before they could obtain a separate house of any sort. They feel that, if they defer their marriage for ten or fifteen years, they will be, at the end of that period, in just the same position as before, and no better off for their waiting. Having then lost all hope of any improvement of their social situation, and all sense of the indelicacy of taking a wife home to the bed-room already occupied by parents, brothers, and sisters, they marry early in life—often, if not generally, before the age of twenty—and very often occupy, for the first part of their married life, another bed in the already-crowded sleeping-room of their parents! In this way the morality of the peasants is destroyed, the numbers of this degraded population are unnaturally increased, and their means of subsistence are diminished by the increasing competition of their increasing numbers.

"A low standard of living always tends to stimulate improvident marriages, to unduly increase the numbers of the population, and to engender pauperism, vice, degradation, and misery.

"As I have said before, the landlords are unwilling to increase the number of cottages in the rural districts, because they fear to increase the numbers of the resident laboring population, and the amount of their poor-rates; and they are generally unwilling, even when they are able, to spend money in improving the size or character of the cottages, because they know that they can easily let any of the existing cottages, no matter how wretched, owing to the great demand for house-room.

"The crowding of the cottages has, therefore, of late been growing worse and worse. The promiscuous mingling of the sexes in the bed-rooms has been increasing very much, and is productive of worse consequences every year. Adultery is the very mildest form of the vast amount of crime which it is engendering. We are told, by magistrates, clergymen, surgeons, and union officers, that in many parts of the country cases of incest, and reports of other cases of the same enormity, are becoming more and more common among the poor. And there is no doubt whatsoever (and in this all accounts and authorities agree) that the way in which the married and unmarried people, and the different sexes, are mingled together in the same bed-rooms, and even in the same beds, throughout the rural districts, is tending to destroy the modesty and virtue of the women, to annihilate the foundations on which are based all the national and domestic virtues, and to make want of chastity before marriage, and want of delicacy and purity after marriage, common characteristics of the mothers and wives of our laboring population.

"But what are the poor to do? So long as the law prevents their purchasing land; so long as they can not obtain ground on which to build their own cottages, as the foreign peasants do; so long, too, as the government will not interfere to educate the children of the peasants in higher tastes and better habits; and so long as they are only the tenants at the will of the agent of a landlord—one does not see how the peasant has a chance of improving the condition of his cottage or the social position of his family.

"I can not too often repeat that the great primary causes of the pauperism and degradation of our peasants are the utter *hopelessness* and *helplessness* of their position. We have done all we can to prevent their helping themselves, and to deprive them of every strong inducement to practice self-denial, prudence, and economy.

"A man will not practice self-denial, economy, and prudence, without an object. What object has an English peasant to practice them?

"A peasant can not possibly buy land as the foreign peasant does. He can not get a farm even as a tenant-at-will of it. He can not buy a house, or a plot of ground on which to build a house. He can not even get the lease of a cottage. He can not buy or get the lease of a garden. He often can not even get the mere occupation of a cottage for himself. He is often obliged to take his wife to his father's or his brother's cottage, and to sleep with her in their bed-room.

"What earthly inducement, then, has such a peasant to practice self-denial and economy? Absolutely none. He does not, therefore, practice any. He says to himself, if I put off my marriage and save, what should I gain by such a course? I'll marry early. If I can not get a cottage, I'll take my wife to my father's cottage; and if bad times come, I'll apply to the union.

"Such is the hideous social system to which we have subjected our poor.

"How different is the condition of the foreign peasant! The majority of even the French peasants who have attained the age of thirty-five possess houses and farms of their own, the latter averaging from five to eight acres in size. The foreign peasant feels that his fate is in his own hands. He knows that, if he postpones his marriage, he will be able to purchase a house and farm of his own, and thus to establish his own complete independence. He is not dependent on agents of landlords or on landlords for the condition of his house, or for its tenure, or for the tenure of his farm, or for the social position of his family. All this, as well as his own future success in life, depends solely and entirely on his own exertions. This stimulates his energies and exertions. This makes his life hopeful and happy. This ennobles and develops his own character. This makes him a good citizen. This makes him a successful farmer. This increases his intelligence; and, while it makes his life hopeful and happy even amid privations, it makes him a good and conservative citizen even in times of suffering and distress.

"I have myself examined, during the present year, the condition of the peasants' cottages in Cambridgeshire, and particularly in that part of Cambridgeshire called the Isle of Ely, in Hertfordshire, and in Leicestershire.

"These are agricultural counties, where the land is very rich and very well cultivated. The farms are generally of considerable size. The peasants have no chance of ever rising to the farmer class. The cottages have scarcely ever a garden attached to them. The land is all divided between great farms and parks.

"Now, what is the condition of the majority of cottages of the peasants of these counties?

"They are almost as wretched as they can be. The majority of them are small, low huts, of one story in hight. The walls are about eight feet high. The roofs are very often thatched. The thatch is very seldom repaired. Through the top of the thatch projects the chimney. There is no cellar beneath the rooms. The floors are made of bricks or flags, which are laid upon the earth, and, as may be conceived, are damp and cold.

"In the middle of one of the side walls there is a door, and on each side of the door a window, which is but too often minus several panes at least, their places being occupied with rags. One-half of the interior of many of these cottages is boarded or walled off, so as to divide the house into two little rooms. One of these rooms is the living room, the other is a bed-room, in which sleep the whole family—parents and daughters. It is by no means rare for the two sexes to sleep not only in the same bed-room, but in the same bed.

"The following remarkable extracts, selected from various sources of the highest authority, will show the miserable condition of the cottages and dwellings of the peasantry in other parts of England and Wales.

"I offer these extracts only as specimens, which I could multiply indefinitely, if my space would allow, of a state of things which exists more or less in every county in England, and as proofs of the wretched way in which the cottages of our peasantry are built; of the miserable lodging and accommodation afforded by them to their poor inmates; of the wretched and unhealthy sites which are often chosen for them by agents and persons who do not care where or how the peasants are lodged; of the want of drainage, ventilation, water-supply, and privies, which distinguishes most of them; and of the sickness and shocking moral degradation caused by this miserable and lamentable state of things.

"The first series of extracts will show the present condition of the peasants' houses in the south-western counties—Wiltshire, Dorsetshire, Devonshire, Gloucestershire, Somersetshire, and Cornwall.

"Mr. Alfred Austin, Special Assistant Poor Law Commissioner, in reporting upon the condition of the peasants' cottages in the counties of Wilts, Dorset, Devon, and Somerset, says:

"'The want of sufficient accommodation seems universal. Cottages generally have only two bed-rooms (with very rare exceptions); a great many have only one. The consequence is that it is very often extremely difficult, if not impossible, *to divide a family, so that grown-up persons of different sexes—brothers and sisters, fathers and daughters—do not sleep in the same room. Three or four persons not unfrequently sleep in the same bed.* In a few instances I found that two families—neighbors—arranged so that the females of both families slept together in one cottage, and the males in the other; but such an arrangement is very rare; and in the generality of cottages, I believe that the only attempt that is or can be made to separate beds with occupants of different sexes, and necessarily placed close together, from the smallness of the rooms, is an old shawl, or some article of dress, suspended as a curtain between them.

"'At Stourpain, a village near Blandford, I measured a bed-room in a cottage consisting of two rooms—the bed-room in question up-stairs, and a room on the ground floor, in which the family lived during the day. The room was ten feet square, not reckoning the two small recesses by the sides of the chimney, about eighteen inches deep. The roof was of thatch, the middle of the chamber being about seven feet high. Opposite the fireplace was a small window, about fifteen inches square—the only one in the room.'

"Three beds were crammed into this little room. There was no curtain or separation between the beds.

"One bed contained the father and mother, a little boy, and an infant.

"The second bed contained *three* daughters—the two eldest, twins, aged twenty years each, and the other aged seven.

"The third bed was occupied by *four* sons, aged respectively seventeen, fifteen, fourteen, and ten.

"Mr. Austin says: 'This, I was told, was not an extraordinary case, but that, more or less, every bed-room in the village was crowded with inmates of both sexes and of various ages, and that such a state of things was caused by the want of cottages.

"'It is impossible not to be struck, in visiting the dwellings of the agricultural laborers, with the general want of new cottages, notwithstanding the universal increase of population. Everywhere the cottages are old, and frequently in a state of decay, and are consequently ill-adapted for their increased number of inmates of late years. The floor of the room in which the family live during the day is always of stone in these counties, and wet or damp through the winter months, being frequently lower than the soil outside. The situation of the cottage is often extremely bad, no attention having been paid at the time of its building to facilities for draining. Cottages are frequently erected on a dead level, so that water can not escape, and sometimes on spots lower than the surrounding ground.'

"Mr. Gilbert, formerly Assistant Poor Law Commissioner for Devonshire and Cornwall, gives the following as an instance of the common condition of the dwellings of the laboring classes:

"'In Tiverton, in Cornwall, there is a large district, from which I find numerous applications were made for relief to the board of guardians, in consequence of illness from fever.

"'One cause of disease is to be found in the state of the cottages.

"'Many are built on the ground, without flooring, or against a damp hill.

"'Some have neither windows nor doors sufficient to keep out the weather, or to let in the rays of the sun, or supply the means of ventilation; and in others the roof is so constructed, or so worn, as not to be weather-tight.

"'The thatch roof is frequently saturated with wet, rotten, and in a state of decay, giving out malaria, as other decaying vegetable matter.'

"The state of the dwellings of many of the agricultural laborers in Dorset, where the deaths from the four classes of disease bear a similar proportion to those in Devon, is described in the return of Mr. John Fox, the medical officer of the Cerne Union, in Dorsetshire, who, remarking upon some cases of disease among the poor whom he had attended, says:

"'I have often seen the springs bursting through the mud floor of some of the cottages, and little channels cut from the center, under the door-ways, to carry off the water, while the door has been removed from its hinges for the children to put their feet on while employed in making buttons. It is not surprising that fever, and scrofula in all its forms, prevail under such circumstances.

"'It is somewhat singular that seven cases of typhus occurred in one village, heretofore famed for the health and general cleanliness of its inhabitants and cottages. The first five cases occurred in one family, in a detached house on high and dry ground, and free from accumulations of vegetable and animal matter. The cottage was originally built for a school-room, and consists of one room only, about eighteen feet by ten feet, and nine feet high. About one-third part was partitioned off by boards, reaching to within three feet of the roof; and *in this small space were three beds, in which six persons slept.* Had there been two bed-rooms attached to this one day-room, these cases of typhus would not have occurred.

"'Most of the cottages are of the worst description, some mere mud hovels, and situated in low and damp places, with cess-pools or accumulations of filth close to the doors.

"'The mud floors of many are much below the level of the road, and in wet seasons are little better than so much clay.

"'In many of the cottages, also, where synochus prevailed, the beds stood on the ground floor, which was damp three parts of the year; scarcely one had a fireplace in the bed-room; and one had a single small pane of glass stuck in the mud wall, as its only window, with a large heap of wet and dirty potatoes in one corner. Persons living in such cottages are generally very poor, very dirty, and usually in rags, *living almost wholly on bread and potatoes, scarcely ever tasting animal food*, and, consequently, highly susceptible of disease, and very unable to contend with it. I am sure, if such persons were placed in good, comfortable, clean cottages, the improvement in themselves and children would soon be visible, and the exceptions would only be found in a few of the poorest and most wretched, who, perhaps, have been born in a mud hovel, and had lived in one the first thirty years of their lives.

"'In my district, *I do not think there is one cottage to be found consisting of a day-room, three bed-rooms, scullery, pantry, and convenient receptacles for refuse and for fuel, in the occupation of a laborer.*'

"The tenor of much information respecting the condition of many of the laboring classes in Somerset is exhibited in the Sanitary Report of Mr. James Gane, the medical officer of the Axbridge Union, in Somersetshire, who states that—

"'The situation of this district, where the diseases therein-mentioned prevail, is a perfect flat, called the South Marsh, in the main road between Bristol and Bridgewater. There are numerous dykes or ditches for the purpose of drainage. The cottages of the poor are mostly of a bad description. The walls are frequently made of mud. They are often situated close to the dykes, where the water, for the most part, is in a state of stagnation. *Oftentimes there is not more than one room for the whole family;* sometimes two, one above the other. With the really poor, *the latter is seldom to be met with* (unless it should happen now and then in a parish where a poor-house was built a short time before the formation of the union). A pig-sty, where the inmates are capable of keeping a pig, is frequently attached to the dwelling, and, in the heat of summer, produces a stench quite intolerable: the want of space, however, prevents it being otherwise. The ordinary houses of the poor peasants (those mentioned above being detached cottages), in most of the parishes in this district, are of a much worse description, several large families existing under the same roof, and *each family occupying only one room*, and having but one entrance door to the dwelling. Here, filth and poverty go hand in hand, without any restriction, and under no control; the accumulation of filth being attributable to the want of proper receptacles for refuse. Owing to the indolent and filthy disposition of the inhabitants, in no instance have such places been provided.'

"The following extract from the report of Mr. Aaron Little, the medical officer of the Chippenham Union, in Wiltshire, affords a specimen of the frequent condition of rural villages which have apparently the most advantageous sites:

"'The parish of Colerne, which, upon a cursory view, any person (unacquainted with its peculiarities) would pronounce to be the most healthy village in England, is, in fact, the most unhealthy. From its commanding position, being situated upon a high hill, it has an appearance of health and cheerfulness, which delights the eye of the traveler, who commands a view of it from the great western road; but this impression is immediately removed on entering at any point of the town.

"'The filth, dilapidated buildings, the squalid appearance of the majority of the lower orders, have a sickening effect upon the stranger who first visits this place. During three years' attendance among the poor of this district, I have never known the small-pox, scarlatina, or the typhus fever to be absent. The situation is damp, and the buildings unhealthy, and the inhabitants themselves inclined to be of dirty habits. There is also a great want of drainage.'

"During the latter part of 1849, some very remarkable and exceedingly able letters were published in the MORNING CHRONICLE, describing the condition of the cottages of the peasantry in different parts of England. I might crowd my pages with extracts from these letters, all proving the truth of the description I have given above of the cottages of our peasantry. It is impossible for me to do more than make one or two extracts from them, to show how the condition of the cottages of the peasantry is *deteriorating*. I must refer my readers to these remarkable letters for further details: they will well repay the most careful study.

"The correspondent of the MORNING CHRONICLE, describing the condition of the laborers in Devonshire, Somersetshire, Cornwall, and Dorsetshire, says:

"'Devon and Somerset have long been classed in the unenviable category of counties presenting the agricultural laborer in his most deplorable circumstances. With Dorset and Wilts they are generally regarded as exhibiting the unfavorable, while Lincolnshire exhibits the favorable, extreme in the laborer's condition.

"'In traversing both counties, more especially Devonshire, I was particularly struck with the utter absence of new cottages. Along the highways and byways their absence is observable; and not only this, but, in many places, there are abundant evidences that cottages, which a few years ago were tenanted, are now, if not altogether untenantable, going rapidly into decay. Many are so rickety and ruined, that to inhabit them any longer is impossible; while, as regards others, the process of demolition or decomposition has only commenced, confining the wretched tenants, who had formerly two rooms, to the only apartment which remains, and which they can with difficulty keep together. In search of these, one has not to go into remote and sequestered parts, where things are done which would not be exposed to the neighborhood of the highways. I have seen specimens of cottages in this state along the line from Exeter to Honiton, and in the district traversed by the high-road to London. . . . . .

"'The cabin is so rude and uncouth that it has less the appearance of having been built, than of having been suddenly thrown up out of the ground. The length is not above fifteen feet, its width between ten and twelve. The wall, which has sunk at different points, and seems bedewed with a cold sweat, is composed of a species of imperfect sandstone, which is fast crumbling to decay. It is so low that your very face is almost on a level with the heavy thatched roof which covers it, and which seems to be pressing it into the earth. The thatch is thickly incrusted with a bright green vegetation, which, together with the appearance of the trees and the mason-work around, well attests the prevailing humidity of the atmosphere. In front, it presents to the eye a door, with one window below, and another window (a smaller one) in the thatch above. The door is awry from the sinking of the wall; the glass in the window above is unbroken, but the lower one is here and there stuffed with rags, which keep out both the air and the sunshine. You approach the door-way through the mud, over some loose stones, which rock under your feet in using them. You have to stoop for admission, and cautiously look around ere you fairly trust yourself within. There are but two rooms in the house—one below and the other above.' The sleeping accommodations 'are gained by means of a few greasy and rickety steps, which lead through a species of hatchway in the ceiling. *Yes, there is but one room, and yet we counted nine in the family!* And such a room! The small window in the roof admits just light enough to enable you to discern its character and dimensions; the rafters, which are all exposed, spring from the very floor, so that it is only in the very center of the apartment that you have any chance of standing erect; the thatch oozes through the wood-work which supports it, the whole being begrimed with smoke and dust, and replete with vermin. But, perhaps, the climax of misery, in this respect, in the district, is to be found in the village of Taversy, about a mile distant from Thame. One house was pointed out to me there with four rooms; each room occupied by a separate family, some of the families being very numerous. It was a two-story house, covered with tiles. There was no communication between the upper and lower stories, the former being approached from the outside by a flight of stone steps, which rose over the door leading into the latter. One of the families counted eight or ten, of both sexes, some of whom had attained maturity. The immorality to which their domestic condition gives rise, I shall have occasion hereafter to refer to.

"'The cottages at Southleigh, in Devon, are, if possible, even worse. One house which our correspondent visited was almost a ruin. It had continued in that state for ten years. The floor was of mud, dipping, near the fireplace, into a deep hollow, which was constantly filled with water. There were five in the family—a young man of twenty-one, a girl of eighteen, and another girl of about thirteen, with the father and mother—all sleeping together up-stairs. And what a sleeping-room! "In places it seemed falling in. To ventilation it was an utter stranger. The crazy floor shook and creaked under me as I paced it." Yet the rent was 1*s.* a week—the same sum for which apartments, that may be called luxurious in comparison, may be had in the model lodging-houses. And here sat a girl weaving that beautiful Honiton lace, which our peeresses wear on Court days. Cottage after cottage, at Southleigh, presented the same characteristics: clay floors, low ceilings, letting in the rain, no ventilation; two rooms—one above, and one below; gutters running through the lower room to let off the water; unglazed window-frames, now boarded up, and now uncovered to the elements, the boarding going for fire-wood; the inmates disabled by rheumatism, ague, and typhus; broad, stagnant, open ditches close to the doors; heaps of abominations piled round the dwellings; such are the main features of Southleigh; and it is in these worse than pig-styes that one of the most beautiful fabrics that luxury demands or art supplies is fashioned. The parish houses are still worse. "One of these, on the borders of Devonshire and Cornwall, and not far from Launceston, consisted of two houses, containing between them four rooms. In each room lived a family night and day, the space being about twelve feet square. In one were a man and his wife and eight children: the father, mother, and two children lay in one bed; the remaining six were huddled 'head and foot' (three at the top, and three at the foot) in the other bed. The eldest girl was between fifteen and sixteen; the eldest boy between fourteen and fifteen." Is it not horrible to think of men and women being brought up in this foul, brutish manner in civilized and Christian England? The lowest of savages are not worse cared-for than these children of a luxurious and refined country.

"'The atmosphere of these houses, and especially of the sleeping apartments, to an unpracticed nose, is almost insupportable. It is, perhaps, worthy of remark, that dishes, plates, and other articles of crockery, seem almost unknown. There is, however, the less need for them, *as grist bread forms the principal and, I believe, the only kind of food that falls to the laborer's lot.* In no single instance did I observe meat of any kind during my progress through the parish. The furniture is such as may be expected from the description I have given of the place—a rickety table and two or three foundered chairs generally forming the extent of the upholstery.'

"It is said that this is the condition throughout the greater part of the counties of Dorsetshire, Wiltshire, and Gloucestershire. Another letter, inserted in the TIMES of the 29th June, 1846, and signed, 'A Country Rector,' says:

'The misery' (described above), 'I am afraid, is not confined to that county (Dorsetshire): if you go to Devonshire, Wiltshire, and the hill country of *Gloucestershire*, you will find him (the peasant) at the point of starvation.'

"The Hon. and Rev. S. G. Osborne, in writing of one of the parishes of Dorsetshire, viz., that of Hilton, which he inspected personally, in company with the vicar of the parish, describes the degradation of the inhabitants, and the wretchedness of the houses, as something almost incredible. He says: 'I despair of giving you any faint idea of the manner these people are pigged together within their dwellings;' and this parish 'closely adjoins the park of Milton Abbey, the beautiful seat of the Earl of Portarlington.'

"'In the first cottage, a man and his wife live, with two children—a son of his by a former marriage; a daughter of hers by a former marriage. This son is married, but, owing to want of room, can not sleep with his own wife and children, who are living in another part of the parish, but sleeps in a small room, the only other bed of which is occupied by the grown girl, the daughter of the woman. They pay the parish 30*s.* a year rent.

"'In one compartment of the large building were dwelling a man, his wife, and five children; five of them had had the fever; the man died of it. With some difficulty, we ascended to a bed-room of this cottage: no one by pen can describe it. You get into it by a sort of ladder; when in it, you find it impossible to stand upright anywhere but in the direct center, for the roof slopes down to the floor at an acute angle; three beds are so placed as to make the base of so many triangles, of which the sides of the roof are the lateral lines; you must cross the first to get at the second—the second to reach the third; the floor is as rotten as possible, full of holes, through one of which the husband's leg had gone on one occasion. I ventured to ask how they got a corpse out of such a place. I found "they had him down stairs to die;" there he was seven weeks, and then they took him, dead, to the church-yard.'

"'The floors of some of the down-stairs rooms are of mud, in pits or holes in many places; where mended at all, it is done with the rough stone of the country. The parish officers regularly, when they can get it, take rent even of the pauper tenants, with the exception of some few.

"'Behind these buildings is a space between them and the broad ditch, varying, perhaps, from twelve to fourteen feet in width; in the said space, in the case of the first two cottages, occupied partly by some out-houses, rank grass is growing, among which is ample evidence of every possible abomination.'"

These extracts from reports occupy about one hundred pages of Mr. Kay's book; they cover nearly the whole field in England and Wales. Their character is so similar throughout, and the statements are from so many independent witnesses (men of high standing), that it is impossible to doubt that here we have a true picture of the general condition of millions of the agricultural laborers of Great Britain; and the worst feature of their case is its hopelessness. The political system of England is absolutely consuming her laborers, body and soul.

England has such a rural population to draw her strength from in that contest in which she has proposed to engage with the United States. Her lands are divided into some fifteen thousand plantations; twenty-two millions of her people are working for wages for the landholding nobility, the millionaires, and the capitalists; and such is the character of these workers and the manner in which they are housed. England is turning her strength into weakness and decay.

There is one fact which shows, more clearly than any yet presented, the moral degradation of portions of the working-classes of the cities and larger towns—a condition which certainly can not be matched, except among the lowest of the heathen. Reference is had to what are called the "Burial Clubs." From Mr. Kay's description of these, the following statements are quoted:

"The accounts of these 'burial clubs,' and of the extent to which infanticide is practiced in some parts of this country, may be found in Mr. Chadwick's able reports upon the sanitary condition of the poor.

"It appears that in our larger provincial towns the poor are in the habit of entering their children in what are called 'burial clubs.' A small sum is paid every year by the parent, and this entitles him to receive from £3 to £5 from the club on the death of the child. Many parents enter their children in several clubs. One man in Manchester has been known to enter his child in *nineteen* different clubs. On the death of such a child, the parent becomes entitled to receive a large sum of money; and, as the burial of the child does not necessarily cost more than £1, or, at the most, £1 10*s*., the parent realizes a considerable sum after all the expenses are paid!

"It has been clearly ascertained that it is a common practice among the more degraded classes of poor in many of our towns to enter their infants in these clubs, and then to cause their death either by starvation, ill-usage, or poison! What more horrible symptom of moral degradation can be conceived? One's mind revolts against it, and would fain reject it as a monstrous fiction. But, alas! it seems to be but too true.

"Mr. Chadwick says: 'Officers of these burial societies, relieving officers, and others, whose administrative duties put them in communication with the lowest classes in these districts' (the manufacturing districts), 'express their moral conviction of the operation of such bounties to produce instances of the visible neglect of children, of which they are witnesses. They often say: "You are not treating that child properly; it will not live: *is it in the club?*" And the answer corresponds with the impression produced by the sight.'

"From a very remarkable letter published in the TIMES of the 18th of January, A. D. 1849, by that indefatigable and earnest man, the Rev. J. Clay, Chaplain of the Preston House of Correction, I collect the following particulars, still further illustrating this horrible symptom of our social state.

"Mr. Clay says: 'Let me recall to your recollection *some* of the murders for burial-money perpetrated since the publication of Mr. Chadwick's admirable report on interment in towns. 1. A Liverpool paper of April, 1846, gives the details of an inquiry before the coroner in a case of "infanticide, at Runcorn, to obtain funeral-money." It appeared, in evidence, that James Pimlet, aged ten months, died on the 6th of March; and that, on the 21st of the same month, died Richard Pimlet, aged four years and a half. On the 27th of the same month, a *third* child was taken ill. The medical man's suspicions were roused. The authorities caused the bodies of the two dead infants to be exhumed. It was found that the *mother* had purchased arsenic before the children's illness. Dr. Brett showed the presence of arsenic in the bodies "in quantities more than sufficient to cause death." The collector of the Liverpool Victoria Legal Burial Society proved that the three children were all enrolled members; that he had paid £1 5*s*. on the death of one child, and £5 on the death of the other. The steward of another society proved the payment of £1 5*s*. and £1 15*s*. on the two deaths. Verdict, "willful murder" against the mother.

"'2. At York assizes, in July, 1846, John Rodda was convicted of the willful murder of his own child, aged one year. The evidence proved that the wretch poured a spoonful of sulphuric acid down his helpless infant's throat. It was proved that he had said he did not care how soon the child died, for, whenever it died, he should have £2 10*s*., as it was in a "dead-list." He said he had another that would have the same when it died, and two others that would have £5 apiece when they died.

"'According to the statement of a leading death-list officer, THREE-FOURTHS of the names on these catalogues of the doomed are names of children. Now, if this be the truth—and I believe it is—hundreds, if not thousands, *of children must be entered each into* FOUR, FIVE, *or even* TWELVE *clubs*, their chances of life diminishing, of course, in proportion to the frequency with which they are entered. Lest you should imagine that such excessive addiction to burial clubs is only to be found in one place, I furnish you with a report for 1846, *of a single club, which then boasted* 34,100 *members—the entire population of the town to which it belongs having been, in* 1841, *little more than* 36,000!

"'I would now bespeak your attention to the infantile mortality in places where burial clubs flourish. In Dr. Lyon Playfair's "Report on the Sanitary Condition of large Towns in Lancashire," (p. 53), it is stated that *among the poor of Manchester, out of one hundred deaths, sixty to sixty-five are of infants under five years old. One man put his children into nineteen clubs!* . . . . Dr. Lyon Playfair again shows (p. 54) that children die in Manchester, when wages are high, at a rate more than that at which they die among the poverty-stricken laborers of Dorsetshire.'"

Such is the condition of the great mass of the people of England. These are the elements of her future progress, and this is the result, for the laboring classes, of her boasted civilization. Her social system, in some main features, is the exact parallel of our Southern slave system. In both, the lands are all in the hands of a few aristocrats, lords of the land; in both, this small class of capitalists and landowners seize for themselves nearly all the earnings of the workers, they becoming enormously rich, and the laborers crushed down in ignorance and poverty. It need not surprise us that the English aristocracy should wish success for the aristocrats of the South. This, too, is the country, whose grave writers, in stately quarterlies, declare that, if an American nation should spread its farms and schools, its printing-presses and Churches, the whole glorious structure of our free Christian civilization, over this continent, God would undoubtedly come down for our overthrow. And this embodies about the average wisdom that England has manifested in regard to American affairs.

The condition of the laborers of Great Britain, as thus presented by English witnesses, furnishes a lesson which Americans should carefully study. It shows us that the abolition of slavery is only one step in our great social and political revolution; and that there can be no broad and permanent basis laid for national prosperity, and no security for the masses, unless the working population are landowners. The laborers must own their own homes, as the general rule, or their condition will be but little above that of the slave or serf, though nominally invested with the rights of freemen.

The laboring classes of England are free, but, with the single exception that they are not chattels, how near does the showing of their own countrymen place them to the condition of the slave! In morality and intelligence, in the manner in which they are housed and fed, there is by no means the wide difference which we once thought between the agricultural laborers of England and Wales, and the slaves on the grain-farms of the South. It shows, in the most conclusive manner, that wherever the lands of a country are in the hands of a few, and beyond the reach of the workers, nothing can save the laboring classes from degradation, poverty, ignorance, and oppression. Unless there can be a land reform for England, unless the process can be arrested by which the small farms are swallowed up by the large estates, it is evident that those who produce the wealth of England must sink ever lower, till nothing is left them but such food, raiment, and shelter as fit a human beast.

This is all that capital and selfishness have left the laborer anywhere when free to oppress, and the English landowner is no worse than the American planter on his great estate, and no better. The fault is in the system; a landless peasantry in any country, in any age, have been, are, and ever will be, either slaves or serfs, or but a single grade above these, when the great estate system has reached its ultimate result.

Let Americans then ponder and act upon the lesson, and,

in the reconstruction of the nation, insist upon planting our workers upon homes of their own, and then give each a rifle and a ballot wherewith to defend them, taking care meanwhile that the free school imparts the needed intelligence. Then shall we have, indeed, an American nation of freemen, placed on an immovable basis, and capable of indefinite growth. These statements of the social condition of England place in a new and equally clear light the necessity of her policy, and the cause of her hostility to Russia and America. She must control the manufactures and commerce of the world; she must be the great money power of earth, or she must decline; and she sees that, if Russia and America are allowed to grow on unchecked, she must soon hold an inferior position, and hence her hostility to both.

Let no one, however, suppose that, because such is the condition of her working population, England is, therefore, weak. On the contrary, she is a mighty power, a most formidable enemy. She is strong, because, having wrung all wealth from her laborers and concentrated it in the hands of a few, it is readily available for the purposes of the Government, and, through her thousand ships, may be used to strike a blow at any time in any quarter of the globe. She is strong for the same reason that Jeff. Davis is strong, when, crushing all opposition, and all individual rights, he seizes all men for his army, and all the wealth of the country to arm, and clothe, and feed them.

Though she holds within the seeds of revolution or decay, for the present, she has at her disposal enormous power wherewith to defend herself or injure others.

It is well, therefore, for Americans at this time to study the military power of England. The following tables are copied from an article in the North British Review for August, 1863, on the national defenses of Great Britain. The writer gives his authority for statements made, showing them to be official, and they may, therefore, be received as an authentic account of the land forces of England only six months since. The article is intended to quiet the fears of the English people in regard to a possible invasion from France, a dread of which hangs like a shadow over Britain. Of course, the national defenses are presented in their most favorable aspect, and Americans will see from this statement how much or how little we have to fear from English armies.

STRENGTH OF BRITISH LAND FORCES AT HOME AND ABROAD.

| | 1805. | 1860–1. | 1863–4. | Increase 1805 to 1863. |
|---|---|---|---|---|
| Asia (exclusive of India and China), | 6,724 | 4,355 | 3,826 | } 1,461 |
| China, . . . . . . . | ...... | ...... | 4,359 | |
| West Indies, etc., . . . . | 16,242 | 4,225 | | |
| Bermuda, . . . . . . . | } 473 | 1,102 | } 24,389 | 3,480 |
| Bahamas, . . . . . . . | | 424 | | |
| North America, . . . . . | 4,194 | 4,329 | | |
| Australia, . . . . . . . | 490 | 1,250 | 1,234 | 744 |
| New Zealand, . . . . . | ...... | 3,626 | 5,538 | 5,538 |
| Falkland Isles, . . . . . | ...... | 35 | | |
| St. Helena, . . . . . . | ...... | 676 | } 2,514 | 2,170 |
| West Africa, . . . . . | 344 | 1,001 | | |
| Cape of Good Hope, . . . . | ...... | 4,840 | 4,719 | 4,719 |
| Corfu, . . . . . . . | ...... | 4,256 | | 4,256 |
| Malta, . . . . . . . . | 6,490 | 7,112 | } 17,008 | 622 |
| Gibraltar, . . . . . . | 4,586 | 5,913 | | 1,327 |
| Total in Colonies (excluding India), | 39,543 | 43,144 | 63,587 | 24,044 |
| Regular Troops in United Kingdom, | 78,426 | 100,218 | 84,655 | 6,229 |
| Total Regular Troops at Home and Abroad, . . . . . . | 117,969 | 143,362 | 148,242 | 30,273 |
| Militia Establishments, . . . | 110,556 | 120,000 | 140,000 | 29,444 |
| Total Regular and Militia Forces in United Kingdom, . . . . | 188,982 | 220,218 | 222,655 | 33,673 |
| General Total Paid Troops at Home and in Colonies (excluding India), | 228,525 | 283,362 | 288,242 | 59,717 |

"These results are, it must be admitted, sufficiently startling. They show that we are now, according to official returns, maintaining a force of 6,000 regulars in this kingdom, and of 24,000 regulars in our colonies (exclusive in both cases of India), beyond what we considered, and found, sufficient for our security when the French eagles were hovering in the air overhead, poising themselves for their swoop. In another view, they show that, were we still to retain the same force of regulars and militia together that we had in 1805 in these islands, we might nevertheless dispatch to-morrow an expedition of 33,000 men, without recruiting a man beyond our present strength, and which would be over and above the war establishment of 18,000 men whom we at present have in Canada."

The conclusion is, that England can, in the opinion of the writer, spare about 33,000 men for foreign service, and maintain her home defenses. This is her full, actual power for foreign war, as tested in the Crimea.

The idea of an English army on American soil needs not a second thought. Whether French and English troops may threaten us from Mexico, is a question to be settled hereafter. When that issue is presented, Europe will probably discover that the Monroe doctrine is not a dead letter in America.

But the English navy, as well as that of France, constitutes a power quite different from the army, and the question, whether we are able to meet this force upon the sea, is a very serious one, involving our national safety.

It is proposed, therefore, to present, first, a general statement of the large navies of Europe as well as our own, and then, by a careful analysis, estimate their comparative strength.

# CHAPTER XXXVI.

## THE NAVIES OF ENGLAND, FRANCE, AMERICA, AND RUSSIA.

MANY varying newspaper reports of the strength of the navies of Europe have been spread abroad. The following statement of the condition of the English and French navies is copied from the NORTH BRITISH REVIEW, for August, 1863.

The writer gives the following in a foot-note as his authority: "The figures for England are from a Return to the House of Commons, 1863, No. 30; for France, from the official statement for 1862, transmitted by our (the English) embassador, (Parliamentary Pap., 1862, No. 177)."

This table is worthly of especial study. It presents the latest official statement of the actual condition of the English iron-clad navy, and from it we are able to form a correct estimate of the force with which England supposes she can blockade our ports and crush our navy. It shows us exactly the character, the size, form, and armament of her most formidable ships, and in which her power, skill, and science are all concentrated. They are, doubtless, among the most powerful broadside vessels in the world, and, perhaps, would find no equal among ships of that class unless in our own New Ironsides, whose armament is much heavier than theirs. Whether they are a match for our Monitors is a question to be considered.

The account, we are informed, includes vessels afloat and building :

| | Armor-plated. | Liners. Screw. | Frigates. Screw. | Frigates. Paddle. | Corvettes. Screw. | Corvettes. Paddle. | Block-ships. Screw. | Other Steam-ships. | Total Steam. | Total Sailing. |
|---|---|---|---|---|---|---|---|---|---|---|
| England, . . . . . . . | 21 | 59 | 44 | 16 | 30 | ... | 9 | 380 | 566 | 103 |
| France, . . . . . . . . | 16 | 37 | 29 | 18 | 7 | 9 | ... | 244 | 360 | 122 |

" At Kinburn the French Emperor proved that iron-clad batteries could, without injury, sustain a fire which would be utterly destructive to wooden vessels. He pursued the conclusions thus arrived at, and finally, in 1858, ordered the construction of four iron-plated frigates—La Gloire, L'Invincible, La Normandie, and La Couronne. The first three are on wood frames; the latter is iron throughout. They are about two hundred and thirty-one feet in length, carrying thirty-six 50-pounders on a single protected deck, with two more on an upper deck, unprotected. Their engines are of nine hundred horse power, and the crew five hundred and seventy men. All these are at sea, and have been found successful; but the ports being only about six feet above the water when at load draught, they are placed at a certain disadvantage in bad weather. Subsequently two others, the Solferino and Magenta, were ordered, which have been launched, but are not yet completed. They are armed with a 'spur,' projecting from the bow, carry their guns in two tiers in the center of the ship, and the lower ports are eight feet from the water-line. Their length is two hundred and eighty-two feet; draught, twenty-five feet; and horse-power, one thousand.

"In November, 1860, ten more were ordered, which are still on the stocks, and are being slowly proceeded with. They are to be of the Gloire type, and all of wood frames, except the Heroine, which is of iron; but the thickness of the plates has been increased from three and a half to four inches of the Gloire, to four and a half to six inches.

All the other iron-plated vessels under construction in France at the present moment are merely floating batteries for harbor defense.

"Our own armor fleet, though more tardily commenced, now stands thus:

| | Hull. | Armor-plated. | Tuns. | Horse Power. | Length. | Draught. | Guns | Men. |
|---|---|---|---|---|---|---|---|---|
| | | | | | feet. | feet. in. | | |
| *At Sea.* | | | | | | | | |
| Warrior, . . . | Iron. | Partially. | 6,109 | 1,250 | 380 | 22 9 | 40 | 704 |
| Black Prince, . . | Iron. | Partially. | 6,109 | 1,250 | 380 | 26 3½ | 40 | 704 |
| Defense, . . . . | Iron. | Partially. | 3,720 | 600 | 280 | 24 11 | 16 | 445 |
| Resistance, . . . | Iron. | Partially. | 3,710 | 600 | 280 | 24 10 | 16 | 455 |
| Royal Oak, . . . | Wood. | Wholly. | 4,056 | 800 | 273 | 25 10½ | 35 | 600 |
| *Launched.* | | | | | | | | |
| Caledonia, . . . | Wood. | Wholly. | 4,125 | 1,000 | 273 | 25 10½ | 35 | 600 |
| Ocean, . . . . | Wood. | Wholly. | 4,047 | 1,000 | 273 | 25 10½ | 35 | 600 |
| Prince Consort, . | Wood. | Wholly. | 4,045 | 1,000 | 273 | 25 10½ | 35 | 600 |
| Hector, . . . . | Iron. | Partially. | 4,089 | 800 | 280 | 24 8 | 32 | 600 |
| Valiant, . . . . | Iron. | Partially. | 4,063 | 800 | 280 | 24 8 | 32 | 600 |
| *To be Launched* 1863. | | | | | | | | |
| Minotaur, . . . | Iron. | Wholly. | 6,621 | 1,350 | 400 | 25 8 | 37 | 704 |
| Achilles, . . . | Iron. | Wholly. | 6,079 | 1,250 | 380 | 26 3½ | 30 | 704 |
| Royal Alfred, . . | Wood. | Wholly. | 4,045 | 800 | 273 | 25 10½ | 35 | 600 |
| Zealous, . . . . | Wood. | Partially. | 3,716 | 800 | 252 | 25 3 | 16 | ...... |
| Royal Sovereign, . | Wood. | Wholly. | 3,963 | 800 | 240 | 22 11 | 5 | 200 |
| Prince Albert, . . | Iron. | Wholly. | 2,529 | 500 | 240 | 20 | 5 | 160 |
| Research, . . . | Wood. | Partially. | 1,253 | 200 | 195 | 14 | 4 | ...... |
| Enterprise, . . . | Wood. | Partially. | 990 | 160 | 180 | 14 4½ | 4 | 80 |
| *To be Launched* 1864. | | | | | | | | |
| Agincourt, . . . | Iron. | Wholly. | 6,621 | 1,350 | 400 | 25 8 | 37 | 600 |
| Northumberland, . | Iron. | Wholly. | 6,621 | 1,350 | 400 | 25 8 | 37 | 600 |
| Favorite, . . . | Wood. | Wholly. | 2,186 | 400 | 225 | 20 5 | 8 | 160 |

Other authorities state the number of iron-clads in the French navy at ninety-four; but, as the English reviewer remarks, all but those enumerated are merely swimming batteries for harbor defense, and small gun-boats, such as were used at Kinburn, in the Crimean war. Of these swimming batteries and gun-boats, the NATIONAL ALMANAC for 1863 enumerates seventy-seven, leaving, of the ninety-four iron-clads, only seventeen for the ocean-going ships, which corresponds very nearly to the statement of the REVIEW.

The condition of the Russian navy is said to have been as follows in 1862:

| STEAM-VESSELS. | No. |
|---|---|
| Ships of the line, | 9 |
| Screw frigates, | 12 |
| Side-wheel frigates, | 8 |
| Corvettes, | 22 |
| Clippers, | 12 |
| Floating battery (iron-clad), | 1 |
| Frigate (iron-clad), | 1 |
| Gun-boat (iron-clad), | 1 |
| Gun-boats, | 79 |
| Yachts, | 2 |
| Schooners, | 25 |
| Transports, | 9 |
| Small steamers, | 68 |
| | 249 |
| Sailing vessels, | 62 |
| | 311 |
| Besides these there were, for port service, small vessels, | 300 |

Such an enumeration, however, of the ships of any nation presents a very imperfect idea of the strength of its navy. The three hundred small ships here set down are, probably, of no value for offensive purposes, or distant service of any kind; and the same may be said of hundreds of the thousand vessels of the British navy, or of the seven hundred ships of France.

Since the spring of 1862, Russia has been actively engaged in enlarging her navy, and its effectiveness has been largely increased. Like other nations, she has begun the construction of an iron-clad fleet; and this, like the American navy, will, it is said, be composed mainly, at first, of ships of the Monitor class, of which many, we are told, are already being built.

The first necessity of Russia is precisely like our own. She needs batteries which will effectually protect her harbors against the iron-clads of England and France; and, at one-fourth the cost of such a ship as the Warrior or the

Minotaur, she can construct a Monitor battery that would demolish either of these.

Russia, having an unlimited supply of material for a navy, whether timber or iron; ship-yards so situated that she can defend them against all Europe; having also the benefit of American experience and skill, is able to construct a navy equal to any in the world; and, with her new and most valuable possessions on the Pacific, nothing can prevent her from becoming, in the immediate future, a great maritime power.

The Monitor forms of battery will give to Russia, as it does to us, an immense advantage for all purposes of defense. Wherever, in her numerous rivers, she has ten feet of water, she can build a Monitor that will be more than a match for any broadside frigate yet afloat, or that can be floated across an ocean.

Defended by these batteries—invulnerable floating forts as they are—neither America nor Russia can be successfully attacked; while within this impregnable line of defense they can construct, to say the least, as many, as swift, and as powerful ocean-going ships as any other nation.

But the policy of Russia, like our own, demands peace and self-development, not war and conquest; and we both need means of defense that will keep our ambitious neighbors at home, and the means on the ocean of defending our growing commerce.

The American navy consists, according to the last report of the Secretary of the Navy, of five hundred and eighty-eight vessels, seventy of which are iron-clad. Of the whole number, one hundred and four are sailing vessels. The general account of these navies will stand as follows:

| | Steam-ships. | Sailing Ships. | Total. |
|---|---|---|---|
| England, . . . . . . | 566 | 103 | 669* |
| France, . . . . . . . | 360 | 122 | 482† |
| America, . . . . . . | ...... | ...... | 588 |
| Russia (1862), . . . | 248 | 65 | 313 |

* Exclusive of small gun-boats and transports; when added, they make 1,014.

† If add swimming batteries and gun-boats, 559.

The NATIONAL ALMANAC says Russia has also four hundred and seventy-four transport and coasting vessels of various kinds, but it does not appear precisely what they are. Russia has also an iron-clad fleet in course of construction, of which no mention is here made. Among her iron-clads are thirteen Monitors of the American pattern, ordered by the emperor after Admiral Lissovsky's report of the trial-trip of the Passaic and of her fifteen-inch guns.

These figures, though copied from official statements, give only approximately the actual number of the ships of these various navies, because changes are being so rapidly made that the statements for 1863 will not apply to the present year. So far as numbers alone are concerned, and including all classes of ships, gun-boats for harbor defense, and floating batteries, these navies may probably be represented in round numbers, with sufficient accuracy, as follows: England, 1,000 ships, including all classes; France, 600; America, 600; Russia, 550 to 600.

Numbers alone, however, afford no sufficient data by which the navies of these nations can be compared. Steam has so completely revolutionized navigation and the construction of war ships, that the efficiency of a navy depends, first of all, upon the number of its steam-ships, then upon their speed and size, then upon their character, whether wooden vessels or plated with armor, and, finally, upon the guns with which they are armed. If we compare the steam navies of these four powers, and take the figures for France and England from the official statements in the NORTH BRITISH, already quoted, the account stands thus:

| | |
|---|---|
| English Steam Navy, . . . . . | 566 |
| French do. do., . . . . . . | 360 |
| American do. do., . . . . . . | 484 |
| Russian (in 1860), . . . . . . | 242 |

Since 1860 the Russian steam fleet has been largely increased. A comparison by numbers, though in no case reliable, would approach more nearly to accurate results with the navies of Europe, than in comparing their numbers with ours. The form, size, and armament of the European vessels are so far alike as to enable us to estimate, approximately, their relative strength by a statement of numbers; but the American navy is so different from all others in the character and armament of its ships, that mere numbers of ships and guns give no true idea of its relative power. For example, the reports state the number of guns in the English navy at about 16,500, while the number in our own is only 4,500; but when we remember that twenty-eight of the guns of England's finest frigate, the Warrior, are 68-pounders, and the remaining twelve 100-pounders, while we have many guns on board our ships which carry a shot of 450 pounds, the apparent disparity disappears.

Thus it is seen that a correct opinion of the relative power and efficiency of the American navy can not be formed without a somewhat minute examination of the character and armament of European war ships in comparison with our own. It must be remembered, these comparisons relate to navies and war ships as they are at present. Inventions can not be monopolized by one nation, and if it appears that our navy and artillery are now, in some important respects, superior to all others, it will depend upon the skill and genius of our countrymen, and the resources of our country, whether this superiority is retained. Judging from the past, however, we have little cause for apprehension. Our mechanics and inventors have never yet failed to protect the country in her hour of need, and we may safely trust them for the future. In estimating the relative strength of navies, we have now to consider an entirely new element of power, the iron-clad ship; and we must add to this the newly-invented heavy artillery. Both these inventions are yet in their infancy, and, astonishing as the results are which are already reached, all estimates must be based upon things as they now are, for no one can foresee how soon our weapons and methods of warfare may be revolutionized again.

The fight between the Merrimac and our wooden frigates, and then between her and the Monitor, closed up one great era in naval warfare. By that battle the wooden navies of the world were virtually annihilated. After that fight the powers of Europe, in calculating their naval force, were reduced to the small catalogue of their iron-clad ships. The London TIMES then said that the navy of England consisted of four ships, and the English statesman was nearly right when he declared, in the House of Commons, that England had no fleet.

In a lecture by J. Scott Russell, Esq., we find the following: "The first question was, were wooden ships worth any thing for purposes of warfare? Sir John C. Hay, the chairman of the committee appointed by Government to make experiments on the effects of artillery upon iron armor, uttered this fatal sentence upon wooden fleets: 'The man who goes into action in a wooden ship is a fool, and the man who sends him there is a villain.' A list of the 'magnificent fleet' which now defends England had been recently published, and it amounted to 1,014 ships of war. This was a very 'formidable inventory,' but he could give them a very simple analysis of the number. Of these 1,014 there were, of wooden ships, 1,010; of fast iron ships, 2; of slow iron ships, 2. A fleet of twenty Warriors would be more formidable than the whole of the 1,010 wooden ships put together."

This is English opinion of high authority in regard to wooden navies.

It is not intended, by this, to assert that wooden ships are, hereafter, to be considered as absolutely worthless, but they must hold, in the future, nearly the same relation to the iron clads that merchant vessels have hitherto done to the frigate and the line-of-battle ship. A wooden ship, of any size, may be regarded as absolutely powerless against a properly armored vessel, and, therefore, except as against other wooden ships, or as transports, the immense wooden navies of the world may be left out entirely in our calculations for the future. This destroys, at a blow, the boasted supremacy of England and France, and places England, France, America, and Russia very nearly upon an equality in regard to naval power, with the advantage thus far, however, on the side of the United States, as will be proved.

When a ship like the Merrimac demonstrated in actual battle that she could smash up and send to the bottom a fleet of wooden ships as the mere sport of a day, or, at most, without impairing her fighting powers, it shows, very conclusively, that wooden navies are already a thing of the past, except for certain limited purposes. It is scarcely too much to say that, with the armament which the navies of the world then carried, the Merrimac might have met and sunk every wooden ship on the ocean, with no material damage to herself. She would have destroyed our finest frigates, the Minnesota and the Niagara, as quickly as she did the Congress and the Cumberland.

No squadron of wooden vessels can hereafter enter and hold a harbor, or blockade a port, in the presence of a single iron-clad, such as every great naval power has already; nor could they attack a fort, with any chance of success, under the fire of the new artillery. They may, possibly, pass a fort without material injury, but they would only pass to certain destruction if they were to meet an armored vessel beyond. Laying out of the account, therefore, the wooden navies, in estimating the actual *fighting* power of the nations, the comparison is reduced to the armored vessels now owned in Europe and America, and the power and resources of this and other countries for the construction of war ships hereafter.

The fact that the armor plate for vessels is an American invention, will strengthen our confidence in the skill of our countrymen for the future. As once before, in the style of their frigates and their heavy guns, now again, in the iron shield and form of the ship, Americans have revolutionized the methods of naval war. We may hope, therefore, that she will also lead the nations hereafter. The following account of the invention is copied from the SCIENTIFIC AMERICAN for February 7, 1863:

"On the 22d ult., Senator Cowan, of Pennsylvania, presented a petition in the Senate from A. Stewart and others, asking for a pension to the widow of Thomas Gregg; it being claimed that he was the original inventor and patentee of iron-clad vessels. This is a new phase of this subject, and a brief history of the invention, according to the information we possess, will, therefore, be of some public interest just now. It is generally admitted by European engineers that, although iron-clad gun-boats were first brought practically into use during the Crimean war, the late Robert L. Stevens and E. A. Stevens, of Hoboken, N. Y., were the inventors of them. Vessels protected with angulated iron plates were proposed by them as early as 1816, and, for coast and harbor defense, a description of such vessels was afterward submitted to a Government board, consisting of Commodores Stewart and Perry and Colonels Thair and Totten, in 1841. It was stated in the document proposing the construction of such a vessel for the defense of New York, that plates of iron four inches in thickness were equal to five feet four inches of oak in resisting a ball at point-blank distance; and, with the guns then in use, it was supposed that none of their shot could penetrate a vessel clad with such armor. In 1843, a contract was formed between our Government and Messrs. Stevens for the construction of such a floating battery, and $500,000 was furnished by Government, and expended on the battery now at Hoboken.

"During the Crimean war, in 1855, it was found that wooden steam frigates were totally useless in attacking granite casemated forts, defended by big guns firing shells. An application of Stevens's invention was suggested, and several iron-clad gun-boats were then built for the French and English navies. A few of these were employed at the siege of Kinburn, and were decidedly successful. This led the Emperor of France to extend the application of iron plates to one of his large frigates—La Gloire—which was completed three years ago, and was the first regular iron-clad war ship ever built. Since then several have been constructed for the French and English navies—the American invention having thus been first carried into practical use in Europe."

In order to mark the progress of the art of mailing vessels, from the first rude application of the American idea by Louis Napoleon to his gun-boats, at Kinburn, to its present condition, and to exhibit the marked peculiarities of the American iron-clads, it will be instructive to trace the different steps. Passing by the small gun-boats which fought at Kinburn, the first important trial of the iron mail was by the French Emperor on the frigate La Gloire, the construction of which was ordered in 1858. She is simply a frigate of the common model, cased with iron plates about four inches thick. The plates are said to be three and a half inches thick at the stern and bow, and four and a half inches in the center, covering the ship's battery.

She is described from French authorities as about 257 feet long, carrying thirty-six 50-pounders on a single protected deck. Her engine is of 900-horse power, and her crew consists of 500 men. Her ports are only six feet above the water. Her width is fifty-six feet, and her speed thirteen and a quarter knots per hour. The French Emperor is constructing ten more iron-cased frigates of this class. Besides these, France has now at sea the Normandie, the Invincible, the Couronne, and two larger iron-clad rams, the Solferino and the Magenta.

These last carry each fifty-two guns, and have a speed of thirteen and a half knots per hour. The lower ports of these are eight feet above the water. It is also stated by the North British Review (August, 1863), that these largest French frigates are plated in the center with iron six inches thick. It may be stated, then, with sufficient

29

accuracy, that Louis Napoleon has at present a fleet of sixteen iron-clad frigates, carrying, each, from thirty-six to fifty-two rifled 50-pounders; that their armor-plates are some four and a half and some six inches thick, and that they have a speed equal to our fastest war ships, with the exception of some of our small and latest built ships, such as the Eutaw and the Sassacus, being much swifter than any of our own iron-clads.

The Normandie has crossed the Atlantic, but no very favorable account has yet been given of the sea-going qualities of any of these French ships. They are said to roll very heavily, and that their batteries can not be used in a heavy sea, because the ports roll under. They are also said to be very unhealthy. These are very likely to be objections to all iron-clads, because, when in action, few of them can be properly ventilated, and the same must be true of them in heavy weather. So far as is known, all the broadside iron-plated ships roll heavily in a rough sea, and the remedy for this does not, as yet, appear.

An inspection of the table already copied from the North British will show that English mailed vessels are, many of them, of much greater size and power than any yet constructed by the French. Nearly all of them are larger than the American Ironsides or Roanoke, and several of them are longer and of greater tunnage than the Dunderberg, our largest iron-clad. A brief description of three of these vessels will enable the reader to compare them with our own iron-plated fleet, and to judge whether we have reason for apprehension should we be compelled to meet them.

The Warrior and the Black Prince are regarded as the model ships of the iron navy of England, and they may be considered as embodying the utmost skill and science of Great Britain at the present time. These ships are 380 feet long; their tunnage is 6,000 tuns; their draught is, of the one, 22 feet 9 inches, and of the Black Prince, 26 feet 3 inches. They each carry forty guns: twenty-eight 68-pounder, and twelve 100-pounder Armstrong guns. Their crew is 704 men. Their armor-plates are four and a half inches thick, and the Warrior, on her trial trip, had a speed of fourteen knots, and the Black Prince ran from twelve to thirteen knots per hour. Their engines are of 1,250-horse power.

These ships are only plated with iron for two-thirds of their length, the bow and stern being, as English writers affirm, more vulnerable than a common wooden ship. The battery only is protected by the iron mail, while about sixty feet of the stern and bow are like a common vessel.

The Minotaur is 400 feet long; her tunnage is 6,621 tuns; her engines are of 1,350-horse power; her draught is 25 feet 8 inches, and she is to carry thirty-seven guns. Her speed has not been ascertained. Portions of the armor of this ship are said to be six inches thick. The Bellerophon is a newly-devised iron-clad, now being built, whose coming is thus heralded by the London TIMES: She will be "as terrible an assailant to iron-clads as an iron-clad would be to wooden ships. The object with which this vessel is designed is, in case of another great war, to avoid repetition of the long, dreary process of blockading an enemy's fleet, by wearisome and dangerous cruising off the mouth of harbors. The Bellerophon is, in short, to a fleet of iron-clads what a fox-terrier is to a pack of hounds. In case of an enemy's iron fleet running into port, she can follow them with impunity."

But in the description which the TIMES gives of what it calls "this monster," one fails to discover the immense superiority which is claimed.

She is 300 feet long, 56 feet beam, has a draught of 25 feet, and her tunnage is 4,246 tuns. "It is hoped," if certain improvements work well, that she will make fifteen knots per hour; but she is on the stocks as yet, and her speed is yet to be determined. Her armor-plates are six inches thick, but they reach to the upper deck for only ninety feet of the ship's length; for the remaining distance of two hundred and ten feet, the plating reaches only six feet above the water, and all above this line and both ends of the vessel are unprotected. She is to be armed with ten broadside guns, of what size we are not informed, and probably that is not yet determined. Of iron-mailed vessels, of the general character described—most of them, however, somewhat smaller—England has between twenty and thirty built, or in process of construction. Like those of France, they are all broadside ships, and, of course, expose an immense surface to an enemy's fire. The importance of this will appear, when they are compared with the American Monitor form of war ship.

The objections made to the French ships are, that they can not use their batteries except when the sea is smooth, and that, in rough weather, they roll so as to render them not only uncomfortable, but dangerous. The English ships require from 25 to 26 feet of water, and are, therefore, unable to enter our principal harbors. From their great size, they are unwieldy; the joints of their armor-plates work in a sea, and leak; they do not steer safely; and, from the general tone of English criticisms, one is led to infer that they are by no means satisfied with the performance of the iron fleet. But, as neither the French nor English ships have been, as yet, tested in battle, no very definite opinion of their qualities can be formed.

We know, however, exactly the effect which certain kinds of artillery will produce upon iron plates, such as those which form their armor; and as the American ships have been exposed, at short range, to the heaviest cannon and the most destructive shot which England could furnish to the rebels, while at the same time our guns have been tried upon armor-plates in action, we have the means of forming a very accurate opinion of our power for attack or defense, as compared with other nations.

The condition and character of the American navy demands a separate chapter, and this will involve, also, a description of our artillery, and then all will be able to make the proper comparison between our navy and those of Europe.

# CHAPTER XXXVII.

## THE AMERICAN NAVY.

At the commencement of Mr. Lincoln's administration our navy consisted of only forty-six vessels. In December, 1863, it numbered 588 vessels, mounted with 4,443 guns. The aggregate tunnage of these ships was about 468,000 tuns.

The creation of such a navy in so short a time, considering the number and character of the vessels, is without a parallel in the history of war. It is at once a most cheering proof of the vast resources of our country, and of the wisdom and energy with which our Navy Department has been conducted. In the brief space between the breaking out of the war and December, 1863, the country has been elevated into a first-class naval power; and, probably, those who have been disposed to criticise the operations of the Secretary would find it very difficult to point out a course by which the safety and honor of the country would have been more securely guarded.

It is no small proof of ability in the management of the navy, that there was skill enough to provide, and independence enough to use, a form of war ship and a kind of cannon before untried, but which time and experience have shown were alone, of all ships and weapons then known, capable of meeting the emergency.

Had there been a frigate built like the Warrior in Hampton Roads at the time of the appearance of the

Merrimac, and armed with the Warrior's guns, there are good reasons for believing that she would have been overmatched by the rebel ship. The Merrimac, with her heavy armament and her sloping armor, could not, probably, *at that time*, have been beaten by any ship afloat, except the Monitor. The Monitors and the fifteen-inch guns have rendered the creation of a rebel navy impossible, and these alone could have done it; and this is a sufficient answer to all by whom they have been condemned.

This subject, however, will be more fully discussed in another place. The American navy is an original creation. In the forms of its most powerful ships, and the character of its armament, it is unlike every other.

A thorough study of all the other navies of the world would give no data from which to judge of the efficiency of the American vessels. One would be entirely deceived by counting their guns, or estimating their length, breadth, and tunnage, or the number of their crews. These things alone do not inform us whether they are superior or inferior to the war ships of other nations. They are modeled after new and strictly American ideas. Whether good or bad, they belong entirely to this new world. They are creations of this Western Republic. Not alone our Monitors, but our other ships, are American in their fitting up, and in the character of their weapons. Judged by the old standards, nothing is more deceitful. An American ship of two guns, of the latest model, may, perhaps, prove a match for a common forty-gun frigate; and it is very certain that we have two-gun vessels, one of which might destroy the whole fleet with which Nelson fought. It is necessary, then, to know both the character and the armament of our war vessels before we can judge of their efficiency. The following statements will furnish the necessary information:

It will, probably, not be denied that, up to the time of the invention of armor-clad vessels, the Americans had been the teachers of the nations in the art of ship-building, whether sail or steam vessels, whether for commerce or for war. Great length, as compared with tunnage, sharpness of bow, and speed, were characteristics of American ships and steamboats. It is not deemed exaggeration that American genius has revolutionized naval architecture, and that the speed of European ships has been obtained by following, in the main, the model of the vessels of the United States. The ocean tub has been displaced everywhere by the long, graceful structure, which first of all bore the Stripes and Stars. The London TIMES sneered at the Niagara when she went over to aid in laying the Atlantic cable; but the finest frigates and corvettes which England has since built have assumed the Yankee form, and their boasted Warrior appears like a Niagara somewhat magnified.

A writer in an English quarterly boasts that the British ocean mail-steamers have driven the American ones from the seas; but he forgets to state that the Collins line furnished the model for her ships, and that the American line failed only because, in a new enterprise, and one so expensive, private capital could not contend against the patronage of the British government.

Had our government given a liberal and steady support to our own vessels, there would have been a different result. The fact that our steamers have obtained a speed of twenty-five miles per hour upon the Hudson; that some of our lake vessels have made twenty-two miles per hour for hours together—such steam-ships as the Vanderbilt and those of the California line; and the fact that our new war steamers overhaul the swiftest steamers that our English friends have built to run the blockade, these things do not indicate that we shall be very soon driven from the ocean by the superiority of the vessels of other nations.

Such of our iron-clads as are yet afloat lack speed, but the main idea in their construction was invulnerability; and the event has shown, that if this had been sacrificed to speed or any other quality, it would have been fatal to our navy and our country's cause.

There is great reason to be thankful that those at the

head of our navy were wise enough, in the first experiment upon which our all depended, to construct ships which no artillery of the enemy could penetrate; for upon that single question the destiny of the country was at that moment hung.

The best and most destructive projectiles of Europe were hurled against our ships at Charleston, and Europe was watching earnestly the result. It would inform England and France whether intervention would be safe.

The only armored vessel of the common form which attacked Fort Darling was ruined by ten-inch shot; and the only Monitor-shaped ship in which speed was aimed at in the construction, was riddled and sunk at Charleston.

Had all our vessels at Charleston been as vulnerable as the Keokuk, the rebel cause would have triumphed at home and abroad, though our fleet had been the swiftest on the ocean.

Four distinct eras appear in the creation of our navy. In one of these we followed the European models, and failed to produce an effective ship. The distinctive American idea has controlled the other three—the placing the heaviest possible armament in the smallest possible space, thus diminishing the size of the ship in proportion to her armament, presenting a smaller surface to an enemy's shot, and lessening the number of the crew. If to this is added the American idea of a heavy shot with a low velocity, rather than a small one with greater velocity, the idea of a *smashing* projectile rather than a penetrating one, the reader will have the leading principles which have governed the construction of the American navy and the manufacture of American cannon. Through various steps and countless experiments, these ideas have led to the Monitors and the fifteen-inch and twenty-inch guns, while, at the same time, every effort has been made to perfect our rifled cannon.

The ships with which the Americans won their first naval renown, in the war of 1812–'15, were constructed with the intention of bringing the armament of a line-of-battle ship within the limits of a frigate. This was so nearly accomplished as to fill England with astonishment and alarm. It was found that the registered rate of our vessels by no means indicated their actual power; and the result was, that when the Guerriere, a British forty-four-gun frigate, was laid along side the Constitution, an American forty-four, the English frigate was demolished in fifteen minutes. Similar results followed, as is well known, in other actions; and though it was conceded that the rapidity of the American fire was generally greater than that of the English, still our almost unbroken success was probably mainly due to the superior weight of the American broadside. The manner in which the American idea of a heavy armament was carried out, will appear from the following comparison between British and American ships which fought in the war of 1812–'15. The figures rest upon the authority of "James's Naval History," and "Cooper," as quoted by Mr. Alison. The weight of the broadside is thus stated:

| | |
|---|---|
| American frigate Constitution, . . . . | 768 lbs. |
| American frigate United States, . . . . . | 864 lbs. |
| British frigate Guerriere, . . . . . . | 517 lbs. |
| British frigate Macedonian, . . . . | 528 lbs. |

The advantage thus gained was decisive, and the results gave an *eclat* and character to the American navy which it has never lost. It was the first triumph of American sagacity on the ocean, and it has shaped since their whole naval policy. The character of the American frigate of that period will more fully appear from another comparison. The NORTH BRITISH, for August, 1863, states, upon the authority of "James's Naval History," the broadside of a hundred-gun ship—the three-decker, such as Nelson fought with—at 1,260 lbs.

The broadside of the United States frigate was 864 lbs., more than two-thirds of that of the English line-of-battle ship with her one hundred guns.

The American and English ideas will appear still more

strongly contrasted by another statement. According to the NORTH BRITISH, in the article alluded to, the English ship of the line in the beginning of this century, in the time of Nelson, averaged about 2,000 tuns burden, and her broadside weighed 1,260 lbs. Now the Warrior's tunnage is more than 6,000 tuns, and the weight of her broadside is no more than 1,612 lbs. The American frigate Minnesota is of 3,300 tuns burden, but the weight of her broadside is about 2,500 lbs.

One of our sloops, like the Brooklyn, throws a broadside equal in weight, and far more than equal in efficiency, to that of the old English hundred-gun ship. The difference between a British and American ship is again illustrated by the American New Ironsides and the English Warrior, both iron-clads, and representative ships. The American frigate is 3,400 tuns burden, the Warrior a little more than 6,000 tuns. The American ship throws a broadside about equal in weight to that of the British vessel, which is nearly double her size; and to make the American idea stand forth more prominent, the New Ironsides mounts only eighteen guns, while the Warrior carries forty.

Again: the turreted frigate Roanoke throws from her *six* guns a weight of metal, at a broadside, almost equal to that of the Warrior when using twenty guns on a side; and, if armed with six fifteen-inch guns, as she can be if needed, her broadside from these six cannon would exceed that of the Warrior's guns by at least one thousand pounds.

These facts present, very clearly, the peculiarities of American ships and American artillery, and the difference between them and the vessels and cannon of Europe. They show that the American mind is not working at random in regard to our weapons of war, but in accordance with original and clearly-defined ideas. The second era in the construction of the United States navy began after the war of 1812–'15, in which an effort was made to follow the European model of the three-deck line-of-battle ship. It resulted in those failures which are now used for receiving-ships, such as the Ohio, the North Carolina, the Pennsylvania, and the Vermont, which are utterly worthless, except as a sort of floating warehouse. The American mind does not work successfully in European harness. In the third era there was a return to the American idea, and it produced such frigates as the Minnesota, the Wabash, the Merrimac, the Roanoke, and the Niagara. They were by no means perfect ships. They failed in speed; but still they were the most formidable frigates afloat. The direction which American improvement has taken is indicated by the Minnesota, whose battery of fifty guns throws more than twice the weight of shot, at a broadside, that was thrown by the hundred-gun ship of Nelson's time, while the British Warrior, three times the size of the old three-decker, uses less than 400 lbs. more shot than the "old liner" in a broadside.

The French and English hundred and hundred-and-twenty-gun ships, that were fought at Trafalgar and the Nile, would be greatly overmatched by such a frigate as the Minnesota, with her heavy guns, and firing shell horizontally, as the Russians did at Sinope, and by which the Turkish fleet was destroyed.

The fourth era in the creation of the navy of the United States has been marked by the introduction of three new classes of ships: the swift, heavily armed, wooden corvette, such as the Lackawanna, the Canandaigua, and the Sacramento; the still swifter, double-bowed steamers, like the Sassacus and the Eutaw, and the various forms of iron-clads, of which the Monitors are the most numerous. This period has also been distinguished by a new form of American cannon; and these new ships and this new artillery have, it is believed, revolutionized the art of war, both by sea and land. The reasons for such a belief will appear from what follows. As has been stated in a previous chapter, France and England began the construction of iron-clad vessels soon after the close of the Crimean war—France in 1858, and England somewhat later.

The general character of these ships has been already described. The rebel leaders, in preparing for rebellion, had made themselves familiar with these operations in Europe, and, almost immediately after the war had begun, turned their attention to the preparation of a formidable iron-clad ship.

They had seized the most important navy-yard of the country—that of Norfolk—though not before the vessels lying there had been scuttled or set on fire and sunk. Among these was the frigate Merrimac, of the class of the Minnesota, of about 3,200 tuns burden. This ship the Confederates soon raised, and proceeded to convert her into an iron-clad battery and ram. In size she was about equal to the New Ironsides, to which ship she bore some general external resemblance. There was nothing original in her construction. Her armor formed an angle with her sides, covering her deck and guns after the manner of a roof, according to a plan which had been proposed but not adopted in England, at least in her first-class vessels.

In the absence of official information, the exact form and thickness of her armor can not be stated. It has been variously described, some believing it to have been formed of railroad iron, and others stating that she was mailed with plates, four inches or four and a half inches in thickness. One important test was, however, applied, which showed more conclusively her powers of resistance than any measuring the thickness of iron plates could have done. She was attacked with nine-inch, ten-inch, and eleven-inch guns, their shot weighing, respectively, about 100 lbs., 128 lbs., and 169 lbs. The heaviest guns of the Minnesota, the Cumberland, and the Congress made no impression upon her, and, although the Monitor engaged her for five hours with eleven-inch guns, and, at times, only a few yards from her side, it is not known, certainly, that her armor was once penetrated, although compelled to haul off and signal for assistance, her hull shattered by the smashing power of the heavy shot that yet did not pass through her armor. This proves that she was a vessel of the most formidable character, and that her mail was equal in resisting shot to that of any French or English vessel which had then been built. Her destructive power was sufficiently shown, by her shattering and sinking, in a few minutes, with perfect ease, and with not the slightest inconvenience to herself so far as is known, two heavily armed wooden ships. She destroyed them as readily as if they had been bark canoes, and no one doubts that the Minnesota would have shared the same fate, had the Merrimac been suffered to approach her. The wooden navies of the world were virtually sunk with the Congress and Cumberland, and from that time it was evident that the ships which were to rule the seas in future were yet to be built. The ocean-scepter of Britain was broken by the blow which crushed in the sides of the Cumberland, and all nations were to start anew in the creation of navies. England, said the TIMES, had but two ships.

The morning after the destruction of the Congress and Cumberland was the most hopeful one, and the proudest one, that ever rose on the slaveholding Confederacy. They seemed to have a war-engine capable of destroying with ease the whole American navy, and of entering any harbor, of capturing or burning all our sea-coast cities. If the Merrimac was indeed a sea-boat, all this was really within reach of the rebels, so far as then was known. It is believed that nothing could have prevented her, if opposed only by our wooden ships, or our forts as they then were, from reaching Washington, Philadelphia, or New York.

Had she succeeded in this, it probably is not too much to say, that the cause of the Union would have been lost. The Christians of the country will never cease to believe that it was the special interposition of God which brought the Monitor to the scene of action just in the hour of the country's greatest need, and put an end to the career of the sea-giant which threatened to crush us at a blow.

The Merrimac had settled, conclusively, the helplessness of a wooden ship, or squadron of ships, when attacked by an iron-clad. This was a mailed ship, patterned in general after the European model, differing mainly in her sloping armor; but the next day she was met by a war ship such as the world never saw before, a fresh invention of the genius of the West, a hurried, rough, imperfect embodying of an idea destined to work another revolution in the structure of ships and the methods of naval war. The reader should remember the size of the Merrimac in order to judge correctly the combat which followed. Her tunnage was more than twice as great as that of the frigates Constitution and United States, with which the victories of 1812–'15 were won, and almost twice as great as that of the hundred-gun ships of the time of Nelson. She ranked with the most formidable iron-clads of Europe, for she was completely mailed, and her angulated armor was thought to give her an advantage even over these.

The next morning after the terrible feat with which she had startled the country, she came forth for the purpose of destroying the Minnesota, and then she intended, as was thought, to proceed at once to Washington and the Northern cities.

As she approached the Minnesota, her progress was interrupted by a strange-looking *something*, no one on board the frigate knew what. "A cheese-box on a raft," they called the queer little boat, raft, or canoe, or whatever it might be. The huge, mailed monster seemed at first disposed to take no notice of this diminutive craft, and steered for the Minnesota. But the first shot from her small adversary was a startling proof of power.

The practiced ear was taught by that report that the new-comer had at least one formidable gun. The Merrimac stopped her engines and paused to observe her little enemy. It came straight on, showing no sign of fear, indicating a wish to come at once to close action. The first shot which struck the Merrimac showed her officers that the Monitor was throwing projectiles of unusual weight, and created some anxiety, which was by no means lessened when they found that their own broadside made no impression upon the little turret, which hurled forth shot in return, whose stroke made the huge ship shudder. Fearing for the result, at length, the Merrimac undertook to do what many think so easily done—to run the Monitor down and sink her. She failed, but in the attempt exposed herself more than before to the Monitor's shot, while the Monitor was uninjured. This first battle of the iron-clads continued for five hours, and then the Merrimac, apparently much injured, drew off, signaled for aid, and was accompanied by some steam-tugs back to Norfolk. This was the end of her career. She was shortly after blown up, rather than risk her in another action.

In its bearings upon naval war, the structure of war ships, and the destinies of this country and Europe, this may be considered the most important naval battle of modern times. The ships engaged in it so far represented the navies of the world, that safe general inferences could be drawn from it in regard to the future.

The wooden navies of Europe and the United States were virtually on trial there, through the Minnesota, the Cumberland, and the Congress. The iron-clads of France and England were so nearly represented by the Merrimac, that an opinion formed of her would equally apply to them with very little modification; while the Monitor presented the rude germ of the turreted navy which the United States has constructed since.

The result was, that while the wooden ships were as egg-shells before the iron-plated one, the little turreted vessel, with her two heavy guns, defeated and drove off, with no injury to herself, a first-class iron-clad broadside frigate, armed with the heaviest guns then known to European war.

This combat not only saved our own navy and our cause, but it prevented the rebels from constructing one, by destroying the basis of it; and showed England and France that the Americans could build a ship in three months which would be a formidable antagonist for their most powerful frigates. To suppose that this fact had no bearing upon their policy, is to believe them less prudent than usual. The Monitor did, indeed, admonish Europe that intervention would be dangerous. Persistent efforts are made to show that the Monitors are all inefficient, an almost worthless class of ships, not worthy to be compared with the broadside frigates of England and France, and that the government is merely wasting the people's money in their construction.

Before entering into a particular discussion of the peculiarities, merits, and defects of the Monitors, it may be well to offer a few suggestions in regard to this now famous battle in Hampton Roads. First, let it be asked, How would that fight have terminated had the Merrimac encountered, instead of the Monitor, a frigate the exact counterpart of the English Warrior? The Merrimac was plated, it is said, all round; the Warrior only for two-thirds of her length. Considering the terrible effect of the shells of the Merrimac upon the Congress and Cumberland, "converting them," as an English reviewer says, "into helpless, burning charnel-houses," how would the Warrior-built frigate have escaped a similar shattering in her unprotected bow and stern? The Warrior is armed with 68-pounder smooth-bores and twelve 100-pounder Armstrong rifles. The batteries of the Cumberland and Minnesota threw heavier shot than these, and made no impression upon the Merrimac; while the shot of the Monitor weighed 169 pounds, and, by some statements, 180 pounds, and these were fired often at the shortest possible range, and yet it is not known that the frigate's armor was pierced.

What reason is there, then, for supposing that such a ship as the Warrior could have seriously injured the Merrimac? and how much reason we have, on the contrary, to think that the rebel frigate would, with her heavier armament and shell-guns, have been victorious!

Our own broadside frigate, the New Ironsides, armed as she now is, would, in all probability, capture or destroy such a ship as the Merrimac; but it would be with far greater risk than was run by the Monitor, because her ends, like those of the Warrior, are not protected by armor. At Charleston, shells pierced these unshielded parts at the distance of a mile; and, in close action with the Merrimac, she might, perhaps, have been seriously injured, or destroyed even, by her shells. The conclusion seems inevitable, that, for the purpose intended, the little Monitor was better adapted than any other ship then afloat.

Indeed, it is very doubtful whether any other vessel then in existence could have stopped and driven back into Norfolk this formidable iron-clad of the rebels. But suppose that one of the new Monitors had encountered the Merrimac with fifteen-inch instead of eleven-inch guns. It is now known, both from the fate of the Atlanta and subsequent experiments, that a few minutes would have sufficed to disable the frigate. While the eleven shot did not pierce the Atlanta's armor, the fifteen-inch gun sent its shot crashing through, and with such a shock, that the crew of the rebel ship could not be brought back to their guns.

It is not, then, exaggeration to say, as the Charleston correspondent of the London Times has done, that the Americans, since the rebellion broke out, have twice revolutionized the art of war—once on the sea, with the Monitors and their enormous guns; and once on the land, with their new rifled artillery.

The invention of the Monitor form of war vessel and the heavy cannon have saved the country, at least for the present, from intervention and foreign war; for they have rendered it certain that no ship known, that can cross the ocean, could withstand an attack from our small Monitors even, armed with fifteen-inch guns, or our heaviest rifled ones. Experiments already made leave no doubt on this point.

The extraordinary performance of the small nondescript craft, that saved from destruction our finest wooden frigate, and beat off the first iron-clad frigate that ever went into action, determined the government to rely mainly upon this class of ship for the present defense of our harbors, and for the reduction of the sea-coast fortifications in the hands of the rebels. As large sums of money have been spent upon this new fleet, and as severe censure has been cast upon the Navy Department on this account, it is important that Americans should fully understand what the peculiarities are of those ships which the government has made so prominent in the creation of our navy.

It will be seen that Mr. Ericsson, in his Monitor ship, has aimed, first, to carry out the American idea of the heaviest possible battery in the smallest possible space; and then to construct an iron-clad vessel with the least possible space exposed to the enemy's shot, and so render it invulnerable by thicker armor than a broadside ship can carry. As an example, the side armor of the Dictator is eleven inches thick, and her turret is fifteen inches thick. She is, consequently, invulnerable to any shot yet known, but no broadside ship could swim a moment cased all round with such an armor as that. Mr. Ericsson then places two heavy guns in a revolving turret, whose walls, in the first Monitor, were nine inches thick. This turret is placed upon an open deck, so that the guns, as the turret revolves, can be fired in any direction. This deck is sunk almost to a level with the water; and the small space above the water-line can be so heavily armored as to be impenetrable, without destroying the buoyancy of the ship. In action, then, the Monitor ship presents a very small mark to an enemy's guns—only her turret, nine feet high, and some twenty or twenty-two feet in diameter, and a very narrow line of her side, just at the water's edge. These ships, in addition to the battle with the Merrimac, have been exposed, at short range, to the heaviest artillery and steel-shot at Charleston, and no shot has yet penetrated either a turret or a side. That they should be injured by a fire which would have sunk any other ship afloat, was a matter of course; but no gun, rifled or smooth-bore, which the rebels yet have tried, with all the skill of England at their disposal, has sent a shot through a turret or the side of a Monitor.

Plates have been cracked and bent, but, with the exception of two or three casualties from bolt-heads, (now guarded against), the Monitors have protected their crews from shot under a fire which no other vessels were ever exposed to, and which there is no reason to believe any other ships afloat could endure.

In the creation of the new navy, the government has constructed—or is building, at least—four classes of Monitors, besides other forms of iron-clad vessels, both for ocean service and for our rivers. A brief description of one of each kind will enable the reader to judge of the present efficiency and probable future of the American iron-clads; and this, with an account of our new wooden ships, will show what claim we have to be considered a first-class naval power, and whether we shall be able hereafter to defend our commerce abroad and our cities at home.

The small Monitor, which encountered and beat the Merrimac, the pioneer ship of her class, was truly an *extempore* vessel, hurriedly built, to meet the emergency which the rebels were preparing for the country at Norfolk; and the great value of the principles upon which she was constructed is shown in the victory which was won over so formidable an adversary.

The following facts in regard to the Monitors are derived from an article in the SCIENTIFIC AMERICAN, one of the best authorities upon such subjects in this or any other country. The dimensions of the original Monitor were as follows:

| | |
|---|---|
| Extreme length on deck, over the armor, | 173 feet. |
| Extreme beam on deck, over the armor, | 41 feet 6 inches. |
| Depth, | 12 feet. |
| Length of iron hull, | 127 feet. |
| Width of iron hull, | 36 feet 2 inches. |
| Projection of armor-shelf forward, | 14 feet. |
| Projection of armor-shelf aft, | 32 feet. |

The thickness of the side armor was five inches, above the water-line, diminishing first to four inches and finally to three inches below the water. The whole armor above the water was two feet three inches of wood, and five inches of iron. The turret was made of eight thicknesses of one-inch iron plates. Its inside diameter was twenty feet, and its hight nine feet. Her armament was two eleven-inch guns, laid side by side, and they revolved with the turret. Such was the diminutive affair which conquered a first-class iron-clad broadside frigate. Her success was due to three things: the invulnerable turret which shielded her guns and crew, the great weight of her shot, and the extremely small surface—little more than her turret—exposed to the enemy's shot. Her defects were many, but they did not affect the main principles of her construction. She was slow, but there is no good reason why a vessel built on the Monitor principle should not be a swift one, and the Puritan and Dictator are expected to be very fast.

She was not a good sea-boat, nor a safe one. The shelf or deck which supported her armor projected over the hull, like the guards of a Western river steamboat; and this projection, being thirty-two feet aft and fourteen feet forward, strained her in a heavy sea, and finally separated the deck from the hull in a storm, and she foundered at sea.

Notwithstanding these serious faults, she had settled the value of the principles of her construction, and the government at once determined to build nine more according to the general plan, with such changes as experience had suggested. The nine vessels of this new Monitor fleet were modeled alike, and their dimensions are as follows:

| | |
|---|---|
| Length on deck, | 200 feet. |
| Width on deck, | 45 feet. |
| Depth on deck, | 12 feet. |
| Length of hull proper, | 159 feet. |
| Width of hull proper, | 37 feet 8 inches. |
| Overhang of armor-shelf forward, | 16 feet. |
| Overhang of armor-shelf aft, | 25 feet. |
| Tunnage, | 844 tuns. |
| Draught of water, | 10 feet. |

The side armor is composed of five one-inch plates. The thickness of the armor and its wood backing is three feet eight inches. The deck is plated with two thicknesses of half-inch iron. The turret is eleven inches thick, made of eleven plates one inch thick. It is nine feet high, and the inside diameter is twenty feet. The armament was originally intended to be two fifteen-inch guns. But this now varies: some carry one fifteen-inch and one eleven-inch gun, and others one fifteen-inch smooth-bore and one Parrott rifle, a 150 or a 200-pounder. These are the ships which were engaged at Charleston.

Still another fleet of nine are, at this time, (March, 1864), about ready for use. They vary little from those last described, except that they are about one-fourth larger, being about 225 feet long and of about 1,000 tuns burden. The projection of the armor-shelf is less, and the vessels are expected to have greater speed, and it is also believed that they will be good and safe sea-boats.

In addition to these, some twenty Monitors of less draught are under way, which, in other respects, are similar to the last described, being 225 feet long and 25 feet wide. They are intended to be fast boats.

Besides these, there is another class of Monitor ships, now nearly finished, differing, in some particular, from those already mentioned. They are much larger, some of them being nearly 1,600 tuns burden. Their side armor is ten inches thick, and the thickness of the turrets is fifteen inches. Some of these have two turrets.

In the frigate Roanoke there is a combination of the turreted and the broadside ship. She is of the same class as the Merrimac. Her upper works were taken off, her sides plated all round with iron four and five-eighths inches thick in the central portion of the ship, and somewhat thinner, as is stated, at the bow and stern. Upon her deck are placed three revolving turrets, of the Ericsson form; and in these she carries six guns—two fifteen-inch, two eleven-inch, and two 150-pounder rifles. The weight of her broadside, as at present armed, is about 1,500 pounds.

But she can carry six fifteen-inch guns if necessary, and then the weight of her broadside would be about 2,500 pounds. She is said to be a slow ship, and it seems not probable that her peculiar form will be adopted in the construction of new vessels, although she has never been tried in action.

The Dictator and the Puritan represent still another class of Monitors, which are intended to be swift sea-going ships; and, if successful—of which no doubt is entertained, except in regard to their speed—they will be the most formidable ships of our navy, and absolutely invulnerable to any artillery yet in service in Europe. These two ships are so nearly alike, in general form and construction, that a description of the Dictator, copied from the New York TRIBUNE, will answer for the Puritan, except that the Puritan is fifty feet longer than the Dictator, and will have two turrets. In other respects, the ships are, in general, alike.

"It having been frequently stated that the Dictator is an ocean iron-clad, the impression prevails that she resembles the New Ironsides and other vessels built for the purpose of going to sea. This is not so. The Dictator has none of the paraphernalia of such ocean vessels as we are in the habit of looking at in our harbors. She has none of the tall bulwarks, no masts, no rigging, no capstan on deck—nothing, in fact, that looks like an ordinary ship. A long-armed man could almost dip his hands into the water from her deck.

"The dimensions of the hull of the vessel are as follows: Extreme length over all, 314 feet. The aft overhang being thirty-one feet, and forward overhang thirteen, it leaves 260 feet between perpendiculars. Extreme breadth fifty, and depth twenty-two and a half feet. Unlike the original Monitor, and the Monitors that are now in course of construction, the Dictator is almost exclusively iron—her frames, beams, etc., being of that metal. A person looking at her in the river can form no idea of her appearance when she is completely out of water. If an ordinary ship were lifted up, and an immense shelf of eleven feet of iron placed on the top of her deck, overhanging for a space of some four feet on each side, she would resemble the Dictator. Every frame and beam is fastened in the most secure manner; and we believe the bolts were all put in red-hot, to render them sufficiently tight. The frames are put together in the same manner as those of the Montauk and Passaic, but they are much more formidable, some parts of them being double. The skin of the ship—that is, the covering of the frames—is of wood, put on in slabs lengthwise, each being about fourteen and a half inches square. These wooden slabs are fastened to the iron frame with screw bolts, which have no nuts, thus rendering it impossible for any such occurrence to take place as that by which the lamented Captain Rogers lost his life. This wooden skin is no less than three feet six inches in thickness. The magnitude of this surface can only be understood when we state that the hull of an ordinary European steamer does not measure more than eighteen to fifty inches in thickness; so that, without the outside armor at all, the hull of the Dictator is nearly twice as thick as that of the Persia. Both forward and aft there are inserted in these wooden slabs immense blocks of iron, to make them still more formidable and powerful. The length of the hull, in the case of this vessel, is the entire length of the ship, as a man can stand on the extreme end of the bow and stern. Taking into account the usual slope of the sea, the Dictator could not be seen four miles off.

"The armor of the original Monitor consisted of four and a half inches of iron, laid on in single plates, each one inch thick. That of the Warrior consisted of four and a half inches of iron, laid on in a solid slab like our own iron-clad frigate Roanoke. The French frigate La Gloire had also four and a half inches of iron laid on in a solid slab. Now, the Dictator has on her sides above eleven inches of iron, and five inches of this is in one solid beam, somewhat like the Warrior, the La Gloire, and the Roanoke, except that the plates of the latter were in very large slabs, while those of the Dictator are in beams five by three inches. Over these five-inch blocks of iron are six one-inch plates of iron; making altogether an armor of eleven inches of iron, the same dimensions as the armor of a turret of the original Monitor, the Passaic, Montauk, etc. The armor begins at the deck and goes down only six feet, which takes it about four feet below water; so that the deck of the ocean iron-clad Dictator will only be about two feet over water. Below this armor there is twenty-two feet of the ship, only two feet of which is covered by the eleven inches of iron mail. There are, therefore, eighteen and a half feet of the hull which has only a skin on of one-inch iron plate. The weight of the armor is about five hundred and twenty-five tuns—the burden of a pretty large-sized steamer. At six cents a pound, the armor would cost about $63,000, without workmanship.

"There will be but one turret, of a very improved pattern. It was originally intended to cover it with twenty-four inches of iron, but the perfection to which its construction has now been brought will render fifteen inches sufficient. This is four inches more than the armor of the original Monitor and the Passaic, and ten inches more than the armored sides of the vessels. The magnitude of the different beams and machinery of the turret is immense, and it is in this magnitude, and in its improved pattern, that it chiefly differs from the old turrets. The apparatus for working the guns will be of a still newer principle than any yet carried out. The revolution in naval artillery, caused by the facility with which four or five men can work the old fifteen-inch gun, will be made still more startling when one or two men can easily handle the immense pieces of ordnance to be placed in the Dictator. The turret will be covered in action when necessary. The new bar, which was recently added to the turrets of the last batch of iron-clads, since the disabling of the Passaic, will be adopted in the new turret on a much more improved principle. The bar is sixteen inches thick, and fastened on with bolts. The gear of the turret is different from that of the other vessels, and is much better. The turret complete will weigh almost five hundred tuns, or thereabout, being as heavy, almost, as the entire armor of the vessel. It is not on board at present, but will be put in its place immediately, as it is completed.

"The ram is the finest piece of mechanism aboard the ship. The ram proper is twenty-two feet of solid oak and iron; unlike the Keokuk, which protruded from the bottom of the hull near the keel, this extends from the top of the deck, being, as it were, an extension of the entire armor of the ship. Another advantage in this ram is, that it could be carried away without any material damage or injury to the vessel, and without her making water.

"The decks are perfectly clear of all incumbrances, except the turret. The same objection made to the other Monitors, relative to their liability to be injured by plunging shot, is valid in the Dictator's case; but it is only just to say, that, of the iron-clad vessels engaged in the attack on Charleston, none has suffered any serious inconvenience from injuries done to the deck. It seems almost impossible, and has proved so, that a projectile fired from an ordinary boat could enter the deck. The armor of the deck consists of one and a half inches of iron, laid on in two plates, in the same manner as in the other vessels.

"The main-deck—that on which the crew and officers are to live—is a very commodious one, being as high as that of any first-class sailing frigate in the navy. A man six feet high, with his hat on, can walk, without stooping, from end to end of it. Of course the different apartments have not been as yet arranged, all that sort of work being left to the last.

"The ship is ventilated by three immense blowers; two for the use of the vessel generally, and one for the express purpose of ventilating the engine-room. These blowers are of immense size, about seventy-two inches by forty-eight inches. An air-trunk, supplying a blower eight feet in diameter, is within about thirty-five feet of the stern. The air to supply the other blowers is drawn from the top of the turret and distributed through the ship.

"The most untraveled individual knows how vessels are steered. 'The man at the wheel' has before him a compass, the hands of which point to the different parts of the globe. In the iron-clads this arrangement is impracticable, the needle refuses to do its accustomed business, surrounded by such masses of iron as are in each turret, acts sluggishly, and is, in fact, perfectly useless. Several means have been adopted to remedy this inconvenience, the most successful of them being that now in use. It is no other than by the help of a looking-glass. The helmsman stands with the wheel in his hands, and before him is a mirror. Seven feet above his head, situated in a copper pipe lifted above the pilot-house, is the compass, which directs the course of the vessel. This compass is so arranged that the movement of its hands is reflected in the mirror, and thus will the Dictator be steered.

"The machinery of the Dictator is of a more extensive character than that of any man-of-war built in this country or in Europe. The cylinders will not be less than a hundred inches in diameter. Cylinders of these dimensions have never, we believe, been built in this city, except once for a side-wheel steamboat called the Petropolis. The cylinders are bolted into two massive wrought-iron kelsons, ten feet deep, and some twenty-four inches or more in width. They are both in line, athwart ships, and have large slide and expansive valves, the latter working over the former. A peculiar feature of the machinery is the absence of guides, cross-heads, and other cumbrous parts. The piston, four feet stroke, has a trunk attached to it. The boilers are immense, six in number, and have fifty-six furnaces, and an aggregate grate-surface of 1,100 feet: allowing twelve pounds of coal per square foot of grate-surface, the vessel will require at least one hundred and seventy-five tuns of coal per day of twenty-four hours steaming at full speed. The weight of these boilers will be almost seventy tuns each, that is, four hundred and twenty tuns altogether, without water; so that when they are completed they will weigh over seven hundred tuns. The cast-iron in the boilers alone, at six cents a pound, will amount to $14,000. The shaft is also a gigantic piece of mechanical work; it weighs something like thirty-six tuns, the burden of an average sloop. The propeller is a right-handed true-screw, twenty-one and a half feet in diameter; has thirty-four feet pitch, and weighs 39,000 pounds. There is no outboard bearing for the shaft. What piston speed will be obtained from the engines remains to be seen. The propeller is in a well, and can not be struck by any projectile, as a shot would have to pass through twenty-six feet of water to strike it. The engines are calculated to be something in the neighborhood of 5,000-horse power.

"One of the greatest difficulties in the way of making the iron-clads permanently useful was that of protecting the bottoms from the filth which concentrated there and prevented them from moving. The original Monitor had to be towed from Fortress Monroe to Washington, on account of her bottoms being so foul. The English frigate Warrior also experienced a similar inconvenience, and we learn that some Monitors at present off Charleston are very foul. All sorts of paints have been tried, and all with want of success. The most popular was a sort of English 'peacock' paint, which was used in some of the mail steamers; but it did very little good. On the bottom of the Dictator, however, and on all of our iron-clads to be built henceforward, and most of the naval-built vessels, a successful remedy has been devised, which will keep the bottoms perfectly clear of all filth. It is called 'ship-zinc' paint, and is perfectly white in color. Some thirty years since a vessel was coated with it in England; she arrived here a few weeks ago, and her bottoms were found in perfect order. The government has responsible parties furnishing the paint, and its purity can be relied on. It is confidently expected that a vessel so complete, with eleven inches of armor and such a heavy battery, will prove herself the Dictator of the ocean."

This description is the latest given of this ship, it having been written at the time when she was launched. Her armament, it is said, will be two thirteen-inch wrought-iron guns, made after the patterns furnished by Mr. Ericsson himself.

The Dunderberg is another monster iron-clad, much larger than either the Puritan or the Dictator, and very different in form, size, and general construction from any previously described. This is being built at the ship-yard of W. H. Webb, New York, and will soon be ready for launching. The following description will give a general idea of this powerful ship. It is copied from the SCIENTIFIC AMERICAN, of March 14, 1863:

"The formidable ram-frigate Dunderberg, now building for the government by W. H. Webb, at his yard at the foot of Sixth Street, this city, is in a very forward state, and being completed as fast as possible. We lately visited this vessel, and are able to furnish a few details of her construction, which we think will prove acceptable to our readers.

"The hull of the Dunderberg is massive, being solid from stem to stern. It is 378 feet long, sixty-eight feet wide, and thirty-two feet deep. The frames are twelve inches thick, and are built of oak, firmly bolted and fastened together. The model of the ship is very peculiar. The floor is dead flat for the whole length, and the sides rise from it at an angle everywhere save forward, where they are very nearly vertical. The bow is as sharp and has as fine lines as it is possible to give it; and the stern and run aft are very clean and handsomely modeled. The hull is divided by several water-tight compartments, both longitudinally and transversely—a precaution common to nearly all modern sea-going ships, which has been found indispensable. The frames are strapped diagonally with heavy irons, five inches wide by seven-eighths of an inch thick, blunt bolted to them. There is a slight sheer on deck, but it is almost invisible to the casual observer at a short distance. There is but one rudder: provision is made, however, for steering by an auxiliary apparatus of a peculiar nature, should the main steering-gear be shot away. The frame timbers, twelve inches thick, are ceiled inside five inches thick, planked outside five inches thick, and over the planking two courses of heavy oak beams, twelve inches thick, are again laid, making in all an aggregate amount of nearly five feet of solid timber on the ram's sides. The planking is all caulked, and the seams payed, before the last protection is applied, and the entire mass is as firmly bolted together as it is possible to do it.

"The ram on the Dunderberg is about as formidable a looking object as one can conceive. The entire fore-foot of the vessel is prolonged thirty feet from the hull proper, and, rising easily upward from the keel about half the distance from the water-line, is there rounded, presenting a blunt end in shape like the profile of an ax-edge; it then runs back toward the stem again. The mass of wood which forms this ram projects inside of the hull almost as far as it does outboard, and is there substantially secured to the main timbers. The sides and edge of the ram will be iron-plated; and even should the whole of it be knocked off in an affray, the builders say that the hull will be water-tight.

"The Dunderberg has, on top of the main-deck, casemated quarters for the guns and crew. This casemate slopes at an acute angle from the sides to the top. It takes up a large portion of the vessel amid-ships, and is an elongated octagon in shape. It is made of heavy timber, plated with iron four and a half inches thick. It is pierced on each side for three broadside guns, and has one port forward and another aft, in the casemate, for bow and stern firing. The hull of the ship is built out from a distance below the water-line to meet the edge of the casemate above, so that the broadside of the Dunderberg will present an acute angle to the line of the enemy's fire. We do not know what the inclination of the casemate and side is, but it can not be less than 45°. The mass of wood and iron presenting a resistance to the enemy's rams or projectiles at this point amounts in all to seven feet. There are to be two turrets on the top of this casemate. The thickness of the turret-walls will be much greater than those of the 'Monitor' batteries, and strong enough to resist the heaviest ordnance.

"The armament of the Dunderberg has been variously guessed at by parties. As it is not publicly known what it will be, we are not able to inform our readers, further than that rumor assigns the twenty-inch guns to the broadside, while each turret will also contain two heavy guns. The deck of the casemate, and also the main-deck, will be plated bomb-proof; and the quarters for the officers and crew, being in the fortress on deck, will be thoroughly ventilated and open to the light and air: there will then be none of that depressing influence which is so marked in the departments assigned to the crews on the other batteries.

"One great and overwhelming advantage that this splendid vessel has is, that she is built of wood. She may leak, become water-logged, roll, pitch, and toss, but there will still be some hope for the crew as long as they stick to her. Iron batteries fill and plunge out of sight with very little warning. The effect of this fact upon sailors morally is not the least important one. Although no men could have behaved better than the crew of the Monitor did in their peril, yet they all felt that their case was hopeless; and if they were saved, it would be more the result of good fortune than any aid which their ship could afford them. The Dunderberg will draw about twenty feet of water. Her speed is not stated. Her engines are estimated at 6,000-horse power. We are not able at present to give particulars of them."

This is one of the largest war ships in the world, and quite different from all others yet devised.

If to these descriptions is added an account of some of the iron-clads intended for the rivers, the reader will have the means of forming a correct opinion of the mailed navy of the United States in its present condition, (March, 1864). The gun-boats Lafayette and Tuscumbia have been selected as types of our most powerful river iron-clads.

The Lafayette is 304 feet long, fifty feet beam, and draws eight and a half feet of water. Her plating is two and a half inches thick, backed by two inches of India-rubber and twelve inches of solid oak. Her armament consists of two 200-pounder Parrott guns, two 100-pounder Parrott guns, and four nine-inch Dahlgrens.

The description of the Tuscumbia is taken from the SCIENTIFIC AMERICAN:

"The Tuscumbia is one among the largest vessels in the Western fleet. In strength of timbers, imperviousness of her coat of iron mail, stanchness of build, and completeness of outfit, she will rank among the very best of the iron-clads yet built. Her length is 182 feet, breadth of beam seventy feet, depth of hold eight feet. She will draw five and a half feet of water with all her armament, stores, coal, etc., aboard.

"Her machinery is of superior finish and extraordinary strength, and is all below the iron-clad deck, and is constructed upon an entirely new plan, lately approved and adopted by the navy. She has two cylinders, thirty inches in diameter, six feet stroke, working two powerful side-wheels twenty-five feet in diameter, twelve feet bucket. She is also supplied with two other cylinders, twenty inches stroke, working two screw propellers six feet six inches in diameter. She is furnished with two small engines for working the capstan; one forward and the other aft. She has six twenty-eight-feet boilers forty inches in diameter, with five flues each, with an auxiliary pumping-engine for filling the boilers. By her pumps the vessel could be flooded in a short time.

"The Tuscumbia has, in addition to her armament, an

apparatus for throwing hot water, capable of ejecting a scalding stream to a distance of two hundred feet. The armament consists of three eleven-inch Dahlgren guns, in battery, forward, and two 100-pounder rifled guns, in battery, aft. The iron plating on the batteries or gun-rooms is six inches in thickness forward, and four inches thick aft. The sides of the vessel are plated with three-inch wrought-iron; the deck with one-inch wrought-iron.

"The cost of the Tuscumbia will be about $250,000. Her magazines are provided with an apparatus by which they can be completely flooded in the short space of one minute. A bulwark of iron, loop-holed, for musketry, is placed around her guards. Her speed will be about twelve miles an hour against the current. She will be manned by 150 marines. Her custom-house measurement is 980 tuns."

It must not, however, be thought that these two boats represent nearly all the Western iron-clads. They are of many different forms, and vary greatly in their armament and general efficiency. Many of them are expensive and powerful vessels. Some of those lately constructed have turrets; and the form of these has been varied, in order to try experiments which might settle important questions of construction. Their armament, in general, is very heavy—nearly all of them carrying one or more guns of greater caliber than can be found on the largest French and English frigates. Eleven-inch smooth-bores and 200-pounder rifles are common guns on board the larger class of the river iron-clad gun-boats. They have been used successfully against fortifications armed with the largest cannon, rifled and smooth-bore, which the rebels have, and have proved a most efficient arm of the nation's power.

The only broadside ocean ships which the Americans have yet plated with iron, except the Roanoke, which has an exposed side and turrets also, are the small corvette Galena and the New Ironsides frigate. It is stated that the Galena was mailed with plates three and a half inches thick.

She was pierced and nearly ruined by ten-inch shot in the fight at Fort Darling, while the same kind of shot made no serious impression on the armor of the Monitor.

The New Ironsides is a first-class frigate, whose tunnage, according to the register, is about 3,500 tuns. She is, therefore, somewhat larger than the Minnesota, and about 1,000 tuns less in burden than the Niagara. Her armor-plates are four and a half inches thick; and her armament consists of fourteen eleven-inch smooth-bores, two 150-pounder rifles, two 50-pounder rifles, and two howitzers.

Her broadside, therefore, is very nearly the same with that of the Warrior in weight; but her principal shot weigh 170 and 150 pounds, while those of the English frigate weigh 68 and 100 pounds—the latter used in Armstrong guns.

Such guns as the New Ironsides carries defeated the Merrimac, though the Monitor had only two of them; while the Ironsides has been exposed at Charleston to far more formidable guns than any yet used on an English, or, indeed, on any European ship, and has received in all those battles no serious injury. The Charleston correspondent of the London TIMES describes her broadside as the most terrible one in its effects ever thrown from a ship. Except in speed, this ship has fully answered the expectation of the country. She was constructed, however, with a more anxious care to obtain a powerful and invulnerable battery than to give her unusual speed. The broadside ship and the Monitor batteries are designed for different spheres of action; and while swiftness is desirable in both, it seems more important for the broadside ship that is intended for an ocean cruiser.

It must be remembered, when comparing the armament of American and European ships, that changes are continually going on; and the indications are that England is disposed to follow our lead in the adoption of heavy guns; and we may expect to see some of her new ships armed with the largest guns which she is able to fabricate. It is announced, for instance, that the Royal Sovereign, a turreted ship, is to carry 300-pounder guns. As yet England has not produced a reliable cannon of this size, much less has she mounted one on the deck of a ship. But if Americans teach her the art, she will do it hereafter. Our largest wooden frigates, such as the Wabash, the Minnesota, and the Niagara, are ships of only medium speed, but they are heavily armed with the most formidable cannon which have ever been used, except those on board the Monitors. As an example, the Niagara, which has been undergoing extensive repairs, in the hope of increasing her speed, lately took on board, as her armament, twenty-four eleven-inch smooth-bore guns and twelve 200-pounder Parrott rifles, with which the weight of her broadside would be 3,200 pounds, twice that, or nearly so, of the English Warrior. This armament, however, was found to sink the ship too low in the water, and it has been changed. The case, however, indicates the direction of American experiments. Our new corvettes, such as the Lackawanna and the Canandaigua, are very swift ships, and, in size, are nearly equal to the old form of the line-of-battle ship, while their armament is far more formidable.

This general survey of the American navy may be completed by stating that among our smaller vessels are some of the swiftest in the world.

### American Artillery.

It will be seen, from the foregoing statements, that the comparative efficiency of the new American navy depends upon two things: the American, or Ericsson form of the turreted ship, and the power of our new artillery. If the Monitor batteries are really invulnerable, yet, if they are not armed with guns that can shatter or pierce the sides of an enemy's ship, they would be nearly worthless, while the superiority and even the safety of our ships of other forms must depend upon the character of their guns.

Other nations as well as our own are earnestly engaged in costly experiments with artillery. What they may hereafter produce, of course, none now can know; but, up almost to the present hour, the effort of the artillerists of Europe has been to obtain the highest possible velocity for the shot, the greatest possible power of penetration, sacrificing to these ends the weight of the projectile.

The American theory, on the contrary, has been to increase the weight of the shot, at the expense of its velocity if necessary—to use, in any event, for breaching walls and smashing armor-plates, a heavy projectile, and then, by rifling or otherwise improving the gun, to increase velocity and range.

Acting upon these opposite theories, the English have mounted, as yet, upon their ships no smooth-bore cannon larger than the eight-inch 68-pounder, which forms the principal broadside guns of the Warrior, while the Americans have already in actual service, on their vessels, nine-inch, ten-inch, eleven-inch, and fifteen-inch smooth-bore guns, while a twenty-inch gun has just been cast at Pittsburg, said to be intended for the Dunderberg; and 200-pounder rifles are found on even our gun-boats, and 300-pounder Parrott rifles are in our batteries at Charleston.

Before stating facts in regard to American cannon which might seem an empty boast, it may be well to present some very late English opinions upon our new artillery. The first extract is from the Richmond correspondent of the London Times, and, of course, not inclined to overestimate an American invention.

"Again I feel tempted to raise a warning voice about the disparity of the armament on board of the English and American navies. It is impossible for those who have been many months absent from England to be well informed as to the actual state of public opinion at the present moment upon this vital subject. But, judging from the officers of Her Majesty's navy who have, at rare intervals, brought vessels of war into Confederate ports, it appears still to be held that the 68-pounder or eight-inch smooth-bore is England's best weapon of offense against iron-clad vessels. The experience gained at Charleston enables me confidently to affirm that as well might you pelt one of the Yankee Monitors or the Ironsides with peas as expect them to be in any way damaged by eight-inch shot.

"Another disagreeable question forces itself upon an Englishman's attention when he is cognizant of the terrific broadside thrown by the eight eleven-inch guns of the Ironsides—one of the most formidable broadsides, in the opinion of the defenders of Charleston, which has ever been thrown by any vessel upon earth. Have we any ship in existence which could successfully resist such a broadside, and respond to it with any thing like commensurate weight and vigor? I should be faithless to my duty if I did not mention that it is the universal opinion of all the English officers serving in the Confederate army, with whom I have conversed, that England is behind America in the weight and power of the guns sent by both nations to sea.

"It is still a matter of the greatest surprise to those who are cognizant of the endless experiments in guns and projectiles which are every day made by the Federal and Confederate States, that England has not thought it worth her while to attach to the armies of both nations such a commission as McClellan had in the Crimean war, with a view to their gaining such scientific information with regard to ordnance and projectiles as at this moment can be gained nowhere else on earth. It is my conviction that from both sections such commissioners would receive nothing but courteous and unreserved information upon all that it imported them to know. It is scarcely creditable to our government that they should be blind to the opportunities for gaining information which this gigantic conflict affords, or that, from Old World pride, they should refuse to avail themselves of the experience to be derived from a continent destined henceforth and evermore to play no secondary part in the drama of the world."

The second opinion is taken from the ARMY AND NAVY GAZETTE (London):

"It may be concluded as certain that the guns used by Gillmore were Parrott's rifled ordnance. Their work has been effectually done. Had such guns been available in the trenches before Sebastopol, the Allies would have made short work, not only of the Redan and Malakoff, and *bastion du mât*, but of the shipping and of the forts at the other side of the harbor. It must not be supposed that Sumter was a flimsy, gingerbread fort. It was constructed of a peculiar kind of hard, close brick, six and seven feet thick; the arches of the casemates and the supporting pillars were of eight and nine feet thickness. The faces presented to the breaching batteries must have subtended, at 3,500 yards, an exceedingly small angle, and the elevation of the fort was low. But so great was the accuracy of the fire that a vast proportion of the shots struck it; so great the penetration, that the brick-work was perforated 'like a rotten cheese;' so low the trajectory, that the shot, instead of plunging into, passed through the fort, and made clean breaches through both walls. Now, the guns that did this work cost, we believe, just one-fourth of our ordnance, cwt. for cwt.; they are light and very easily handled. The gun itself is finely rifled, with grooves varying from four and five in number, for small calibers, to six and seven for the larger; but, as Mr. Parrott is still 'experimenting,' no settled plan has been arrived at, and all we know is that the pitch is not so sharp as is the case in our rifled guns. The projectile is like the conical Armstrong, and has a leaden sabot and coating—at least it is coated and based with some soft metal.

"In this journal the attention of the government authorities has been called, again and again, to the Parrott and Dahlgren guns. The Americans have constructed cannon of calibers which to us are known only as of theoretical and probable attainment, and they have armed batteries hundreds of miles from their arsenals, with the most powerful guns ever used in war, which have been carried by sea and in stormy waters to the enemy's shores. Before such projectiles as these guns carry, the breaching of masonry, whether of brick or stone, is a question of short time. And, in face of these facts, we are obliged to record that our scientific officers are of opinion that our 'best gun for breaching purposes is the old 68-pounder!' Why, we know what that can do! We know that at 3,500 yards its fire would be about as effectual as that of Mons. Meg. These trials at two hundred yards are perfectly fatuous, if no other results than these, or such as these, be gained by them. It is of no use saying Sumter was of brick; it was at least as good a work as most of our existing fortifications, and infinitely less easy 'to splinter up' than a work of granite or rubble masonry. In substance it resembled very much our martello-towers on the beach at Hythe. Have we any gun which could breach one of these at 3,500 yards? . . . The authorities have had no experience of the effect of such shot as the Dahlgrens propel. They have not got the guns to discharge them. When next the ordnance officers and gentlemen meet, let them apply their minds to the little experiments the Americans have been making for their benefit at Sumter. It is astounding to see what progress has been made in artillery since the Crimean war."

Another English periodical, by no means favorable to Americans, makes the following observations upon the operations at Charleston:

"'The Swamp Angel,' as the Federals call the big gun of General Gillmore, has surely bellowed loud enough at Sumter to wake up some of our critics at home *to what is a fact in despite of them.* As they have underestimated the civil contest, so they have overlooked the Titanic character of the military duel, peddling and muddling over strategics on the map, and blind, meanwhile, to the revolution which these giant combatants are accomplishing in the art of warfare. If the Americans are vain of being 'big,' why not do them the justice of confessing that they attain that adjective, in their contentions, their sufferings, and their engines and methods of warfare? Twice in the course of this two-years struggle they have altered the complexion of the science of destruction—once on the water, and once on land. The Monitor and Merrimac confessedly initiated a new era in naval tactics. The plates of both are hardly rusted by the salt water into which they went down so soon; but already every country that pretends to keep the sea armed is fitting out vessels after their kind. Now, it is a revolution in the art of attack by battery and defense by battlements, which these energetic fighters have developed. Sumter is down—breached and shattered into such a ruin that hardly one stone stands upon another. And this, after repeated failure with such artillery as could be made to float aboard ship, has been accomplished by enormous cannon fixed on a land-battery, discharging bolts of two hundred pounds weight, at a range of four thousand four hundred yards. Six hundred of these Olympian thunderbolts were hurled across this interval upon the walls and parapets of Sumter during the course of three days, and with such deadly accuracy that the proud key-stone fortress of Charleston Harbor withered under them; and an eye-witness writes, that a moldy cheese fired at for a month with pistols could not present a more forlorn appearance than Fort Sumter at the close of the bombardment. No arsenal is safe, no empire secure which is too proud to study this lesson. Nevertheless, what is chiefly remarkable about the destruction of Sumter is the range at which it was accomplished, and the precision of the fire by which these huge bolts were flung. The 200-pounders are said to have gone through and through, till the further channel of the fort could be seen between the gaping rents and fissures of the double wall. Neither Mr. Whitworth nor Sir William Armstrong has shown us any thing in range and accuracy like this. The American officers have, first in their profession, laid, and kept at work throughout three days, siege-guns the like of which for weight were last used when Mohammed besieged Constantinople. We do not hesitate to say that our Spithead forts must be reconsidered, as to structure and position, if our enemies, whoever they may be, can be made to fire these American guns from their floating batteries."

The facts upon which these Englishmen have been compelled to review and change their opinions of American affairs are such as all Americans should know and study, and they are presented to the reader, in order that he may feel confidence in American genius, and know the nature and power of our new weapons of war. It is proposed to confine these statements to our largest cannon, for they alone are peculiarly American. The 300-pounder Parrott gun is the most destructive one, at long ranges, which has as yet been used, either in this country or elsewhere.

Its range is between five and six miles, and Charleston has been effectually shelled at a distance of five miles. This gun, as is said, has thrown its shot through nine inches of solid iron.

The 200-pounder Parrott rifle has a range scarcely less than the former; and with these guns Sumter was riddled and demolished at the distance of two miles and a half, a feat before unheard of in all the records of war. In the destruction of Fort Sumter the Monitors and the New Ironsides assisted, but the work was performed mainly by the land-batteries, because the destruction was certain without exposure of the fleet, and with little loss of life. Some of the Monitors are armed with one of these guns, and one fifteen-inch one. The shot of the fifteen-inch gun weighs 425 pounds, and the shell 334 pounds. These monster guns, being as yet experiments, have been handled very cautiously in regard to the charges of powder. In the trial of this gun at Fortress Monroe, General Barnard, of the Engineer Corps, says the shell, with a charge of forty pounds of large-grained powder, had an initial velocity of 1,328 feet per second, and a range of more than three miles, with 28° 35′ elevation.

He gives his opinion that the maximum range of this gun is "considerably beyond four miles." It has been lately found that these, as well as our other large cast-iron smooth-bores, will bear charges heavier than those hitherto used. The French armor-plates are said to be superior in resisting power to the English ones. A French plate, six inches thick, and prepared especially for a target, was lately, at the Washington Navy-yard, smashed in pieces by a single shot from one of these fifteen-inch guns.

"While rifle sea-coast guns give vastly increased accuracy, range, and penetration at the higher elevations, the effect upon armored vessels of their projectiles of relatively smaller diameter is very much less destructive than the smashing shock of the immense iron spheres projected from the thirteen, the fifteen, or the twenty-inch.

"There is no longer any question of the fact, that the introduction of guns which project such enormous spheres of iron have restored to forts their pristine superiority over ships. No *sea-going* armored vessel can withstand the shock of a fifteen-inch shot; and it is believed that a thirteen-inch, or even a ten-inch solid shot will be found to be quite as effective. It is, therefore, safe to assert, that our harbors, defended by forts armed with such guns, and having the advantage of artificial submarine obstructions, are securely barred against any ship that can cross the ocean. The wreck produced by the impact of these mighty spheres will set at defiance the most energetic efforts of ships'-pumps or ship-carpenters' plugs; and, as in the case of the brief but eloquent duel of the Weehawken and the Atlanta, the men of which latter vessel were driven below from their guns, and could not be induced to return to them, it produces a moral effect as irresistible as it is fatal."

The armor of the Atlanta, equal, as is said, to five inches

of solid iron, was pierced by a shot from a fifteen-inch gun, and the ship captured.

The government has lately constructed a thirteen-inch gun of the same external dimensions, or nearly so, as the fifteen-inch gun. It is supposed that this will bear a much heavier charge of powder, and the velocity and range of the shot be proportionately greater. To test the penetrating and smashing power of cannon-shot, a ten-inch gun was lately loaded heavily and fired at an iron target ten inches thick, and the ball pierced it through.

The heavy Parrott rifles will pierce armor-plates of four inches and five inches thickness with ease. The 300-pounder smashes a nine-inch plate; and Stafford's projectiles, thrown from a cast-iron smooth-bore, have gone through seven inches of solid iron, with only fourteen pounds of powder.

These facts, in connection with what has been before stated, will enable one to judge of the comparative power of our navy, and our means of attack and defense. The reader must remember that the results already reached are the first fruits only of American genius when earnestly applied to the arts of war; and that experiments are even now going on which promise still more formidable cannon than any now in use.

In estimating the power of our weapons, the reader must not forget that the old solid cast-iron spherical shot and the spherical shell are no longer the most formidable projectiles used in cannon. Elongated shot and shells of many different forms are used in our rifled cannon, and lately such projectiles have been used in our smooth-bores, and even in the fifteen-inch guns. According to Captain Rodgers' report, it was a conical shot from a fifteen-inch gun which smashed the side of the Atlanta, and drove the crew in a panic from their guns—the eleven-inch gun having failed to injure her.

Some of these elongated missiles, whose length is about twice and a half their diameter, are rounded like a cone, some are flat-headed, some have the end formed like a punch, some are cast-iron, some are of chilled-iron, some have case-hardened ends, some are of wrought-iron, and some are of steel. These last are said to be the most destructive shot which have yet been tried, so far as penetration is concerned; but whether these or the smashing heavy shot—a 425-pounder—would soonest destroy a ship or fort, is a question yet to be tried.

The reader can now form an intelligent opinion of the comparative power for attack and resistance of the American and the European iron-clad. But before the direct comparison is made, let the following statement be carefully read. It is the opinion of one of the most competent judges of such matters in this country—the editor of the SCIENTIFIC AMERICAN—upon the condition of the Monitors after the attack upon Sumter; an opinion formed, as is shown, after a personal inspection of the vessel most injured in the fight:

"Now that the smoke of battle has cleared away, and the fearful cannonading at Fort Sumter, which so annoyed the twittering reporters, has ceased, we may review the event dispassionately and with reason, at least in so far as it concerns the offensive and defensive powers of the Monitors. The daily press, through its accredited representatives, made great haste to assure the public that their favorite batteries, those in which (not unwisely) they placed the greatest confidence, were altogether unsuitable, and, in fact, were not available against heavy artillery. At the time we were compelled, against our judgment, in view of the overwhelming representations of these self-constituted authorities, to accept as a fact that we were beaten in the contest, and compelled to retire from the fort by sheer force alone. Even at the time of the action, and in days supervening, that portion of the press of the country who criticised the conduct of the attack were immediately frowned down, and, to say the least, sent to 'Coventry' by other papers, whose interests or opinions led them to sustain the part our commanders took on that occasion. We were treated with graphic accounts of the effects of the rebel shot on the Monitor's turrets; and it was asserted that the most destructive shot that was fired on the occasion struck the Passaic's turret near the top, and, after scooping out an immense portion of it, broke all the eleven plates, and spent its force on the pilot-house, which it very nearly demolished. This is the spirit, if not the exact letter, of the accounts furnished. Now, we have examined the turret of the Passaic since her arrival here for repairs, and, with all due respect for the reporter's rhetoric and his sensational paragraph, we must say that it is *bosh*. The shot *did* strike the turret, *did* scoop out a portion, (which might weigh twenty-five pounds), and did strike the pilot-house with great force, besides breaking the turret-plates in its passage. But what of all this? When iron meets iron, (as when Greek meets Greek), then comes the tug of war; and it is not to be supposed that a shot, moving at the rate of say 1,500 feet per second, will strike an iron structure in its weakest part and not damage it.

"The simple facts of this loudly-trumpeted performance of the rebels are, that the shot which struck the Passaic did not endanger her safety in the least; for all the effect they had on her externally, she might have been fighting away till this hour, and, in reality, have been none the worse for it. We have examined the shot-marks on the Passaic, said to be sixty-eight in all, though we did not count them, and find an accurate representation of the Whitworth shot impressed in the turret in many places. If these much-boasted projectiles are not able to do any greater damage than they did, we may safely defy all the English iron-clads and their armaments. The Whitworth shot, or *fac-similes* of them, in a majority of cases, struck sideways; they reached the turret in all possible positions, and show very poor shooting on the part of the rebels. There were several bolts driven in on the turret, which injured the persons within; but the majority of the indentations and scars could be covered by and filled with a common tea-saucer. These are, simply, the 'terrible' effects of the rebel shot. Now, what person possessing ordinary judgment and at all conversant with the properties of iron, could conscientiously report that the Monitors were unable to cope with artillery? For our own part, we assert that the favorable opinions hitherto expressed in regard to those vessels have been greatly strengthened, and we do not hesitate to say, that, with the present artillery, they can successfully defy any fort or any iron-clad afloat. So far as the impregnability of their armor is involved, we would not hesitate an instant to confide our personal safety to the thickness of their walls. We have no desire to disparage any official in connection with this subject; but, so far as the Monitors being disabled (except temporarily) in the late attack is concerned, we must avow our utter skepticism. The Passaic is the only iron-clad sent North; *ergo*, the Passaic must be the one most injured. What injuries are those that merely indent iron plates! and what terrible shot those must be which strike and leave no sign internally to tell the story of their spent force and impotent rage! We think a much better sensational report could have been made on the occasion by writing the facts: How the minions of the rebel government did their utmost to demolish the Monitors, and how signally they failed; how, backed and aided by English capital and skill, they hurled their powerful projectiles against the impenetrable iron-clads, and were worsted in the encounter; how grandly those little vessels withstood the enemy's fury; and how, saving one poor little egg-shell craft, they bore unflinchingly the most furious cannonading that was ever known in the shortest space of time. These features would have been worth commenting upon; and were we in the rebels' situation, we should prefer a naval assault to take any shape but that proceeding from a fleet of those vessels. Properly handled and armed, they can defy any ship now floating; and improvements are being made which will render their utility past all doubt.

"We have considered in this light merely the question

of the impregnability of the Monitors—supposed to be the first requisite of a modern war vessel. That they have other objectionable features, we do not deny; but, taking them as representatives of fighting machines—the greatest offensive power in the very smallest compass—they can not be excelled, and the nation does well to estimate them among its stanchest defenses.

"It is singular, in viewing the effects of the shot on the Passaic's turret, to note that they exhibit none of the characteristics of a plunging fire. The shot that 'scooped out a tremendous portion' of the top of the Passaic's turret, struck the pilot-house at nearly the same hight, showing that it must have been fired at point-blank range, or nearly so. So also those that struck the base of the turret—no marks are visible on the deck which would lead the observer to suppose that the missiles were fired from such an elevation as the barbette of Fort Sumter; and we conjecture that the batteries on Morris Island and Battery Bee must have taken a hand in the engagement, although we think it is stated in the reports that those batteries were silent."

Let it be remembered that every form of missile, shot, and shell which English skill and capital could supply was hurled at the Monitors in that fight, and at short range, and then, in the light of the foregoing statement, judge of their powers of endurance. Let it now be supposed that one of these our smallest Monitors were to engage such a ship as the English Warrior, and let us observe the combatants. Let them be placed so that each is within range of the other's guns. The Monitor carries two guns; the Warrior has forty. Of the Monitor's guns, one is a fifteen-inch smooth-bore, the other a 200-pounder Parrott rifle. The Warrior has twenty-eight 68-pounder smooth-bores and twelve 100-pounder Armstrong rifles. First observe the difference in the surface which each presents to the other's fire when lying broadside opposed to broadside. This would not often be the case in action, perhaps, but it is the only method of making a comparison. The exact hight of the Warrior above the water is not known to the writer. The battery of the Gloire is said to be six feet above the water, and the lower battery of the Normandie is eight feet, and these are said to be lower than in the English frigates, and too low for service in a rough sea.

Without pretending to entire accuracy—nor is this necessary—it will probably be safe to estimate the sides of the Warrior as rising eighteen feet above the water, from the water-line to the top of her bulwarks. She is about three hundred and eighty feet long, and her broadside presents, therefore, in round numbers, 6,800 square feet to an enemy's fire. The small Monitors, such as those at Charleston, are two hundred feet long. Their decks are, at most, it is said, not more than twelve inches above the water, and this narrow strip of hull and the turret are all that is exposed. The turret is about twenty-two feet outside diameter, by nine feet high, presenting a surface of not quite two hundred feet. The hull and the turret together, then, offer a surface of about four hundred square feet to fire, compared with the more than 6,000 square feet of the Warrior's broadside.

Here, then, is at once an immense advantage in favor of the Monitor. Her chances of being struck, at the distance of a mile, would be exceedingly small, while at that distance the huge hull of the broadside frigate would be almost certainly hit by a majority of shots fired. It is doubtless true that the ships in action would not often thus be exposed broadside to broadside; and yet it would seem that this might be the Warrior's safest position, for her bow and stern are unprotected with armor, and are as vulnerable as any wooden ship.

Let their comparative vulnerability be now considered. Experiment has conclusively shown that no gun now on board the Warrior, or any other European ship, can pierce the turret of a Monitor, or even materially injure her side. The bombardment from the Charleston forts has proved this beyond all contradiction. A Monitor, therefore, could not be materially injured by the Warrior's guns. On the other hand, the 200-pounder Parrott gun pierces armor like that of the Warrior with ease; the shot from the fifteen-inch gun pierced the Atlanta's armor, and a fifteen-inch gun has smashed plates much thicker than the armor of the English ship; and we have the opinion of General Barnard, already quoted, that no *sea-going*, armored ship can withstand the shock of a fifteen-inch shot.

All these facts go to show that the boasted Warrior would be overmatched by one of our small Monitors, like those at Charleston. This would inevitably be the case, if she were restricted to the use of her guns only. But it is said that such a frigate could easily run down and sink a Monitor. It should be remembered that the huge frigate, almost four hundred feet long, is unwieldy, while the Monitors, only half as long, are easily maneuvered. It requires, as is said, fifteen minutes to turn the Warrior, and it may be seen, therefore, that it is probably a very difficult instead of an easy thing for a long, heavy frigate to run down a Monitor. The attacking ship would be much more likely to miss her foe, and receive the fifteen-inch and 200-pounder rifled shot at short range. It is true, a slow Monitor can not pursue and capture a swift frigate like the Warrior; but when a pet ship of the English navy shall avoid a combat with a diminutive craft like a Monitor, it will do more to establish our supremacy on the sea, than to capture that frigate in battle. Should a European iron-clad ever visit our shores on a hostile errand, it will not endeavor to save itself from a Monitor by flight. In such a case the issue of battle must be tried.

But the Warrior is, probably, not now the most formidable ship in the English navy. As none of those iron-clads have been yet tested in battle, it is impossible to judge correctly their comparative merits. There are some new frigates, however, of about the Warrior's size, whose armor over the battery is stated to be, for one five inches, for another five and a half inches, and for still another six inches in thickness; and these ships are reported to have a speed of about twelve knots per hour. This was on the trial trip, and, as with our own vessels, it will be much less in actual service.

Let it now be supposed that the most formidable one of this class, with an armor six inches thick in the central portion of the ship, the vessel being of the Warrior's size, were matched against one of our new Monitors, like the Agamenticus, the Monadnock, or the Miantonomoh.

These Monitors have a side-armor, as is stated, of ten and a half inches in thickness, while the turrets are fifteen inches thick. No shot yet fired, either here or in England, has penetrated such an armor as this; and such an armor can not be placed upon a broadside ship of the common form: it would sink her at the dock. Between the English frigate Minotaur, part of whose armor is said to be six inches thick, and such a Monitor as the Agamenticus, there would be the same disparity before mentioned, in the surfaces exposed to shot. The Minotaur is more than four times the tunnage of such a Monitor, and while the deck of the Monitor lies almost level with the water, the Minotaur presents her huge broadside high above the water-line, and four hundred feet long. The Monitor, besides having this immense advantage in the chances of being hit by shot, is herself invulnerable to any cannon now in use; while the fifteen-inch gun she carries smashes through a six-inch plate of the best French manufacture, and her Parrott shot goes through plates six inches and even nine inches thick. How, then, will the Minotaur withstand the Monitor's attack? Nothing is plainer than that she can not do it with her guns. Can the frigate run the Monitor down? It is useless to speculate upon the issue of such an experiment. The Monitors are also rams of a very formidable kind, and the broadside frigate, considering the effect of the Monitor's guns at short range, would, to say the least, be in as great peril as the American vessel. But if the Minotaur can not run down such a Monitor, and should choose to continue the combat, it is a matter of

32

certainty that she would be captured or sunk. But again: suppose any European ship of which we have any account, should engage the Dictator, now nearly ready for sea. Her side-armor, more than eleven inches thick, and her turret, fifteen inches, can not be pierced by any shot now known.

She, too, lies almost level with the water, presenting a small mark to her adversary, and, with half the tunnage of the Minotaur, she has engines of 5,000-horse power, while English official papers, quoted in the NORTH BRITISH REVIEW, state the horse power of the Warrior's engines at 1,250, and those of the Minotaur at 1,350. The Dictator, then, ought to be much the fastest vessel, but this must be determined by trial. Certainly, however, she can not, with such engines, be a slow ship. She is built especially for a ram, and she will carry two guns of no less power than the fifteen-inch gun and the 300-pounder Parrott, because we know that we have those at command. But Mr. Ericsson is making his own guns for this new ship, and expects them to be more formidable than any now in use. Should he not succeed in this, we already have cannon for her that, in the opinion of our best engineer officers, no sea-going ship can withstand. What chance would the Minotaur have with the Dictator?

Or, finally, select the most powerful broadside ship in the English navy, and place her by the side of Mr. Webb's immense frigate and ram combined, the Dunderberg. Her size is equal to the Minotaur, or nearly so. Her turrets can not be penetrated; her casemates and sides are as well protected as those of the English ships; she will have engines of far greater power; and her guns will crash through any armor that a broadside ship can float. The reader can judge what the result of an engagement would be between any European ship now known, and either the Dictator, the Puritan, or the Dunderberg.

Compared with their tunnage and displacement, these ships have, by far, the most powerful engines ever placed on a war ship. They ought to be the swiftest armed vessels afloat. This remains to be tried. Should they prove so, however, it is easy to see that England and France will once more be compelled to begin their navies anew, if they intend to attack the United States.

Such is the navy which the United States government has created in a little more than two years; and, gigantic and efficient as it already is, it is but the first step in our new career—only the earnest, the first fruits, of what the nation is capable of performing. American genius has not yet reached the limit of its inventive power, and we have no reason to fear that it will not hereafter, as it has hitherto done, keep pace with the progress of Europe.

Mr. Ericsson's invention not only saved the country in an hour of great peril, but it will revolutionize the structure of war ships, for the Monitors and the big guns, smooth-bore and rifled, have rendered it certain that no broadside ship can cross the ocean which our vessels can not sink; and Mr. Webb's monster sea-going ram seems likely to present another American idea, which will attract the attention of the world.

The government has been severely criticised for constructing so many Monitors, and no broadside and swift vessels. Events will probably vindicate the wisdom of those who have controlled the navy. The country needed, first of all, not so much swift ships, nor large ocean cruisers, to match the European navies, as batteries, for coast service, as nearly invulnerable as human skill and science *then* could make them.

This want was undeniably met by the Monitors better than it could have been by any other vessels yet known. It needed, at the same time, gun-boats for the rivers. It will be conceded that these have done admirable service, and, so far as yet appears, the best of them will be used as models for future fleets. The broadside type of ironclads was followed in the New Ironsides, and, notwithstanding she is one of the finest frigates of this class afloat, yet, as the improvements in cannon show how easily her armor can be pierced, no one will regret that these experiments in artillery have been made before we had expended $250,000,000, as England has done, in constructing broadside ships. If a fleet of iron-clad broadside ships is needed at any time hereafter, we can construct it with all the added light derived from the experiments of the world.

The country needed swift wooden cruisers for the work of the blockade, and the Navy Department has furnished from its own yards some of the fastest ships that float—vessels that overhaul the swiftest blockade-runners that ever left an English port; and these ships are the beginning of a new class of American ships which, in speed and power of armament, are not yet matched elsewhere. Having produced such a navy in a little more than two years, and which is only the germ of the future American navy, with a commercial marine already greater than that even of England, with unlimited resources at command, with two great oceans washing a coast-line of thousands of miles, nothing seems too great to anticipate in regard to the future naval power of America.

We want, however, no fleets for conquest; we have no wish to interfere with the affairs of other nations—as England and France have threatened, and still desire, in regard to us—and enough is already known to show them that, until some new war ship shall be invented in Europe, no fleet can be sent to invade us that can not be destroyed with the means we already have; and we may feel entire confidence that the genius of our inventors and the skill of our workmen will hereafter devise ships and guns that will protect, on every sea, the Stripes and Stars, which will represent, hereafter, a Free and Christian American Nation.

SINCE the foregoing chapter was written, letters have been addressed to the Secretary of the Navy, upon the subject of the Monitors and the fifteen-inch guns, by three of our most distinguished naval officers—Commodore Rodgers, Commodore Porter, and Admiral Dahlgren—whose opinions are so important that extracts from them are added here, for the views of such men in high official stations should be considered as decisive upon subjects with which they are perfectly familiar. Every American will feel encouraged, in regard to the present and future of the American navy, by these letters, while they can not fail to make a profound impression on Europe.

In describing the difference between the ordinary ship and the Monitor model, Commodore Rodgers says:

"In the Ironsides class, the hull of a wooden man-of-war, as constructed for general purposes, is clad with iron. It is true, some modification of shape and increase of size is required to meet the additional weight which she has to carry; but still, in essentials, she is a vessel of the ordinary model; she has the advantage of ample quarters for her crew, with free access to her decks in storms; with natural ventilation; with abundance of light; with numerous guns, giving her a rapidity of fire unattainable in a Monitor, and essential in battering forts; and she is as able to carry canvas as other men-of-war.

"The Monitor class, as far as I know, is new. If I understand the idea, it is to cut off all the surface above water, except that which may be necessary to flotation, and to carry the guns in a revolving turret, or turrets, near the center of motion, supported upon the keel and kelsons.

"The plans upon which Mr. Ericsson has worked out this idea of his may be modified by further experience; but the idea itself will be employed while iron-clad vessels are used in warfare."

He describes the advantage of the Ericsson model as follows:

"It has these advantages:

"The Monitor has the least possible surface to be plated, and therefore takes the least possible tunnage to float armor of a given thickness, or, with a given tunnage, allows the greatest possible thickness of armor, and, consequently, the greatest possible impregnability. The ability to carry armor is proportionable to the tunnage, but the Monitor of 844 tuns has actually thicker plating than the Ironsides of 3,480 tuns, and than the Warrior of 6,000; and yet the Ironsides and Warrior have only the middle portion of their hulls plated, their ends being merely of wood without armor.

"The guns of the Monitors, near the center of motion, are supported upon the keel and kelsons, upborne by the depth of water under them, and carried by the whole strength of the hull.

"In Monitors heavier guns are, therefore, practicable than can ever be carried in broadside out upon the ribs of a ship.

"In the Monitors, concentration of guns and armor is the object sought.

"In them the plating is compressed into inches of elevation; while in the Ironsides class it is extended over feet; and the comparatively numerous guns distributed over the decks of the Ironsides class are molded into a few larger ones in the turrets of the Monitors."

In speaking of the principle upon which the Monitors are armed, he says:

"When power enough is required in the individual guns to crush and pierce the side of an adversary at a single blow, the most formidable artillery must be employed—and fifteen-inch guns are the most formidable which, so far, we have tried; but no vessel of the Ironsides class can carry these guns, and the Monitors actually do carry them. If target experiments are reliable, a shot from a fifteen-inch gun will crush in the side of any vessel of the Ironsides class in Europe or America. A single well-planted blow would sink either the Warrior, La Gloire, Magenta, Minotaur, or the Bellerophon."

Commodore Porter says, also, that the Monitors roll very little in a seaway, and relates the following incident to show their steadiness. A bottle of claret, he says, remained standing for an hour on the dinner-table of the Weehawken at a time when no one could stand on the deck of her convoy, the Iroquois, a fine sea-boat, without holding on to the life-lines.

Admiral Dahlgren declares that, to meet the wants of the government in this war, the Monitors are far better than the broadside models adopted by France and England; and that, if contractors had met the government demand, every Southern port would, ere this, have been in our possession.

Commodore Porter says that, with one of our Monitors, he could begin at Cairo, and, going down the Mississippi, destroy every vessel we have on the Western waters, unless they should escape by flight.

Commodore Rodgers states his conclusions as follows:

"To sum up my conclusions, I think that the Monitor class and the Ironsides class are different weapons, each having its peculiar advantages—both needed to an iron-clad navy—both needed in war; but that, when the Monitor class measures its strength against the Ironsides class, then, with vessels of equal size, the Monitor class will overpower the Ironsides class; and, indeed, a single Monitor will capture many casemated vessels of no greater individual size or speed: and as vessels find their natural antagonists in forts, it must be considered that upon the whole the Monitor principle contains the most successful elements for plating vessels for war purposes.

"I have the honor to be, very respectfully, your obedient servant,

"JOHN RODGERS, *Commodore U. S. N.*

"Hon. GIDEON WELLES, *Secretary of the Navy.*"

The importance of these statements from experienced

naval officers, who have been eye-witnesses of the performance of the Monitors, and the effect of the shot of the fifteen-inch guns, can not be overrated. They seem to insure our nation from foreign attack, at least, until great changes are made in naval war. No ship of the broadside class, Commodore Rodgers thinks, can carry a fifteen-inch gun safely, while the Monitors do carry them; and one well-directed shot from one of these guns, he says, would sink any broadside vessel, even the last and most powerful ones of England or France.

Every American should reflect upon the bearing which these facts have upon the future of our nation. It is proved, beyond dispute, that we can build vessels of the Monitor class which can traverse, safely, the whole American coast, which no artillery carried on a broadside ship can penetrate, while the cannon which a Monitor can carry, and with which even our small Monitors are armed, can sink any broadside ship that floats.

The fleets of France and England can not, therefore, approach our coasts without almost certain destruction. Such a ship as the Dictator, or the Puritan, according to the opinions stated by these eminent officers, would be able to destroy the whole iron-clad navies of France and England, if their ships could be encountered singly, and the only danger from a squadron would be that of being run down. The solution of a mathematical problem is not more certain than that even such a Monitor as the Catawba, now lately launched at Cincinnati, would destroy any ship in the British or French navy, unless (a thing most improbable) she could be run down before she could use her guns. The side-armor of the Catawba, a ship of about eleven hundred tuns, is equal to ten inches of solid iron on the hull above the water-line, while her turret is eleven inches thick, and she is, therefore, absolutely invulnerable to any artillery which a broadside ship can carry.

The government, then, has acted most wisely in adopting the Monitors for its present need. They have secured the nation against foreign attack, and rendered it certain that, within the lines defended by these impregnable floating batteries, we can safely develop our national life, free from all external danger.

In the mean time the two finest broadside iron-clads in the world have been built in America—the Ironsides and the Italian frigate; and we are able to produce any form of vessel which the nation may need, and to any extent that may be required.

In order to give the reader a complete view of our navy, a full list is added here of all the vessels in it March 12, 1864. This is from the official catalogue, published by the government in answer to a resolution of the Senate. It will be found very valuable for future reference, as it is alphabetically arranged, and shows the character, the size, the rate, and the armament of every one of our national ships, and the location of each at the time of its publication.

## COMPLETE LIST OF THE VESSELS OF THE AMERICAN NAVY, MARCH 12, 1864.

### RATES.

FIRST RATES.

Sailing ships of 2,000 tuns and upward.
Screw steamers of 2,500 tuns and upward.
Paddle-wheel steamers of 2,400 tuns and upward.
Iron-clad steamers of 2,500 tuns and upward.

SECOND RATES.

Sailing ships from 1,300 to 2,000 tuns.
Screw steamers from 1,200 to 2,500 tuns.
Paddle-wheel steamers from 1,000 to 2,400 tuns.
Iron-clad steamers from 1,200 to 2,500 tuns.
Purchased screw steamers of 1,400 tuns and upward.
Purchased paddle-wheel steamers of 1,500 tuns and upward.

THIRD RATES.

Sailing ships from 700 to 1,300 tuns.
Screw steamers from 600 to 1,200 tuns.
Paddle-wheel steamers from 700 to 1,000 tuns.
Iron-clad steamers from 500 to 1,200 tuns.
Purchased screw steamers from 700 to 1,400 tuns.
Purchased paddle-wheel steamers from 900 to 1,500 tuns.
Receiving-ships.

FOURTH RATES.

Sailing ships under 700 tuns.
Screw steamers under 600 tuns.
Paddle-wheel steamers under 700 tuns.
Iron-clad steamers under 500 tuns.
Purchased screw steamers under 700 tuns.
Purchased paddle-wheel steamers under 900 tuns.
Store and supply vessels.

| Name. | Rate. | Class. | Guns | Tunnage. | Station. |
|---|---|---|---|---|---|
| Abraham | Fourth | Paddle-wheel | 0 | 700 | Mississippi Squadron. |
| Acacia | Fourth | Screw | 4 | 300 | South Atlantic Squadron. |
| Adela | Fourth | Paddle-wheel | 6 | 583 | East Gulf Squadron. |
| Admiral | Fourth | Screw | 5 | 1,248 | Supply Steamer, W. Gulf Squadron. |

| Name. | Rate. | Class. | Guns | Tun-nage. | Station. |
|---|---|---|---|---|---|
| Adolph Hugel...... | Fourth | Schooner...... | 3 | 269 | Potomac Flotilla. |
| Agamenticus...... | Second | Iron-clad...... | 4 | 1,564 | Building at Portsmouth, N. H., navy-yard. |
| Agawam | Third.. | Paddle-wheel | 10 | 974 | Waiting for crew, at Portsmouth, N. H. |
| A. Houghton....... | Fourth | Bark............ | 2 | 326 | South Atlantic Squadron. |
| Alabama............ | Third.. | Paddle-wheel | 10 | 1,264 | Repairing at Portsmouth, N. H. |
| Albemarle ......... | Fourth | Schooner...... | 0 | 200 | N. Atlantic Squadron ordnance-ship, Newbern, N. C. |
| Albatross............ | Fourth | Screw ......... | 6 | 378 | West Gulf Squadron. |
| Alert.................. | Fourth | Screw ......... | 2 | 65 | North Atlantic Squadron. |
| Alexandria......... | Fourth | Paddle-wheel | 2 | 60 | Mississippi Squadron. |
| Alfred Robb........ | Fourth | Paddle-wheel | 4 | 86 | Mississippi Squadron. |
| Algonquin ......... | Third.. | Paddle-wheel | 10 | 974 | Building at New York. |
| Allegany............ | Third.. | Screw ......... | 10 | 989 | Receiving-ship, Baltimore. |
| Althea................. | Fourth | Screw ......... | 1 | 72 | Fitting for sea, at N. York. |
| America............. | Fourth | Yacht ......... | 3 | 100 | School-ship, Newport, R. I. |
| Ammonoosuc....... | First... | Screw ......... | 10 | 3,200 | Building at navy-yard, Boston. |
| Anacostia .......... | Fourth | Screw ......... | 4 | 217 | Potomac Flotilla. |
| Annie.................. | Fourth | Schooner...... | 1 | 27 | East Gulf Squadron. |
| Antelope............ | Fourth | Paddle-wheel | 6 | 173 | Mississippi Squadron. |
| *Antietam ......... | Second | Screw ......... | 20 | 2,200 | |
| Antona............... | Fourth | Screw ......... | 4 | 565 | West Gulf Squadron. |
| *Arapaho........... | Second | Screw ......... | 8 | 2,200 | |
| Argosy .............. | Fourth | Paddle-wheel | 8 | 219 | Mississippi Squadron. |
| Arkansas............ | Third.. | Screw ......... | 6 | 752 | West Gulf Squadron. |
| Aries.................. | Third.. | Screw ......... | 7 | 820 | North Atlantic Squadron. |
| Ariel.................. | Fourth | Schooner...... | 1 | 19 | East Gulf Squadron. |
| Arizona ............. | Third.. | Paddle-wheel | 6 | 959 | West Gulf Squadron, (Mississippi Squadron temporarily). |
| Arletta............... | Fourth | Schooner...... | 3 | 199 | N. Atlantic Squadron ordnance-ship, Beaufort. |
| Aroostook........... | Fourth | Screw ......... | 7 | 507 | West Gulf Squadron. |
| Arthur .............. | Fourth | Bark............ | 6 | 554 | West Gulf Squadron. |
| Ascutney ........... | Third.. | Paddle-wheel | 10 | 974 | Building at New York. |
| Ashuelot ............ | Second | Paddle-wheel | 10 | 1,030 | Building at Boston. |
| Atlanta ............. | Third.. | Iron-clad ..... | 4 | 1,006 | North Atlantic Squadron. |
| Augusta............. | Third.. | Paddle-wheel | 10 | 1,310 | Waiting crew at N. York. |
| Augusta Dinsmore | Third.. | Screw ......... | 2 | 850 | West Gulf Squadron. |
| Avenger ............ | Third. | Ram ............ | 7 | 750 | Building at N. Albany, Ind. |
| Baltimore .......... | Fourth | Paddle-wheel | 2 | 500 | Ordnance vessel, Washington. |
| Banshee............. | Fourth | Paddle-wheel | 5 | 533 | Fitting for service at N. Y |
| Beauregard ........ | Fourth | Schooner...... | 1 | 101 | East Gulf Squadron. |
| Benton .............. | Third.. | Iron-clad...... | 16 | 1,033 | Mississippi Squadron. |
| Ben Morgan........ | Fourth | Ship............ | 0 | 407 | North Atlantic Squadron ordnance-ship. |
| Bermuda............ | Fourth | Screw.......... | 3 | 1,238 | Supply steamer for West Gulf Squadron. |
| Bienville ........... | Second | Paddle-wheel | 11 | 1,558 | Repairing at New York. |
| Black Hawk....... | Third.. | Paddle-wheel | 11 | 902 | Mississippi Squadron. |

| Name. | Rate. | Class. | Guns | Tunnage. | Station. |
|---|---|---|---|---|---|
| Bloomer ............ | Fourth | Paddle-wheel | 2 | 130 | West Gulf Squadron. |
| Blue Light.......... | Fourth | Screw ......... | 1 | 103 | Building at the navy-yard, Portsmouth, N. H., (powder tug). |
| Bohio................ | Fourth | Brig............ | 6 | 196 | West Gulf Squadron. |
| Brandywine........ | Fourth | Frigate......... | 1 | 1,726 | Store-ship, Norfolk navy-yard. |
| Braziliera........... | Fourth | Bark............ | 6 | 540 | South Atlantic Squadron. |
| Brilliant ............ | Fourth | Paddle-wheel | 6 | 226 | Mississippi Squadron. |
| Britannia........... | Fourth | Paddle-wheel | 4 | 495 | North Atlantic Squadron. |
| Brooklyn............ | Second | Screw ......... | 26 | 2,070 | Ready for sea at N. York, (waiting crew). |
| Buckthorn.......... | Fourth | Screw ......... | 1 | 128 | Ready for sea at N. York, (waiting crew). |
| Cactus............... | Fourth | Paddle-wheel | 1 | 176 | Waiting crew at N. York. |
| Calhoun ............ | Fourth | Paddle-wheel | 5 | 508 | West Gulf Squadron. |
| Calypso.............. | Fourth | Screw ......... | 6 | 630 | North Atlantic Squadron. |
| Camanche........... | Third.. | Iron-clad ..... | 2 | 844 | San Francisco, California. |
| Cambridge.......... | Third.. | Screw ......... | 10 | 858 | North Atlantic Squadron. |
| Camellia ............ | Fourth | Screw ......... | 2 | 198 | South Atlantic Squadron. |
| Canandaigua ...... | Second | Screw ......... | 11 | 1,395 | South Atlantic Squadron. |
| Canonicus ........... | Third.. | Iron-clad ...... | 2 | 1,034 | Ready for sea at Boston. |
| Carmita ............. | Fourth | Schooner...... | 0 | 61 | East Gulf Squadron. |
| Carnation .......... | Fourth | Screw ......... | 2 | 82 | South Atlantic Squadron. |
| Carondelet.......... | Third.. | Iron-clad ..... | 11 | 512 | Mississippi Squadron. |
| Carrabasset......... | Fourth | Paddle-wheel | 6 | 202 | West Gulf Squadron. |
| Casco................. | Third.. | Iron-clad ...... | 2 | 614 | Building at East Boston. |
| Catawba ............ | Third.. | Iron-clad ...... | 2 | 1,034 | Building at Cincinnati. |
| Catskill ............. | Third.. | Iron-clad ...... | 3 | 844 | South Atlantic Squadron. |
| Cayuga.............. | Fourth | Screw ......... | 7 | 507 | West Gulf Squadron. |
| Ceres ................ | Fourth | Screw ......... | 4 | 144 | North Atlantic Squadron. |
| Champion .......... | Fourth | Paddle-wheel | 4 | 115 | Mississippi Squadron. |
| Charlotte ............ | Fourth | Schooner...... | 2 | 70 | West Gulf Squadron. |
| Chas. Phelps........ | Fourth | Ship............ | 1 | 362 | North Atlantic Squadron, (coal vessel). |
| Chattanooga........ | First... | Screw ......... | 8 | 3,000 | Building at Philadelphia. |
| Chenango .......... | Third.. | Paddle-wheel | 10 | 974 | Ready for sea at N. York, (waiting crew). |
| Cherokee............ | Fourth | Screw ......... | 6 | 606 | Ready for sea at Boston, (waiting crew). |
| Chickasaw.......... | Third.. | Iron-clad ...... | 2 | 970 | Building at St. Louis. |
| Chickopee........... | Third.. | Paddle-wheel | 9 | 974 | Ready for sea at N. York. |
| Chillicothe.......... | Fourth | Iron-clad ...... | 3 | 203 | Mississippi Squadron. |
| Chimo ............... | Third.. | Iron-clad ...... | 2 | 614 | Building at South Boston. |
| Chippewa .......... | Fourth | Screw ......... | 4 | 507 | South Atlantic Squadron. |
| Choctaw............. | Third.. | Paddle-wheel | 8 | 1,004 | Mississippi Squadron. |
| Chocura............. | Fourth | Screw ......... | 5 | 507 | West Gulf Squadron. |
| Chotank............. | Fourth | Schooner...... | 0 | 53 | Navy-yard, New York, (laid up). |
| Cimarron............ | Third.. | Paddle-wheel | 10 | 860 | South Atlantic Squadron. |
| Cincinnati.......... | Third.. | Iron-clad ...... | 13 | 512 | Mississippi Squadron. |
| Circassian ......... | Fourth | Screw ......... | 6 | 1,750 | Supply steamer, repairing at Boston. |
| Clara Dolsen....... | Fourth | Paddle-wheel | 1 | 852 | Mississippi Squadron. |

| Name. | Rate. | Class. | Guns | Tun-nage. | Station. |
|---|---|---|---|---|---|
| Clover | Fourth | Screw | 2 | 128 | South Atlantic Squadron. |
| Clyde | Fourth | Paddle-wheel | 2 | 294 | East Gulf Squadron. |
| Cœur de Lion | Fourth | Paddle-wheel | 3 | 60 | Potomac Flotilla. |
| Cohasset | Fourth | Screw | 2 | 100 | North Atlantic Squadron. |
| Cohoes | Third | Iron-clad | 2 | 614 | Building at Greenpoint, N. York. |
| Colorado | First | Screw | 52 | 3,425 | Navy-yard, Portsmouth, N. Hampshire. |
| Columbine | Fourth | Paddle-wheel | 2 | 133 | South Atlantic Squadron. |
| Commodore | Fourth | Paddle-wheel | 4 | 80 | West Gulf Squadron. |
| Com. Barney | Fourth | Paddle-wheel | 7 | 513 | North Atlantic Squadron. |
| Com. Hull | Fourth | Paddle-wheel | 6 | 376 | North Atlantic Squadron. |
| Com. Jones | Fourth | Paddle-wheel | 6 | 542 | North Atlantic Squadron. |
| Com. McDonough | Fourth | Paddle-wheel | 6 | 532 | South Atlantic Squadron. |
| Com. Morris | Fourth | Paddle-wheel | 6 | 532 | North Atlantic Squadron. |
| Com. Perry | Fourth | Paddle-wheel | 5 | 513 | North Atlantic Squadron. |
| Com. Read | Fourth | Paddle-wheel | 6 | 650 | Potomac Flotilla. |
| Conemaugh | Third | Paddle-wheel | 9 | 955 | West Gulf Squadron. |
| Conestoga | Fourth | Paddle-wheel | 5 | 512 | Mississippi Squadron. |
| Connecticut | Second | Paddle-wheel | 11 | 1,800 | North Atlantic Squadron. |
| Constellation | Second | Sloop | 24 | 1,425 | Mediterranean. |
| Constitution | Second | Frigate | 17 | 1,607 | School-ship, Newport, R. I. |
| Contoocook | Second | Screw | 8 | 2,200 | Building at Portsmouth, N. Hampshire, navy-yard. |
| Cornubia | Fourth | Paddle-wheel | 3 | 600 | Ready for sea at Boston, (waiting crew). |
| Corypheus | Fourth | Sloop | 2 | 82 | West Gulf Squadron. |
| Courier | Fourth | Ship | 4 | 554 | Store-ship, on way to Pensacola. |
| Covington | Fourth | Paddle-wheel | 8 | 224 | Mississippi Squadron. |
| Cowslip | Fourth | Paddle-wheel | 3 | 220 | West Gulf Squadron. |
| C. P. Williams | Fourth | Schooner | 4 | 210 | South Atlantic Squadron. |
| Cricket | Fourth | Paddle-wheel | 6 | 156 | Mississippi Squadron. |
| Crusader | Fourth | Screw | 7 | 545 | North Atlantic Squadron. |
| Curlew | Fourth | Paddle-wheel | 8 | 196 | Mississippi Squadron. |
| Currituck | Fourth | Screw | 5 | 193 | Potomac Flotilla. |
| Cyane | Third | Sloop | 19 | 972 | Pacific Squadron. |
| Dacotah | Third | Screw | 7 | 996 | North Atlantic Squadron. |
| Daffodil | Fourth | Paddle-wheel | 2 | 160 | South Atlantic Squadron. |
| Dahlia | Fourth | Paddle-wheel | 0 | 50 | Mississippi Squadron. |
| Dai Ching | Fourth | Screw | 7 | 520 | South Atlantic Squadron. |
| Daisy | Fourth | Paddle-wheel | 0 | 50 | Mississippi Squadron. |
| Dale | Fourth | Sloop | 3 | 566 | East Gulf Squadron (ordnance-ship). |
| Dandelion | Fourth | Screw | 2 | 111 | South Atlantic Squadron. |
| Dan Smith | Fourth | Schooner | 7 | 149 | South Atlantic Squadron. |
| Darlington | Fourth | Paddle-wheel | 0 | 300 | South Atlantic Squadron, (quarter-master's service). |
| Dart | Fourth | Schooner | 1 | 94 | West Gulf Squadron. |
| Dawn | Fourth | Screw | 3 | 391 | North Atlantic Squadron. |
| Daylight | Fourth | Screw | 8 | 682 | North Atlantic Squadron. |
| Decatur | Fourth | Sloop | 0 | 566 | San Francisco, Cal. |
| Delaware | Fourth | Paddle-wheel | 3 | 357 | North Atlantic Squadron. |
| De Soto | Second | Paddle-wheel | 10 | 1,600 | East Gulf Squadron. |

| Name. | Rate. | Class. | Guns | Tunnage. | Station. |
|---|---|---|---|---|---|
| Dictator | First | Iron-clad | 2 | 3,033 | Building at New York. |
| Dragon | Fourth | Screw | 2 | 118 | Potomac Flotilla. |
| Dunderberg | First | Iron-clad | 10 | 5,090 | Building at New York. |
| Eastport | Third | Iron-clad | 8 | 800 | Mississippi Squadron. |
| E. B. Hale | Fourth | Screw | 6 | 192 | South Atlantic Squadron. |
| Elk | Fourth | Paddle-wheel | 6 | 162 | West Gulf Squadron. |
| Ella | Fourth | Paddle-wheel | 2 | 230 | Potomac Flotilla. |
| Ellen | Fourth | Paddle-wheel | 4 | 341 | South Atlantic Squadron, (laid up). |
| Emma | Fourth | Screw | 8 | 350 | North Atlantic Squadron. |
| Essex | Third | Iron-clad | 12 | 614 | Mississippi Squadron. |
| Estrella | Fourth | Paddle-wheel | 5 | 438 | West Gulf Squadron. |
| Ethan Allen | Fourth | Bark | 9 | 566 | South Atlantic Squadron. |
| Etlah | Third | Iron-clad | 2 | 614 | Building at St. Louis. |
| Eugenie | Fourth | Schooner | 1 | 150 | East Gulf Squadron. |
| Eureka | Fourth | Screw | 1 | 50 | Potomac Flotilla. |
| Eutaw | Third | Paddle-wheel | 10 | 955 | North Atlantic Squadron. |
| Exchange | Fourth | Paddle-wheel | 7 | 211 | Mississippi Squadron. |
| Fahkee | Fourth | Screw | 3 | 699 | North Atlantic Squadron. |
| Fairplay | Fourth | Paddle-wheel | 7 | 156 | Mississippi Squadron. |
| Farallones | Fourth | Screw | 6 | 382 | Pacific Squadron, store-ship, Acapulco. |
| Fawn | Fourth | Paddle-wheel | 7 | 174 | Mississippi Squadron. |
| Fearnot | Fourth | Ship | 1 | 1,012 | Store-ship, W. Gulf Squadron. |
| Fern | Fourth | Paddle-wheel | 0 | 50 | Mississippi Squadron. |
| Fernandina | Fourth | Bark | 8 | 297 | South Atlantic Squadron. |
| Flag | Third | Screw | 8 | 963 | South Atlantic Squadron. |
| Flambeau | Third | Screw | 5 | 900 | Repairing at New York. |
| Florida | Third | Paddle-wheel | 7 | 1,261 | North Atlantic Squadron. |
| Forest Rose | Fourth | Paddle-wheel | 8 | 260 | Mississippi Squadron. |
| Fort Donelson | Third | Paddle-wheel | 5 | 900 | Fitting for sea at Boston. |
| Fort Henry | Fourth | Paddle-wheel | 7 | 519 | East Gulf Squadron. |
| Fort Hindman | Fourth | Paddle-wheel | 7 | 286 | Mississippi Squadron. |
| Fort Jackson | Second | Paddle-wheel | 7 | 1,770 | North Atlantic Squadron. |
| Fortune | Fourth | Screw | 2 | 350 | Building at Boston. |
| Fox | Fourth | Schooner | 2 | 80 | East Gulf Squadron. |
| Franklin | First | Screw | 50 | 3,684 | Building at Portsmouth, N. H., navy-yard. |
| Fredonia | Fourth | Sloop | 0 | 800 | Pacific Squadron, store-ship at Callao. |
| Fuchsia | Fourth | Screw | 3 | 180 | Potomac Flotilla. |
| Galena | Third | Iron-clad | 14 | 738 | At Baltimore. |
| Galatea | Third | Screw | 11 | 1,244 | West India Squadron. |
| Gazelle | Fourth | Paddle-wheel | 6 | 117 | Mississippi Squadron. |
| Gem of the Sea | Fourth | Bark | 5 | 371 | East Gulf Squadron. |
| Gemsbok | Fourth | Bark | 7 | 622 | West India Squadron. |
| Genessee | Third | Paddle-wheel | 8 | 803 | West Gulf Squadron. |
| General Bragg | Fourth | Paddle-wheel | 2 | 950 | Mississippi Squadron. |
| General Lyon | Fourth | Paddle-wheel | 2 | 468 | Mississippi Squadron. |
| General Pillow | Fourth | Paddle-wheel | 2 | 38 | Mississippi Squadron. |
| General Price | Fourth | Paddle-wheel | 3 | 633 | Mississippi Squadron. |

| Name. | Rate. | Class. | Guns | Tunnage. | Station. |
|---|---|---|---|---|---|
| G. W. Blunt | Fourth | Schooner | 2 | 121 | South Atlantic Squadron. |
| George Mangham | Fourth | Schooner | 5 | 274 | South Atlantic Squadron. |
| Geranium | Fourth | Paddle-wheel | 3 | 222 | South Atlantic Squadron. |
| Gertrude | Fourth | Screw | 8 | 350 | West Gulf Squadron. |
| Gettysburg | Fourth | Paddle-wheel | 5 | 726 | Fitting for sea at N. York. |
| Glasgow | Fourth | Paddle-wheel | 6 | 252 | West Gulf Squadron. |
| Glaucus | Third | Screw | 11 | 1,244 | North Atlantic Squadron. |
| Glide | Fourth | Paddle-wheel | 6 | 232 | West Gulf Squadron. |
| Gov. Buckingham | Third | Screw | 6 | 886 | North Atlantic Squadron. |
| Grampus | Fourth | Paddle-wheel | 0 | 300 | Receiving-ship, Cincinnati, Ohio. |
| Grand Gulf | Third | Screw | 11 | 1,200 | North Atlantic Squadron. |
| Granite | Fourth | Sloop | 1 | 75 | North Atlantic Squadron. |
| Granite City | Fourth | Paddle-wheel | 7 | 315 | West Gulf Squadron. |
| Great Western | Fourth | Paddle-wheel | 3 | 800 | Mississippi Squadron. |
| *Guerriere | Second | Screw | 20 | 2,200 | |
| Hartford | Second | Screw | 28 | 1,900 | West Gulf Squadron. |
| Harvest Moon | Fourth | Paddle-wheel | 3 | 546 | South Atlantic Squadron. |
| *Hassalo | Second | Screw | 8 | 2,200 | |
| Hastings | Fourth | Paddle-wheel | 8 | 293 | Mississippi Squadron. |
| Heliotrope | Fourth | Paddle-wheel | 1 | 238 | Waiting crew at N. York. |
| Hendrick Hudson | Fourth | Screw | 6 | 460 | East Gulf Squadron. |
| Henry Brinker | Fourth | Screw | 1 | 108 | North Atlantic Squadron. |
| Henry Janes | Fourth | Schooner | 3 | 261 | West Gulf Squadron. |
| Hetzel | Fourth | Paddle-wheel | 2 | 301 | North Atlantic Squadron. |
| Hollyhock | Fourth | Paddle-wheel | 3 | 300 | West Gulf Squadron. |
| Home | Third | Screw | 3 | 713 | South Atlantic Squadron. |
| Honduras | Fourth | Paddle-wheel | 3 | 376 | East Gulf Squadron. |
| Honeysuckle | Fourth | Screw | 2 | 234 | East Gulf Squadron. |
| Hope | Fourth | Schooner | 1 | 134 | South Atlantic Squadron. |
| Horace Beals | Fourth | Barkantine | 2 | 296 | New York. |
| Howquah | Fourth | Screw | 4 | 397 | North Atlantic Squadron. |
| Hunchback | Fourth | Paddle-wheel | 7 | 517 | North Atlantic Squadron. |
| Huntsville | Third | Screw | 4 | 817 | East Gulf Squadron. |
| Huron | Fourth | Screw | 4 | 507 | South Atlantic Squadron. |
| Hyacinth | Fourth | Paddle-wheel | 0 | 50 | Mississippi Squadron. |
| Hydrangea | Fourth | Screw | 2 | 224 | Ready for sea at N. York, (waiting crew). |
| Ida | Fourth | Screw | 1 | 104 | West Gulf Squadron. |
| Idaho | First | Screw | 8 | 2,500 | Building at Brooklyn. |
| *Illinois | Second | Screw | 20 | 2,200 | |
| Independence | Third | Frigate | 50 | 2,257 | Receiving-ship, navy-yard, Cal. |
| Ino | Third | Ship | 11 | 985 | Hampton Roads. |
| Ion | Fourth | Paddle-wheel | 0 | 230 | Mississippi Squadron, (Receiving-ship, Cairo). |
| Iosco | Third | Paddle-wheel | 10 | 974 | Ready for sea at Boston, (waiting crew). |
| Iris | Fourth | Screw | 2 | 159 | South Atlantic Squadron. |
| Ironsides, jr | Fourth | Bark | 0 | 200 | South Atlantic Squadron, (store vessel). |
| Iroquois | Third | Bark | 9 | 1,016 | Repairing at Baltimore. |
| Itasca | Fourth | Bark | 4 | 507 | West Gulf Squadron. |
| Iuka | Third | Screw | 4 | 940 | Waiting crew at N. York. |

| Name. | Rate. | Class. | Guns | Tun-nage. | Station. |
|---|---|---|---|---|---|
| Ivy.................... | Fourth | Paddle-wheel | 0 | 50 | Mississippi Squadron. |
| Jacob Bell.......... | Fourth | Paddle-wheel | 5 | 229 | Potomac Flotilla. |
| J. C. Kuhn......... | Fourth | Bark........... | 4 | 888 | West Gulf Squadron. |
| James L. Davis.... | Fourth | Bark........... | 4 | 461 | East Gulf Squadron. |
| Jas. S. Chambers.. | Fourth | Bark........... | 6 | 401 | East Gulf Squadron. |
| Jamestown ......... | Third.. | Sloop .......... | 22 | 985 | East Indies. |
| James Adger....... | Third.. | Paddle-wheel | 9 | 1,151 | Repairing at Philadelphia. |
| Jasmine............. | Fourth | Sloop........... | 2 | 122 | Tender to Pensacola navy-yard. |
| *Java................ | Second | Screw.......... | 20 | 2,200 | |
| John Adams........ | Third.. | Sloop........... | 8 | 700 | South Atlantic Squadron. |
| Jno. L. Lockwood.. | Fourth | Paddle-wheel | 3 | 180 | North Atlantic Squadron. |
| John Griffith....... | Fourth | Schooner...... | 3 | 246 | West Gulf Squadron. |
| John Hancock ..... | Fourth | Screw ......... | 1 | 382 | Navy-yard, San Francisco. |
| J. N. Seymour...... | Fourth | Paddle-wheel | 2 | 133 | North Atlantic Squadron. |
| John P. Jackson... | Fourth | Paddle-wheel | 6 | 777 | West Gulf Squadron. |
| Jonquil.............. | Fourth | Screw.......... | 2 | 90 | South Atlantic Squadron. |
| Judge Torrence... | Fourth | Paddle-wheel | 1 | 700 | Mississippi Squadron. |
| Julia.................. | Fourth | Sloop........... | 0 | 10 | East Gulf Squadron. |
| Juliet................. | Fourth | Paddle-wheel | 6 | 157 | Mississippi Squadron. |
| Juniata.............. | Second | Screw ......... | 9 | 1,240 | Repairing at Philadelphia. |
| Kalamazoo.......... | First .. | Iron-clad...... | 4 | 3,200 | Building at navy-yard, New York. |
| Kanawha............ | Fourth | Screw ......... | 4 | 507 | West Gulf Squadron. |
| Kansas.............. | Fourth | Screw ......... | 8 | 593 | North Atlantic Squadron. |
| Katahdin............ | Fourth | Screw ......... | 7 | 507 | West Gulf Squadron. |
| Kearsarge .......... | Third.. | Screw ......... | 8 | 1,031 | Special service. |
| Kennebec ........... | Fourth | Screw ......... | 5 | 507 | West Gulf Squadron. |
| Kensington......... | Third.. | Screw ......... | 4 | 1,052 | Repairing at New York. |
| Kenwood ............ | Fourth | Paddle-wheel | 6 | 232 | Mississippi Squadron. |
| *Keosauqua ........ | Second | Screw ......... | 8 | 2,200 | |
| *Kewaydin.......... | Second | Screw ......... | 20 | 2,200 | |
| Keystone State.... | Third.. | Paddle-wheel | 13 | 1,364 | North Atlantic Squadron. |
| Key West........... | Fourth | Paddle-wheel | 9 | 207 | Mississippi Squadron. |
| Kickapoo ........... | Third.. | Iron-clad...... | 4 | 970 | Building at St. Louis. |
| Kineo................ | Fourth | Screw ......... | 6 | 507 | West Gulf Squadron. |
| Kingfisher ......... | Fourth | Bark............ | 7 | 450 | South Atlantic Squadron. |
| King Philip........ | Fourth | Paddle-wheel | 0 | 500 | Attached to navy-yard, Washington. |
| Kittatinny.......... | Fourth | Schooner...... | 6 | 421 | West Gulf Squadron. |
| Klamath ............ | Third.. | Iron-clad...... | 2 | 614 | Building at Cincinnati. |
| Koka................. | Third.. | Iron-clad ..... | 2 | 614 | Building at Camden. |
| Lackawanna ...... | Second | Screw ......... | 14 | 1,533 | West Gulf Squadron. |
| Lafayette .......... | Third.. | Paddle-wheel | 8 | 1,000 | Mississippi Squadron. |
| Lancaster........... | Second | Screw ......... | 30 | 2,362 | Pacific Squadron, (Flag-ship). |
| Larkspur ........... | Fourth | Screw ......... | 2 | 125 | South Atlantic Squadron. |
| Laurel ............... | Fourth | Paddle-wheel | 0 | 50 | Mississippi Squadron. |
| Lehigh............... | Third.. | Iron-clad...... | 2 | 844 | South Atlantic Squadron. |
| Lenapee ............ | Third.. | Paddle-wheel | 10 | 974 | Building at New York. |
| Leslie ............... | Fourth | Screw ......... | 1 | 100 | Navy-yard, Washington, (Tender). |

| Name. | Rate. | Class. | Guns | Tunnage. | Station. |
|---|---|---|---|---|---|
| Lexington .......... | Fourth | Paddle-wheel | 7 | 448 | Mississippi Squadron. |
| Lilac.................. | Fourth | Screw ......... | 2 | 129 | North Atlantic Squadron. |
| Linden .............. | Fourth | Paddle-wheel | 6 | 177 | Mississippi Squadron. |
| Little Rebel ....... | Fourth | Paddle-wheel | 4 | 151 | Mississippi Squadron. |
| Lodona............... | Third.. | Screw ......... | 7 | 861 | South Atlantic Squadron. |
| Louisiana........... | Fourth | Screw ......... | 5 | 295 | North Atlantic Squadron. |
| Louisville........... | Third.. | Iron-clad ...... | 13 | 527 | Mississippi Squadron. |
| Lupin ................ | Fourth | Screw ......... | 0 | 68 | Tender to New York navy-yard. |
| Macedonian ........ | Second | Sloop........... | 16 | 1,341 | Practice-ship, Newport, Rhode Island. |
| Mackinaw........... | Third.. | Paddle-wheel | 10 | 974 | Fitting for sea, Baltimore. |
| Madawaska.......... | First... | Screw ......... | 10 | 3,200 | Building, navy-yard, N. Y. |
| Magnolia............ | Fourth | Paddle-wheel | 5 | 843 | Waiting crew at N. York. |
| Mahaska............. | Third.. | Paddle-wheel | 8 | 832 | South Atlantic Squadron. |
| Mahopac............. | Third.. | Iron-clad ...... | 2 | 1,034 | Building at Jersey City. |
| Malvern.............. | Fourth | Paddle-wheel | 3 | 627 | North Atlantic Squadron. |
| Manayunk .......... | Third.. | Iron-clad ...... | 2 | 1,034 | Building at Pittsburg. |
| Manhattan .......... | Third.. | Iron-clad ..... | 2 | 1,034 | Building at Jersey City. |
| *Manitou ........... | Second | Screw ......... | 8 | 2,200 | |
| Maratanza .......... | Third.. | Paddle-wheel | 6 | 786 | North Atlantic Squadron. |
| Marblehead......... | Fourth | Screw ......... | 6 | 507 | Repairing at New York. |
| Maria................. | Fourth | Screw ......... | 2 | 170 | Building at New York. |
| Marietta............. | Fourth | Iron-clad...... | 2 | 479 | Building at Pittsburg. |
| Marigold............ | Fourth | Screw ......... | 2 | 115 | East Gulf Squadron. |
| Marion............... | Fourth | Sloop ......... | 8 | 566 | Naval Academy, Newport. |
| Marmora ............ | Fourth | Paddle-wheel | 8 | 207 | Mississippi Squadron. |
| Maria A. Wood... | Fourth | Schooner...... | 2 | 344 | West Gulf Squadron. |
| Mary Sanford...... | Third.. | Screw ......... | 3 | 757 | South Atlantic Squadron. |
| Massachusetts ..... | Fourth | Screw ......... | 5 | 1,155 | Supply steamer for South Atlantic Squadron. |
| Massasoit ........... | Third.. | Paddle-wheel | 10 | 974 | Waiting for crew at Boston. |
| Mattabesett ........ | Third.. | Paddle-wheel | 10 | 974 | Ready for sea at N. York, (waiting crew). |
| Matthew Vassar .. | Fourth | Schooner...... | 3 | 182 | Potomac Flotilla. |
| Maumee ............ | Fourth | Screw ......... | 5 | 593 | New York, (receiving engines). |
| Mayflower ......... | Fourth | Screw.......... | 2 | 350 | Building at Boston. |
| Memphis............ | Third.. | Screw.......... | 7 | 791 | South Atlantic Squadron. |
| Mendota ............ | Third.. | Paddle-wheel | 10 | 974 | Waiting crew at N. York. |
| Mercedita........... | Third.. | Screw.......... | 9 | 776 | North Atlantic Squadron. |
| Mercury ............ | Fourth | Paddle-wheel | 2 | 187 | Repairing at New York. |
| Merrimac ........... | Fourth | Paddle-wheel | 6 | 684 | Fitting for sea at N. York. |
| Metacomet.......... | Third.. | Paddle-wheel | 10 | 974 | West Gulf Squadron. |
| Meteor............... | Fourth | Paddle-wheel | 6 | 221 | West Gulf Squadron. |
| Miami ............... | Third,. | Paddle-wheel | 8 | 730 | North Atlantic Squadron. |
| Miantonomoh...... | Second | Iron-clad ..... | 4 | 1,564 | Building, navy-yard, N. Y. |
| Michigan............ | Fourth | Paddle-wheel | 18 | 582 | On the Lakes, (Erie, Penn.) |
| Midnight............ | Fourth | Bark............ | 7 | 386 | South Atlantic Squadron. |
| Mignonette......... | Fourth | Paddle-wheel | 0 | 50 | Mississippi Squadron. |
| Milwaukie.......... | Third.. | Iron-clad ...... | 4 | 970 | Building at St. Louis. |
| Mingoe.............. | Third.. | Paddle-wheel | 10 | 974 | Building, Bordentown, N.J. |
| Minnesota .......... | First... | Screw.......... | 52 | 3,307 | North Atlantic Squadron, (Flag-ship). |
| *Minnetonka ...... | Second | Screw.......... | 20 | 2,200 | |

| Name. | Rate. | Class. | Guns | Tun-nage. | Station. |
|---|---|---|---|---|---|
| Mistletoe | Fourth | Paddle-wheel | 0 | 50 | Mississippi Squadron. |
| Modoc | Third | Iron-clad | 2 | 614 | Building at New York. |
| Mohawk | Fourth | Screw | 9 | 459 | South Atlantic Squadron. |
| Mohican | Third | Screw | 7 | 994 | Special service. |
| Mohongo | Second | Paddle-wheel | 10 | 1,030 | Building at New York. |
| Monadnock | Second | Iron-clad | 4 | 1,564 | Building at navy-yard, Philadelphia. |
| *Mondamin | Second | Screw | 8 | 2,200 | |
| Monocacy | Second | Paddle-wheel | 10 | 1,030 | Building at Baltimore. |
| Monongahela | Second | Screw | 12 | 1,378 | West Gulf Squadron. |
| Montauk | Third | Iron-clad | 2 | 844 | South Atlantic Squadron. |
| Monterey | Fourth | Screw | 1 | 87 | San Francisco, California. |
| Montgomery | Third | Screw | 6 | 787 | North Atlantic Squadron. |
| Monticello | Fourth | Screw | 7 | 655 | North Atlantic Squadron. |
| Moose | Fourth | Paddle-wheel | 6 | 189 | Mississippi Squadron. |
| Morse | Fourth | Paddle-wheel | 6 | 513 | North Atlantic Squadron. |
| *Mosholu | Second | Screw | 8 | 2,200 | |
| Mound City | Third | Iron-clad | 14 | 512 | Mississippi Squadron. |
| Mount Vernon | Fourth | Screw | 5 | 625 | North Atlantic Squadron. |
| Mt. Washington | Fourth | Paddle-wheel | 5 | 500 | North Atlantic Squadron. |
| Muscoota | Second | Paddle-wheel | 10 | 1,030 | Building at Boston. |
| | Fourth | Paddle-wheel | 0 | 50 | Mississippi Squadron. |
| | Fourth | Screw | 7 | 541 | North Atlantic Squadron. |
| Nahant | Third | Iron-clad | 2 | 844 | South Atlantic Squadron. |
| Nansemond | Fourth | Paddle-wheel | 4 | 340 | North Atlantic Squadron. |
| Nantucket | Third | Iron-clad | 2 | 844 | South Atlantic Squadron. |
| Napa | Third | Iron-clad | 2 | 614 | Building at Wilmington. |
| Narcissus | Fourth | Screw | 2 | 101 | West Gulf Squadron. |
| Narragansett | Third | Screw | 6 | 809 | Pacific Squadron. |
| National Guard | Fourth | Ship | 1 | 1,046 | West India Squadron, coal-ship, Cape Haytien. |
| Naubuc | Third | Iron-clad | 2 | 614 | Building at Williamsburg. |
| Naumkeag | Fourth | Paddle-wheel | 6 | 250 | Mississippi Squadron. |
| Nausett | Third | Iron-clad | 2 | 614 | Building at East Boston. |
| Neosho | Third | Iron-clad | 2 | 523 | Mississippi Squadron. |
| Neptune | Third | Screw | 11 | 1,244 | West India Squadron. |
| Nereus | Third | Screw | 11 | 1,244 | Waiting crew at N. York. |
| Neshaminy | First | Screw | 10 | 3,200 | Building, navy-yard, Phil. |
| Nettle | Fourth | Paddle-wheel | 0 | 50 | Mississippi Squadron. |
| Newbern | Fourth | Screw | 6 | 948 | Supply steamer, North Atlantic Squadron. |
| New Era | Fourth | Paddle-wheel | 6 | 157 | Mississippi Squadron. |
| New Hampshire | First | Ship | 10 | 2,633 | Fitting at Portsmouth, N. H., for a store vessel. |
| New Ironsides | First | Iron-clad | 20 | 3,486 | South Atlantic Squadron. |
| New London | Fourth | Screw | 5 | 221 | West Gulf Squadron. |
| New National | Fourth | Paddle-wheel | 1 | 379 | Mississippi Squadron. |
| New Orleans | First | Ship | 84 | 2,805 | On stocks at Sackett's Har. |
| Niagara | First | Screw | 15 | 4,582 | Ready for sea at N. York, (waiting crew). |
| Nightingale | Fourth | Ship | 1 | 1,000 | West Gulf Squadron, coal-ship. |
| Nina | Fourth | Screw | 2 | 350 | Building at Chester. |
| Niphon | Fourth | Screw | 9 | 475 | North Atlantic Squadron. |

33

| Name. | Rate. | Class. | Guns | Tun-nage. | Station. |
|---|---|---|---|---|---|
| Nipsic | Fourth | Screw | 5 | 593 | South Atlantic Squadron. |
| Nita | Fourth | Paddle-wheel | 4 | 210 | East Gulf Squadron. |
| Norfolk Packet | Fourth | Schooner | 5 | 349 | South Atlantic Squadron. |
| North Carolina | Third | Ship | 6 | 2,633 | Receiving-ship, New York. |
| Norwich | Fourth | Screw | 6 | 431 | South Atlantic Squadron. |
| Nyack | Fourth | Screw | 7 | 593 | Building at New York. |
| Nyanza | Fourth | Paddle-wheel | 6 | 203 | West Gulf Squadron. |
| Octorara | Third | Paddle-wheel | 10 | 829 | West Gulf Squadron. |
| Ohio | Third | Ship | 17 | 2,757 | Receiving-ship, Boston. |
| Oleander | Fourth | Paddle-wheel | 2 | 263 | South Atlantic Squadron. |
| O. H. Lee | Fourth | Schooner | 3 | 199 | West Gulf Squadron. |
| O. M. Pettit | Fourth | Paddle-wheel | 2 | 165 | South Atlantic Squadron. |
| Oneida | Third | Screw | 10 | 1,032 | West Gulf Squadron. |
| Oneoto | Third | Iron-clad | 2 | 1,034 | Building at Cincinnati. |
| Onondaga | Second | Iron-clad | 4 | 1,250 | Preparing for sea at N. Y. |
| *Ontario | Second | Screw | 20 | 2,200 | |
| Onward | Third | Ship | 9 | 874 | Special cruise. |
| Orvetta | Fourth | Schooner | 3 | 171 | West Gulf Squadron. |
| Osage | Third | Iron-clad | 2 | 523 | Mississippi Squadron. |
| Osceola | Third | Paddle-wheel | 10 | 974 | Waiting crew at Boston. |
| Ossipee | Second | Screw | 13 | 1,240 | West Gulf Squadron. |
| Otsego | Third | Paddle-wheel | 10 | 974 | Building at New York. |
| Ottawa | Fourth | Screw | 5 | 507 | South Atlantic Squadron. |
| Ouachita | Fourth | Paddle-wheel | 14 | 720 | Mississippi Squadron. |
| Owasco | Fourth | Screw | 4 | 507 | West Gulf Squadron. |
| Ozark | Third | Iron-clad | 2 | 578 | Mississippi Squadron. |
| Pampero | Fourth | Ship | 6 | 1,375 | West Gulf Squadron. |
| Panola | Fourth | Screw | 4 | 507 | West Gulf Squadron. |
| Pansy | Fourth | Paddle-wheel | 0 | 50 | Mississippi Squadron. |
| Para | Fourth | Schooner | 3 | 190 | South Atlantic Squadron. |
| Passaconaway | First | Iron-clad | 4 | 3,200 | Building at navy-yard, Portsmouth, N. H. |
| Passaic | Third | Iron-clad | 2 | 844 | South Atlantic Squadron. |
| Patapsco | Third | Iron-clad | 2 | 844 | South Atlantic Squadron. |
| Paul Jones | Third | Paddle-wheel | 7 | 863 | South Atlantic Squadron. |
| Paul Jones, jr | Fourth | Steam launch | 1 | 30 | South Atlantic Squadron, (Tender). |
| Pawnee | Second | Screw | 11 | 1,289 | South Atlantic Squadron. |
| Pawpaw | Fourth | Paddle-wheel | 8 | 175 | Mississippi Squadron. |
| Pawtuxet | Third | Paddle-wheel | 10 | 974 | Building at Providence. |
| Pembina | Fourth | Screw | 6 | 507 | West Gulf Squadron. |
| Penobscot | Fourth | Screw | 4 | 507 | West Gulf Squadron. |
| Penguin | Fourth | Screw | 7 | 389 | West Gulf Squadron. |
| Pensacola | Second | Screw | 24 | 2,158 | West Gulf Squadron. |
| Peoria | Third | Paddle-wheel | 10 | 974 | Building at New York. |
| Peosta | Fourth | Paddle-wheel | 14 | 233 | Mississippi Squadron. |
| Pequot | Fourth | Screw | 11 | 593 | North Atlantic Squadron. |
| Perry | Fourth | Brig | 9 | 280 | South Atlantic Squadron. |
| Petrel | Fourth | Paddle-wheel | 8 | 226 | Mississippi Squadron. |
| Philadelphia | Fourth | Paddle-wheel | 2 | 500 | South Atlantic Squadron. |
| Philippi | Fourth | Paddle-wheel | 2 | 311 | Fitting for sea at Boston. |
| Pilgrim | Fourth | Screw | 2 | 170 | Building at Wilmington. |
| Pink | Fourth | Screw | 1 | 184 | Waiting crew at N. York. |

| Name. | Rate. | Class. | Guns | Tunnage. | Station. |
|---|---|---|---|---|---|
| Pinta | Fourth | Screw | 2 | 350 | Building at Chester. |
| *Piscataqua | Second | Screw | 20 | 2,200 | |
| Pittsburg | Third | Iron-clad | 14 | 512 | Mississippi Squadron. |
| Pocahontas | Fourth | Screw | 7 | 694 | Ready for sea at Phila. |
| Pompanoosuc | First | Screw | 14 | 3,200 | Building at navy-yard, Boston. |
| Pontiac | Third | Paddle-wheel | 10 | 974 | Building at Philadelphia. |
| Pontoosuc | Third | Paddle-wheel | 10 | 974 | Building at Portland, Me. |
| Poppy | Fourth | Screw | 2 | 93 | North Atlantic Squadron. |
| Portfire | Fourth | Screw | 1 | 103 | Building at Portsmouth, N. H., navy-yard, (powder tug). |
| Port Royal | Third | Paddle-wheel | 8 | 805 | West Gulf Squadron. |
| Portsmouth | Third | Sloop | 20 | 1,022 | West Gulf Squadron. |
| Potomac | Fourth | Frigate | 32 | 1,726 | West Gulf Squadron, (store-ship). |
| Potomska | Fourth | Screw | 6 | 287 | South Atlantic Squadron. |
| Powhatan | First | Paddle-wheel | 21 | 2,415 | West India Squadron, (Flag-ship). |
| Prairie Bird | Fourth | Paddle-wheel | 8 | 171 | Mississippi Squadron. |
| Primrose | Fourth | Paddle-wheel | 2 | 94 | Potomac Flotilla. |
| Princess Royal | Third | Screw | 7 | 828 | West Gulf Squadron. |
| Princeton | Third | Screw | 0 | 990 | Receiving-ship, Philadel'a. |
| Proteus | Third | Screw | 11 | 1,244 | Waiting for crew at N. Y. |
| Puritan | First | Iron-clad | 4 | 3,265 | Building at Greenpoint, New York. |
| Pursuit | Fourth | Bark | 7 | 603 | East Gulf Squadron. |
| *Pushmataha | Second | Screw | 8 | 2,200 | |
| Quaker City | Second | Paddle-wheel | 7 | 1,600 | North Atlantic Squadron. |
| Queen | Fourth | Screw | 7 | 630 | At New York. |
| Queen City | Fourth | Paddle-wheel | 9 | 212 | Mississippi Squadron. |
| Quinsigamond | First | Iron-clad | 4 | 3,200 | Building at navy-yard, Boston. |
| Racer | Fourth | Schooner | 3 | 252 | South Atlantic Squadron. |
| Rachel Seaman | Fourth | Schooner | 2 | 303 | At New York. |
| Rattler | Fourth | Paddle-wheel | 6 | 166 | Mississippi Squadron. |
| Red Rover | Fourth | Paddle-wheel | 1 | 787 | Mississippi Squadron. |
| Reindeer | Fourth | Paddle-wheel | 6 | 212 | Mississippi Squadron. |
| Release | Fourth | Bark | 3 | 327 | North Atlantic, store-ship, Beaufort. |
| Relief | Fourth | Ship | 3 | 468 | At Boston, receiving stores. |
| Renshaw | Fourth | Schooner | 0 | 80 | Ordnance vessel, Newbern, North Carolina. |
| Rescue | Fourth | Screw | 1 | 111 | South Atlantic Squadron. |
| Resolute | Fourth | Screw | 2 | 90 | Potomac Flotilla. |
| Restless | Fourth | Bark | 7 | 265 | East Gulf Squadron. |
| Rhode Island | Second | Paddle-wheel | 12 | 1,517 | West India Squadron. |
| Richmond | Second | Screw | 24 | 1,929 | West Gulf Squadron. |
| Roanoke | First | Iron-clad | 6 | 3,435 | North Atlantic Squadron. |
| Rocket | Fourth | Screw | 0 | 127 | Ordnance vessel, N. York navy-yard. |
| Rodolph | Fourth | Paddle-wheel | 6 | 217 | West Gulf Squadron. |
| Roebuck | Fourth | Bark | 5 | 455 | East Gulf Squadron. |
| Roman | Fourth | Ship | 1 | 350 | North Atlantic Squadron. |

| Name. | Rate. | Class. | Guns | Tunnage. | Station. |
|---|---|---|---|---|---|
| Romeo | Fourth | Paddle-wheel | 6 | 175 | Mississippi Squadron. |
| Rosalie | Fourth | Sloop | 1 | 28 | East Gulf Squadron. |
| Rose | Fourth | Screw | 1 | 96 | Ready for sea at N. York, (waiting crew). |
| R. R. Cuyler | Third.. | Screw | 12 | 1,202 | Ready for sea at N. York, (waiting crew). |
| Sabine | Second | Frigate | 52 | 1,726 | In ordinary, Boston. |
| Saco | Fourth | Screw | 8 | 593 | Building at Boston. |
| Sacramento | Second | Screw | 14 | 1,367 | Special cruise. |
| Sagamore | Fourth | Screw | 4 | 507 | East Gulf Squadron. |
| Saginaw | Fourth | Paddle-wheel | 4 | 453 | Pacific Squadron. |
| Sandusky | Fourth | Iron-clad | 2 | 479 | Building at Pittsburg. |
| Sangamon | Third.. | Iron-clad | 2 | 844 | South Atlantic Squadron. |
| San Jacinto | Second | Screw | 14 | 1,446 | East Gulf Squadron, (Flag-ship). |
| Santee | Second | Frigate | 49 | 1,726 | School-ship, Newport, R. I. |
| Sam Houston | Fourth | Schooner | 1 | 66 | West Gulf Squadron. |
| Samson | Fourth | Paddle-wheel | 0 | 600 | Mississippi Squadron. |
| Samuel Rotan | Fourth | Schooner | 3 | 212 | North Atlantic Squadron. |
| Santiago de Cuba | Second | Paddle-wheel | 10 | 1,567 | Repairing at Boston. |
| Sarah Bruen | Fourth | Schooner | 3 | 233 | West Gulf Squadron. |
| Saranac | Second | Paddle-wheel | 13 | 1,446 | Pacific Squadron. |
| Saratoga | Third.. | Sloop | 22 | 882 | South Atlantic Squadron. |
| Sassacus | Third.. | Paddle-wheel | 10 | 974 | North Atlantic Squadron. |
| Saugus | Third.. | Iron-clad | 2 | 1,034 | Building at Wilmington. |
| Savannah | Third.. | Sloop | 7 | 1,726 | Instruction-ship, N. York. |
| Scioto | Fourth | Screw | 5 | 507 | West Gulf Squadron. |
| Sea Bird | Fourth | Schooner | 1 | 57 | East Gulf Squadron. |
| Sea Foam | Fourth | Brig | 4 | 264 | West Gulf Squadron. |
| Sebago | Third.. | Paddle-wheel | 10 | 832 | West Gulf Squadron. |
| Seminole | Third.. | Screw | 9 | 801 | West Gulf Squadron. |
| Seneca | Fourth | Screw | 4 | 507 | South Atlantic Squadron. |
| Shakamaxon | First .. | Iron-clad | 4 | 3,200 | Building, navy-yard, Phila. |
| Shamokin | Second | Paddle-wheel | 10 | 1,030 | Building at Chester. |
| Shamrock | Third.. | Paddle-wheel | 10 | 974 | Building at New York. |
| Shark | Fourth | Schooner | 0 | 87 | South Atlantic Squadron. |
| Shawmut | Fourth | Screw | 5 | 593 | Building, Portsmouth, N. H. |
| Shawsheen | Fourth | Paddle-wheel | 3 | 180 | North Atlantic Squadron. |
| Shawnee | Third.. | Iron-clad | 2 | 614 | Building at East Boston. |
| Shenandoah | Second | Screw | 10 | 1,378 | North Atlantic Squadron. |
| Shiloh | Third.. | Iron-clad | 2 | 614 | Building at St. Louis. |
| Shokokon | Fourth | Paddle-wheel | 6 | 700 | North Atlantic Squadron. |
| Signal | Fourth | Paddle-wheel | 6 | 190 | Mississippi Squadron. |
| Silver Cloud | Fourth | Paddle-wheel | 6 | 236 | Mississippi Squadron. |
| **Silver Lake** | **Fourth** | **Paddle-wheel** | **6** | **212** | **Mississippi Squadron.** |
| Snowdrop | Fourth | Screw | 2 | 125 | Waiting crew at N. York. |
| Somerset | Fourth | Paddle-wheel | 6 | 521 | East Gulf Squadron. |
| Sonoma | Third.. | Paddle-wheel | 7 | 955 | South Atlantic Squadron. |
| Sophronia | Fourth | Schooner | 3 | 217 | Potomac Flotilla. |
| South Carolina | Third.. | Screw | 8 | 1,165 | South Atlantic Squadron. |
| Southfield | Fourth | Paddle-wheel | 7 | 751 | North Atlantic Squadron. |
| Sovereign | Fourth | Paddle-wheel | 0 | 440 | Mississippi Squadron. |
| Speedwell | Fourth | Screw | 2 | 350 | Building at Boston. |
| Springfield | Fourth | Paddle-wheel | 6 | 146 | Mississippi Squadron. |
| Squando | Third.. | Iron-clad | 2 | 614 | Building at East Boston. |

| Name. | Rate. | Class. | Guns | Tun-nage. | Station. |
|---|---|---|---|---|---|
| Standish | Fourth | Screw | 2 | 350 | Building at Boston. |
| St. Clair | Fourth | Paddle-wheel | 6 | 203 | Mississippi Squadron. |
| St. Lawrence | Fourth | Frigate | 12 | 1,726 | North Atlantic Squadron, (ordnance-ship). |
| St. Louis | Third | Sloop | 18 | 700 | Special service. |
| St. Mary's | Third | Sloop | 28 | 985 | Pacific Squadron. |
| Stars and Stripes | Fourth | Screw | 5 | 407 | East Gulf Squadron. |
| State of Georgia | Third | Paddle-wheel | 8 | 1,204 | North Atlantic Squadron. |
| Stepping Stones | Fourth | Paddle-wheel | 5 | 226 | North Atlantic Squadron. |
| Stettin | Fourth | Screw | 5 | 600 | South Atlantic Squadron. |
| Stockdale | Fourth | Paddle-wheel | 6 | 188 | West Gulf Squadron. |
| Stonewall | Fourth | Schooner | 1 | 30 | East Gulf Squadron. |
| Suncook | Third | Iron-clad | 2 | 614 | Building at South Boston. |
| Sunflower | Fourth | Screw | 2 | 294 | East Gulf Squadron. |
| Supply | Fourth | Ship | 7 | 547 | South Atlantic Squadron. |
| Susquehanna | First | Paddle-wheel | 16 | 2,450 | Repairing at New York. |
| Suwanee | Second | Paddle-wheel | 10 | 1,030 | Building at New York. |
| Sweetbrier | Fourth | Screw | 2 | 240 | South Atlantic Squadron. |
| Tacony | Third | Paddle-wheel | 10 | 974 | North Atlantic Squadron. |
| *Tahgayuta | Second | Screw | 8 | 2,200 | |
| Tahoma | Fourth | Screw | 6 | 507 | East Gulf Squadron. |
| Tallahoma | Third | Paddle-wheel | 10 | 974 | Building at New York. |
| Tallahatchie | Fourth | Paddle-wheel | 6 | 171 | West Gulf Squadron. |
| Tallapoosa | Third | Paddle-wheel | 10 | 974 | Building at New York. |
| Tawah | Fourth | Paddle-wheel | 8 | 108 | Mississippi Squadron. |
| Teaser | Fourth | Screw | 1 | 90 | Potomac Flotilla. |
| Tecumseh | Third | Iron-clad | 2 | 1,034 | Preparing for sea, N. York. |
| Tennessee | Third | Paddle-wheel | 5 | 1,275 | West Gulf Squadron. |
| Tensas | Fourth | Paddle-wheel | 2 | 150 | Mississippi Squadron. |
| Thistle | Fourth | Paddle-wheel | 0 | 50 | Mississippi Squadron. |
| Thos. Freeborn | Fourth | Paddle-wheel | 3 | 269 | Potomac Flotilla. |
| T. A. Ward | Fourth | Schooner | 5 | 184 | South Atlantic Squadron. |
| Ticonderoga | Second | Screw | 20 | 1,533 | Ready for sea at Phila. |
| Tioga | Third | Paddle-wheel | 8 | 819 | East Gulf Squadron. |
| Tippecanoe | Third | Iron-clad | 2 | 1,034 | Building at Cincinnati. |
| Tonawandah | Second | Iron-clad | 4 | 1,564 | Building, navy-yard, Phila. |
| Triana | Fourth | Screw | 2 | 350 | Building at New York. |
| Tritonia | Fourth | Paddle-wheel | 1 | 202 | Ready for sea at N. York, (waiting crew). |
| Tulip | Fourth | Screw | 5 | 183 | Potomac Flotilla. |
| Tunxis | Third | Iron-clad | 2 | 614 | Building at Chester. |
| Tuscarora | Third | Screw | 10 | 997 | North Atlantic Squadron. |
| Tuscumbia | Third | Iron-clad | 5 | 565 | Mississippi Squadron. |
| Two Sisters | Fourth | Schooner | 1 | 54 | East Gulf Squadron. |
| Tylor | Fourth | Paddle-wheel | 10 | 575 | Mississippi Squadron. |
| Umpqua | Third | Iron-clad | 2 | 614 | Building at Pittsburg. |
| Unadilla | Fourth | Screw | 7 | 507 | South Atlantic Squadron. |
| Union | Fourth | Screw | 1 | 1,114 | Supply steamer for East Gulf Squadron. |
| Valparaiso | Fourth | Ship | 0 | 402 | South Atlantic Squadron. |
| Vandalia | Third | Sloop | 22 | 700 | Receiv'g-ship, Portsmouth, New Hampshire. |
| Vanderbilt | Second | Paddle-wheel | 15 | 3,360 | Repairing at New York. |

| Name. | Rate. | Class. | Guns | Tun-nage. | Station. |
|---|---|---|---|---|---|
| Valley City......... | Fourth | Screw.......... | 6 | 190 | North Atlantic Squadron. |
| Vermont............ | Third.. | Ship............ | 18 | 2,633 | South Atlantic Squadron, (store and receiv'g ship). |
| Vicksburg.......... | Third,. | Screw ......... | 6 | 886 | North Atlantic Squadron. |
| Victoria............. | Fourth | Screw ......... | 3 | 254 | North Atlantic Squadron. |
| Victory.............. | Fourth | Paddle-wheel | 6 | 160 | Mississippi Squadron. |
| Vincennes ......... | Third.. | Sloop.......... | 10 | 700 | West Gulf Squadron. |
| Vindicator.......... | Third.. | Ram............ | 4 | 750 | Building, N. Albany, Ind. |
| Violet................ | Fourth | Screw ......... | 2 | 146 | North Atlantic Squadron. |
| Virginia ............ | First... | Ship............ | 84 | 2,633 | On the stocks, Boston. |
| Virginia ............ | Fourth | Screw ......... | 7 | 581 | West Gulf Squadron. |
| Wabash.............. | First .. | Screw ......... | 48 | 3,274 | South Atlantic Squadron. |
| Wachusett.......... | Third.. | Screw ......... | 10 | 1,032 | Coast of Brazil. |
| Wampanoag ....... | First... | Screw ......... | 8 | 3,200 | Building, navy-yard, N. Y. |
| Wamsutta .......... | Fourth | Screw ......... | 6 | 270 | Repairing at Philadelphia. |
| *Wanaloset......... | Second | Screw ......... | 8 | 2,200 | |
| Wanderer .......... | Fourth | Schooner...... | 3 | 300 | East Gulf Squadron. |
| Wassuc.............. | Third.. | Iron-clad ..... | 2 | 614 | Building at Portland, Me. |
| *Watauga........... | Second | Screw ......... | 8 | 2,200 | |
| Wateree ........... | Third.. | Paddle-wheel | 14 | 974 | On the way to the Pacific. |
| Water Witch....... | Fourth | Paddle-wheel | 4 | 378 | South Atlantic Squadron. |
| Wave................. | Fourth | Paddle-wheel | 6 | 229 | West Gulf Squadron. |
| Waxsaw.............. | Third.. | Iron-clad...... | 2 | 614 | Building at Baltimore. |
| Western World.... | Fourth | Screw.......... | 5 | 441 | Potomac Flotilla. |
| Whitehead.......... | Fourth | Screw ......... | 4 | 136 | North Atlantic Squadron. |
| Wild Cat............ | Fourth | Sailing vessel | 1 | 30 | South Atlantic Squadron. |
| *Willamette........ | Second | Screw ......... | 8 | 2,200 | |
| Wm. Bacon......... | Fourth | Schooner...... | 5 | 183 | Potomac Flotilla. |
| Wm. Badger........ | Fourth | Ship............ | 1 | 334 | North Atlantic Squadron. |
| Wm. G. Putnam... | Fourth | Paddle-wheel | 4 | 149 | North Atlantic Squadron. |
| Wm. H. Brown..... | Fourth | Paddle-wheel | 1 | 235 | Mississippi Squadron. |
| Wm. G. Anderson. | Fourth | Bark........... | 8 | 593 | West Gulf Squadron. |
| Winnebago ......... | Third.. | Iron-clad ..... | 4 | 970 | Building at St. Louis. |
| Winnipec............ | Second | Paddle-wheel | 10 | 1,030 | Building at Boston. |
| Winona ............. | Fourth | Screw.......... | 6 | 507 | South Atlantic Squadron. |
| Winooski............ | Third.. | Paddle-wheel | 10 | 974 | Building at New York. |
| Wissahickon........ | Fourth | Screw.......... | 5 | 507 | South Atlantic Squadron. |
| Wyalusing ......... | Third.. | Paddle-wheel | 10 | 974 | North Atlantic Squadron. |
| Wyandank ......... | Fourth | Paddle-wheel | 3 | 399 | Potomac Flotilla. |
| Wyandotte.......... | Fourth | Screw ......... | 5 | 458 | North Atlantic Squadron. |
| Wyoming............ | Third.. | Screw ......... | 7 | 997 | East Indies. |
| Yankee.............. | Fourth | Paddle-wheel | 4 | 328 | Potomac Flotilla. |
| Yantic ............... | Fourth | Screw ......... | 5 | 593 | Building, navy-yard, Phil. |
| Yazoo................ | Third.. | Iron-clad...... | 2 | 614 | Building at Philadelphia. |
| Young America... | Fourth | Screw ......... | 2 | 173 | North Atlantic Squadron. |
| Young Rover...... | Fourth | Screw ......... | 5 | 418 | North Atlantic Squadron. |
| Yuma ............... | Third.. | Iron-clad...... | 2 | 614 | Building at Cincinnati. |
| Zouave ............. | Fourth | Screw ......... | 2 | 127 | North Atlantic Squadron. |

* Machinery contracted for in November, 1863. Hulls about being commenced.

# CHAPTER XXXVIII.

## THE ARMIES OF ENGLAND, FRANCE, AND AMERICA.

The reported numerical strength of the armies of the four great powers which are under discussion, is, in round numbers, as follows:

| | |
|---|---|
| France, . . . . . | 500,000 |
| England, . . . . . . | 200,000 |
| Russia, . . . . . | 950,000 |
| United States, North and South, say, . | 900,000 |

These figures, though obtained mainly from official sources, do not, of course, express the exact truth. They merely present, in a general way, the relative military strength of these nations. Each of them could command a far greater number to resist an invasion of its territory, while neither could send from home, on distant service, one-fourth of the number here set down. France and Russia could maintain large armies on the fields of Europe, but neither they, nor any other power, could send a formidable force to operate here.

Still, with France controlling Mexico and Central America, it might be possible, at any time, with a French army as a nucleus, to assemble a very formidable force upon our Southern borders.

The character of the Russians, as soldiers, has been already considered, because Americans should know the quality of those who, alone, among all nations, can now be regarded as our cordial friends, and whose interests may yet ally them with us, against the central despotisms of Europe.

The soldiers of France and England have written their own history on the battle-fields of modern Europe, and their distinguishing traits are known to all. None will dispute their courage or their skill. Those who expect to meet them with success, must be masters of the science of slaughter.

But America is now, for the first time, assuming the character and position of a great military power. For the first time we have gathered great armies, and have fought battles on a scale proportioned to the great conflicts of Europe. It is, therefore, important to inquire, whether our armies and our soldiers have exhibited an individual, a national character? Can we speak of the American soldier and the American army as having characteristics of their own, distinctive and peculiar? If we can, what are the military traits of the American nation? Are they such as give us confidence in our ability to meet the troops of other nations should they invade our shores?

In attempting to answer this question, it will be assumed as certain, that this rebellion will soon be over, and our military strength will be drawn from the whole territory of the Union, and from every portion of the population.

This being so, the armies of the United States will, hereafter, be drawn from the following elements: the white population of the North, the whites of the South, the blacks both North and South, and the foreign population. The foreign element in our armies requires but a passing notice. These soldiers will certainly be equal to those of Europe, while we have every reason to expect that those who are to come, like those who are already among us, will exhibit, under the influence of free institutions, a higher form of manhood than their countrymen who remain behind.

When the proper manhood of the blacks is fully acknowledged, and their rights as citizens are sanctioned and protected by law and by practice, we can easily draw from them, at any time, an army of two hundred and fifty thousand men, and perhaps double that number in case of a pressing emergency. The war, by the emancipation of the slaves, will add this to our effective fighting force, and enough is already known of these soldiers, from the sternest experience of battle, to show that, with proper encouragement and discipline, they will not be inferior to any.

Great injustice will be done to the race if we judge them only by what they have done when they have barely escaped from the brutehood of slavery, with all its crushing influences still bearing them down; but even in this condition their record has been a noble one, and we know that, if we do our duty, if, as a nation, we prove true to God and humanity, we shall have at our disposal an immense force, which will be invaluable to us should Louis Napoleon compel us to operate upon our Southern border, or in Mexico.

Two hundred and fifty thousand stalwart men, who can brave unharmed both the Southern malaria and the yellow fever, and guided by skillful officers, would present a very effectual barrier to all the schemes of France in Mexico. These black soldiers are to form a most important element hereafter in the American army and navy, and, although their capabilities have not yet been fully tested, what they have already done gives noble promise for the future, and it is perhaps not fanatical to believe that God has delivered them just at the time when they will be needed most for the defense of the country which they have enriched by their toils, their blood, and their tears.

No candid man, even at the North, will deny that the Southern troops have fought, in general, with desperate courage; all will confess that their chief leaders have exhibited skill, daring, and energy, while the fortifications of the Southern cities are, for the purpose designed, masterpieces of engineering science. These qualities, these talents, this skill and science, now used for the destruction of the Republic, are all American, and will in the future all be available for the defense of the country against a common foreign foe. Probably no troops were ever hurled with more impetuous bravery upon defensive lines, than was Lee's army at Gettysburg, or Bragg's at Chickamauga. The rush of the successive assaults was more like the spring of the tiger than the march of columns, and of a tiger foiled and hurled back, only to spring again.

There is an intensity of passion in the Southern charge that gives the utmost possible effect to the material power, and which, it is thought, will scarcely find a parallel in the movements of any of the regular troops of Europe. Americans would not expect that the veterans of Lee and Longstreet would be defeated by an equal number of the best soldiers of any nation in Europe. The defense of Fort Wagner was a marvelous instance of persistent heroism, certainly not often surpassed in the history of war. Such a terrible storm of shot and shell as swept over and into, and tore through those defenses, man never saw before, and yet the garrison held bravely out, till forced to evacuate by a regular siege. History surely has not many stories like that of the defense of Sumter, where such an immense work was defended till its massive masonry was all leveled with the sea, a heap of rubbish, and yet the flag was kept defiantly hoisted over its foundation-stones. This engineering skill, and this unyielding tenacity of courage, are all to be available for the defense of the future American nation. They are examples of what the South will do in a better cause, and supported by the sympathies and arms of the North. They admonish Europe of the reception which invaders will meet.

What this fiery semi-barbarism which slavery has produced will yet become, when quickened by general intelligence, and balanced and molded by free institutions, and when its energy springs from principle instead of passion, does not now appear; but none can doubt that it will be a nobler and more reliable power than it now is—a firmer basis on which to build a nation.

The Southern people have borne the privations and

hardships to which they have been subjected, through the desolations of war and the rigor of the blockade, with a firm endurance that awakens admiration in all who forget the atrocity of their treason and the savage cruelty of their spirit; and the wretched food and clothing of the rebel soldiers often astonish our Northern men, presenting an appearance of extreme hardship heroically borne; but it may be doubted, perhaps, whether the common people and the private soldiers suffer as severely as many suppose. They know little or nothing of the comforts and luxuries of Northern homes; most of them have lived in the log hut only, and have been accustomed to the coarsest food, and to little variety in that.

Their endurance of hardship partakes more of the sullen indifference of the savage than the lofty heroism of the cultivated man; and yet, with all needed deductions, the people of the South have exhibited qualities which, when cleansed from the defilement and curse of slavery, and ennobled by the influences of freedom, will become a mighty power in the State.

The worst condition of the rebel soldier is not so far below his ordinary home-life, as the best aspect of a camp is inferior to the every-day comforts of the home of the Northern laborer; and, therefore, with far better fare, the actual privations of the Northern soldier have been greater, and the endurance which springs from true heroism has been more fully exhibited by the army of the North.

The true American life is found only in the free States, and the army of the North is the only true representative of the military power of the Republic—the American nation of the future; because this Northern life-power will assimilate and mold after its own image the whole material of the nation. The vital force of the free States will energize and transform the whole population, and the nation will be quickened, guided, and glorified by the indwelling spirit of Christian freedom. Among the peculiar traits of the real American army, the most prominent is its intelligence. In this respect it stands alone among armies. It has been drawn from the whole population, and every class, and all forms of business, and all mechanical arts have their representatives in every Northern regiment. Such an army is not a mere aggregation of human puppets or machines under the direction of an engineer in shoulder-straps, but it is a body of thousands of individual thinkers, combining thought, skill, and experience, for a common purpose. A majority of Northern regiments could furnish from their ranks mechanics that could build or repair a locomotive, or construct a bridge or a steamboat, or repair a watch; and with them are associated lawyers, and physicians, and ministers, printers, editors, painters, and authors. No army ever gathered before has embodied such an amount of educated, thinking power, and such a variety of gifts and attainments.

It is not only a fighting engine, but it is a thinking machine of the highest order. And precisely those qualities from which the aristocrats of Europe, and the slave-lords of the South, predicted its ruin, have made it the most admirable army of the world. They predicted that such men would not fight. The slave-owner, blinded by his own false system, believed that common soldiers must be half-brute, half-savage, in order to be brave, and that an officer must be a tyrant in order to command.

The nobility of Europe have adopted a military maxim suited to their ideas of man, and their false notions of courage: "the worse the man the better the soldier," and, therefore, they, too, believed that the men of the North would not fight, and would be scattered by the fiery onset of a Southern army. They forgot that the highest forms of courage, the sternest and most persistent bravery, spring directly from intelligence and principle. They ought to have known that these are stronger than passion, or hate, or revenge. They thought that these freemen of the North, accustomed to no restraint, and insisting upon thinking for themselves, would submit to no discipline, and that the Northern army would be only an armed mob. The first letter-writers and observers from Europe, having known only the machine-movements of military puppets, saw only tumult, disorder, and inefficiency in the Northern troops.

They knew nothing of the true nature of freedom. They ought to have known that what they saw, and censured so eagerly, were indications of real power, and that the intelligence of these men would, of itself, soon render them the most obedient of soldiers, because they would obey from principle, and as a means of safety and success.

Perhaps the peculiar and sterling qualities of American troops have never been exhibited under circumstances which could test more severely the spirit of men, than by the Army of the Potomac. Since its first organization after the battle of Manassas, it has shown no cowardice, no faltering in the face of an enemy, nor in the performance of any duty; it has fought more than half of the great and bloody battles of the war, and, though never wholly defeated, it has never been completely victorious. Victory, fairly earned by its own valor, has been repeatedly lost to them by the incompetency or treachery of some of its commanders, and yet it has maintained its faithfulness, its discipline, its courage, and its confidence in itself and in its cause.

Its steadfast courage is based on intelligence and principle, and therefore it survives disaster, and springs up afresh after the severest disappointment. The career of the Army of the Potomac is, in many respects, a mortifying one, and yet it is a very noble exhibition of the military capabilities and qualities of the freemen of the North, and to it yet may be given, as its final reward, the crowning victories of the war.

These qualities have been exhibited in a more brilliant light by the armies of the West, because they have been more ably and faithfully led, and therefore led to victory. Many suppose there are marked differences between Eastern and Western troops. The freer, more expansive life of the West gives somewhat more, perhaps, of impetuosity to the men of the West; but wherever Eastern and

Western troops have been associated, they blend at once into one homogeneous mass, and all differences vanish, and no one could tell, from their manner of fighting, whether they came from the prairies or the New England hills.

Eastern and Western soldiers have fought under very similar circumstances, with results so similar as to forbid either boasting or complaint. They sustained alike the honor of our flag. Gettysburg and Chickamauga were not only the great battles of the war, but, in each case, the best troops of the South were matched against the best of the North. The North and the South were fairly represented on these bloody fields, and the main features of the fighting were the same. One was fought mainly by Eastern troops, and the other mostly by soldiers of the West. In each battle the fiery and yet orderly rush of the Southern veterans, led by their most trusted generals, was checked and rolled back with terrible slaughter by the persistent firmness, the long-enduring courage and skill of the Northern troops; and the two battles were a true type of the war.

The Southern charge comes with the sweep and roar of a headlong torrent, but the Northern lines are granite, upon which it dashes and breaks. The men of the West fought, it is true, under great disadvantage at Chickamauga. They were outnumbered nearly two to one from the first, according to the statement of General Rosecrans, and nearly half of the army on the second day was shaken from its position; but the left, under Thomas, showed the true qualities of Northern soldiers, by hurling back charge after charge of Longstreet's chosen men, the very *elite* of the Southern army, and in numbers more than double their own, and compelling them to withdraw after five hours of the bloodiest fighting of the war.

In these two battles the fighting qualities of the North and South were tested, with the advantage of numbers on the side of the South, and with results that show the superior steadfastness and endurance of Northern troops. The

South will not believe, hereafter, that it can beat a Northern army on an equal field.

Nor are Northern soldiers at all deficient in those qualities which most distinguish the armies of the South. The storming of Fort Donelson, the rush of Grant's army round to the rear of Vicksburg, and the running of the batteries at New Orleans, Port Hudson, and Vicksburg, have not been matched by any Southern exploit, while the history of war scarcely shows any thing more brilliant than the dash up the steeps of Mission Ridge, and the storming of Lookout Mountain. The South has performed nothing which can bear comparison with these, and the military superiority of the North has, at length, been fully established.

The conclusion, then, which is fairly reached from the facts presented, is, that the American nation will be able, at any time after this rebellion is over, to command an army, in numbers, in variety of its qualifications, and in effective power, that will, to say the least, be second to that of no other nation, and abundantly sufficient for our complete protection. With this army, and with our new navy, with exhaustless supplies of all kinds, whether of food or munitions of war, with railways and navigable rivers which enable us to concentrate troops and supplies when and where they are needed, we shall come forth from this struggle a great military power, quite able not only to defend ourselves from attack, but to compel the powers of Europe to relinquish all pretensions to this Western World.

There are many, who are decidedly in favor of prosecuting the war until the last vestige of rebellion is swept away and the authority of the government is re-established over every foot of our territory, who, nevertheless, are exceedingly anxious in regard to the future, expecting, after the close of the war, a long period of depression for every branch of industry, and general commercial disaster. They know that the country will then be burdened with an enormous debt, and they think that the South, being desolated by the war, the supply of her great staples cut off, the producing power of the North largely diminished by the destruction of life, our resources in measure exhausted, and our currency at the same time largely inflated, there must be a season of universal prostration and embarrassment.

Others, however, take a far more hopeful view of the future, and believe that the country will pass out of the war almost immediately into a more prosperous state than it has ever known. It is admitted that the South will be left by the war a comparative desert; that she will be stripped of nearly all the accumulations of her previous life; she will be destitute of almost every article that belongs to civilized life.

The land, however, remains undiminished in fertility, and even refreshed by its rest, and the laborers of the South have been mostly preserved, by the good providence of God, amid the ravages of the war, and that which oppressed labor and hindered production has been taken out of the way. It can not be doubted that, so soon as the labor system of the South can be reorganized upon the principles of a free society, the production of Southern staples will be increased far beyond what it was before the war. And when we consider that this reorganization has already begun, and is making rapid progress; that thousands of plantations of sugar and cotton will be wrought by free laborers this very year; and that this process of reconstruction will go forward almost equally with the progress of the war, it will be seen that, immediately and before the war closes, the great staples of the South will begin to reappear in the markets of the world. As fast as territory is reconquered and made secure, it will be occupied by the superior producing power of free labor, and the prosperity of peace will thus gradually return with the decline of the war, and there will be no abrupt and disastrous transition from a state of war to a condition of peace.

The waste of the South is, indeed, to be repaired; her railroads are to be reconstructed and furnished anew; tools and machinery, dwellings and household furniture are to be supplied for the whole country which the war has swept over; but the teeming soil, under the wise culture of free labor, will pay for it all; and the supply of these wants for so vast a territory will furnish full and profitable employment for Northern capital, skill, and labor, as the return of peace shall diminish the demand for the material of war. The manufacture of locomotives and cars, and sugar-mills and cotton-gins, of agricultural machinery, and tools of all kinds, of dwellings and furniture, of steamboats for our Southern and Western rivers, will take the place of the work of the government, while the products of the South will be ready to pay for all. Under the system of Northern industry, moreover, this Southern trade will be as safe, and will pay as promptly as that of the North. It will aid us to form a correct estimate of the condition of the country after the war, and of the ability which the nation will then have to pay interest and principal of its debt, and to expand with a sure and healthy growth, if we study the rate of progress at which the country has advanced thus far, and the amount and character of our resources.

Fortunately, the statistical information which has been gathered by the government, and by individual effort, is so varied, so full, and so exact, as to present with accuracy the actual progress and present condition of the nation, and from these facts the future may be safely predicted. In September, 1863, an International Statistical Congress assembled at Berlin, at which Hon. Samuel B. Ruggles, of New York, was present as a delegate from the United States, and presented a report, which is a condensed history of the progress and condition of this country. From this the reader will be enabled to see what resources we shall probably have at our disposal for the next quarter of a century, for the payment of our debt, and for general national progress. Some extracts from this report are here given:

"I. The territorial area of the United States at the peace of 1783, then bounded west by the Mississippi River, was 820,680 square miles, about four times that of France, which is stated to be 207,145, exclusive of Algeria. The purchase from France of Louisiana, in 1804, added to this area 899,680 square miles. Purchases from Spain, and from Mexico, and the Oregon treaty with England, added the further quantity of 1,215,907 square miles—making the total present territory 2,936,166 square miles, or 1,879,146,240 acres.

"Of this immense area, possessing a great variety of climate and culture, so large a portion is fertile, that it has been steadily absorbed by the rapidly increased population. In May last there remained undisposed of, belonging to the government of the United States, 964,901,625 acres.

"To prevent any confusion of boundaries, the lands were carefully surveyed and allotted by the government, and are then granted gratuitously to actual settlers, or sold for prices not exceeding $1.25 per acre to purchasers other than settlers. It appears, by the report of the Commissioner of the General Land-office, a copy of which is herewith furnished, that the quantity surveyed and ready for sale in September, 1862, was 135,142,999 acres. The report also states, that the recent discoveries of rich and extensive gold-fields in some of the unsurveyed portions are rapidly filling the interior with a population whose necessities require the speedy survey and disposition of large additional tracts. The immediate survey is not, however, of vital importance, as the first occupant practically gains the preemptive claim to the land after the survey is completed. The cardinal, the great continental fact, so to speak, is this: that the whole of this vast body of land is freely open to gratuitous occupation, without delay or difficulty of any kind.

"II. The population of the United States, as shown by the census of 1860, was 31,445,080; of which number 26,975,575 were white, and 4,441,766 black, of various degrees of color; of the blacks, 3,953,760 being returned as slaves. Whether any or what proportion of the number are hereafter to be statistically considered as 'slaves,' depends upon contingencies, which it would be premature at the present time to discuss.

"The increase of population since the establishment of the government has been as follows:

| | | | |
|---|---|---|---|
| 1790 . . . | 3,929,827, | | |
| 1800 . . | 5,305,937, | increase . | 35.02 per cent. |
| 1810 . . . | 7,239,814, | increase . | 36.45 per cent. |
| 1820 . . | 9,638,191, | increase . | 33.13 per cent. |
| 1830 . . . | 12,866,020, | increase . | 33.49 per cent. |
| 1840 . . | 17,069,453, | increase . | 32.67 per cent. |
| 1850 . . . | 23,191,876, | increase . | 35.87 per cent. |
| 1860 . . | 31,445,080, | increase . | 35.59 per cent. |

"This rate of progress, especially since 1820, is owing, in part, to immigration from foreign countries.

"There arrived in ten years—

| | |
|---|---|
| From 1820 to 1830 . . . . . . . . . . | 244,490 |
| From 1830 to 1840 . . . . . . . . . | 552,000 |
| From 1840 to 1850 . . . . . . . . . . | 1,558,300 |
| From 1850 to 1860 . . . . . . . . . | 2,707,624 |
| Total . . . . . . . . | 5,062,414 |

"Being a yearly average of 126,560 for the last forty years, and 270,762 for the last ten years.

"The disturbances in the United States, caused by the existing insurrection, and commencing in April, 1861, have temporarily and partially checked this current of immigration, but during the present year it is again increasing.

"The records of the Commissioners of Emigration of New York show that the arrivals at that port alone have been for

| | From Ireland. | From Germany. | Total, includ'g all other countries. |
|---|---|---|---|
| 1861 . . . . . . . | 27,754 | 27,159 | 65,529 |
| 1862 . . . . . . . . | 32,217 | 27,740 | 76,306 |
| 1863, up to August 20, 7⅔ months, | 64,465 | 18,724 | about 98,000 |

"The proportions of the whole number of 5,062,414 arriving from foreign countries, in the forty years from 1820 to 1860, were as follows:

| | | |
|---|---|---|
| From Ireland, . . . . . . . . | 967,366 | |
| From England, . . . . . . . . | 302,665 | |
| From Scotland, . . . . . . . . | 47,800 | |
| From Wales, . . . . . . . . . | 7,935 | |
| From Great Britain and Ireland, . . | 1,425,018— | 2,750,784 |
| From Germany, . . . . . . . . | 1,546,976 | |
| From Sweden, . . . . . . . . | 36,129 | |
| From Denmark and Norway, . . . . | 5,540— | 1,588,145 |
| From France, . . . . . . . . | 208,063 | |
| From Italy, . . . . . . . . . | 11,302 | |
| From Switzerland, . . . . . . | 37,732 | |
| From Spain, . . . . . . . . . | 16,245 | |
| From British America, . . . . . . | 117,142 | |
| From China (in California almost exclusively), | 41,443 | |
| From all other countries, or unknown, . | 291,558— | 723,485 |
| Total, . . . . . . . . . . . | | 5,062,414 |

"It is not ascertainable how many have returned to foreign countries, but they probably do not exceed a million.

"If the present partial check to immigration should continue, though it is hardly probable, the number of immigrants for the decade ending in 1870 may possibly be reduced from 2,707,624 to 1,500,000.

"The ascertained average increase of the whole population, in the seven decades from 1790 to 1860, which is very nearly 33⅓ per cent., or one-third for each decade, would carry the present numbers (31,445,080)

| | |
|---|---|
| By the year 1870 to . . . . . . . . . | 41,926,750 |
| From which deduct for the possible diminution of immigrants, as above . . . . . . . . | 1,207,624 |
| There would remain . . . . . . . | 40,719,126 |

"Mr. Kennedy, the experienced Superintendent of the Census, in the Compend published in 1862, at page 7, estimates the population of 1870 at 42,318,432, and of 1880 at 56,450,241.

"The rate of progress of the population of the United States has much exceeded that of any of the European nations. The experienced statisticians in the present Congress can readily furnish the figures precisely, showing the comparative rate.

"The population of France in

| | | | |
|---|---|---|---|
| 1801 | 27,349,003 | 1841 | 34,230,178 |
| 1821 | 30,461,875 | 1851 | 35,283,170 |
| 1831 | 32,569,223 | 1861 | 37,472,132 |

Being about 37 per cent. in the sixty years. It does not include Algeria, which has a European population of 192,746.

"The population of Prussia has increased since 1816 as follows:

| | | | |
|---|---|---|---|
| 1816 | 10,319,983 | 1849 | 16,296,483 |
| 1822 | 11,664,133 | 1858 | 17,672,609 |
| 1834 | 13,038,970 | 1861 | 18,491,220 |
| 1840 | 14,928,503 | | |

Being at the rate of 79 per cent. in forty-five years.

"The population of England and Wales was, in

| | | | |
|---|---|---|---|
| 1801 | 9,156,171 | 1841 | 16,035,198 |
| 1811 | 10,454,529 | 1851 | 18,054,170 |
| 1821 | 12,172,664 | 1861 | 20,227,746 |
| 1831 | 14,051,986 | | |

"Showing an increase of 121 per cent. in sixty years, against an increase in the United States, in sixty years, of 593 per cent.

"III. The natural and inevitable result of this great increase of population, enjoying an ample supply of fertile land, is seen in a corresponding advance in the material wealth of the people of the United States. For the purpose of State taxation, the values of their real and personal property are yearly assessed by officers appointed by the States. The assessment does not include large amounts of property held by religious, educational, charitable, and other associations exempted by law from taxation, nor any public property of any description. In actual practice, the real property is rarely assessed for more than two-thirds of its cash value, while large amounts of personal property, being easily concealed, escape assessment altogether.

"The assessed value of that portion of property which is thus actually taxed increased as follows: In 1791 (estimated) $750,000,000; 1816 (estimated) $1,800,000,000; 1850 (official valuation) $7,135,780,228; 1860 (official valuation) $16,159,616,068, showing an increase in the last decade alone of $9,023,835,840.

"A question has been raised in some quarters as to the correctness of these valuations of 1850 and 1860, in embracing in the valuation of 1850 $961,000,000, and in the valuation of 1860 $1,936,000,000, as the assessed value of slaves, insisting that black men are persons and not property, and should be regarded, like other men, only as producers and consumers. If this view of the subject should be admitted, the valuation of 1850 would be reduced to $6,174,780,000, and that of 1860 to $14,223,618,068, leaving the increase in the decade $8,048,825,840.

"The advance, even if reduced to $8,048,825,840, is sufficiently large to require the most attentive examination. It is an increase of property over the valuation of 1850 of 130 per cent., while the increase of population, in the same decade, was but 35.99 per cent. In seeking for the cause of this discrepancy, we shall reach a fundamental and all-important fact, which will furnish the key to the past and to the future progress of the United States. It is the power they possess, by means of canals and railways, to practically abolish the distance between the sea-board and the wide-spread and fertile regions of the interior, thereby removing the clog on their agricultural industry, and virtually placing them side by side with the communities on the Atlantic. During the decade ending in 1860 the sum of $413,541,510 was expended within the limits of the interior central group, known as the 'food-exporting States,' in constructing 11,212 miles of railway to connect them with the sea-board. The traffic-receipts from those roads were:

In 1860 . $31,335,081 | In 1861 . $35,305,509
In 1862 . . . $44,908,405

"The saving to the communities themselves, in the transportation, for which they thus paid $44,908,405, was at least five times that amount, while the increase in the exports from that portion of the Union greatly animated not only the commerce of the Atlantic States, carrying those exports over their railways to the sea-board, but the manufacturing industry of the Eastern States, that exchange the fabrics of their workshops for the food of the interior.

"By carefully analyzing the $8,048,825,840 in question, we find that the six manufacturing States of New England received $735,754,244 of the amount; that the middle Atlantic, or carrying and commercial States, from New York to Maryland, inclusive, received $1,834,911,579; and that the food-producing interior itself, embracing the eight great States of Ohio, Indiana, Illinois, Michigan, Wisconsin, Minnesota, Iowa, and Missouri, received $2,810,000,000. This very large accession of wealth to this single group of States is sufficiently important to be stated more in detail. The group, taken as a whole, extends from the western boundaries of New York and Pennsylvania to the Missouri River, through fourteen degrees of longitude, and from the Ohio River north to the British dominions, through twelve degrees of latitude. It embraces an area of 441,167 square miles, or 282,134,688 acres, nearly all of which is arable and exceedingly fertile, much of it in prairie, and ready at once for the plow. There may be a small portion adjacent to Lake Superior unfit for cultivation, but it is abundantly compensated by its rich deposits of copper and of iron of the best quality.

"Into this immense natural garden, in a salubrious and desirable portion of the temperate zone, the swelling stream of population from the older Atlantic States and from Europe has steadily flowed during the last decade, increasing its previous population from 5,403,595 to 8,957,690, an accession of 3,554,095 inhabitants gained by the peaceful conquest of nature, fully equal to the population of Silesia, which cost Frederick the Great the seven years' war, and exceeding that of Scotland, the subject of struggle for centuries.

"The rapid influx of population into this group of States increased the quantity of the improved land, thereby raising farms, more or less cultivated within their limits, from 26,689,361 acres in 1850 to 51,826,395 in 1860, but leaving a residue to be improved of 230,398,290 acres. The area of 25,146,054 acres thus taken in ten years from the prairie and the forest is equal to seven-eighths of the arable land in England.

"The effects of this influx of population in increasing the pecuniary wealth as well as the agricultural products of the States in question are signally manifest in the census. The assessed value of their real and personal property ascended from $1,116,000,000 in 1850 to $3,926,000,000 in 1860, showing a clear increase of $2,810,000,000. We can best measure this rapid and enormous accession of wealth by comparing it with an object which all nations value, the commercial marine. The commercial tunnage of the United States

In 1840 was . 2,180,764 tuns. | In 1850 was . 3,535,454 tuns.
In 1860 was . . 5,358,808 tuns.

"At $50 per tun, which is a full estimate, the whole pecuniary value of the 5,358,808 tuns, embracing all our commercial fleets on the oceans and the lakes and the rivers, and numbering nearly thirty thousand vessels, would be but $267,940,000; whereas the increase in the pecuniary value of the States under consideration, in each year of the last decade, was $281,000,000. Five years' increase would purchase every commercial vessel in the Christian world.

"But the census discloses another very important feature, in respect to these interior States, of far higher interest to the statisticians, and especially to the statesmen of Europe, than any which has yet been noticed, in their vast and rapidly increasing capacity to supply food, both vegetable and animal, cheaply and abundantly, to the increasing millions of the old world. In the last decade their cereal products increased from 309,950,295 bushels to 558,160,323 bushels, considerably exceeding the whole cereal product of England, and nearly if not quite equal to that of France. In the same period the swine, which play a very important part in consuming the large surplus of Indian corn, increased in number from 8,536,182 to 11,039,352, and the cattle from 4,373,712 to 7,204,810. Thanks to steam and the railway, the herds of cattle that feed on the meadows of the Upper Mississippi are now carried, in four days, through eighteen degrees of longitude, to the slaughter-houses on the Atlantic.

"It is difficult to furnish any visible or adequate measure for a mass of cereals so enormous as 558,000,000 of bushels. About one-fifth of the whole descends the chain of lakes, on which 1,300 vessels are constantly employed in the season of navigation. About one-seventh of the whole finds its way to the ocean through the Erie Canal, which has already been once enlarged for the purpose of passing vessels of two hundred tuns, and is now under survey, by the State of New York, for a second enlargement, to pass vessels of five hundred tuns. The vessels called 'canal-boats,' now navigating the canal, exceed five thousand in number, and, if placed in a line, would be more than eighty miles in length.

"The barrels of wheat and flour alone, carried by the canal to the Hudson River, were,

In 1842 . . 1,146,292 | In 1852 . . 3,937,366
In 1862 . . 7,516,397

"A similar enlargement is also proposed for the canal connecting Lake Michigan with the Mississippi River. When both the works are completed, a barrel of flour can be carried from St. Louis to New York, nearly half across the continent, for fifty cents, or a tun from the Iron Mountain of Missouri for five dollars. The moderate portion of the cereals that descends the lakes, if placed in barrels of five bushels each, and side by side, would form a line five thousand miles long. The whole crop, if placed in barrels, would encircle the globe. Such is its present magnitude. We leave it to statistical science to discern and truly estimate the future. One result is, at all events, apparent. A general famine is now impossible; for America, if necessary, can feed Europe for centuries to come. Let the statesman and philanthropist ponder well the magnitude of the fact, and all its far-reaching consequences —political, social, and moral—in the increased industry, the increased happiness, and the assured peace of the world."

These facts may well give us great confidence in the future of the United States, and dispel our fears of being crushed by the weight of our debt, or of being seriously embarrassed at the close of the war. Some of these statements and calculations are worthy of particular attention. It is estimated that our population in six years (in 1870) will be about 42,000,000; for the great increase, now probable in immigration, will prevent our general rate of advance from being materially lessened by the waste of the war. Should we close the war in 1864, the national debt will not be far from $2,000,000,000. We shall have then, in 1870, a population from three millions to four millions larger than France, with about the same amount of debt, and with general resources far greater than hers. Our population will then be about ten millions larger than that of Great Britain, and our debt little more than half as great.

But another important fact is, that, while the rate of increase of our population for the last decade was about 36 per cent., the rate of increase of our wealth for the same period was 130 per cent. The wealth of the country in 1860 was estimated at about fourteen thousand two hundred and twenty-five millions. If the same rate of increase should continue during this decade, the aggregate property of the United States in 1870 would be about equal to the present estimated wealth of Great Britain, while we shall have little more than half her debt.

The war has destroyed an immense amount of property in the South; but, in the meanwhile, the wealth of the free States has been increasing, probably, at a more rapid rate than ever; for new inventions in agricultural machinery keep up the rate of production for our cereals, while they are selling at greatly enhanced prices.

Such calculations can only be regarded as approximately correct; but they may be so far relied upon as to give us great confidence in the future ability of the country to meet all its obligations, and to keep up, at least, the usual rate of progress. To these statements the report of the Commissioner of the General Land-office should be added in regard to the metalliferous regions of the United States:

"The report of the Commissioner of the Land-office shows on what a grand scale God has laid here the foundation of power, and provided abundantly all the elements of national greatness. The facts presented prove that our mineral wealth is in full proportion to the extent of territory, and that the supply of the precious metals in particular will meet every want of the country, even when its population shall amount to hundreds of millions; that it will supply a specie basis for the whole business of the continent when it shall be as densely populated as Europe, and when America, placed between India and Europe, shall control the commerce of the 'exhaustless East,' when, through steamers on the Pacific, and railroads across the continent, our cities will be nearer to Asia than London or Paris.

"Among the elements of national wealth and power, iron and coal hold, perhaps, the first place, inasmuch as both these must be so largely used hereafter, not alone in commerce and the arts, but in all the operations of war.

"Upon this point the Commissioner's report is full of interest. He says:

"'The extent of the twelve coal-bearing States east of the Mississippi holds but a small proportion to the immense coal-fields west of that region, as we have information reporting the existence of coal in Dacotah, Kansas, Nebraska, Colorado, Utah, Nevada, California, Oregon, and Washington.'

"It is impossible to overestimate the importance of these immense coal-fields in the future progress of our country; and when we remember how coal is almost constantly associated with iron, we see on what a vast scale God has prepared the materials of civilization over millions of square miles, where these stored-up riches wait for the coming of the people.

"The following statements in regard to the gold region will doubtless attract great attention. Though based on well-ascertained facts, they seem almost like fable:

"'It stretches on the western portion of the continent from 40° north latitude to 31° 30′, and from the 102° of longitude to the Pacific Ocean, embracing portions of Dacotah, Nebraska, Colorado, all of New Mexico, with Arizona, Utah, Nevada, California, Oregon, and Washington Territory. Its breadth is about 1,100 miles from north to south, and of nearly equal longitudinal extension, making an area of more than a million of acres. This vast region is traversed from north to south, on the Pacific side, by the Sierra Nevada and the Cascade Mountains, then by the Blue and Humboldt; on the east by the double ranges of the Rocky Mountains, embracing the Wasatch, Wind River chain, and the Sierra Madre, stretching longitudinally and in lateral spurs—crossed and linked together by intervening ridges connecting the whole system by five principal ranges, dividing the country into an equal number of basins, each being nearly surrounded by mountains, and watered by mountain streams and snows, thereby interspersing this immense territory with bodies of agricultural lands equal to the support of not only miners, but of a dense population.

"'These mountains are literally stocked with minerals—gold and silver being interspersed in profusion over their immense surface, and daily brought to light by new discoveries. The precious metals are found embedded in mountains of quartz, rich washings marking the pathways of rivers and floods. Besides their wealth in gold, no part of the world is so rich in silver-mines as Nevada and New Mexico; yet these may be estimated only in proportion to the gold-fields which are in process of development with amazing results. The recent discoveries in the Colorado region of California, and in the region stretching thence away up to and north of Salmon River, in Washington Territory, are every day stimulating the mining enterprise of our people.'

"In order to show what an amount of labor may find profitable employment in this mining region, the Commissioner states that what is called a claim, in the quartz region, is one hundred feet square. If only one-hundredth part of the mountain district is suitable for mining, there will still be room for three million six hundred thousand claims.

"By another estimate, based upon a calculation of Governor Evans, of Colorado, he shows that the gold-bearing region of our country will give employment to twenty millions of miners. He says that quartz which yields $12 per tun will pay, under favorable circumstances. There is, however, much quartz which will yield from $20 to $500 per tun. There is some which yields from $500 to $3,000 per tun, and some recent discoveries are estimated as high as $20,000 per tun.

"'In addition to the deposits of gold and silver, various sections of the whole mineral region are rich in precious stones, marble, gypsum, salt, tin, quicksilver, asphaltum, coal, iron, copper, and lead; together with mineral, medicinal, thermal, and cold springs and streams. None of these mines have been worked for a great length of time, except the placers of California, and much the largest portion of them are comparatively recent discoveries; yet the deeper the mine is worked, the richer is the ore or rock. Enormous profits are derived from operations at depths of 150 to 200 feet.'

"The Commissioner states that, prior to the discovery of gold in 1848, the gold product of the world was only, on the average, $18,000,000; now the annual yield of our own mines is $100,000,000, and the working of our gold-bearing region has only just begun."

The Commissioner estimates that "within ten years (from 1863) the annual product of these mines in the precious metals alone will be two hundred millions of dollars; and in coal, iron, tin, lead, quicksilver, and copper, half that sum." He says: "With an amount of labor relatively equal to that expended in California, applied to the gold-fields already known to exist outside of that State, the production even now, including that of California, would exceed four hundred millions of dollars per year." He is confident that these mines may be relied upon to pay principal and interest of the national debt, besides supporting the government. These estimates do not appear extravagant to those who have made our mineral resources a subject of study, and the facts should be known by the whole American people, in order to remove all anxiety in reference to the future.

A debt of $2,000,000,000 would require for the payment of its interest probably $100,000,000 annually. If, then, our other expenses are reduced to the proper rates of peace, can any man doubt our ability to provide for these amounts and an additional sinking-fund, which would extinguish our debt within a quarter of a century? The extent of our unoccupied lands, and their great fertility, and the increasing inducements for immigration, warrant the belief that the rate of increase of our population will be nearly as great for the next half-century as it has been in the last fifty years. Our ability to pay a debt may be compared with that of France, whose debt is equal to ours, or nearly so, and with that of England, who owes nearly twice as much as we, by comparing our respective rates of progress. The population of France increased 37 per cent. in sixty years, ending in 1861, according to Mr. Ruggles. The increase of England and Wales was 121 per cent. in the same time; while, in this period, the increase in the United States was 593 per cent. Mr. Kennedy, in his Compendium of the Eighth Census, estimates the population, twenty-six years from this time (1864), at more than seventy-seven millions. If this should prove true, it will add some forty-seven millions to the present population; and Mr. Ruggles has shown that the rate in which wealth increases in this country is about four times the rate of the progress of population; and this rate of production would bring the aggregate wealth of the country in 1880 to more than seventy-five thousand millions of dollars.

These calculations are based upon actual results already reached, and upon rates of progress which the country has as yet maintained, and which men of attainment and experience assume are likely to be maintained in the future. The certain increase of the amount of the Southern staples through free labor and machinery, our unlimited capacity for cereal production, our mineral wealth, our manufacturing and commercial resources, should convince all that the national debt will scarcely be felt in our future progress. It has been said by many that Europe will not, hereafter, purchase as largely as heretofore of our agricultural productions. It is evident, however, that unless new grain-fields are opened in the old world, its population must receive yearly more and more of its food from America; and, in regard to the supply of cotton, unless England and France can obtain elsewhere an article fully equal in quality to that of American growth, they must either buy our cotton or we shall manufacture it ourselves, and then they must meet us with our superior fabrics in the markets of the world.

Let those who fear that national bankruptcy is approaching, consider what the material progress of the country must be for the next quarter of a century while nearly fifty millions are being added to our population.

There are certain great improvements, of a national character, which are certain to be made before half that period has elapsed, if this war shall be speedily closed. At least one great trunk-line of railway will be finished to the Pacific, with Eastern branches reaching the Northern lakes, the central Mississippi Valley, and the Southern sea-coast, and with lateral branches shooting out into the vast mineral regions of the far West.

The railway intended to connect the Ohio Valley with East Tennessee and with Charleston will be finished, and the North Carolina Railway will be carried westward until it connects with some branch of the Pacific Road, and the now ruined railroads of the South will be put in complete order again. That internal coast-line of navigation, even now almost continuous from Long Island Sound to Florida, will be perfected by connecting the bays, sounds, and channels, until our coastwise commerce can pass from New York to Florida by this inland route, safe alike from an enemy, and from ocean storms. There will be a ship-canal around the falls of Niagara, and from the lakes to the Mississippi, and the Ohio River will be rendered navigable through the year. In addition to this, the government must soon bring its mineral lands into the market in the same manner as it does all other lands, and give a title in fee to the purchaser.

While these things are in progress, the tide of our population will set strongly in upon the South, and the mineral lands of the Western mountains, and industry will plant itself precisely where it is most needed to sustain our finances, where it will produce the great staples of the South and silver and gold as the basis of our currency, while, at the same time, the riches of the Eastern commerce will flow in through the golden gate of California. Any amount of debt which this war can create will press lightly upon such a country as this will be, almost in the immediate future.

Nor are any of the predictions so freely made, at home and abroad, in regard to future divisions of our country, likely to be fulfilled.

No one of the great geographical divisions of the land is complete in itself. Each is a necessary part of one great whole.

The mineral region, the great agricultural basins, the coast-lines for commerce on the two oceans, fronting Europe and Asia, the long lines of hill-country for manufactures; in the East the Alleghanies, stretching from Canada to central Alabama, and, in the far West, the Rocky Mountains and the Nevada, all bear a due proportion to each other, and stand so related to each other as to be bound inseparably together to form one grand national whole, in which each part, like members of a living body, will be necessary to all the rest.

The manufacturers of the country will purchase the staples of the South and the South-west. Commerce will make the exchanges, the agricultural regions will supply the food, and the mines will furnish the silver and the gold as the money basis of the whole; and, bound together as we shall be by railways and canals, and all the interlacing bonds of kindred and business and social relations, warned by the experience of this rebellion, and having learned the value of a great nationality, we shall remain henceforth "one and inseparable."

# CHAPTER XXXIX.

## SUMMARY OF THE RELATIONS OF ENGLAND, FRANCE, RUSSIA, AND AMERICA, TO THE WORLD AND TO EACH OTHER.

FROM what has been already stated, it is not difficult to see in what direction the great forces of the world are to be exerted in the future, and the bearing which the four powers named above will have upon the progress of civilization.

France is the great military power of Western Europe. With Louis Napoleon and his political and military associates, this is the one ruling idea; the chief, if not the sole object of every wile of state-craft, as well as every movement in war. The extending and consolidating the Papal power is with them a means to an end. The common religious sentiment and the ties of race are being used to combine the Catholic nations into one grand organization, with its head at Paris; a vast military power, supported by the prestige and authority of the Romish Church, and strong enough, as is hoped, to give civil and ecclesiastical law to Europe, and perhaps, also, to this Western world.

France desires manufactures and colonies, not for the benefit of the people, but to create a wealth which may support the army, the navy, and the splendor of the imperial government. The people, like the slaves on a plantation, are regarded simply as machines for the production of wealth which the government may use.

The Emperor adorns his capital with regal magnificence; he constructs such fortifications and dock-yards as those at Cherbourg; he creates navies and armies; he concentrates, in short, all the wealth of the empire in the hands of the rulers whom he directs, but he does little or nothing for the education, the comfort, the general progress of the people. One fact, already stated, is a whole volume of history for France. Her population has increased only thirty-seven per cent. in sixty years. Sixty years ago she had more than twenty-seven millions of inhabitants; she has about thirty-nine millions now. This shows conclusively how heavily the government policy presses upon the laboring classes, and how little hope the empire can have of keeping pace in *growth* with either Russia or America, and hence the need of seeking combinations of power which she can herself direct.

The empire is, in no sense, of or for the people. The elections are simply a farce and an imposition. The Emperor and his officers are the State; they are France, the only France with which the world without has any relations. The government has really no popular element in it; the bayonets alone vote, and in accordance with the orders given.

The government virtually owns say thirty millions of laborers, whose earnings, excepting only common food and clothing, it consumes in navies, armies, and in imperial pomp.

Such, politically, is France: a military despotism, seeking to dominate both over Europe and America. The leaders of the Papal Church are, equally with the Emperor, intent upon the military aggrandizement of France; but with them this military power is not an end, but a means to extend, in both hemispheres, the exclusive dominion of the Romish Church. Thus the Jesuits use the military strength of the empire to advance the Church, and Louis Napoleon, on his part, sustains the Church, and excites her ambition, and extends her influence, in order that he may use it all to create, consolidate, and secure a military empire that shall, if possible, rule the world. Unless France is again revolutionized, she will very soon embody the three forms of despotism which have cursed the world: the ecclesiastical, the political, and the military.

Should Louis Napoleon succeed in so allying all the Papal States of Europe to France that he could wield the military power of all combined, and then this force should be controlled by Jesuit statesmen, it would, of course, be used everywhere to repress free institutions, whether religious or political; it would become, in both hemispheres, the most formidable foe of freedom and human progress that has arisen in modern times.

The Papal Church is bound by her nature her principles, and all her past history, to the monarchical form of government—to the theory that the people have no right of choice in rulers, nor authority to shape the laws by which they are governed; her spirit is that of a despotism from which the people can have no appeal, and in this she can not change, for that would annihilate the Papacy, and sink it to the level of a mere religious denomination. The Romish Church must and will, from its very nature, compel obedience to itself as the only true Church, to the full extent of her power, and, therefore, the most alarming feature in the immediate future of Europe is the rapid growth of the military power of France, the swift yet steady increase of her political influence, and the old persecuting power of the dark ages, now become a part of the empire's life, growing with its growth and strengthening with its strength.

No conspiracy so formidable as this has been formed for many centuries against popular civil rights and religious freedom. Its ramifications already extend to every nation, but the two chief objects at which it proposes to strike are, Russia and the Greek Church in the East, and the American Republic, with its free institutions and its Protestant faith.

The French occupation of Mexico, and the letter of the

Pope to Jeff. Davis, are inspired by the same spirit, a desire for the overthrow of this Republic.

The traitor President has the sympathies both of the Emperor and the Pope, because they hope that, through him and their own efforts, this free Republic and the Protestant faith will be destroyed together. Such is the France of to-day, aiming at the universal supremacy of the military empire and the Roman Catholic Church; a double-headed despotism, ready to tread down the people of every land, occupying Mexico already as a point from whence to make its spring at the United States.

It is only necessary to refer to the quotations already made, setting forth the condition of the laborers of England, to show that Great Britain, though boasting of a free constitution and chartered liberties, has, in the practical working of her policy, ground her people down with a more crushing despotism than that of France, and that, according to the showing of her own witnesses, there are very few countries in Europe where the condition of the laborers, as a whole, is as wretched as in England.

Only about one million in England have the privilege of voting, or have any direct influence upon the laws or the government; and this fact, with the other already stated on the authority of Mr. Kay, that in England fifteen thousand persons own all the land, is quite sufficient to prove that the English system, whatever it may be in theory, in its practical working forces the laborers down to very near the level of the slave, and shuts up completely the path of progress and the door of hope. As France uses her laborers as so much machinery for war and to aggrandize the government, the empire, so England employs her people to create wealth for the titled landholding few. England, then, is a despotism of wealth and rank; the government is a combination of capital and the titled and privileged few, to whose support the earnings of the laboring millions must contribute all except what is needed to support a life only a grade above that of the slave.

The France and the England with which the world has to deal, whose diplomatic craft, whose armies and navies the world must meet, are alike the representatives and watchful defenders of despotism, seeking alike to establish or maintain everywhere governments in which the people have no controlling share—governments founded upon the theory that no rights whatever inhere in the people, that the laboring classes have no rights except such as the government chooses to bestow. To this theory the soul of the Holy Alliance, England, has constantly given assent by her acts, and, therefore, France and England both are the deadly foe of republican or democratic freedom, and represent and defend the old despotic forms of government that in all ages have cursed and trodden down the people.

England is a despotism of the aristocracy, a tyranny of title and capital, which, in its workshops of Mammon, is grinding up the people as surely as the material upon which the machinery works, the mills and the agricultural systems producing poverty and degradation as regularly as they do the cotton fabrics of Lancashire or the cutlery of Sheffield.

These powers belong to a period now closing and passing away, and they seek to retard, by all means, the progress of that new era of popular freedom which is dawning upon the nations. For this purpose they will probably unite their strength hereafter as they have hitherto done, for it is difficult to see how England can safely separate from or oppose France in any of her ambitious schemes. The Papal element is strong, and growing daily stronger, in Great Britain, and it is at least very doubtful whether England could this day be induced to rally to the defense of the Protestant faith, against any attack which France might choose to make. The hazard is too great, and her enthusiasm for truth too small.

Precisely as she left France to work her will in Mexico, and even encouraged her, knowing perfectly her designs, so will she do hereafter, if her own interests can be promoted thereby. The England which would make war to defend a religious principle we may well fear is gone forever. The England of to-day is paralyzed by the spell of France, and chilled by Mammon selfishness. These are the two great powers which now present themselves on the theater of nations as the special antagonists of Russia and America, the champions of political and ecclesiastical despotism, massing their banded strength against Russia and the Greek Church on the one hand, against this Protestant American Republic on the other.

It is perfectly evident, therefore, that, as Europe now stands, the only hope for her of arresting or resisting this new combination which France is forming—and of which England is almost certain to become a part, unless prevented by popular revolution—must rest on Russia.

The Protestant portion of Germany is in a state of chaos: we may hope that it may yet be organized and find a fitting leader, raised up as Luther was of God; but, as things now are, Russia alone has power, if any thing human has, to save the people of Europe from this new conspiracy against civil and religious freedom.

Russia has committed herself openly, fully, deliberately, to the cause of popular progress. Her new policy in freeing, elevating, and educating her people, and in making the laborers landowners, is very far in advance of any thing done or proposed by England or France. Her theory is not a democratic one, but it is, that the government should be administered so as to promote the highest welfare of the people, instead of using the people as machines or plantation slaves, merely to add to the pomp and splendor of an empire or an aristocracy.

Strange as it may at first thought appear, it is nevertheless true, that Russia is the true point of support for liberal opinions or popular progress in Europe. She, in the Greek Church, can present to Europe and the East a religious organization powerful enough to compete with the Papacy; and that Church has a spiritual life, a liberality, a spirit of toleration, of which the Church of Rome knows nothing. The cordial friendship between Russia and America will incline the national Church to affiliate hereafter with at least our American form of Protestantism, and the Protestant faith may, in its coming struggle with Rome, find that support in Russia which England, entangled as she is, and largely Catholic as she is already, may be unable or unwilling to give.

Russia alone has the military and naval strength to resist the attack of France and her allies. The battle of our iron-clads effected for Russia precisely what it did for us. It delivered her from the fear of the great navies of France and England. Thanks to the genius of Ericsson, and our American artillery, Russia can construct mail-clad batteries that no ocean-going ship can resist. She has a fleet of these already, and she can defy the utmost effort of France and England combined, and her late reply to France, on the Polish question, is proof that she knows her strength.

She alone of all Europe can give freedom to the down-trodden East; she alone can re-establish on the historic plains of the old Greek Empire a nation with popular rights and religious freedom; and mankind will have reason to rejoice when the national banner of the Greek Church shall take the place of the Crescent on the towers of St. Sophia. Who can foresee the changes which will be wrought in Europe, and especially upon all the branches of the Sclavonic race, now that the imperial and religious head of that race has planted himself on the side of the people, the advocate and defender of popular progress. There are many who are deeply prejudiced against Russia because of her course in Poland; but even there, when she is fully understood, she will be justified, at least in her general course, by even the friends of freedom. First, the insurrection in Poland was a rebellion of the nobility, and not of the people; it was, like our own rebellion, an attempt of the aristocracy to secure and extend their power over the laboring classes. Second, it is now asserted, by good authority, that this outbreak received its inspiration from Paris, and was an attempt, on the part of Louis

Napoleon and his Jesuits, to obtain a foothold within the Russian dominions, from whence Russia and the Greek Church might be attacked when the opportunity should offer. It was a covert attempt to flank Russia by a French Catholic outpost, as he is flanking the United States by the occupation of Mexico.

The Russian Minister did not hesitate to inform the French Emperor that the Polish insurrection was fomented in his own capital; and Russia knew, and America ought to know, that she was called to meet, in Poland, not an uprising of the people, but an insidious effort of France and the Catholic leaders to wrest from her a portion of her dominions, and strike a blow also at her national Church.

Russia is now the grandest spectacle in the old world. She stands the center of a hundred millions of people, and head of that Church which for a thousand years had its chief seat at Constantinople, and made it the second city of the East; and while France and the Latin nations and the Papacy are together preparing to create an overwhelming despotism, and England seems caught in the toils of the conspiracy, Russia confronts them with her gigantic power and nobler aspirations, and, standing in that light of freedom with which she is scattering her own darkness away, she turns to a new era and a nobler life.

Russia has professedly undertaken an experiment which has not been tried since the time of the Jewish theocracy. She declares that she will use the powers of the government and the influence of a national Church to instruct, to elevate, to enrich, and bless the masses of the people. The Czar assumes the position of Father and Priest of his people, and proposes to govern for their benefit; and therefore he invests them all with the proper rights of citizenship, and offers to aid them in every effort at improvement by the advice and influence and treasure of the government itself. Doubtless there will be many mistakes and shortcomings in the carrying out of this plan, but it is the noblest announcement of the true Christian theory of government which Europe has heard in modern times.

In all ages, and everywhere except in Judea and here, the people have been used to aggrandize the monarch, the nobility, and the Church. Russia proposes now to reverse this, and use both Church and State power to ennoble and bless the people at large.

The progress of her experiment will be watched with intense interest by every friend of the Gospel and of human progress. She presents at all points an illustrious antagonism to the movement which now controls all Western Europe.

She has cut herself loose from the traditions and policy of the past, and proposes henceforth to act upon the principle that governments are instituted for the good of the citizens. This new policy has brought Russia, so far as general purpose is concerned, into close sympathy with the United States, as no other European power can be until Germany is reconstructed, and God sends her a leader.

The national purpose in this Republic, also, is to use the powers of the State and of religion to promote the welfare of the people, to spread intelligence among the laboring masses, and to multiply their comforts.

In our republican State we propose to accomplish this object by civil institutions created by and dependent upon the people themselves, and by Churches having no connection with the State, receiving from it no support of any kind, being merely voluntary religious associations, depending for support upon the free-will offerings of the people. This is the American form of Christian civilization, while Russia proposes to attain the same end by a government both patriarchal and kingly in its character, while at the same time the Church is an integral part of the State and the Czar is its imperial head.

These two forms of government, so different and yet aiming at the same result, present the two great experiments of modern times for the elevation of the working masses of the nation, and it remains to be seen which will achieve the most signal success. The tendency of the one will, of course, be toward despotism and oppression of the people, such as characterizes every other monarchy; that of our free government is toward lawlessness, an undue assertion of individual right, or, in times of great peril like the present, toward a military despotism; but if these two experiments in popular progress are faithfully carried out, they will help to settle the great problem of Christian civilization, whether a strong central government and a national Church, faithfully administered for the good of the citizens, will promote the general welfare and secure the general progress equally with those democratic forms, both in the State and the Church, which have been adopted here. However this may be, Russia and America now stand before the world as the leaders of the two great forms of popular progress, and both are confronted and threatened by the civil and ecclesiastical despotisms of Western Europe. Their interests are identical, their fields of action so remote from each other as to render unlikely any future collision, their enemies are the same, and it is not improbable that they may yet unite to free themselves and the nations, on land and on the sea, from the arrogant assumptions of France, England, and the Papacy.

# CHAPTER XL.

## THE MONROE DOCTRINE.

THE subjects treated of in the preceding chapters lead naturally to the consideration of what is called "The Monroe Doctrine," and to inquire whether that announcement of the American government was intended only to serve an occasion, or whether that declaration sets forth a policy upon which our national safety, and even our existence as a Republic, depends.

It is necessary to the full understanding of this matter, that one should consider the causes which induced our government thus to declare its intentions.

The history of Europe presents many examples of combinations among different nations to repress the growing power or ambition of some monarch or kingdom that threatened the peace or liberty of the rest, but no regular system for such a purpose was formed and agreed upon until the Congress of Vienna. The career of Napoleon had shown Europe the necessity of some kind of union among the powers for mutual protection against any future Bonaparte that might arise; and after his overthrow and at the Congress of Vienna, the so-called Holy Alliance was formed, by which Europe was placed under the joint supervision and control of five "Great Powers," Great Britain, France, Austria, Russia, and Prussia. By the decisions of these the nations were to be bound. They constituted themselves the guardians and trustees of

Europe, and had, of course, ample power to enforce their opinions upon all the rest.

Moreover, any three of these, or any two, if Great Britain or France were one, could act in any case for the whole. England, for private reasons, did not become, *in form*, a party to this arrangement, but she shared in all the negotiations of the Congress, approved of the system as adopted, and has ever maintained and relied upon it since—a cordial, active partner of the Alliance, though without signing her name to the paper. These self-constituted guardians of Europe assumed the right to interfere with the concerns of any State whose government or policy did not please them, and compel it, by force of arms, if necessary, to shape all its concerns according to their judgment of the case. They were the European Supreme Court of Nations, and their armies and their navies were always ready to execute their decrees.

A cardinal principle of these kingly custodians of Europe was, to maintain everywhere, so far as possible, one only form of government, an absolute monarchy, hereditary, and supported by due military power. If a constitutional government were already in existence, strong enough to resist, such as England was, it was to be endured while it must be; but it was a primal object with these Holy Allies to repress and put down everywhere all popular institutions and power, to deny entirely any right in the people to choose their own rulers, or to frame their own laws and institutions. It was a part of the contract between these five powers to establish and support, wherever they had the power, a form of government directly opposed, both in essential principles and in every form and feature, to the free institutions of our own Republic. They were bound to put us down whenever the occasion should offer, and the intervening ocean alone has saved us from intervention and destruction while we were yet in our infancy.

But the absolute rulers of Western Europe and the Jesuits have never ceased to hope that this Republic might yet be destroyed. Many have been the schemes to render us subservient to their designs before the use of steam on the sea had brought us within the reach of their arms. The first Napoleon sold us Louisiana in order that we might become a maritime rival of England. Subsequently, England, under Canning, approved of our Monroe Doctrine, in order to exclude France from the American continent, and now England unites with France, both to occupy Mexico and destroy the Republic, in the very spirit of the Holy Alliance, and because she wishes to crush a rival. Bonaparte overthrew the government of Spain, and her American colonies, freed from her yoke, declared their independence. There was also a popular movement in Spain, and the Cortez demanded a constitution for the people. The Holy Alliance interfered, put down the popular party, and restored absolute authority to Ferdinand. The independence which the South American States had just declared, then received the attention of the Allies, and a scheme was formed, first for reconquering South America for Spain, and then to determine whether any thing could be devised for checking the young Republic of the North. This was the time selected by Mr. Monroe to announce the policy which stands connected with his name as the "Monroe Doctrine." This doctrine was presented in his message of December, 1823, in the following words:

"In the wars of the European powers, in matters relating to themselves, we have never taken any part, nor does it comport with our policy so to do. It is only when our rights are invaded, or seriously menaced, that we resent injuries, or make preparations for our defense. With the movements in this hemisphere we are of necessity more immediately connected, and by causes which must be obvious to all enlightened and impartial observers. The political system of the Allied Powers is essentially different in this respect from that of America. This difference proceeds from that which exists in their respective governments. And to the defense of our own, which has been achieved with so much expense of blood and treasure, and matured by the wisdom of their most enlightened citizens, and under which we have enjoyed most unexampled felicity, this whole nation is devoted. We owe it, therefore, to candor and to the amicable relations subsisting between the United States and these powers, to declare, that we should consider any attempt on their part to extend their system to any portion of this hemisphere as dangerous to our peace and safety. With the existing colonies or dependencies of any European power we have not interfered, and shall not interfere. But with the governments who have declared their independence, and maintained it, and whose independence we have, on great consideration, and on just principles, acknowledged, we could not view any interposition, for the purposes of oppressing them, or controlling in any other manner their destiny, by any European power, in any other light than as the manifestation of an unfriendly disposition toward the United States. In the war between these governments and Spain, we declared our neutrality at the time of their recognition, and to this we have adhered, and shall continue to adhere, provided no change shall occur which, in the judgment of the competent authorities of this government, shall make a corresponding change on the part of the United States indispensable to their security."

"The deep interest which we take in their independence, which we have acknowledged, and in their enjoyment of all the rights incident thereto, especially in the very important one *of instituting their own governments,* has been declared, and is known to the world. Separated as we are from Europe by the great Atlantic Ocean, we can have no concern in the wars of the European governments, nor in the causes which produce them. *The balance of power between them, into whichever scale it may turn in its various vibrations, can not affect us.* It is the interest of the United States to preserve the most friendly relations with every power, and on conditions fair, equal, and applicable to all. But in regard to our neighbors our situation is different.

It is impossible for the European governments to interfere in their concerns, especially in those alluded to,"—[of *instituting their own governments*]—"which are vital, without affecting us; indeed, the motive which might induce such interference in the present state of the war between the parties, if war it may be called, would appear to be equally applicable to us. It is gratifying to know that some of the powers with whom we enjoy a very friendly intercourse, and to whom these views have been communicated, have appeared to acquiesce in them."—*Message of Dec.* 7, 1824.

These messages, as well as the general political history of that time, show in the clearest light the character and designs of that European movement against which the protest was directed. Its avowed object was to bring the American continent under the control of the allied monarchs of Europe, to trample out all popular rights, put down all popular governments, and restore the reign of absolutism over all this Western world.

Mr. Monroe and his associate statesmen knew well that the coming blow was to be aimed at the very life of this Republic, and, indeed, at republican institutions on both the American continents, and with a courage, boldness, and firmness which might have been profitably imitated in our later dealings with Europe, and especially with France, they declared that they were resolved to resist all attempts to impose the European system upon part of America, and, if necessary, they would do this by force of arms.

A writer in the NEW ENGLANDER for October, 1863, in a very clear and able article upon "The Monroe Doctrine," thus sums up its principles:

"1. That the American continents, (leaving out the islands), are henceforth not to be considered subject to any future colonization by any European nation.

"2. That we shall consider any attempt on the part of the European powers to extend their political system to any portion of this hemisphere as 'dangerous to our peace and safety,' and of course to be counteracted or provided against as we shall deem advisable in any case.

"3. That for any European power to interfere with any American government for the purpose of oppressing or dictating to them unjustly, or of controlling their destiny by force or threats, would be viewed by us as 'the manifestation of an unfriendly disposition toward the United States,' which we should be called upon to notice by protest or remonstrance, or in such way as we should think our honor and interest required."

In this conspiracy against free institutions on this continent, Russia was then engaged, as earnestly engaged as the rest, having offered to assist Ferdinand in recovering his colonies; but Russia, under Alexander and under Nicholas, was not the liberal Russia which she is to-day. The whole aspect of Europe has changed; the Crimean war taught her that her deadliest foes were among the Allied Powers; she saw clearly that her true interests are quite independent of absolutism and of Western Europe; that her aims are identical with those of the Western Republic, and that the enemies of America are equally her own. The Papacy strikes alike at Protestantism and the Greek Church, and those who hate and fear our free America are equally hostile to a liberal Russia, throbbing and expanding with a new popular life.

France and England, when they had resolved, for purposes of their own, to make an attack on Russia, gave to their plan, at first, the aspect of a joint movement of four of the great *regulators* of Europe, to check the ambition of one of their own associates in the Holy Alliance; but, so soon as they saw that they could not thus produce a war, they abandoned Austria and Prussia, and made the attack alone, for reasons which have been presented in the previous chapters of this work; and now these same powers, in connection with Spain, have undertaken anew the very scheme against which Mr. Monroe, supported by the whole country, protested so earnestly and firmly in

1823, and by their manly courage averted, for a time, the danger.

When this Southern conspiracy first disclosed itself in Europe, it was carefully nourished and strengthened; and when the outbreak of the rebellion gave the occasion, every crowned and titled foe of popular rights prepared for what they believed would be the final overthrow of free institutions, and the restoration of the Western continent to European control, England taking the grand initiatory step, which made all the rest easy, by recognizing the traitors as lawful belligerents and on an equality with the regular government.

As has been already stated, commercial ambition on the part of England, the purpose so coolly selfish of crippling her American rival, and with France a desire to aggrandize the Papacy and the Latin races, enter largely into this new attempt to subjugate America, and these greatly increase our danger. This rebellion, of itself, could not have lived through a twelvemonth unaided from abroad, and this its leaders have confessed; and it has been cherished and aided by France and England, simply as their instrument to carry out their own designs. Through the Confederates, England and France cunningly wage a secure war upon the United States, the arms, powder, supplies of all sorts, being furnished to the traitors with as much good-will as if they were for their own armies, and the traitor ships are sent forth as if they belonged to their own navies; and, to crown all, France seizes Mexico as a point of support for the Confederacy, and as a spot to which can be rallied every foe of the United States, for an assault upon us whenever the favorable hour shall come.

The secessionists in Europe are already rallying to the support of that tool of France and the Pope, called the Emperor of Mexico, and receiving titles of nobility at his hands, and the fearful, cautious steps by which this war has been prolonged, and the want of any firm remonstrances to the course of France, have brought us at this time (March, 1864) within a step of the position where the Southern rebels will be supported by a consolidated government in Mexico, backed by the sympathies and the arms of France.

A policy which has nothing positive, which lacks every element of courage and boldness, which commits itself to the drift of circumstances, has brought the nation face to face with this deadly peril, and it now remains to be seen whether the American people will rouse themselves in season and demand from our rulers the swift crushing of our home-traitors by the energetic use of every war-power, by treating them as traitors in justice to the loyal, and then reassert the principles set forth by Mr. Monroe, in the same spirit of comprehensive statesmanship and calm courage with which they were asserted at first.

The country has not now one moment to lose. This Congress should annihilate slavery; the rebellion should be crushed by our blows in the spring and early summer, if there is force enough in the whole North to do it; the property of the South, real and personal, should be placed forever beyond the reach of a traitor; and, at the same time, let the proper admonition be given to Maximilian, France, and Europe.

Thus only, as is believed, can our Republic be saved, and all America be secured against European control, and preserved as the grand theater for the expanding life of free institutions.

Let Maximilian once be established firmly on our border, and when we have broken the armies of the South, the chief conspirators, with all whom they can influence, will rally in Mexico to renew the war.

The manner and spirit with which Louis Napoleon entered Mexico are well set forth by the writer in the NEW ENGLANDER, already referred to, Rev. Dr. Joshua Leavitt. He says:

"Our government is generally regarded in Europe as a mere aggregation of individuals, to and from which men may come and go at pleasure, without incurring any moral obligation or violating any moral principle.

"It is upon this ground that we are to explain what appeared to Americans so shameless in the conduct of the French Emperor, when, in his letter to General Forey, he directed him to treat any government he might find in Mexico as merely provisional. The government of President Juarez is unquestionably the constitutional government of Mexico, and it has been supported by the great body of the people as such—the malcontent priests and their followers, and a few factious chiefs, only excepted. But it originated solely in the voice of the people, and neither had nor asked any other sanction than the popular will; and, therefore, Europe pronounces it only provisional, and hence liable to be replaced by another of equal authority by any faction which could get possession of the capital, so as to wield for a moment the forms of government at the accustomed seat of government. Another point gained by this subtilty is to give color to the pretext by which Mexico is held to be bound by the acts of the transient usurper, Miramon; for if Juarez's government is only provisional, Miramon's had as much authority as his. And, on no better ground than this, the Three Great Powers, Great Britain, France, and Spain, formed a coalition to invade Mexico, just as it was recovering from the disorders of a long revolution, in order to coerce the payment of Miramon's bonds, for which the scoundrel bankers had paid the plundering brigand only at the rate of four or five cents on the dollar. And, by the same rule, if Jeff. Davis had been smart enough to seize Washington City in 1861, and inaugurate himself as President of the United States, they might by and by be making war against us to compel the payment of his loans, for his government would have been provisional, and Europe decides in the case of Mexico that a constitutional government, sanctioned alone by the will of the people, is 'only provisional.'

"If there had been any doubt as to the real intent of

the language employed in the diplomatic correspondence of the Allied Powers and in the Emperor's letter, it is all now dispelled by the action of the French commander since he got possession of the city of Mexico. He knew the object of the expedition, and what his master meant by his orders. He has treated the constitutional government of Mexico as no valid government, as a merely provisional arrangement, a *locum tenens*, until military power could come in and grant to the people a government conformed to the fundamental ideas of Europe. He first appoints, by his own authority, a commission of three persons, one a renegade Mexican, the instigator of the invasion, Almonte; the second, the Archbishop, a servant of the sovereign of Rome, to give the sanction of the Pope to the proceeding; the third, Salas, the most unprincipled of all the chiefs who have aided to keep Mexico in a turmoil for a generation. These three convene a Council of Notables, selected by themselves, who proceed at once to declare Mexico an Empire, and designate the Archduke Maximilian, of Austria, for Emperor, with the provision that, if he declines, the Emperor of France shall designate a person to be their monarch. Here we have the true intent of the ambiguous phraseology which was used throughout by the Allied Powers, of their intention to secure to unfortunate Mexico the blessings of a *stable* government. They meant a frame of government not originating with the people in the exercise of their own inherent rights, and which they were always at liberty to change for good cause, but one *granted* to the people by some authority above them. It is a legitimate outgo of the political system of Europe, as adjusted by the Congress of Vienna."

The invasion of Mexico was made under the merest shadow of a pretext, a vail so thin as not to cover one feature of its real purpose from any discerning eye. To enforce the payment of Miramon's worthless bonds was a monstrous atrocity; but to make this a pretense under which to subjugate a whole country, overthrow its institutions, and impose upon it, by force of arms, a foreign despot, is a still deeper crime against God and humanity. Americans will make a very perilous mistake if they fail to regard this armed occupation of a sister Republic as any thing less than one important part of the scheme for the hoped-for subjugation of the United States. The invasion of Mexico and the rebellion are the two grand features of this French and English plot; and, while England has devoted her energies more particularly to protecting and aiding our home-conspirators, France has been equally busy with her allotted share in the attempt to dismember the Republic, and reconquer America. It is a blow at our national life, and in defense of that life we are bound to use all honorable means which may be at our disposal. It is aimed by the monarchies of Western Europe against free institutions on this continent; it is aimed by the Papacy against our Protestant faith; it is aimed at our commerce with Asia through excluding us from the Isthmus and Central America, and with the ultimate intention of wresting from us our possessions on the Pacific, and our whole mineral territory, which Louis Napoleon has surveyed and mapped out already. So far back as 1847, the French Emperor unfolded his plan for the occupation of the Isthmus of Panama and Central America, and for a ship-canal between the oceans, for the purpose of planting a European power in the center of the continent to check our southward progress and control the American route to India. England, having changed her views since the time of Canning, and fearing the rapid growth of the Republic, adopted his, and hence her operations in Central America, and also her approval of the attack on Mexico. Whatever may be the external aspect or attitude of these two powers, their purposes remain unchanged; they are perfectly agreed as to their American policy, and, until the relations of Europe are materially changed, we can count with certainty upon their covert or open hostility. To permit France, under such circumstances, to obtain a firm foothold on our Southern border, would be nothing less than national suicide.

In warning Americans against the establishment or the strengthening of the Papal power on this continent, one explanation should be made. No true American will object to a Church of the Catholic form in this country—a Church which should be one among others, one of the religious denominations merely, and on a level with the rest. With the religious belief of any man, or with his mode of worship, Americans propose not to interfere. But it is quite another thing to stretch over this continent, and over this Republic, the power of that politico-ecclesiastical despotism called the Papacy, of which Louis Napoleon is one head and the Pope the other—of which the Jesuits are the inspiring soul, and French and other Latin armies and navies are to be the executive powers. Could Europe and America, as France and the Jesuits design, be brought under the control of the Papacy again, it would bring upon the world a more fearful despotism, a bitterer curse than it felt under Hildebrand and the Innocents. Let Americans consider this subject in its relations to our Pacific States, and our commerce with Asia. The Isthmus will soon be the great transit-point over which the Asiatic trade of the Americas and a part of Europe must go, and every rule of national safety demands that this route should be under the control of an American power.

With Mexico, Central America, and Cuba permanently in the hands of European powers, they could doom us to a second-rate position in spite of our every effort. They could control, to suit themselves, the commerce of the world, and absorb its wealth. Besides, the nations of Europe have their own home-routes to Asia.

France is preparing, in union with England, to cross Suez with the ship-canal now nearly finished. Russia is extending her lines from the Black Sea, by the Caspian and the Aral, while she also proposes to divert a part of the trade of Asia up the Amoor, and cross the continent by railroad and water to Moscow. Surely, then, this

American route belongs to Americans; and to permit any European power to hold *our own keys* of Asia would be to sink from the position of a power among nations.

Let England and France confine themselves within their appropriate limits, and then, in the natural course of events, by peaceful growth and fair contract, we shall obtain, in due time, whatever we require. Their officious, arrogant, and hostile interference will not be endured, unless we are either blind to our most important interests or have lost the spirit of our fathers.

The sun is not more certain to rise than that France, in possession of Mexico and Central America, would, with the help of England, exclude us from the routes of the Isthmus, and this would first destroy our participation in the commerce of the East, and then, with the Pacific ports of Mexico and Central America in the hands of a hostile power, what could save California, connected with us only by the Cape or two thousand miles of railway? Viewed from any point, the movement of France involves the question of life or death for this Republic.

Let us thank God that just in the hour of our need and peril he has provided for us the means of defense. Before the war we should have seen no method by which such an attack as Europe now threatens could have been resisted, in the face of their overwhelming navies. They could have sealed up our whole coast, burned our cities, and landed any number of troops safely under cover of their fleets.

But the revolution which we have wrought in naval warfare, by our Monitors and improved artillery, has changed all this. Our harbors can not now be entered, our cities can not be burned, no fleet can maintain its position here for the landing of troops, or for blockading our coast. No vessels that can cross the ocean can withstand batteries and ships that we can prepare for home defense, and these ships on the coast of Mexico, and such an army as we can easily place there, would soon solve the question of European occupation; and then, when Europe has been taught that these Americas are the rightful and exclusive domain of Americans, the theater for an American civilization, which will brook no foreign dictation, the United States, as the leader of a grand alliance of American States, may present to all nations the type and model of a Christian Republic, while Russia, let us hope, will exhibit to Europe and the East, a Christian monarchy and a national Church administered so as to bless, instruct, and elevate the people.

If so, America and Russia will be the two great powers of the future.

# CHAPTER XLI.

## CONCLUSION.

CHARACTERISTICS OF THE ERA UPON WHICH WE ARE ENTERING: THE ERA OF POPULAR POWER AND POPULAR PROGRESS—THE FORCES WHICH WORK IN HARMONY WITH THE SPIRIT OF THE NEW AGE—THE POWERS THAT STILL CLING TO AND STRIVE TO RETAIN AND STRENGTHEN THE DESPOTISMS WHICH ARE PASSING AWAY—PROBABLE RESULTS.

ALTHOUGH the whole movement of society may be regarded as a progress from a definite starting point toward a definite end, yet this movement is so marked off into divisions, stages in the grand march, that we are able to see where one great system ends and another begins. There is hardly room for doubt that the nations are just now standing at the close of a political era, just at the beginning of one of those revolutions in which old institutions, having lived beyond their time, either silently crumble or are shattered by violence and swept away, and the world enters upon the life of a new age; and the spirit of that age embodies itself in new forms of social, political, and perhaps religious life.

At such periods the powers which have ruled the world through an age, and which have controlled and divided among them its authority, its honors, and emoluments, struggle desperately to maintain their position. The wealth, the power, the rank, the religious institutions, in short the external forces of society, are at first all at their disposal, and these for a time are used to force back the coming age, to trample out the light of new truth, to perpetuate the old abuses, and retain the vanishing past.

In such a struggle the era of the old military despotisms closed; Rome, the last of these, fell and crumbled away, and the feudal system was built upon its ruins. Nationalities then almost disappeared. The European populations were a loosely joined conglomerate of baronial tribes nearly independent of each other, a structure of society which presented no basis on which to rear a civilization.

This era was followed by what may be called the period of national consolidation; the age in which the monarchies of modern Europe assumed their present forms, and the power of the crown swallowed up that of the great nobles, and the separated tribes—for they were little more—became a united nation, the population crystalized upon the throne. Thus was laid the foundation upon which modern civilization has been raised. This system is distinguished by the mingled despotism of capital and classes, the never-ending attempt to subject the laborers, nominally free, to the dependence, the degradation, the ignorance, and the poverty of slavery, without its name.

The spirit of the Gospel, and especially since the Reformation, has exerted against this whole system a counterworking force, by separating the individual man, declaring his worth, setting forth and demanding his rights, instructing and elevating him, until these monarchies and aristocracies no longer suit the spirit of the age. They belong to the past, their limit of life is nearly reached, and we are just about entering upon a new era, in which popular institutions must take the place of thrones, and despotism must give place to freedom. Here, and elsewhere, this is the meaning of the world's struggle, and Europe will probably be the theater of a conflict as fierce and desperate as that which is raging here; but through this agony of nations, the era of the people will be born.

Since the first chapters of this book were written, the decided progress which has been made in putting down the rebellion, and the character of our recent military operations in Virginia and Georgia, have produced a profound impression in Europe. Not only has it been rendered certain that our free institutions are to triumph over a slaveholding despotism, though so powerfully sustained by European sympathy and aid, but the powers of the old world are amazed at the strength and resources of our Republic, at the gigantic character of our military operations, and the courage, skill, and matchless endurance of our soldiers.

Our bitterest enemies, who at first assailed us both with reproaches and sneers, are compelled to admit that all the previous history of war shows no parallel to this American fighting; and, much as they are disposed to lavish all their praise upon the armies of the South, they can not conceal the fact that the soldiers of the free North are steadily pressing them back, and are showing on every battle-field a decided superiority.

The ennobling power of freedom is manifested, also, in the delivered slaves. Touched by this transforming spell of liberty, they have risen, at a single step, from brutehood to a manhood which compels our admiration. By common consent they are heroes; respected by their fellow-soldiers and trusted by their commanders, they form a very important part of our national army even now, and it is easy to see that this enfranchised race will be invaluable in defending America from foreign aggression.

These things have caused already a marked change in the sentiments of Europe, and a new impulse has been given to the hopes and the power of the people. The friends of liberal institutions, encouraged by our success, are devoting themselves with new energy to their work, and some among the ranks of power are, like Mr. Gladstone, keen-sighted enough to discern the coming change, and are preparing themselves to be leaders in a revolution which they are convinced must come, either by sudden violence or peaceful reform.

In England, France, Italy, Germany, Sweden, and Denmark, the popular power is making swift progress, and our final success will be a signal for important movements, which may end in the overthrow of the present institutions of Western Europe.

There is, however, little reason to hope that such a change can be speedily made, or without such bloody convulsions as usually occur at the close of an era—the earthquakes that heave and shatter the foundations and the structures of society. Our own rebellion shows with what desperation privileged classes will defend their wealth wrung from unrequited labor, their social rank, and their political power; and the thrones and aristocracies, the rulers and owners of Western Europe will, in like manner, fill their lands with all the horrors of modern war, sooner than yield to the just demands of the people. The spirit of the English aristocracy, in regard to the progress of popular freedom here, indicates the intensity of passion and hate with which they will oppose a similar movement at home; and the leaders of the Papacy, dazzled with the new prospects which are opening before them through the policy of France, will be as eager for blood as they have been in the ages past. In Europe, moreover, the liberal movement will be made at a great disadvantage compared with our own. With us, in the North, the life and power of our great conflict are derived from the religious sentiment of the country. It is supported by the cordial sympathies, the teachings and prayers, of the evangelical Churches; it receives its impulse from the faith of the people.

But in Europe the popular revolution must proceed, for the most part, against the established Churches and the prevailing religious sentiment; and, as in the former French revolution, the tendency will, almost from necessity, be not only against the present ecclesiastical despotisms, but against Christianity itself.

Here, as the old structures, social and political, pass away, the vigorous religious sentiment forms, speedily and safely, new ones that fit the spirit of the new era; but in Europe we have reason to fear that society may be reduced to chaos, thrones, aristocracies, and hierarchies crushed together, with no religious power to shape a new creation. Should this be so, then the example and united power of Russia and America may, under God, prove the salvation of the nations, presenting, as they will, two stable forms of government, both based upon and animated by the spirit of a true Christianity, and both using alike political and religious power to bless, instruct, and elevate the people.

These two great powers will work in harmony with the spirit of the new age upon which we have entered, and, consequently, will be in alliance with each other; the one seeking the regeneration of the East, the other the helper and protector of these Western worlds.

England clings, with as much desperation as the slaveholders here, to systems that are passing away, and dreams as vainly of binding the nations to her mills and workshops as they did of ruling the world by their cotton. Lord Palmerston, eighty years old, and struggling to force back the future, is a fit representative of the present England. Great Britain, as it would seem, is committed to a struggle against popular progress, and she must bide the issue.

France is preparing to head the last onset of the Papacy against religious liberty and the civil rights of man. Satan is striving to rally the people of Europe under an anti-Christian banner, and thus it appears as if the elements of a world-wide battle were being prepared and arranged, and as if the shock could not be long delayed. In this coming conflict, it is clear that the general interests of Russia and America will be identical, whether they are formally allied or not; and some of the results may, perhaps, be foreseen without any pretension to prophetic vision, or even uncommon intelligence.

It is evident that the events of our war have essentially changed the relative power of the great nations. The naval supremacy of England and France is gone, to return no more. It is impossible for them, henceforth, to regain their former ascendency over the United States or Russia. Our own navy is, in efficiency for home defense, far more than the equal of that of England or France. Neither power can attack us with any reasonable hope of success, and the new American floating-battery and the new artillery have rendered Russia invulnerable. France and England are effectually shut out from her harbors and her territory. They are equally excluded from ours.

Among the results of a general war, which seems inevitable, are the occupation of Constantinople by Russia, and the expelling of every European power from this Western continent. England can scarcely escape being drawn into the wake of France, and sinking, in consequence, into a second-rate power, France, meanwhile, controlling the consolidated Latin races and the Papal Church. What the ultimate result of this tripartite division of Christendom may be, can only be determined when the scroll of human destiny is somewhat more unrolled, and when the prophetic record shall become more clear. It is, however, settled already, that the two powers which have hitherto played a subordinate part in the world's affairs, will be the chief and most powerful actors in the new period now commencing, while it is also clear that Western Europe, under the lead of France, will be capable of waging a most formidable battle against Protestantism in the West and the Greek Church in the East.

How the Protestant faith is to be defended in Europe, with France and the Papacy controlling all but Russia, does not now appear. No Protestant leader appears among the European nations in the visions of the future. The England, whose power was wielded by Cromwell in defense of religious freedom, and whose voice was heard through Milton, is gone. The England of to-day is too selfish, or too weak, to appear, any-where, the assertor or defender of the right.

She follows France, copartner in a causeless, heartless attack on Russia; she proposes to tread down China, as she has done India; she escorts Louis Napoleon over the ocean to Mexico, and bids him God-speed in the most criminal invasion of modern times; she throws all her influence in favor of the slaveholding rebels of our own country, and coolly leaves Denmark to her fate.

Such a government, of course, is incapable of playing any great or noble part in the stormy future; and where the Protestants of Europe are to look for a leader, a central power around which to gather for organization and defense, none now can tell. If England, as she now is, could obtain the control of Europe, she would make of it one empire of Mammon, in which selfishness, unchecked by one great moral or religious principle, or one generous impulse, would shape all her policy. If she could succeed in what she aims at now, she would become one vast commercial despotism, the money tyrant of the earth, making spoil of all human industry to enrich her nobles and to make her merchants princes. Perhaps it would be better for the people to be ruled by the Papacy, than to be ground up as England's laborers are, even now, in the mills of Mammon. The hope of our own country is in holding firmly to the faith of our fathers in endeavoring to make, by the blessing of God, a true Christian faith the life of our national institutions. Even while these closing pages were being written another grand step has been taken in our progress toward Christian freedom, another glorious triumph has been won for the right in the repeal of the "Fugitive-slave Law," and God and man have both been honored. We are taking no backward step. Every month we commend ourselves more and more strongly to the people of Europe.

Let Americans hope and pray, and add earnest labor to the prayer, that our afflicted land, more dear to us now than ever, because of this sorrowful baptism of blood and tears, may present herself, in the new era, a new-born Christian power, consecrated to Christ and Christian freedom, an instrument chosen by our Lord for the elevation of our whole humanity.

www.ingramcontent.com/pod-product-compliance
Lightning Source LLC
LaVergne TN
LVHW021229110826
845150LV00002B/280

* 9 7 8 1 4 2 5 5 6 3 1 5 8 *